A PECULIAR TREASURE

Books By
EDNA FERBER

Autobiography
A PECULIAR TREASURE

Short Stories
NOBODY'S IN TOWN
BUTTERED SIDE DOWN
CHEERFUL—BY REQUEST
HALF PORTIONS   GIGOLO
MOTHER KNOWS BEST
THEY BROUGHT THEIR WOMEN

The Emma McChesney Stories
ROAST BEEF MEDIUM   PERSONALITY PLUS
EMMA McCHESNEY & COMPANY

Novels
DAWN O'HARA
FANNY HERSELF   THE GIRLS
SO BIG   SHOW BOAT   CIMARRON
AMERICAN BEAUTY   COME AND GET IT

Plays
THE ROYAL FAMILY
(with George S. Kaufman)
MINICK
(with George S. Kaufman)
DINNER AT EIGHT
(with George S. Kaufman)
$1200 A YEAR
(with Newman Levy)
STAGE DOOR
(with George S. Kaufman)

Seven—and Stage-struck.

A PECULIAR TREASURE

By
EDNA FERBER

E. F.

NEW YORK

The Literary Guild of America, Inc.

1939

To
Janet Fox
and
Mina Fox
with the hope that my reason
for having written this book
may soon seem an
anachronism.

E. F.

"NOW, THEREFORE, IF YE WILL OBEY MY VOICE INDEED, AND KEEP MY COVENANT, THEN YE SHALL BE A PECULIAR TREASURE UNTO ME ABOVE ALL PEOPLE; FOR ALL THE EARTH IS MINE; AND YE SHALL BE UNTO ME A KINGDOM OF PRIESTS, AND AN HOLY NATION."

Exodus: XIX, 5

Illustrations

A PECULIAR TREASURE

1

Wʜᴇɴ I ᴡᴀs ᴀ sᴍᴀʟʟ ɢɪʀʟ living in Appleton, Wisconsin, I often was sent with a quart tin pail to the creamery which was three blocks away on the wrong side of the railroad tracks. The Ferber family, I hastily and grandly add, lived on the right side of the tracks. Any native Middle West American will get the social significance (and the revolting snobbery) of that statement. I didn't much relish the errand because the creamery had a curdled smell like that of a baby who has just had a digestive surprise. Where Morrison Street met the tracks there was a sign, hydra-headed. It spoke in large black painted letters to the little girl with the milk pail:

R. R. CROSSING
STOP!   LOOK!
LISTEN!

And always, though I might be deep in the weighty thoughts and plans of a twelve-year-old, I would pause for a hasty glance right and left before setting foot across the shining steel rails over which a swift iron monster might descend upon me from who knows where.

The little girl of twelve in the clean gingham dress, her bushy black curls tied back with a ribbon bow, is middle-aged now and the curls are iron-gray. Bewildered, she stands looking at the sign which still states its warning to STOP! LOOK! LISTEN! But where the tracks used to be there is nothing. They've pulled them up. Only the warning remains, and if you heed it you can plainly hear the thunder of the iron monster approaching. But there is no knowing how to escape it, for it is trackless now and running wild.

There are many others standing bewildered at the place where the tracks used to be, so straight and shining and plain to see. Some of them rush ahead, recklessly. Some turn left and others turn right and thousands are doomed to be caught by the onrushing monster. You can hear their screams as it crushes them.

Hesitating there, confused, by the side of the road, I see an occasional face that is wise and kind and experienced. I pluck this one by the sleeve and I say, "Pardon me, mister, but I seem to have lost my way. Can you show me the road to the creamery?"

Invariably the other shakes his head. "I'm sorry. I'm afraid I can't be of any help. I'm a stranger here myself."

Perhaps, I say to myself, if I go back to the spot from which I started, and retrace my steps ever so carefully, I may learn where and how I lost my bearings and missed the way.

A like feeling may account for the wave upon wave of autobiographical books with which the United States has been flooded in the past few years. Some have been written by professional writers; others by people to whom sustained writing is an unfamiliar pursuit. It is as though a panic-stricken world were trying to pin down on paper a dear and accustomed way of life that rapidly is slipping out of its grasp. There! it says in triumph, there it is, plain as a blueprint. That's the way things are. But even as it looks, the pattern changes and dissolves before its eyes.

Usually these life stories are glittering with high adventure. Vicariously the reader hobnobs with royalty and millionaires. Interviews with potentates, dictators and tycoons are relieved by eyewitness descriptions of battles whose outcome decides the fate of the world (for the moment). Safaris wend their way

[2]

through the African jungle, leopard-strewn. A Russian spy disguised as a femme fatale works her wicked wiles from Istanboul to Stockholm; fortunes are made and lost; revels are held in the prewar bohemias of Paris, London and New York.

I've never met a king or queen socially, unless you care to count as royalty Liliuokalani of Hawaii, a sad and ancient black lady in a Mother Hubbard. Her tiny lush kingdom had been snatched from her years before, and all that remained to her was a rickety wooden building dignified by the name of palace, and on her dusky hand an emerald. Immediately thereafter she died. Mine seems to be the evil eye when cast upon rulers. I saw William of Germany tootling down Unter den Linden in his chocolate-colored motorcar, his outriders blowing blasts from golden horns as he came. Very soon thereafter he was skedaddling for Doorn and the sawbuck. At a bull fight in San Sebastian I looked up to see Alphonso of Spain seated in the royal box just over my head. Next thing I knew he was burning up the road in his Hispano-Suiza toward France and safety. I wonder if the evil eye would work when applied to dictators. It's worth trying.

In all my life I've seen only one President of the United States while in office, and he was on his way out, weary and bewildered. The one duchess I ever met was American-born and wore a terrible red hat at luncheon in London. She talked unceasingly in a voice that sounded like hailstones on a tin roof. It beat down mercilessly on the conversation of the man at my left to whom I so passionately wanted to listen. He was a little leather-colored man with great soft eyes and a gentle Scotch voice. Chap by the name of Barrie.

Handicapped for reminiscence thus on the one hand by having failed to mingle sufficiently with the royal and powerful, I am equally at a loss on the other hand through never having known the alleged picturesqueness of poverty. Want has never squatted, a toothless yellow hag, on the doorstep of my childhood or later life. I never have married. I have borne no child. I come of American middle-class Jewish family life. For thirty or more years I have sat daily for hours with my face in a typewriter. I have been conventional, thrifty, hard-working, respectable. Certainly, these are no attributes for a life story. Yet if I were to die tomorrow (which, being middle-aged and neurotic, I feel fairly certain I shall), I should say today that I have had an enchanting time of it; a rich, gay, exciting and dramatic life.

It may be only I who would find it so. Who doesn't think his own life dramatic? In the day's miscellany of mail every professional writer finds a letter or two saying:

No doubt you will be surprised to get a letter from someone who is a complete stranger to you. I am writing to you because I feel sure you are the person who can write a book I have in mind. It is an idea for a great book, but I do not feel that I can write it myself because I am too busy. It is the story of my life. All of my friends say that if I would just write down the story of my life it would make a wonderful book.

Well, you think (though you toss the letter into the wastebasket), and so it doubtless would. The story of any life, told with truth, selection and a dramatic sense, would make an arresting book. Surely romance and agony, humor, adventure and tragedy lie within the span of any ordinary lifetime.

Since I was seventeen I have been a professional writer, yet only once have I deliberately taken a large piece of my own life as the subject of a book. This was the novel entitled Fanny Herself, and even that is so changed and colored by the thick glaze of fiction as to be almost unrecognizable. I am more than a little embarrassed to find myself doing this. It always has seemed to me that a writer of fiction should work almost as does a chemist or a research-laboratory scientist, experimenting with the action of this on that to get the desired effect. The writer himself is only a test tube, a retort and a lamp through which the chemicals are mixed and from which they emerge, transformed. That he himself should be the substance and the subject of the experiment has seemed to me akin to the case of the strange insect that eats itself for nourishment.

There exists, of course, a writing cult which is concerned only with a rather adolescent self-revelation. It might be called the emetic or regurgitation school of writing. The disciple of this

writes his first book all about his first school, his first sex experience, his first love affair, his first job, his first marriage, his first
divorce, his first trip to Europe, in terms of thinly disguised fiction. This finished, he then begins his second novel, which is all
about his second love affair, his second marriage, his second
divorce. The trip this time is to Mexico. The third book depends
upon whether or not he goes through these performances a third
time.

For two or three years I fought the desire to put down this
rather haphazard account of my own life because to do so seemed
definitely silly. In the beginning I said, dishonestly, that I would
put down these things for my own perusal only. I'll never want
them published, I said to myself. Besides, who'd want to read
them? I'm only doing it to clear my mental vision so that I may
see a little way ahead in the darkness. What a lie! Perhaps as
much as any professional writer can mean this, I meant it. But
writers write to be read. Only amateurs say that they write for
their own amusement. Writing is not an amusing occupation. It
is a combination of ditch-digging, mountain-climbing, treadmill
and childbirth. Writing may be interesting, absorbing, exhilarating, racking, relieving. But amusing? Never!

Since the impulse would not abate, I gave way to it. I want
more than anything to write about myself, and my Family, and
about Train Riding, and America, and Jews, and Writing, and
the Theater, and Fun, and Friends, and Work, and Food and
Hope and Hate and Ambition. Everything I put down will be
true, but I make no promise to Tell All. Sores displayed in the
market place are seldom fascinating or even interesting. A bandage is mysterious. Removed, it may reveal only a hangnail. The
soul-baring school of autobiography is more embarrassing for the
reader than for the writer. When one innocently opens a door
and comes unexpectedly upon a nude occupant, it is infinitely
more painful for the door-opener than for the person within the
room. For he or she already is naked, and knows it. Nakedness
of the soul is interesting to the psychiatrist, the physician, the
ethnologist and the patient. To all others it is likely to be boring.

This, then, isn't a story of my life, written because I am fatuous enough to think that anyone is interested. It is the story of an American Jewish family in the past half-century, and as such is really a story about America which I know and love.

Since I was seventeen, and a reporter on the Appleton, Wisconsin, Daily Crescent (sworn circulation 2,389, Samuel Ryan, Editor and Prop.), I have written for hours daily about America as I saw it, and felt it. It is the one country I really understand. I understand its courage, its naïveté, its strength, its childishness, its beauty, its reality. I find it more thrilling to ride through the flat prairie land of Kansas or Nebraska than through the most glorious Swiss or Italian mountain passes. Not more beautiful, please note, but more stimulating, more interesting, more vital. It is the difference between going through a cemetery and going through a school yard in which children are shouting, playing, scuffling. The cemetery is tree-shaded, beautiful, majestic and dead. The school yard may be ugly, utilitarian and makeshift, but it is full of life, it is being used, it is progress, hope, everything in it shows chance for improvement. I have no notebook, I have no diary, I have no scrapbook. All these years of my writing life I have meant to keep a record of reassuring items which would tell, in large black print, all about my books and plays, with photographs of myself staring out from every page. To feed on these stale scraps in middle age must be sustaining; otherwise so many people would not do it. But I always have felt that to reread praise of work long finished is poor fodder, containing about as much nourishment as a leaf of wilted lettuce. After all, the things that stay fresh in the mind through the years are the happenings, large and small, made of tender or dramatic or stern or colorful stuff.

I would rather have lived these last twenty-five years than any other period in the world's history. It has been a perpetual three-ring circus in which spectators and performers, animals and humans, trapeze artists and side-show freaks have been inextricably mingled. Haggard, disheveled and wild-eyed though I am from both beholding and participating in this kaleidoscopic show, I have enjoyed it enough to be willing to stay another twenty-five years—but only if they change the acts. Certainly those of us who remain that long will see the end of this show and the beginning of a new one. It is rarely given to a people to see the end of an epoch—perhaps the end of a civilization—clearly defined. Certainly a new cycle is being born; or an old one is dying without progeny. That means the end. But even that, though doubtless painful, will be interesting to see.

Those of us who found ourselves in the spotlight of success about twenty-five years ago, blinking a little in the unexpected glare, but liking its warmth, are still able to perform the new steps if we've kept limber through the years. Lately we may have puffed a little, trying to keep up, for the world formations have got into the habit of changing between the Home Edition and the Sports Edition of the evening papers.

The writer who can turn back the leaves far enough to include the past twenty or twenty-five years finds the World War of 1914–1918 staring out at him, a dirty obscene blob of grease on the printed page. From this he recoils. Scurrying past, he finds himself in the Jazz Age, which is too recent to be picturesque and too dated to be vital. He may find shelter in the Mauve Decade, the Civil War period, or the Covered Wagon days. From this excursion into the past he emerges with a Nostalgia Novel which is offered as a sedative to a jittery world. It is called the Escapist School of writing. It is a school held in deepest contempt by the one-syllable novelist of the Shock or Slut-and-Cup School. He, in turn, is considered less than the dust by the Propaganda or Boiler Factory School of novelist who writes with a hammer, and ignores both past and present to concentrate upon the future, which he finds rosy but which the world calls red.

We who were born in the late '80s and early '90s are now men and women in our late forties and early fifties. Only a handful of years, yet we remember when the horseless carriage was a freak; when the airplane was a hoax called the flying machine; when the Germans were considered a nation of poets, music lovers, scientists and homebodies; the French, according to our history books, were "a gay people, fond of dancing and light wines." Britannia ruled the waves. The motion picture was a thing

[7]

called a nickelodeon to which no one gave a thought except dirty-faced little boys and bums with a nickel.

I feel sorry for anyone born after 1918. To have been an adult before the World War of 1914–1918 and to have lived twenty years after it is to have known two worlds in one lifetime. The boys and girls born after 1918 sprang full-grown from a Jovian forehead. They missed, somehow, all the fun of growing up in a placid normal world. I'm a quarter of a century distant from being an old lady, but I remember when I thought the telephone was pretty amazing. They take for granted airplanes, television, radio, streamliners. Yesterday is as unreal to them as though a blanket fog had blotted it out. Perhaps it will be rather thrilling for them to discover it when they are fifty and the fog has lifted. One advantage they have that we had not. They are the first generation, surely, that has not sneaked, smirked, gloated and whispered about the biological facts of the human race. If television isn't a shock to them, neither is sex.

Never before, I should think, in the history of the world, has there been a time when middle age and old age did not envy youth. Always the rich, the powerful, the successful, the failures, the poor, having passed the hilltop of life, with the downward slope ahead of them, have looked back at youth. "How I envy you!"

"Envy *me!*" youth has exclaimed. "I've got nothing."

"You've got youth. You have the world ahead of you. Youth, the most precious thing in the world. I'd give everything I have for it."

But who now envies youth? Not I. And that this should be so is the most terrible indictment of the human race, and of the once civilized world.

I should like, in this book, to write about being a Jew. All my life I have been inordinately proud of being a Jew. But I have felt that one should definitely not brag about it. My Jewishness was, I thought, something to wear with becoming modesty, calling attention to it no more than to my two good physical points which were a fine clear skin and an abundant head of vigorous curly hair. Perhaps someone—it may have been my grandfather

Neumann, but I do not remember it—had told me this. As I grew older and became a woman the feeling was intensified. This is inexplicable, because my early childhood was spent, for the most part, in an anti-Semitic Middle Western town, and mine was not and is not a religious family. But I have felt that to be a Jew was, in some ways at least, to be especially privileged. Two thousand years of persecution have made the Jew quick to sympathy, quick-witted (he'd better be), tolerant, humanly understanding. The highest compliment we can pay a Christian is to say of him that he has a Jewish heart.

All this makes life that much more interesting. It also makes life harder, but I am perverse enough to like a hard life. I like a fighting life. I like overcoming things. Maybe a psychiatrist could tell me why, and it might not prove flattering. Being a Jew makes it tougher to get on, and I like that. The highest apple on the branch is the sweetest, and nearest the sun. But, I hasten to add, there's such a thing as overdoing it. The Nazis' little plan has made things just a shade too tough. A joke's a joke.

It may be that being a Jew satisfied the frustrated actress in me. It may be that I have dramatized myself as a Jew. I am fond of referring, especially of late, to two thousand years of persecution. The fact remains that hundreds and thousands of years of continued ill-treatment must stamp its mark upon a people. Primarily, to be a Jew meant to belong to a religion, not a race. But a religious sect, persecuted through the centuries, takes on a certain resemblance, one to another, in countenance, in habits, in feeling, much as one often notes that a husband and wife, through years of common experience and companionship, grow to look alike. The Jewish eye is a melancholy eye, the mask is tragic. He has acquired great adaptability, nervous energy, ambition to succeed and a desire to be liked.

It irks me to hear people say that Jews are wonderful people or that Jews are terrible people. Jews are wonderful and terrible and good and bad and brilliant and stupid and evil and spiritual and vulgar and cultured and rich and poor and beautiful and ugly and gifted and commonplace. Jews, in short, are people.

Anti-Semitism has, through the centuries, become a behavioristic habit, like stealing or arson or murder. It is a way of thinking that has been handed down from generation to generation, like tainted blood. It is a criminal weapon used against society by the unsuccessful, the bigoted, the depraved, the ignorant, the neurotic, the failures. It thrives on terror, hunger, unemployment, hate, resentment. It is mob psychology displayed at its lowest and most unreasoning. It is a thing to fill one with a profound sadness and pity for the whole struggling human race.

Quite a few hundreds of years before Christ a largish group of human beings decided that, instead of worshiping idols made of stone and wood and metal as the rest of the world was doing and had done for centuries, they would acknowledge a higher Power, a Power that was the Spirit, a Power for good. This Power, they felt, would rule the universe if only one would accept It in humbleness and sincerity. That Power they called God, the One God. Those human beings were the Jews. It constantly astounds me afresh to learn how little the so-called civilized world knows about their origin and history. As the Christian religion was founded on the Jewish religion, this is all the more inexplicable. When people express a mild curiosity I refer them to a book called History and Destiny of the Jews, by Josef Kastein.

America—rather, the United States—seems to me to be the Jew among the nations. It is resourceful, adaptable, maligned, envied, feared, imposed upon. It is warmhearted, overfriendly; quick-witted, lavish, colorful; given to extravagant speech and gestures; its people are travelers and wanderers by nature, moving, shifting, restless; swarming in Fords, in ocean liners; craving entertainment; volatile. The *schnuckle* among the nations of the world.

What a country it is! And what a superb time I have had writing about it these last twenty-five years! Violent, varied; tropical, arctic; vast, insular, spectacular. Sequoia trees, Grand Canyon, Niagara Falls, Rocky Mountains, Painted Desert, Great Lakes, Mississippi, black prairies; metal, water, forest, grain, all on a Gargantuan scale. In the very quality of the soil itself there seems to be something that makes for vitality and excitement, an electric element very disconcerting to the European visitor. I have seen staid and conservative Englishmen full of bad British cooking step off an English transAtlantic ship as stuffy as Dundreary, only to be transformed one week later into bounding fauns, eyes alight, step frisky, conversation snapping with what they fondly hope is the newest American slang.

America has been a work hive since the fifteenth century. All over the hundreds of thousands of miles of virgin land the tents went up, the cabins went up, the wooden houses went up, then the brick, the stone, the fantastic cloud-scraping shafts of concrete and steel. Wagon roads cut across Indian trails, railroads blotted out wagon roads across mountains and through forests, automobile roads crisscrossed the railroads, airplane routes zigzagged above them all. The workshop became a mill, the mill became a factory, the factory became a vast plant, the plant grew into a solid town composed of works and workers and owners of works.

With millions of others I have been a work worshiper. Work and more work. Work was a sedative, a stimulant, an escape, an exercise, a diversion, a passion. When friends failed or fun palled or spirits flagged, there was my typewriter and there was the world, my oyster. I've worked daily for over a quarter of a century, and loved it. I've worked while ill in bed, while traveling in Europe, riding on trains. I've written in woodsheds, bathrooms, cabins, compartments, bedrooms, living rooms, gardens, porches, decks, hotels, newspaper offices, theaters, kitchens. Nothing in my world was so satisfactory, so lasting and sustaining as work.

America turned out a million little gadgets, and I and my fellow writers turned out a million little stories, and we all were as merry as grigs. (Note. A grig is a cricket, and it has the reputation for merriness when in reality it is only making a lot of noise.)

We were so busy being workers and merry little grigs that we forgot all about a region which was one of the first to be cleared and settled in America. It had grown into a jungle, weed-ridden, snake-infested. It was called the Soul and Spirit of America and at one time was thickly inhabited and very highly thought of, though fallen into disrepute and even ridicule now.

[11]

Long years ago I vainly disputed those cheery ones who said, "Just a temporary unpleasantness. Mere little recurrence of the hard times this country always has, periodically. Good for us, really. Like a purge." I tried to say that this was no mere economic sickness. It was a sickness of the soul and of the spirit that might well usher in the end of our world. Oh, hush, they said, oh, hush your croaking. Be a merry little grig like us, not a croaking cricket.

But the mills and the plants and the works and the towns took on an awful stillness. And the typewriters of the little grigs ceased their clatter, too.

The imaginary world of creative writing has vanished because the real world of today is so much more fantastic than anything the mind could conceive. The pages of any newspaper today make fiction seem absurd.

So, baffled, we turn to autobiography. Psychologists tell us it is our attempt to creep back into the shelter of the womb, where life held no problems. It isn't necessary to go back quite that far to remember a measure of peace and serenity. We who were in our twenties when the World War began knew the days when a passport was something they used in that backward country, Russia; when the income tax was unheard of; when your Irish, Hungarian, Swedish, German, Bohemian houseworker came over by the hundreds in every ship; when people were folks, and not The People. When a man who worked was a working man, and not The Worker.

A legitimate reason makes me reluctant to use my own life as the subject for a book. The element of surprise and the possibility of change are here absent for the writer. In writing a book of fiction or a play the most astonishing things may happen to a character or a situation overnight; may happen, for that matter, in a split second. Your heroine may be as blonde as Brunhilde and as virtuous as Penelope on Monday morning at ten, only to turn into a black-haired Carmen at eleven, with a dagger in her garter. The scene which was a garden may turn out to be a bedroom. I have started a novel with a secondary character who became so dominant that I had to kill her in the middle of the book in order to save the heroine's face. But in this tale, day after day, week after week, month upon month, I must deal with actual events, bare facts, real people. Imagination has no chance here; fancy is not free, but shackled. The plump and determined seventeen-year-old reporter on the Appleton, Wisconsin, Crescent will not be permitted to turn into a thing of lithe loveliness at sight of whose beauty strong men turn pale and women bite their handkerchiefs and faint. The road back which I must travel is inflexible. The one chance is that, in retracing it, I may find by the wayside and on the path itself small flowers, lovely vistas, and even fellow travelers whose existence as I traveled the road forward I was too hurried, too self-centered or too blind to see clearly.

So then, with this slight warning of what is to come, I go back to that faintly improbable-sounding town called Kalamazoo, Michigan, where I was born to Jacob Charles Ferber and Julia Neumann Ferber. In that way perhaps I may be able to discover what I am doing at a typewriter in a penthouse apartment on top of a roof on Park Avenue, New York.

2

When Dr. Hochstein came back into the bedroom the patient was alert and tidy, being a woman of great vitality. Besides, it had been what they called an easy birth. His tone was professionally hearty.

"Well, Mrs. Ferber, you have another fine baby girl!"

"Girl!" shrieked the young mother in angry disappointment. "But it can't be. His name is Edward Victor Ferber. Oh, Doctor, are you sure!"

He was sure.

So they called her Edna.

From time to time I learned that I was born in Ottumwa, Iowa; in Appleton, Wisconsin; in Chicago, Illinois. I even have heard that I was born somewhere in the more unpopular parts of Europe. But as no bronze tablets are to be found in any of these places with the name of Ferber elaborately engraved thereon, I may as well break down and confess that I was born in Kalamazoo, Michigan, shortly before the turn of the nineteen hundreds. I hate to give the date because I haven't yet become reconciled to being middle-aged. The garment still sets awry on my unwilling shoulders. Incidentally, there are no bronze tablets in my birthplace, either. I have immensely enjoyed having hailed from so improbable-sounding a place as Kalamazoo. It is an

Indian name meaning boiling pot. In America all town names beginning with the letter K (oddly enough, they are for the most part Indian names) are considered comic and used to be a sure-fire laugh in the days of vaudeville. Kankakee, Kokomo, Kewaskum, Kansas, Kewaunee, not to speak of Oshkosh whose "k" comes in the middle. After the World War it used to be very exhilarating to witness the bewilderment of pompous passport officials at European frontiers as they looked at the strange word. Kalamazoo, Michigan, U.S.A. These crazy Americans. They would study it, glance up at me, shake their heads in pity and contempt and give up.

My father's name was Jacob Charles Ferber. He was born in a small village called Oylso, near Eperye, in Hungary, which he left at seventeen to come to America. The Ferber family from which he came lived on a large farm which they owned. It was the type known as a *gute,* which meant that portions of it were rented out by the year to small tenant farmers. My father hated the hard dull routine of farm life. Like every intelligent European youngster he had heard of the opportunities in America, the dream-world across the ocean. He made straight for it, became a citizen as soon as possible, and never left it until the day of his death in 1909. In time his father and mother, his sisters and brothers joined him in this new land. They were good middle-class people of no outstanding quality of mind or achievement. Of the three brothers my father was the only one who brought offspring into the world—my sister Fannie and myself.

He was a man both gentle and irascible, my father. A real Hungarian. He wasn't at all the hustling energetic type of American Jewish businessman. He liked to smoke his cigar and hold long desultory talks with his fellow townsmen on any topic other than business. A man rather on the handsome side, of medium height and medium build and medium intelligence, and the clearest finest most exquisite complexion I've ever seen, set off by bright brown eyes. He was completely engulfed by his family of three energetic high-vitality females—my mother, my sister and myself. As we argued and bounced and rushed about, "Peace!" he used to say, plaintively. "Peace!" He and I were great friends and I like to think that in later life, when deep tragedy came upon him, I was of some comfort to him.

Now, the Neumanns—the family of Julia Neumann Ferber, my mother—there were birds of a different feather. To write about them would be to create a saga resembling that of G. B. Stern's books The Matriarch and A Deputy was King. For the Neumann family is interwoven with Miss Stern's dazzling Viennese tribe that were to be found in Berlin, London, Paris. The annals of that amber merchant appear in my family story, too; and that hoity-toity artist of G. B. Stern's book who refused to sell a charming bit of her own sculpture to Kaiser William of Germany, who coveted it, simply because she didn't like the fellow, is my mother's cousin.

My mother's people make up a glamorous background full of romance, tragedy, drama. To set down these pages of my immediate family without including that picturesque crew would be to leave the raisins, citron, butter and icing out of a fruitcake. And the nuts.

My annals of them go back a couple of hundred years in Germany, and those years are packed with fantastic goings-on. Merchants and bankers, they branched into big-game-hunting expeditions in Africa when Africa was not a society playground; they flew when airplanes were little more than a myth; they wrote plays, fought duels, blew themselves up in chemistry laboratories. Great-great-uncle Max is a meal in itself. It was he who was offered a title and barony by Kaiser Frederick with the understanding that he must first renounce his Judaism. It must have been tempting to a wealthy and ambitious old boy such as he was, but I am proud to state that no Von appears before his name, then or thereafter. It was my great-grandfather Israel Neumann who, when the family lived in Breslau, before moving to Berlin, entertained at dinner a great lady of the theater. Rachel, with her troupe, found herself booked to play Breslau on the Day of Atonement, Yom Kippur, the holiest of the Jewish holy days. She sat, fasting, all day long in the synagogue, and when sunset came she dined as a guest at the bountiful table of the Neumanns and then went off, replete, to give her show.

My Mother and Father. Julia Neumann Ferber, the Bride, and Her Husband, Jacob Ferber.

Curiously enough, I didn't know this tale when, in 1914, I spent hours in Père La Chaise cemetery in Paris, searching until I found the grave of the famous tragedienne, Rachel; or when I went to the Carnavalet Museum only that I might gaze upon her touching little souvenirs there—the watch, the fan, the buskins (very long in the foot).

My only reason for being here today is that in the 1840s my grandfather, Louis Neumann, listened to Carl Schurz and agreed with him to such an extent that he, together with all the others of that famous fighting Schurz crew, came to America from Germany to escape political persecution. He went first to Milwaukee, and there he met and married a dainty and diminutive girl of eighteen named Harriet Lichtenstein. My mother, Julia Neumann Ferber, was born in Milwaukee, the first of five children. Shortly after that the family moved to Chicago, and there they stayed through that incredible town's mud-wallow days, through the Civil War and the Chicago fire. My mother remembers her mother and the other housewives of the neighborhood preparing great boilers of hot coffee for the weary footsore Northern soldiers passing through the town and pausing, spent, by the roadside. (Some of this I used in a novel called The Girls.)

The Neumann family fled the Chicago fire, on and on as its hot tongue licked at their heels. They tell some entertaining stories of it. Harriet Neumann had given birth to a child just a few days before, and was still ill and weak. Louis Neumann finally succeeded in getting a horse-drawn wagon whose driver consented to let the young mother lie on the wagon-bed as he drove. The sum demanded for this was prodigious. After hours of lying thus, parched with thirst, Grandma Neumann begged for a swallow of water. The driver had some, carefully guarded. He consented to give her a drink of water for a goodly price, but first he gave his horse a drink from the pail. In fleeing the house Grandma Neumann had shown (mistakenly) the only evidence of thrift she ever was known to display, then or thereafter. At the child's birth she had been presented by her husband with a fine new mink coat. She felt that she couldn't possibly wear this handsome new garment in a dirty wagon. Besides, the Neumann house wouldn't burn. The fire was still distant, and everyone said it would be stopped in no time. So they locked the house and off she went without the mink coat. It made fine fuel.

On this Chicago's North Side my mother grew up, a high-spirited harum-scarum girl; fun-loving, original, self-willed so far as one can be in a family ruled by a matriarch like Harriet Neumann, her mother. When the man who was to be my father came along, Jacob Ferber, young, good-looking, well-to-do, with twenty-five thousand dollars tucked away (a fortune in that day) ready to be invested in a new business venture, Harriet Neumann considered him a great catch for her daughter. That lively young lady was very much in love with someone else, not a Jew. But parental pressure and conservative middle-class upbringing proved too strong. The girl respected and liked this young Ferber well enough. There was an engagement, and she thought in her careless way that between engagement and wedding something or other would happen to stop the whole thing. But nothing did. And to her helpless amazement she found herself standing there in a plum silk gown being married to the wrong man. The young husband had decided that the thriving small town of Kalamazoo, Michigan, was the place in which to invest part of his comfortable capital. The way in which he happened to be possessed of this tidy sum is important as bearing on the young couple's later life. Jacob Ferber was not then, and never was, a shrewd or even fairly capable businessman. He was well meaning and possessed of singularly bad judgment. Like most people of unsound judgment, he called this bad luck. The twenty-five thousand had been paid him by his astute business partner in Crawfordsville, Indiana, as a means of buying outright his interest in the business.

So off the young couple went, ill-assorted, to Kalamazoo and life. There my father opened a dry-goods store. The young Chicago bride, with her flashing black eyes, her fine figure and her city trousseau, caused quite a furore in the placid Michigan town. She never had lived in a small town and had not learned to change her gait and garb to suit its more provincial standards. In fact she never learned this (or scorned to) and when, fifteen years later, she wore the first short skirt in Appleton, Wisconsin, in a day when trained skirts swept the streets, she was considered too advanced to be quite respectable. In her bridal wardrobe was a large "picture" hat with a sweeping plume, and a flowing cape whose hood was lined with red satin. Dressed in this she went downtown, only to find herself being followed by an assorted rabble of small boys, idlers, and the curious generally. It happened that there was a burlesque troupe in town, billed to play an evening performance. This was known as a "leg show" in that day, and the gaping townspeople mistook the very respectable young bride for one of the members of this lively company. She laughs now as she tells it, but she says she wept then.

Here in Kalamazoo my sister Fannie was born. Three years later I had the bad judgment to be born a girl. There can be nothing in prenatal influence, because I never have wished that I had been born a man, or thought myself handicapped because I hadn't been. At my birth my father presented my mother with the deed to the Park Street house which it had been her dream to possess. It looked as if the family were settled there for life. Less than three years later we were on our way, lock, stock, and barrel.

Being little more than a baby when we left Kalamazoo, I remember very little about it, but certain things there are which I do recall clearly. There are others which have been told me, but I have not confused the two. Mine is an almost photographic memory, and the camera began to click early. I remember a little boy, older than I, called Morgan Smith whose name, in my unaccustomed tongue, became Monkey Mitt. I remember being dressed up by the larger children of the neighborhood in a suit of Monkey Mitt's pants and coat and being taken, charmed with my dramatic prominence, to be viewed by the neighborhood families. I don't know why this was done, or why it made such a lasting impression on my maiden mind. A psychiatrist is welcome to that bit of deep-well information.

I remember Dr. Hochstein, too—the same who had broken the news of my unmistakably feminine sex to my mother's unwilling ears. His dignity ruffled, he called one day to complain that whenever he passed our house where I was at play in the yard, or when he encountered me on the street with the housemaid or an older child, I invariably stuck my tongue out at him as far as it would go, accompanying this rude gesture with a suitably dreadful expression of repulsion. I was brought in and proved the truth of his accusation by promptly proceeding to go through the whole obnoxious performance as described. After a slightly stormy scene it turned out that my baby memory was again to blame. On the two or three professional visits he had made in my healthy infant life I had been told to put out my tongue. I didn't know what a doctor was. I had merely set him down as a visitor with an odd taste in greetings, and was good-naturedly obliging with the best I could manage, on sight.

One more memory of Kalamazoo. That is the Willow Rocker, Champagne Charlie, and Ten Little Indians. The willow rocker, which squeaked on its back swing, was the chariot in which I rode to sleep as I lay in my mother's arms. Champagne Charlie was one of two songs which served as lullabies. The songs were as tempestuous as the singer. I don't know why I didn't turn out a Floradora Girl or dipsomaniac. My mother had, and has, no voice and almost complete inability to carry a tune. Some of the verses I think she made up. But the chorus was legitimate. The lyricist had a simple task in those days:

> *I have a beau,*
> *I'd have you know,*
> *And Charlie is his name.*
> *A fine young lad,*
> *And fond of game,*
> *I wish his name to claim.*

> *Fo-or—*
> *Champagne Charlie is his name,*
> *Champagne Charlie is his name,*
> *Good for any game at night, my boys,*
> *Good for any game at night, my boys,*
> *Who'll come and join him in a spree.*

On the second Champagne Charlie of the chorus her voice reached for an unattainable high note that ended in a screech, the rocker swayed violently backwards and forwards, the runner squeaked, and I fell gently asleep and slept eight hours, a charming gift which I still retain. I think the song satisfied something in this gay, high-spirited woman and was an unconscious protest against the humdrum life she was living in this small Michigan town. Ten Little Indians was a greater favorite with me. It had a stronger dramatic touch.

Telescoped, it ran something—no, exactly—like this:

> *Ten little Indians standing in a line,*
> *One fell down and then there were nine.*
> *Nine little Indians swinging on a gate,*
> *One tumbled off and then there were eight.*
> *Eight little Indians never heard of Heaven,*
> *One kicked the bucket and then there were seven.*

Between the demise or unfortunate accident of every alternate little Indian the chorus came in, very lilting and quick. I waited for it, charmed. I never tired of it:

> *One little, two little,*
> *Three little, four little,*
> Five *little Indian boys.*
> *Six little, seven little,*
> *Eight little, nine little,*
> Ten *little Indian boys.*

This was sung with mounting effect. The last Indian was romantically disposed of.

> *One little Indian,*
> *Left all alone.*
> *He got married.*
> *Then there were none.*

One little, two little, three little, four little, *Five* little, etc.

Sometimes my mother substituted some original variation of the fortunes of the Ten Little Indians, but I liked the familiar lines best. To the tune of their adventures, or those of the devil-may-care Champagne Charlie, I sank blissfully into dreamland.

By now my mother, a city girl born and bred, had, with her ready adaptability, made a place for herself in the little Michigan town. She had a circle of friends, a pleasant and ample house, two small children. My father's business was prospering well enough. In the same inexplicable way by which Jacob Ferber had decided to invest his tidy little fortune in Kalamazoo, he now announced his intention of turning his back on that town. He would sell his business and invest his money in Chicago. The World's Fair, in the process of construction, was to be opened in Chicago in 1893. This was the place for him. The whole of America would pour into Chicago, he argued. Where could a fortune be made more quickly? The fact that the people who poured in would pour out again didn't occur to him. Marshall Field had made his fortune in Chicago; and Netcher, of the Boston Store; and Carson Pirie Scott & Company.

My mother was enchanted at the prospect. Kalamazoo had been pleasant enough, but Chicago was her home, Chicago was not a provincial town where, if you wore a hat with a plume and a cape with a scarlet-lined hood, they thought you belonged to a fly-by-night burlesque troupe. The Neumann family, her mother, her father, her sister Josephine, her three unmarried brothers, all lived in Chicago. Her girlhood friends were there. Joyously she packed the household goods, my father sold his store stock and good will and off we trooped for Chicago, to settle down like locusts on Grandma and Grandpa Neumann in the four-story house on Calumet Avenue, Chicago. It was one of those high-stooped white-stone-front Chicago houses of the '90s, with a small square of grass plot in front and a longish stretch of back yard going back to the alley. The alley, by the way, has perhaps done as much as anything to make crime easy in Chicago. Every Chicago block is alley-intersected, and the alleys themselves are pitch-black at night, which makes for a very cozy and comfortable life on the part of the underworld. Crime had not become a prosperous business in the Chicago of that day. The back yard and the alley were sources of fun and play for me.

Adults never dreamed of sitting in the rear yard, even if it had its rows of flowers and shrubs as Grandma Neumann's had. Grownup Chicago sat on the high front stoop summer evenings. In Grandma Neumann's back garden were growing nasturtiums, mignonette, sweet William, four-o'clocks, besides mint and parsley for the kitchen. The yard ended in a woodshed or stable which gave on the alley. In that alley there sounded through the day the calls of the peddlers with their clarion voices, their gongs, their bells, their horns of trade. Flowers, fruits, vegetables, rags, junk made up the varied stock. The words of their chant would have been incomprehensible to unaccustomed ears. Ra-a-agsalarn! Ra-a-agsalarn! Bna-noooooo! Straw-aw-aw-awb! Straw-aw-aw-aw-b! Ding-dong, ding-dong, ding-dong. It was an opera of small trade. In the evening, on the front stoop, the popcorn man trundled by with his brightly lighted cart that gave off such a tantalizing smell. Chicago was much more exciting than Kalamazoo. I began to be aware of the shape and sound and meaning of things. People took on form and made sense. The mists of my baby vision were clearing.

We must have made them hideously uncomfortable, that family of Neumanns, with four seemingly permanent guests—a man and woman and two small children—plumped down in their midst. Yet I do not recall a single word of remonstrance or impatience. I think I should have remembered it, for I was keenly alive to new sounds and sights. There were a number of bedrooms, but someone, I know, slept in the back parlor on a folding bed that was miraculously transformed into a writing desk by day. It must have been Aunt Josephine. I recall thinking the front parlor very grand. It was a long narrow room furnished with a deep crimson stamped plush parlor set of sofa, armchairs and side chairs complete. There was a picture of The Wedding Party over the mantel and a pale carpet, rose-garlanded, on the floor. I used that room, too, in a description of the Thrifts' front parlor in the novel The Girls. We stayed a full year.

Here I can no longer endure keeping Grandma and Grandpa Neumann in the background. Grandpa Neumann, scholar, gentleman, and complete old darling. Grandma Neumann, the high-tempered, the gadabout, the born mimic.

Old Jewish gentlemen of fiction and history invariably are depicted as Fagins or as bearded patriarchs full of Talmudic wisdom and pious ways. I remember Grandpa Neumann with the utmost clarity, though I was a very small child when he died. White Burnside whiskers, which were called sideburns, very dapper. Benevolent myopic blue eyes behind gold-rimmed spectacles, neat dark suits and a flat bow tie. He always carried a gold-headed ebony cane and walked with short rather springy steps that gave the effect of a slightly bouncing trot, very engaging. When, later, I plunged head over heels in love with the works of Charles Dickens I always envisaged the Cheeryble brothers in Nicholas Nickleby as looking exactly (both of them) like Grandpa Neumann. His wife never called him Louis. I can see her, standing at the foot of the stairs and calling in her high sharp voice, "Neumann! Neumann! Come down."

"Yes, yes, Harriet."

During that year of our stay in Chicago the house was always full of friends and relatives and hangers-on. It was an extravagant household, and a lavish table was hospitably set. The house always was stretched to its capacity. The dining-room table was the sort which could be made larger or smaller as fitted boards were inserted or removed. I don't remember ever seeing it set for dinner when it was not stretched to the fullest. Twelve or fourteen were considered a comfortable tableful.

The soup was served in a tureen. The meat was carved at the table, the vegetables dished. I have that old soup tureen, a creamy china with a tawny oak-leaf pattern. I never see it that my mouth does not water. The soup was almost always chicken soup with noodles (hand-rolled, homemade, hair-fine) or beef soup with marrow balls, a clear strong golden brew. When the cover was removed a fragrant steam arose. It seems to me an excellent custom—now largely discarded by modern households—that of serving and carving the food at the table. The eyes feasted on it first and immediately they sent their message to the stomach. "Get ready, boys!" they telegraphed to the gastric juices. "Gather,

Sister Fannie and Little Sister Edna, Looking Sort of Adenoidal.

Kalamazoo, Michigan, Birthplace. The Young Lady on the Front Porch Is Distinctly Not Me.

all you fluids of digestion. Here comes the soup! Look at this roast stuffed chicken, brown and crisp. I can see the slices melting away from the glittering carving knife."

There always was interesting talk at the table, and I never was banished from it as is the modern child. I suppose I must have heard and remembered a great deal of adult conversation and gathered quite a vocabulary in the process.

After the evening dinner Grandpa Neumann sometimes followed an enchanting custom with which he used to delight his own children many years before the arrival of my sister Fannie and myself, his only grandchildren. Directly after the dinner table was cleared he would place upon it a large box with the name of Koelling & Klappenbach, Importers and Stationers, printed upon it. In that box was a tiny theater made of cardboard. It was exquisitely complete and needed only to be set up. Clouds floated. Waves rolled (by hand). Pasteboard men and women slid on and off along tiny grooves, the figures manipulated by a string. There was a crimson curtain on a weighted roller with a little gold fringe, and the thing actually rolled up and down like a regular theater curtain. It was perfection. Perhaps that diminutive playhouse accounts for the fact that, to this day, my heart beats faster when the theater lights go down, that little hush falls, the golden glow of the footlights suffuses the proscenium, and the curtain goes silently up. Certainly I have been stage-struck all my life.

Sometimes it was a play that Grandpa Neumann presented to us, but more frequently it was an opera. He loved to give a one-man show. He knew and sang entire scores from beginning to end. He played the piano. He sang in French, in German, in Italian. Sometimes he played the violin, too, for good measure. He gave us, as we sat open-mouthed and wide-eyed, Mozart's Don Giovanni; Bellini's Somnambuliste; Le Prophète and Les Huguenots of Meyerbeer. By now the whole family knew the scores and characters and were likely to join in, but Grandpa Neumann definitely wished they wouldn't.

One of my delights was to have him take me on his knee and tell me stories of Edelvard and Kunigunda. This went on and on.

I never tired of them. "More!" I would demand. "More!"

"They're sleeping now," he finally would say. "Sh-sh! Edelvard and Kunigunda are asleep."

There is another story about this charming old gentleman that will bear telling. He never was a shrewd or even a passable businessman. He had had a fine cultural education but never a practical one, there in his youth among the Berlin Neumanns. Neither Louis nor Harriet had a head for figures. His Harriet was a spendthrift. She gave money away to anyone who asked for it, and to many who didn't. The Calumet Avenue house was overrun with idlers, hangers-on, relatives. One day, when they both were young, shortly after their marriage, a scholarly young friend joined Grandpa Neumann in Chicago, having arrived lately from Berlin. He had become a citizen and was about to take the examinations that would secure for him a teacher's certificate. Nervous, apprehensive, still a little unused to American ways, the young fellow pleaded with my grandfather to accompany him to the examination rooms. Grumbling a little, but always the *schnuckle,* Louis went as moral and spiritual support. Sitting there, waiting for his studious friend to complete his paper, he idly glanced at the questions posted up on the board and decided to have a try at answering them, just for the fun of it. You have by now guessed the joke. He turned in his paper and passed the examination. His friend didn't.

This mildly elated him, and he dreamily announced to his wife that he thought he would take up teaching as a profession. Grandma Neumann, materialistic and something of a scold, stormed the idea away.

It was a lively dramatic family, as middle-class Jewish families of education and imagination are likely to be. Every one of them liked the theater, but Grandpa Neumann was stage-struck. He never got theater seats for himself and his Harriet alone. No, the entire family must go. I remember the first theater-seat talk of which I was really conscious. He came home one day in high spirits.

"Well, Neumann, did you get good seats?" Harriet asked. Evidently it was to be a play for which there was great demand.

He shook his head. "Nothing in the whole theater left down-stairs." Then, as the family groaned in disappointment, "But look!" He held up a whole handful of tickets. "I've got something better. We'll all sit in a box."

In the general hubbub of joy my own personal shock did not register. I went off to be alone with my humiliation. That my adored grandfather, Louis Neumann, should sit at the theater in a box! I visualized him stuffed into a pine dry-goods crate.

Harriet Neumann was a natural and acid mimic. A plump tiny woman, overhospitable, a gadabout, my clearest memory of her is as she sat at about eleven in the morning at the far end of the dining-room table. She had been up and out for hours, she was wearing her snug basque dress with the velvet binding, her little black velvet bonnet with the jet aigrette atremble on one side. The bonnet strings were untied from beneath her chin for greater ease, as well they might be. Not only was she talking with her usual volubility but she was partaking of her customary second breakfast—the zweite Frühstück of her German background. Between bites of cheese sandwich and draughts of cold beer she would re-enact her morning's encounter with market man, with neighbor, with a chance friend met by the way. A sharp tongue, a sense of comedy, a flexible voice, a wicked gift of impersonation combined to give us a fine performance. I loved to watch this pink-faced bright-eyed little mimic as she ate and drank and postured.

All this time, and from the time I first learned to talk, I was a demon reciter. I was forever speaking pieces, and I must have been very good or very funny, because there always was a crowd of grownups and older children around me. If I turned up missing at bedtime someone of the household would just go down the block where there was a little crowd gathered about some unseen object under the lamppost. There, I regret to state, would be I, reciting, with appropriate gestures, Jolly Old St. Nicholas or Little Orphan Annie. The final line of this offering was accompanied by the wagging of a fat and warning forefinger. "And the gobble-uns'll git *you* if you don't watch out!"

I must have been a revolting and exhibitionistic little brat. As my sister Fannie was quiet and shy, I think she must have loathed me at this period. I, swollen with approval, had a fine time. My theater ego was being fed.

Years later, when I became a newspaper reporter in Milwaukee, I was interested to learn that various German plays then being given by the Pabst Theater Stock Company had been written by Hugo Bürger, a cousin of Grandpa Neumann, and that these plays were of the vintage of the late '70s. I was enchanted to learn that he had been a well-known German playwright of Berlin, and I now treasure the little brown cloth-bound volume of Der Frauenadvokat, one of his comedies produced in the Königliche Schauspielhaus in Berlin in May, 1875. As his play Das Fünfte Rath was done by the Pabst Stock Company when I was a reporter in Milwaukee in 1909 I felt a smug family satisfaction in concluding that he must have been rather good.

Nothing, I suppose, could more definitely date me than to say that I actually remember the Chicago World's Fair to which I was taken on one occasion only. I remember the peristyle, fountains playing, a lagoon, and lunches done up in a shoebox. I remember my mother in a blue serge Eton suit trimmed with soutache braid. She looked happy, young and gay. But I became cross and tired, my feet lagged, I whimpered and was a horrid nuisance. That ended my education at the World's Fair. They left me home after that and gave me a penny for candy. Instead of spending the penny legitimately thus for candy I always perversely bought instead a horror called a copper pickle. The family never knew this, and I can't understand why I liked it or wanted it. It was a large cucumber pickle so prepared that it emerged (from a copper jar, I suppose) a brilliant and poisonous green, and sour enough to twist the mouth of a rattlesnake. Those copper pickles of my very early childhood may have been the foundation for a rather delicate digestion with which I always have been annoyed. There is an old wives' tale to the effect that my mother craved pickles before I was born.

Of my paternal grandfather and grandmother I saw very little. It is, usually, the grandparents on the distaff side who are most closely in touch with the grandchildren. I know this was so in my case. Besides, Grandma and Grandpa Ferber had none of the vivacity and bounce of the Neumanns. On a visit to them in Milwaukee, where they lived, we were served with chicken soup in which the succulent portions of chicken were afloat. I cast questioning glances at my mother, wretched little snob that I was. Eating one's meat out of a soup dish, after the soup! Years later, in Munich, at the excellent Park Restaurant I learned that the famous spécialité de la maison was Huhn Suppe, which was nothing more than Grandma Ferber's chicken stewed and served in the soup dish. I ate it with appreciation and a considerable feeling of guilt.

3

My FATHER HAD DECIDED that Chicago was not, after all, the ideal spot on which to lay the foundations of our future fortunes. A year had gone by during which we had stayed on in the house on Calumet Avenue. During that year my father was off for days at a time looking for a business location. He realized that he might much better have stayed on in Kalamazoo, but it was too late to think of that now. Perhaps he had discovered that the steps toward becoming a second Marshall Field or Carson Pirie Scott & Company were not so simple. He had, after all, been a small-town man always. Some miracle of mischance led him to a small Iowa coal-mining town distinguished by the Indian name of Ottumwa. The word is said to mean Place of Perseverance. Whatever Ottumwa means in the Indian language, it meant only bad luck for the Ferbers. My father had been told that there was absolutely no general store in the town. Ottumwa clamored, apparently, for Ferber's Bazaar. He inspected the place (he must have been blindfolded) and returned with glowing stories of this Iowa town in a farming and coal-mining district. The fact that it boasted more than sixteen thousand population without a decent shop for china, toys, notions and all sorts of household goods should have been significant enough to serve as a warning.

My mother was anguished. She had left Kalamazoo happy at the thought of again becoming a Chicagoan. Now she was to live in an Iowa coal-mining town apparently for the rest of her days. Heavy-hearted with misgivings she gathered up her household goods and her two children, left Chicago and her people behind her, and came to Ottumwa. As soon as she had a good look at the sordid, clay-and-gully Iowa town, she knew. There it lay flanked by the muddy Des Moines River; unpaved, bigoted, anti-Semitic, undernourished. Julia Ferber's days of youth and peace and happiness were over.

Those next seven years—from 1890 to 1897—must be held accountable for anything in me that is hostile toward the world in which I live. Child though I was, the brutality and ignorance of that little town penetrated to my consciousness, perhaps through casual talk as I heard it between my young parents; certainly as it was visited upon me.

I have since visited the town once, some ten years ago, and I found it a tree-shaded, sightly, modern American town of its size; clean, progressive. I had planned to stay overnight in the new and comfortable hotel. Memory was too strong. At eight that evening I drove through the starlit night back to Des Moines, past the rich black-loam farmlands of Iowa, past the substantial square-built fine farm homes, certainly the most modern and even luxurious farmhouses in the world. It was a purple velvet spring night; the air was rich with the smells of freshly turned earth and the first flowers; the highway ran its flawless length, mile on mile; the sky was lavish with brilliants.

For the first time in my life, out of the deep well of repression where they had so long festered, I dragged those seven years of my bitter little girlhood and looked at them. And the cool clean Iowa air cleansed them, and I saw them then, not as bitter corroding years, but as astringent strengthening years; years whose adversity had given me and mine a solid foundation of stamina, determination and a profound love of justice.

My mother kept a sort of skeleton diary through the years, and the scant line-a-day covering the Ottumwa years forms a human document, bare as it is, containing all the elements of courage, vitality, humor, sordid tragedy, high tragedy. Through it all, I may add, the Ferber family went to the theater. Bitter Iowa winters, burning Iowa summers; death, business crises, illness—the Ferber family went to the theater when any form of theater was to be had in the boundaries of that then-benighted little town.

We moved into a new eight-room house on Wapello Street at the foot of a steep hill. The town ran from almost perpendicular hill streets to the flats near the Des Moines River. In the wintertime it was thrilling to be able to coast, gaining rocketlike velocity, down the length of Wapello or Marian street hill. It was before the day of automobiles, there was little danger of being run down as you whizzed past street intersections. An occasional team, plop-plopping along in the snow, pulled up at the hill street crossings. In the summer Wapello hill was almost as exciting because you could count on the runaways. There were runaway horses every few days and, as we lived at the foot of the hill, they usually wound up with a grand flourish and splintering of wood and screaming of occupants practically in our laps. Faulty brakes, steep hill and frightened horse combined to bring about this state of affairs. The best runaway I remember was a heavily laden hay wagon whose driver, helpless, sat perched atop his precarious load. I still can see the unwieldy mass careening wildly down the hill like a vast drunken fat woman. The usually phlegmatic farm horses, teased by the overladen wagon nipping at their heels, had taken fright, had galloped frantically down the steep slope, the mass had overturned, and the farmer lay unconscious, his head bleeding, his arm dislocated at the shoulder and broken. It was midmorning. There were no men about. I remember the doctor, hastily summoned, looking about him in his shirt sleeves for likely help in this emergency.

"Which one of you ladies will pull this man's arm with all your strength while I set it?"

Julia Ferber came forward. "I will." And she pulled with all her strength while the sweat poured down the doctor's face and that of the groaning farmer.

My sister Fannie and I were left increasingly alone as my

Grandmother Harriet Neumann, Great-Grandfather Israel Neumann and Grandfather Louis Neumann.

mother realized that there was more to my father's business than opening a store, stocking it and waiting for customers. With instinctive common sense, though she knew nothing of business, she felt that something was amiss, and she set about finding out what this might be. She was still too young, too newly married, and too life-loving to admit that the whole structure was wrong. She got into the way of going to the store early after midday and staying there through the afternoon. There was the hired girl to look after my sister and myself, and we lived the normal outdoor life of small-town children.

The American maid-of-all-work, known then as the hired girl, was an institution in the middle-class life of that day and until the emigration restrictions largely stopped her. She should have a rich, colorful and important book all to herself. The American hired girl was, in that day, a farm girl, daughter of foreign-born parents; or she was an immigrant newly landed; perhaps at most of five years' standing in this country. She was any one of a half-dozen nationalities: Irish, German, Swedish, Bohemian, Hungarian, Polish. Poverty, famine, persecution, ambition, a spirit of adventure—any one of these may have been the force which catapulted her across the ocean and into the melting pot. She brought into the Eastern and Midwestern middle-class American household a wealth of European ways, manners, customs in speech, cooking, religion, festivals, morals, clothing. If Hungarian, she brought the household such dishes as goulash and strudel; if Irish, stew and shortbread; if Bohemian, noodle-kraut; if Swedish, meat balls and flaky pastry; if Austrian, wienerschnitzel and the best of coffee. She brought her native peasant costume overseas in her funny corded trunk and could be coaxed to don it for the entertainment of the children of the household. To them, too, she brought old-world folk tales, dances, myths, songs. She was warmhearted, simple, honest, and had to be taught to brush her teeth. Her hair, tightly braided, was wound around her head or skewered into an eye-straining knot. She rose at five-thirty to start the kitchen fire; she rose at four on Mondays to do the family wash. Numbers of her you will see queening it now in American so-called society. She loved to dance, she

loved to sing, she loved to work. She might be uncouth or graceful, sullen or sunny, neat or slovenly, but she was the American
hired girl of the '50s, '60s, '70s, '80s and '90s, and as such she
influenced the manners, morals and lives of millions of American-born children. I always have thought that English children
brought up by English maids, French children cared for by
French maids, and so on through the countries of Europe, have
missed a lot of variety and fun.

Of the Ottumwa hired girls the first I remember is Sophy.
Sophy was swarthy, rather heavily mustached, a superb cook and
definitely "touched." Her mental maladjustment was, however,
confined to one narrow theme. She thought all men were in love
with her. I don't know whether she was Polish or Hungarian.
She was somewhere in her forties, very plain. She spoke with an
accent, and she was always rushing in, after her days off, with
an account of the passionate advances of some strange male encountered in her girlish perambulations. These stories were
considered very amusing as told among the married couples of
my parents' acquaintance. My sister and I listened, awe-struck,
while she regaled us with accounts of her amorous adventures.

"I vass walking on the street and pretty soon I know somebody
vass following after me, so I hurry but he catch up wiss me, he
is tall and handsome wiss black mustache and black eyes and
curly hair. And he says, 'So! You are de vooman I am seeking.' "
This last word became sikking in her accent. " 'You must come
wit me, my beauty, or I will keel you.' " In those simple and
rather cruel days this story was repeated with the accent complete, and greeted by shrieks of mirth. No one seemed to realize
that here was a middle-aged virgin in the throes of a mild sex
mania. She was devoted to us children and we loved her, but it
was not our childish love she wanted.

After Sophy there was Sarah, a dear Welsh girl. Sometimes I
used to go to early Mass with her. During my childhood I often
went to early Mass when the household maid happened to be
Catholic. I liked the drama of it; the color, the rich robes, the
procession, the choir boys' fresh young voices; the sweetish prick
of incense. Once or twice I went with Sarah to the little cottage

where her parents lived, near the mines, and my first trip down into the deep black shaft of a coal mine was made with Sarah and her father. We stumbled through the eery galleries where the men were at work, their tiny cap lamps casting weird shadows. I remember being shocked to learn that people worked in the earth like grubs. I felt sorry for them, and when we came up into the open air again I was relieved. I somehow had felt doomed never to see daylight again.

More and more of my mother's time was spent at the store, though she did little but watch and learn. It was as though scales and scales were falling from her eyes and she were seeing the hard world as it was for the first time. On Saturdays she was there until nine or ten o'clock waiting for her husband, for Saturdays and Saturday nights were the busy times. The farmers and their wives would come in to sell their produce and put in supplies; and the miners would spend their pay. The coal mines lay very near the town. The miners were, for the most part, Welshmen, brought over from the black pits of Cardiff. I would see them coming home from work in the evening, their eyes grotesquely rimmed with black, their trade caps, with the little miner's lamp, on their heads, their tin lunch pails in their tired hands. A lean gaunt lot with few enough quarters and half-dollars to exchange for goods at Ferber's Bazaar.

The town swirled down Main Street on Saturday night. On Saturday afternoon my sister and I went to a matinee if there happened to be a stock company in temporary residence. On Saturday night I was allowed to sit in a tiny chair in a corner and survey the crowds shuffling by. This I insisted on doing. I don't know why a child of five or thereabouts should have enjoyed this diversion, but I did, and I do to this day. My notion of bliss would be to sit in an armchair at the corner of Broadway and 42nd, or State and Madison, or any other busy intersection in America, and watch the town go by. The passer-by does not notice you or care about you; they, the people, are intent on getting somewhere, their faces are open to the reader; they betray themselves by their walk, their voices, their hands, clenched or inert; their feet, their clothes, their eyes.

[35]

Well, there I sat at my ease, an intent and obnoxious little student of the human race, fascinated, God knows why, as I saw this cross section of America go shuffling by in a little Iowa town. At about nine o'clock my sister and I would be sent home, either with the hired girl who had come for us, or hand in hand alone through the dark streets and into the empty house. Perhaps that's why I don't understand what women mean when they say that they are timid about being alone on the street at night. All my life I've walked at night. It is my favorite tramping time.

If it was not too late we were allowed to read at night. Our reading was undirected, haphazard. By the dining-room kerosene lamp we read and read and read. We read the Horatio Alger books in which the newsboy helped the white-headed gentleman with the gold-headed cane across perilous Lexington Avenue, and was promptly adopted by the old gentleman (who later turned out to have been his long-lost grandfather all the time). By the time I was nine I had read all of Dickens, but I also adored the Five Little Pepper books, the St. Nicholas Magazine, all of Louisa Alcott, and the bound copies of Harper's Bazaar; Hans Brinker and the Silver Skates; the novels of The Duchess (the Kathleen Norris of her day); Thelma; Between Two Worlds; The First Violin. Good and bad, adult or infantile, I read all the books in the house, all the books in the store stock, all the books in the very inadequate little public library, for this was before the day of Andrew Carnegie's omnipresent Greek temple. I remember that when Fannie and I were simultaneously stricken with measles, and lay in separate rooms, she in the spare bedroom, I in our everyday bed, my mother sat in the hall between the two rooms so that we both might hear plainly as she read aloud from A Texas Steer, a gusty tale which we relished enormously. Of the stand-bys in the household bookcase there was one book of which I never tired. It was known familiarly as the Green Book, because of the color of its worn binding. Its official name was The World of Wit and Humour. I read it to tatters. I still have it, its worn pages held together now by skillful binding, its leaves yellow and dog-eared, but its cover still the old original bilious cloth of the Green Book. Between those boards I was introduced to Bret

Harte and George Eliot, Samuel Lover and William Allen Butler, author of the immortal Flora M'Flimsey of Madison Square. There I read of Samuel Warren's Tittlebat Titmouse; Oliver Wendell Holmes' Ballad of the Oysterman; there were Artemus Ward, Charles Lever, Mark Twain. Jokes, poems, Mrs. Caudle's Curtain Lectures—the Green Book was a mine of riches, and is to this day. Curiously enough, a friend of my mother subscribed to Puck and the English humorous magazine, Punch. These she saved for me, and I spent an occasional Saturday afternoon curled up, ecstatically happy, with a pile of these papers. In Puck there was one series I particularly loved. It depicted its characters as very plump, round-cheeked pop-eyed creatures, in type a good deal like the Betty Boop cartoons, but infinitely more human and varied.

Of my few agreeable memories of Ottumwa perhaps the pleasantest is that of Sallie Ainley, one of my mother's friends. She was English-born and lived with her father, for whom she kept house, in a cottage by the river on the other side of the bridge that spanned the Des Moines. Ainley père was a miller, and the mill was just next the house. I adored visiting the mill. I never shall forget the kindness of the miller, his beard and face white with flour; or of his daughter Sallie, who put up with Fannie and me for whole Saturdays, while my mother was busy in the store. We watched the grinding of the grain in the mill, we were fed strange delightful dishes, we picked apples from the tree in the yard, we read all the books and magazines on the Ainley shelves. I can't imagine how they came to be residents of Ottumwa. How good, how kind they were, this father and daughter.

If all this sounds stuffy I hasten to say that it wasn't. Ottumwa of that day was a tough town. There were seven murders in it one year, and no convictions. This annoyed certain of the citizenry. They decided to take steps. Consequently, one day as I was rounding the corner on Main Street I saw people running and I was aware of a strange and blood-curdling sound, not human. It was like the sound made by animals as I remembered them in Chicago's Lincoln Park Zoo at their mealtime. I quickened my steps and cleared the corner just in time to see an odd bundle jerking its way in mid-air up the electric light pole. It had legs and arms that waved like those of an insect, then they ceased to wave, the thing straightened itself and became decorous and limp, its head drooping as though in contrition. The animal sounds from the crowd below swelled, then ceased. Suddenly they melted away, seeming to flow up and down the streets in all directions. I heard the clang of the police patrol wagon.

Whatever there was to see I saw. Yearly there were held Methodist camp meetings in a great tent. People "got religion," they came down the aisle clapping their hands and shouting, rolling their eyes, shrieking and sobbing in an hysteria of induced emotion. They would drop to the floor at the foot of the platform. I was astonished to learn that these frenzies were occasioned by religious fervor. I had thought of religion as something dignified, solemn and a little sad.

Somehow or other I attended Chautauquas, revival meetings, political rallies, political parades, ten-twenty-and-thirties, the circus. We always went to the circus at night because my parents could not very well get away in the daytime. I pitied my small friends who were obliged to be content with the afternoon performance. I thought it must be very dull to see this strange world by daylight exposed beneath a blazing sun. Under the gas flares it was mysterious, romantic. Spangles glittered, color blazed, there was more menace in the snarls and growls of the wild animals. Then, too, there was the added thrill of being up so late. When we stumbled out after the performance, drunk with sound and color and dazzling sights, the smaller tents already had been whisked away like an Arabian Nights dream; hoarse men were shouting to one another and charging about with poles and weird canvas bundles. One heard the thick rich sound of heavy circus wheels on the roadway, like no other sound in the world. It stirred something in me, vague and terrible—something that went back, back, perhaps, to Egyptian days and the heavy wheels of chariots.

The political parades were fine things. The marchers carried torch flares and wore colored hatbands and ribbons fastened crosswise from shoulder to waist, and there were huge signs and painted banners on poles held high in the air. I was in the dense crowd that heard Bryan's Cross of Gold speech. He spoke at the Opera House; the throng waiting for the door to be opened was unmanageable. It was then I came by my lifelong horror of close-packed crowds. The doors were opened, the eager hundreds surged forward, I lost my father's hand, I felt myself suffocating, being trampled, I screamed at the top of a none-too-dulcet voice, a man picked me up out of the welter of trampling feet and crushing knees and swung me up to his shoulder, where I sat perched above the heads of the mob and from which vantage point I calmly listened to the impassioned Mr. Bryan in his historic speech, not a word of which I can recall, for some hidden reason.

I saw Coxey's Army, a pitiful tatterdemalion crew, floating down the muddy Des Moines River on flat boats and rafts, hungry, penniless, desperate, on their way to demand food and work of a government which, at that time, had not even dreamed of Relief, of Social Security, of Old Age Pensions, of PWA Projects. The Panic of 1893 had struck America a violent blow, and the whole country was writhing in terror and misery.

It is not for me to say whether all this was good or bad for me. Probably bad and good. Certainly it made for an interesting childhood. Perhaps it is just as well that I never have had a child. I am afraid I should have wanted to bring him or her up in this way—fending for itself, moving from place to place, seeing all that there is to see. I hear mothers and fathers debating whether or not to allow their offspring to see Snow White and the Seven Dwarfs. They discuss its possible psychological and physical effects on little Junior or Sister. I know they're modern and right and wise and oh, how glad I am that I was not thus sheltered in my childhood. Always to be cared for and serene seems to me to be much like living in a climate where it is always summer. Never to know the bitter nip of winter's cold, and to brace oneself against it and fight it; never to long for the coming of spring and then to witness, in ecstasy, the marvel of the first pale lemon-green haze; not to know the voluptuous luxury of rare hot summer sun on basking flesh. No. Summer's only fun if winter is remembered.

Going to school, playing with Ora Burney and Maude Hayward and the Trost boys, I had plenty of normal childish pleasure. But there in Ottumwa it was smirched with constant and cruel persecution. Through the seven years during which we lived in Ottumwa I know that I never went out on the street without being subjected to some form of devilment. It was a fine school for a certain sort of fortitude, but it gave me a strong dash of bitterness at an early age, together with a bewildered puzzlement at what was known as the Christian world. Certainly I wasn't wise enough or old enough at five, six, seven, eight, nine, ten, to philosophize about this. But these people seemed to me to be barbarians.

On Saturdays, and on unusually busy days when my father could not take the time to come home to the noon dinner, it became my duty to take his midday meal down to him, very carefully packed in a large basket; soup, meat, vegetables, dessert. This must be carried with the utmost care so as not to spill or slop. No one thought of having a sandwich and a cup of coffee in the middle of the day, with a hot dinner to be eaten at leisure in the peace of the evening.

This little trip from the house on Wapello Street to the store on Main Street amounted to running the gantlet. I didn't so much mind the Morey girl. She sat in front of her house perched on the white gatepost, waiting, a child about my age, with long red curls, a freckled face, very light green eyes. She swung her long legs, idly. At sight of me her listlessness fled.

"Hello, sheeny!" Then variations on this. This, one learned to receive equably. Besides, the natural retort to her baiting was to shout, airily, "Red Head! Wets the bed!"

But as I approached the Main Street corner there sat a row of vultures perched on the iron railing at the side of Sargent's drugstore. These were not children, they were men. Perhaps to me, a small child, they seemed older than they were, but their ages must have ranged from eighteen to thirty. There they sat, perched on the black iron rail, their heels hooked behind the lower rung.

The Bernhardtian Pose at Two.

They talked almost not at all. The semicircle of spit rings grew richer and richer on the sidewalk in front of them. Vacant-eyed, they stared and spat and sat humped and round-shouldered, doing nothing, thinking nothing, being nothing. Suddenly their lackluster eyes brightened, they shifted, they licked their lips a little and spat with more relish. From afar they had glimpsed their victim, a plump little girl in a clean starched gingham frock, her black curls confined by a ribbon bow.

Every fiber of me shrieked to run the other way. My eyes felt hot and wide. My face became scarlet. I must walk carefully so as not to spill the good hot dinner. Now then. Now.

"Sheeny! Has du gesak de Isaac! De Moses! De Levi! Heh, sheeny, what you got!" Good Old Testament names. They doubtless heard them in their Sunday worship, but did not make the connection, quite. They then brought their hands, palms up, above the level of their shoulders and wagged them back and forth, "Oy-yoy, sheeny! Run! Go on, run!"

I didn't run. I glared. I walked by with as much elegance and aloofness as was compatible with a necessity to balance a basket of noodle soup, pot roast, potatoes, vegetable and pudding.

Of course it was nothing more than a couple of thousand years of bigotry raising its hideous head again to spit on a defenseless and shrinking morsel of humanity. Yet it all must have left a deep scar on a sensitive child. It was unreasoning and widespread in the town. My parents were subject to it. The four or five respectable Jewish families of the town knew it well. They were intelligent men and women, American born and bred, for the most part. It probably gave me a ghastly inferiority, and out of that inferiority doubtless was born inside me a fierce resolution, absurd and childish, such as, "You wait! I'll show you! I'll be rich and famous and you'll wish you could speak to me."

Well, I did become rich and famous, and have lived to see entire nations behaving precisely like the idle frustrated bums perched on the drugstore railing. Of course Ottumwa wasn't a benighted town because it was cruel to its Jewish citizens. It was cruel to its Jewish citizens because it was a benighted town. Business was bad, the town was poor, its people were frightened, resentful and stupid. There was, for a place of its size and locality, an unusually large rough element. As naturally as could be these searched for a minority on whom to vent their dissatisfaction with the world. And there we were, and there I was, the scapegoat of the ages. Yet, though I had a tough time of it in Ottumwa and a fine time of it in New York, I am certain that those Ottumwa years were more enriching, more valuable than all the fun and luxury of the New York years.

New England awoke, horrified and ashamed, after its orgy of witch-burning. Ottumwa must feel some embarrassment at the recollection of its earlier ignorance and brutality. A Nazi-infested world may one day hide its face at the sight of what it has wrought in its inhuman frenzy.

There was no Jewish place of worship in Ottumwa. The five or six Jewish families certainly could not afford the upkeep of a temple. I knew practically nothing of the Jewish people, their history, religion. On the two important holy days of the year—Rosh Hashana, the Jewish New Year; and Yom Kippur, the Day of Atonement—they hired a public hall for services. Sometimes they were able to bring to town a student rabbi who had, as yet, no regular congregation. Usually one of the substantial older men who knew something of the Hebrew language of the Bible, having been taught it in his youth, conducted the service. On Yom Kippur, a long day of fasting and prayer, it was an exhausting thing to stand from morning to sunset in the improvised pulpit. The amateur rabbi would be relieved for an hour by another member of the little improvised congregation. Mr. Emanuel Adler, a familiar figure to me as he sat in his comfortable home talking with my parents, a quaint long-stemmed pipe between his lips, a little black skullcap atop his baldish head as protection against drafts, now would don the rabbinical skullcap, a good deal like that of a Catholic priest. He would open on the high reading stand the Bible and the Book of Prayers containing the service for the Day of Yom Kippur; and suddenly he was transformed from a plump middle-aged German-born Jew with sad kindly eyes and a snuffy gray-brown mustache to a holy man from whose lips came words of wisdom and of comfort and of hope.

The store always was closed on Rosh Hashana and Yom Kippur. Mother put on her best dress. If there were any Jewish visitors in the town at that time they were invited to the services and to dinner at some hospitable house afterward. In our household the guests were likely to be a couple of traveling salesmen caught in the town on that holy day. Jewish families came from smaller near-by towns—Marshalltown, Albia, Keokuk.

I can't account for the fact that I didn't resent being a Jew. Perhaps it was because I liked the way my own family lived, talked, conducted its household and its business better than I did the lives of my friends. I admired immensely my grandparents, my parents, my uncles and aunt. Perhaps it was a vague something handed down to me from no one knows where. Perhaps it was something not very admirable—the actress in me. I think, truthfully, that I rather liked dramatizing myself, feeling myself different and set apart. I probably liked to think of myself as persecuted by enemies who were (in my opinion) my inferiors. This is a protective philosophy often employed. Mine never had been a religious family. The Chicago Neumann family sometimes went to the temple at Thirty-third and Indiana, but I don't remember that my parents ever went there while in Chicago. In our own household there was no celebration of the informal home ceremonies so often observed in Jewish families. The Passover, with its Sedar service, was marked in our house only by the appearance of the matzos or unleavened bread, symbolic of the hardships of the Jews in the wilderness. I devoured pounds of the crisp crumbling matzos with hunks of fresh butter and streams of honey, leaving a trail of crumbs all over the house, and thought very little, I am afraid, of the tragic significance of the food I was eating or of that weary heartsick band led by Moses out of Egypt to escape the Hitler of that day, one Pharaoh; or of how they baked and ate their unsalted unleavened bread because it was all they had, there in the wilderness. I still have matzoth (matzos, we always called them) in my house during the Passover, and just as thoughtlessly. Now they come as delicate crisp circlets, but they seem to me much less delicious than the harder, tougher squares of my childhood munching. Ours were not Jewish ways. My father and mother and sister Fan and I exchanged many friendly little calls with the pleasant Jewish families of the town—the Almeyers, the Adlers, Feists, Silvers, Lyons, living in comfortable well-furnished houses, conducting their affairs with intelligence and decorum, educating their children. They saw a little too much of one another. There was a good deal of visiting back and forth, evenings. At nine there would be served wine or lemonade and cake, a moment which I eagerly awaited. The Ferber specialty was a hickory-nut cake, very rich, baked in a loaf, for which I was permitted to crack the nuts and extract the meats. This was accomplished with a flat-iron between my knees and a hammer in my hand. The nuts went into the cake and into me fifty-fifty. Once baked, it was prudently kept under lock and key in the cupboard of the sitting-room desk, rather than in the free territory of the pantry.

My mother, more modern than most in thought and conduct, had numbers of staunch friends among the non-Jewish townspeople, and these enormously enjoyed her high spirits, her vitality, her shrewd and often caustic comment. She, too, was an omnivorous reader, so that when life proved too much for her she was able to escape into the reader's Nirvana. Certainly she was the real head of the family, its born leader; unconsciously she was undergoing a preliminary training which was to stand her in good stead when she needed it.

It is interesting (to me) to note that all this time I never wrote a line outside my school work and never felt the slightest urge toward original composition. But the piece-speaking went on like a house afire. I recited whenever I could. In school we had recitations every Friday afternoon, and a grand burst of entertainment at the end of each term and on that world-rocking occasion, the Last Day of School, in June. I was by this time a confirmed show-off and a chronic reciter. At the slightest chance I galloped to the front of the room and began my recitation, with gestures. My bliss was complete on those days when we went from room to room giving our programs as visiting artists before an entire class of helpless listeners. To a frustrated actress like myself it is significant now to read a phrase that recurs again and again in that hastily scribbled line-a-day kept by Julia Ferber. Edna recited, it says. No comment, no criticism. Edna recited.

During the Ottumwa period my sister and I used to be taken to Chicago once a year, in the summer, to visit Grandma and Grandpa Neumann. By this time money was scarce, and we—my mother and the two of us—sat up all night in the coach. Children of six were allowed to ride free. I was bundled up in a shawl for a supposed nap, and told to make myself very small. There I lay, trembling and sweating, until the conductor had passed on his ticket-collecting trip. He always looked exactly the same, though perhaps he wasn't. Perhaps he only followed the pattern of the Midwest American train conductor—grizzled, spectacled, brownish spots on the backs of his hands; an Elks and a Masonic emblem; service stripes on his sleeve; a worn, patient and rather benevolent face, strangely unembittered by the pettiness, bad manners and vagaries of the American traveling public.

He would cast a doubting eye on the plump mound under the shawl. "Looks like a big girl to me, ma'am."

"She's big for her age."

Which I undeniably was.

Always I watched and waited with enormous anticipation for the first glimpse of the Mississippi River. I can't explain why it held such fascination for me. Perhaps I had been impressed by what I had learned of it in school—three thousand miles long, tributaries, floods, currents, Mark Twain. For an hour before it was time to cross the great bridge that spanned the stream my face was pressed against the car window. With my own eyes I had seen its ruthless power reflected in the wild antics of our Des Moines River, its tributary. Every year, in the spring, we heard stories of the Mississippi's wild career, how it went berserk and destroyed farms and lives with a single lash of its yellow tail, or gobbled up whole towns in one dreadful yawning of its gigantic jaws. It was always a living thing to me. A monster. When we actually sighted it I eagerly knelt up at the window and watched it out of sight—its broad turbulent bosom, its swift current, its eddies, its vast width, like a mighty lake rather than a river.

The lowlands of Ottumwa, and especially the low-lying Main Street which embraced the chief business section of the town, frequently were flooded. I am here rather embarrassed to admit that I was quite old enough to have known better—such was the terror of the rivers in that part of the country—before I realized that the long laden trains of boxcars and flatcars that crept and puffed so slowly and cautiously along the tracks by the side of the Des Moines River were not 'fraid trains, but freight trains.

It was because of these floods that I knew how rivers behaved. I saw bridges as they swayed, cracked, then, with screams of despair, were swept downstream in the flood. I saw houses tossing like toys in midstream, while sheep, cows, pianos, rocking chairs, bedsteads floated and bobbed by. People sat marooned on rooftops as their houses took to the nautical life.

In the beginning chapters of the novel Show Boat there is a description of the Mississippi at floodtime. I found I did not need to consult books or ask old-timers to relate their river experiences. I just took my childhood memories of the Mississippi and the Des Moines at floodtime out of the back of my head where they had been neatly stored for so many years and pinned them down on paper.

It is a method every writer can use and one which all experienced writers do use. Sometimes (this may be scientifically disputed, but I believe it nevertheless) the memory goes back, back, beyond one's actual lifetime experience, into the unknown past. Most writers must have had the odd sensation of writing a line, a paragraph, a page about something of which they have had no actual knowledge or experience. Somehow, inexplicably, they know. It writes itself. Of course the everyday storehouse method is merely a matter of having a good memory and a camera eye, with the mental films all neatly filed away for future development when needed. That is why, no matter what happens, good or bad, to a professional writer, he may count it as just so much velvet. Into the attic it goes. This can better be illustrated, perhaps, by describing a shabby old yellow trunk kept in the store-room of the Ferber household in my childhood. When you lifted the rickety lid there was wafted to you the mingled odor of mothballs, lavender, faint perfumery, dyes, and the ghostly emanation peculiar to castoff garments. Inside, the trunk foamed with every shade and variety of material. There were odds and ends and scraps and bolts and yards of silk, satin, passementerie, beads, ruchings, insertion, velvet, lace, ribbon, feathers, flower trimmings, bits of felt, muslin. When my mother needed trimming for a dress or a hat for herself or for my sister Fannie and myself she merely dived into the old trunk, fished around in the whirlpool of stuffs, and came up with just the oddment or elegancy she needed.

4

THE PIECE-SPEAKING PROPENSITY must now have assumed serious proportions, because I began to take elocution lessons of a Miss Zangs. I recall a pale rather mystic woman with pale golden hair and unexpectedly deep blue eyes. I think she could not have been very gifted dramatically, because I do not remember one single line of any poem or recitation taught me by Miss Zangs. Unconsciously I must have dismissed the whole experience as having been no good.

Sex, as it filtered into my mind at this time, was a mysterious, secret and shameful thing, not to be discussed or, if possible, even thought of. From my childhood to young womanhood I don't recall one word of decent enlightenment that ever was said or revealed to me on the subject of sex. In a vague way the sex act and childbirth filtered into my consciousness, but I shoved such thoughts away after some attempt at questioning my elders. I was told that these were things little girls shouldn't talk about. What I surreptitiously learned shocked me. I decided that such goings-on certainly were never even thought of for a moment by kings and queens and my own mother and father. In my reading, made up of good material and trash, certain things bewildered me. In the novels (including Dickens) the young bride, trembling and blushing, would hide her head on her husband's shoulder while she whispered her secret. Well, this completely baffled me. If things were as I'd heard slyly rumored, how did he happen to know nothing about all this! Then there were the stories in which beautiful but impoverished maidens were wed to hated but highly pecunious middle age. Of this wretched union children would be born. Such proceedings left me with no ground at all to stand on.

The child of today has an enormous advantage in being rid of the Victorian secrecy and whispered nastiness of my childhood days.

Now tragedy that had been stalking so close behind unhappiness in this grisly little town finally caught up with us.

First, there was the Lawsuit. The Lawsuit was an ogre, a demon in the house. An employee had been accused of systematic theft. Witnesses who had sworn to the truth of the accusation suddenly, in the courtroom, denied all knowledge of it. At home I heard endless talk about that wretched trial. My parents discussed it in sadness and disillusionment. I wasn't conscious that it affected me particularly at the time. It is a neat plan that nature has—that of limiting in very small children and very old people the capacity to experience extreme emotional pain. Without this anodyne, so wisely administered by nature, the human race probably could not bear to contemplate the beginning of life and its end—those first years up the long hill and the final years down it. Still, it must have made a lasting impression on me. My horror of all legal complications doubtless stems from that early spectacle of two people whom I most loved made sad and miserable because of the courts. Lawyers, witnesses, courtrooms, legal terms all were fraught with terror for me. Every writer of any recognized standing finds himself involved in legal entanglements from time to time. If he is successful he is more than likely to find himself accused of plagiarism, of libel, of contractual breaks. I am now accustomed to these by-products of a writing career, and a letter stating that I have stolen someone's (unpublished) manuscript of which I never have heard leaves me quite unruffled. But after the publication of Show Boat, which had a rather spectacular success, I found myself at the point of being sued by practically everyone from show-boat captains to river-front saloonkeepers' descendants. This threw me into a terrible state until I realized that my fears were traceable, not to terror of present or future miscarriages of justice, but to a past injustice suffered by my parents.

The verdict went against them, my father was made to pay some thousands of dollars to the employee alleged slandered. It was a staggering sum to him at that time. It was during this period that I saw him come home one noonday with a flaming scarlet patch on his cheek. It stood out painfully against the clear fine texture of his skin. His soft dark eyes were hot and bright. The family of the accused thief had ganged him. Violence was no part of our lives. Ours always had been a courteous way of conduct. That anyone should dare to lay hands on this gentle man, my father, filled me with an agony of protective resentment. I clung to him, I patted his poor bruised cheek, but he put me from him and turned away his head so that I should not see the anguish in his face.

It is a dreary business, being obliged to put all this down. But it is soon over. Ottumwa, which had all the sordidness of a frontier town with none of its picturesqueness; where I can't recall ever hearing (outside my own family and its circle) a gracious word, or seeing a lovely act, or hearing a beautiful sound; or knowing laughter, careless happiness, gay freedom, fades from the picture.

It was after five years here that my father noticed his eyes were bothering him. He was conscious of a rather blurred vision and some head pains. From time to time a traveling optician came to the town and set up temporary shop at the Ballingal Hotel, on Main Street. He was known as an "eye doctor." He advertised his coming in the Ottumwa Courier, with the statement that he would test eyes and fit glasses. It was to this man that my father went. He must have been a very decent kindly fellow, that itinerant eye doctor. He examined my father's eyes in the routine way, looked at him intently for a moment, then said that perhaps he needed rather special lenses and should come back to get them next day. He asked a few questions. Had he had a shock? Had he been troubled by something? Was he married? What was his business? Where did he live? He put these questions casually, this man with the little case of sample lenses and the cheap metal frames.

That day he wrote a letter to my mother, asking her to come to see him at once, and to say nothing to her husband about it. She came, with premonition wrapping its icy fingers around her heart.

"Madam, I didn't give your husband glasses."

"I know. He said you didn't——"

"I thought—I think maybe you'd better take him to a better eye man than I am. I think you'd better take him to Chicago or New York."

"New York!"

"Well, somebody first rate. Of course, there's Dr. Schneider in Milwaukee."

"But what is it? What is it?"

"It's more the—uh—optic nerve. Atrophy, they call it. Shrinking."

"Shrinking." She was repeating words after him like a child.

"It's dying."

"Dying." The meaning of this came to her slowly. "Dying." Then, with sudden full knowledge, "And when it's dead he'll be——"

He nodded. He did not finish her sentence for her.

Well, the long years of traveling from doctor to doctor began. A losing—a lost—fight, from the beginning. Eyedrops. Electricity. Osteopathy. Massage. Rest. Sleep. Exercise. Milwaukee. Chicago. Even New York. There's a wonderful doctor up in Battle Axe, Michigan, they say he cures with herbs. Listen, I know a man he couldn't see his hand in front of him, he went to a man in Omaha, he treats through the feet . . .

My sister and I were alone, now, for weeks at a time, but I don't recall that we were lonely. We had only a hazy idea of the tragedy that was being played. We were living safely in the unreal world of childhood. My mother always had encouraged us to cook little messes of this or that for make-believe tea parties to which we were permitted to ask our neighborhood playmates. We loved to dress up. This was called "playing grownup." We would don our mother's long skirts, pinned tight around our hips, top this by a discarded waist, all revers and braid and high collar; skewer with long hatpins a two-story hat of that day; ferret out a sunshade and gloves if possible, and in this regalia go flouncing down the street, walking with a mincing gait, speaking in an affected tone, discussing our children, our hired girls, our cookery, our clothes, our husbands in unconscious and deadly imitation of our elders. This was, of course, a favorite diversion of mine, but the game I liked best was playing show. I suppose that hundreds of thousands of children playing show through the years of their childhood have constituted the real Little Theater movement in America. Curiously enough, they still do it though many of them never have been inside a real theater. It seems to me that as long as this persists the living theater is safe. The urge to act is strong, the imitative instinct is stronger, the desire to be seen and heard and to express oneself is still stronger. The shows were given in the woodshed, we charged pins for admittance, our goings-on were as authentic and legitimate as Thornton Wilder's Our Town, but there was no Pulitzer Prize in the world of the Woodshed Theater of Wapello Street, Ottumwa, Iowa.

After school, and at noon, and at night when the hateful home lessons were finished I read and read and read. Somehow, in between school hours, play hours, mealtimes, sleeping hours, I managed to read a book a day for years and years. It would be very gratifying to be able to say that at this time I precociously read Addison, Fielding, Sophocles and a sprinkling of Keats, Gibbon, Shelley and the gloomier Russians. I truthfully can't. I certainly should have if they had come within my reach. No printed page was safe from me. It is with considerable pride that I am able to state that I loathed the Elsie Dinsmore books, and found the lachrymose Elsie a bloody bore.

At school I never was a good student, and my term reports would indicate that I wasn't even quite bright. In mathematics particularly I seemed to be mentally lacking. Those arithmetical problems in which A, B and C dig a well, paper a room or fence a field completely baffled me. I hated those alphabetical workmen with a deep personal loathing. If A can dig a well 9½ feet wide and 23 feet deep in 18 days how long will it take B to dig a well 11 feet wide and 27½ feet deep? I wished their well would cave in on them. Then, and later, I found that I was naturally clever at such studies as English, grammar and history, probably because of my years of omnivorous reading. I used to come to these classes completely unprepared and get away with it.

As the misfortunes of the Ferber family now mounted to an almost comic crescendo it is significant that they blithely persisted in attending the theater whenever theatrical fare offered itself in the town. Ottumwa had to be content with shoddy, usually; companies known as Ten-Twent-and-Thirt. I rarely had a seat of my own, but was allowed to view the drama from my perch on my mother's lap. From this vantage point I saw some of the most incredible plays and certainly some of the worst acting in the history of the theater. But we got our money's worth. There always were songs or dance numbers between the acts. The soubrette would come out in sunbonnet and curls, or the leading man in a character song. There was one stand-by I loved. It was the story of a gambler's fate, told in song. The actor always used a deck of cards, a table and a pistol as props in order to give the number its proper dramatic effect:

> *"You lie! I saw you turn that ace."*
> *A smashing blow right in the face,*
> *A pistol shot, and death's disgrace,*
> *Was in that pack of cards.*

A favorite form of entertainment in that day was the minstrel show. It seems to have passed entirely out of the theater. I loved it. When the curtain went up, revealing those rows of red-and-white candy-striped satin pants, those absurd wing collars, those black faces and rolling eyes, I began to laugh in anticipation. I knew the ritual by heart. First, the opening song. Then the classic line of the interlocutor:

"Gentlemen, be seated!"

The jokes were simple classics, too. "Who dat lady Ah seen you wid last night, Mistah Bones?"

There was always the cakewalk in the second half, as American (or as American Negro) as jazz itself.

Oculists here, there, everywhere had taken all the Ferber spare money, and more. In the enforced absence of my parents on their hopeless search for a doctor who would stay the black fate that was so inevitably to creep upon my father, the store had been run by careless clerks. Things were at sixes and sevens. Financial loss, death, accident, disaster, flood, illness—but the Ferber family went to the theater. In Julia Ferber's spartan diary you read, from day to day, such swift mounting of horror as: Deathly sick with headache. Cut my finger. Mrs. Almeyer died (her best friend). Had two teeth filled and one pulled. Jake brought home with two ribs fractured. Canned two crates of raspberries and a bushel of peaches, then went down to the store all day. Both the girls sick, and I have the grippe. Got word that Jake's mother is dying. To see Tim Murphy in Old Innocence. To see The Factory Girl. To see Our Boys. To see Uncle Daniel. To see Ole Oleson. All of us to the theater to see A Family Affair —A Fallen Candle—The Pulse of New York.

I suppose it was color, escape, in that dour unlovely town.

It was in 1897 that I glimpsed the first faint flicker of that form of entertainment which was to encircle the world with a silver sheet. We all went to see the newfangled thing called the animatograph. You actually saw people walking down the street; and the fire engine, pulled by plunging wild-eyed horses, rolling practically into your lap. It was hard on the eyes, what with a constant flicker and a shower of dancing black and white spots over everything. But the audience agreed that it was a thousand times more wonderful than even the magic lantern.

By now even so blundering a businessman as my father and so inexperienced a young woman as my mother plainly saw that there was no going on in this town. The third mistake must be put down on the wrong side of the ledger of life. Again, for the fourth time, the young couple, with two children now, must start afresh to seek their fortunes.

While my father was spending endless days in the waiting rooms of Milwaukee and Chicago oculists, or traveling about the Midwest looking for that ideal business location, it was left to Julia Ferber to have the store stock disposed of or packed, and the household goods as well. There it is in that meager diary. Auction afternoon and evening. Packing. Packing. Packing all day and evening.

Then the inevitable dash of bravado: To the theater with the girls to see A Freak of Nature. To the theater to see (ironically enough) Confusion. Feeling blue. But the thing ends on a note of quiet triumph, of work well done.

February 24th. Got all through. DID IT ALONE.

That interval between Ottumwa, which was part of our past, and the Next Town, which was our unknown future, must again be spent with the long-suffering Chicago Neumanns. They must have dreaded it, poor dears, but I looked forward to it with enormous anticipation. It was a busy exciting household. Of course, there were certain hours when one must walk muted because Uncle Julius was practising. Hour on hour the skilled fingers ranged the keys, and a little triangular box atop the piano went tick-tock tick-tock. He had studied for four years with the masters of Europe, had Uncle Julius. The house was music haunted and the family life was largely lived in deference to his talent. But Uncle Ed and Uncle Isidore were made of different stuff. Ed, like Grandma Neumann, was a born actor and mimic. Ed and Isidore had joined the growing cult of bicyclists. They were known as "scorchers," and every Sunday they used to bicycle furiously out to Pullman and back, or to some equally remote and unattractive spot. They rode in jerseys and tight pants snugly held by clips at the ankles. Their backs were doubled over low-hung handle bars, and their eyes peered out from beneath long-visored caps. The unnatural position, the speed maintained, the long senseless grind all are probably responsible for the fact that both died as the result of weak hearts long before their time, while the frailer Julius, the musician, lives on into his seventies, reading his beloved French and German books, listening to music, walking in the leafy paths of Chicago's Jackson Park.

So now the Ferber family were off again to Chicago to plump themselves once more upon the Neumann household while Jacob Ferber, like Micawber, waited for something to turn up.

The high-spirited Neumann girl—she of the plumed hat and the scarlet-hooded cape—was launched midstream into life now, out in a very small and leaky boat indeed, with only herself to man it and, for passengers, a husband rapidly going blind and two small girls. It sounds like deepest gloom, yet I remember high spirits, laughter, air-clearing quarrels, fun; pretty challis dresses for my sister and myself, good food, books to read, a tricycle to ride; and always, whether sick or well, hard up or affluent, traveling or stay-at-home, Chicago, Kalamazoo, Ottumwa or Appleton, Wisconsin—our next stop—always: Edna recited at the church sociable. Edna recited at the school exercises. Went to the theater to see Woman Against Woman. To see Eddie Foy in Off the Earth. Went to the theater.

God bless the theater for what it gave to a frightened fun-loving family of four.

5

Two SEPARATE RIVERS winding through two separate towns may serve as well as anything to illustrate the difference between the two towns themselves. The Ottumwa which we had so gladly left behind us was harried rather than helped by the muddy turbulent Des Moines River that bit its savage way between resentful shores. The townspeople feared it. Yearly it took its toll of lives and property like some mythical monster of the Dark Ages. Appleton, Wisconsin, our future home, lay in the Fox River Valley. The Fox River ran cool and swift and strong, a willing beast of burden, a benign giant whose power turned mill wheels, energized factories, created industry, brought prosperity.

Perhaps pioneer families of sixty years before, coming upon a cool green oasis after heart-breaking days through parched desert and wind-swept plains, must have felt much as the Ferber family did as it arrived in Appleton, Wisconsin, and looked about at the smiling valley in whose arms the town so contentedly nestled. A lovely little town of sixteen thousand people; tree-shaded, prosperous, civilized. Its waterways hummed with huge paper mills fed by the forests of Michigan and Wisconsin. All about it lay small prosperous towns like itself—Kaukauna, Neenah,

Menasha, Little Chute. Giant elms and oaks, arching overhead, made cool green naves of the summer streets. The townspeople owned their houses, tended their lawns and gardens. They were substantial, intelligent, progressive. They read, they traveled, they went to the theater, heard music, educated their children at the local college, a Methodist institution called Lawrence University, or sent them to Beloit College, or Notre Dame, or the University of Wisconsin at Madison.

My parents rented a comfortable white frame house on Drew Street, across from the quiet tree-shaded City Park, and immediately the hospitable town came calling.

There never was such a town for sociability. At the least provocation Japanese lanterns burst into bloom on a hundred lawns, and lemonade-punch bowls were encircled by organdie-clad girls, and boys in white duck pants (peg-top) and blue serge coats (with silk revers). The dour days—the seven lean years through which we had just passed—were dispelled like fog before the sun of Appleton's warm-generous friendliness. If Ottumwa had seemed like some foreign provincial town in its narrowness and bigotry, Appleton represented the American small town at its best. A sense of well-being pervaded it. It was curiously modern and free in the best sense of the words. Cliques, malice, gossip, snobbishness—all the insular meannesses—were strangely lacking in this thriving community. Trouble, illness and death were to come upon us there in the next few years, but sympathy and friendship leavened them and made them bearable.

The mayor of Appleton that year, and for many years thereafter, was old David Hammel, a Jew. A handsome patriarch with a high-bridged nose, a bearded leonine head, ruddy color, a superb physique. He and his handsome white-haired wife and their sons and daughters lived in a big Victorian frame house on North and Durkee streets. Later, when we moved to North Street, just across the way from the Hammel house, I saw much of their family life as I read and rocked and munched cookies and played on our own front porch. It was a lesson in loyalty and family devotion.

There were about forty Jewish families living in the town. Of these perhaps thirty families were German-born or of German ancestry. The rest were Russian or Polish. At that time the German-born Jew practised the most absurd snobbery toward the Russian or the Polish Jew. Much of this still persists in America, even in these days when the Jews of the world are combating a fresh outburst of medieval persecution. To the average Gentile a Jew is a Jew. In the mind of the Jew himself there exist gradations based on ridiculous standards. The Polish Jew is looked down upon by the Russian Jew; the German and Hungarian Jew feels himself superior to the Russian; and the Spanish and Portuguese Jew feels himself above all the tribe. It may be that this was not, in the past, quite so ridiculous as it appears, since it was based on hundreds of years of difference in the freedom, economic condition, customs, occupations, habits, health and education of the various nationalities.

In Appleton most of the Jewish families were interrelated and even intermarried. With the exception of ourselves and two or three other families they hailed from the little German town of Gemünden. There was a snarl of brothers, sisters, uncles, cousins, very puzzling to the outsider. The children and grandchildren had been born in Appleton. The men were, for the most part, in the business of buying and selling Wisconsin farm lands and horses—all sorts of horses from beautiful spirited carriage chestnuts or blacks to mammoth pudding-footed draught animals. They were a full-blooded open-handed sort, these husbands and fathers. They smelled too pungently of the horse barns even when dressed in their Sabbath blacks. Their wives were placid, home-loving; their sons and daughters well educated and intelligent. The children did not stand spectacularly high in their studies, in the athletic field, or in any of the arts, probably because they never had experienced racial or religious oppression. It is usually the persecuted Jew who naturally tries to compensate for oppression. It always has been my contention that the Jew, left in peace for two hundred years throughout the world, would lose his aggressiveness, his tenacity and neurotic ambition; would be completely absorbed and would vanish, as a type, from the face of the earth. The Jew, like the Protestant or the Catholic, fights the battles of his own country, be it America, Germany, Italy, France, England; he works for his living, educates his children, travels, lives the normal life of his country as richly as his condition permits. Suddenly, from the headlines of every newspaper in the so-called civilized world, blaring out of the radio, screaming from a thousand platforms, he sees and hears quoted, to his amazement and heartsick despair, "Jew! Jew! Jew! Down! Down!" If these fools really want to destroy us they need only leave us alone. Incredibly adaptable, gregarious, imitative, we soon would be absorbed by the world about us. Yet invariably, just as we are slipping into the world mass, our identity to be forever lost, along comes a despot who singles us out as an object on which to vent his hate or to satisfy his own or his country's psychological perversion. So then, outnumbered but terribly persistent, we again muster what defense we can, draw close together for protection, the stronger helping the weak as we stumble along. Thus for centuries we have been saved from complete absorption or utter oblivion by such fanatics, megalomaniacs or perverts as Pharaoh, Hitler, Ivan of Russia, Philip of France or Edward I of England. If one must build bricks without straw or die, one contrives, somehow, to build bricks without straw. So, through the centuries, the weakest of us have perished; the strong, the courageous, the cunning, the tenacious have survived the repeated blasts of hatred and prejudice. Any biologist or horticulturalist will tell you that that is not the way to weaken or destroy a strain; that is the way to strengthen it. If, in past centuries, the Jew has grown pale of skin, undersized, rather badly articulated, overeager, oversensitive, it is because the ghetto to which he was condemned was the tenement of the Middle and Dark Ages—crowded, airless, mean, dark. Tenements then and now do not make for stature, beauty, health or self-confidence. The German Jew, following these past few years of torture, will need a century to recuperate, if ever he is given the opportunity at all.

So, then, again and again deprived of property, of liberty, of land, of human rights, we have turned to the one thing of which only death can rob us: creative self-expression. An old Chassidic book says:

There are three ways in which a man expresses his deep sorrow: the man on the lowest level cries; the man on the second level is silent, but the man on the highest level knows how to turn his sorrow into song.

So then, because of a Hitler, the Jew of Europe (and of the world) has perforce become more intensely racial. In the mercantile class and in the professions he has clung to the last to his rights; he will emerge more tenacious, more aggressive unless he is completely destroyed. But before that happens let us hope that, seeking in self-expression some relief for our pain, we may again, as in the past, produce for the delight of the whole world another Mozart, another Mendelssohn, another Bernhardt, golden-voiced; another Heifetz, another Rachmaninoff, another Menuhin, another Zimbalist, another Gershwin, turning centuries of sorrow into song. And by that legacy of beauty justify our living and our dying; justify even those who, by torturing us, have produced our poignantly beautiful death cry. For, paradoxical though it may seem, in spite of the degradation of the body, the humiliation of the spirit, the agony of mind, the torture of the soul which has been visited upon the Jews of the so-called civilized world in the past five years, the gorgeous irony of it is this: Adolf Hitler has done more to strengthen, to unite, to solidify and to spiritualize the Jews of the world than any other man since Moses.

I never have heard a satisfactory answer to the riddle of the world's attitude toward the Jew. I remember my shock of horror when, having been taken to an early-morning Mass by the hired girl Sarah, in Ottumwa, I looked upon my first sight of agony and bloodshed—a church statue of the crucifixion. I have wondered many times since just how deep and widespread an effect in later life this same experience has had upon hundreds of millions of children.

It is generally accepted among intelligent people that very early impressions, deeply implanted, influence us for the remainder of our lives. Certainly the psychiatrist is interested in fishing up, not the events and people and thoughts that occupied us at fifteen, twenty, twenty-five, but when we were three years old, four, five, six.

Small children are ordinarily shielded from sights and sounds of horror. Even the rhymes and the pictures in Mother Goose are sometimes seriously debated.

There was a man in our town,
And he was wondrous wise.
He jumped into a bramble bush,
And scratched out both his eyes.

Dear me! says the child-psychologist. No good can come of that. The child will grow up suspecting hidden horrors in every bush it encounters, and probably will develop eye trouble at fifteen. But at the age of four or five this child is deliberately confronted with its first vision of sanguine tragedy. In a picture or a statue he sees a man's nude figure drawn and distorted in agony. Nails through the hands and feet pin him to a cross of wood. On his head is a crown of thorns. From head, hands and feet the scarlet blood streams over the tortured body.

The child's face is a mask of fascinated revulsion. "What is that?"

"That is Our Lord Jesus Christ."

"What is the matter with him? Why is he like that?"

"He is nailed to the cross. He died for you and me."

"Who nailed him?"

"The Jews."

This has gone on for hundreds of years. The fact that Jesus was tried by Pontius Pilate, the Roman governor, and sentenced by law according to the court proceedings of that day, and that he was then crucified by Roman soldiers is universally ignored. He was one of thousands of that period who died on the cross. The life and death of this Jew, distorted through the centuries, has deeply affected the life and death of millions of Jews, and will until the historical truth is generally accepted.

These Appleton townspeople of Jewish faith—first-, second-

and third-generation Americans—owned big comfortable houses, richly furnished; they lived well, had carriages and horses. The horses were well matched high-stepping beauties, the carriages beige- or plum-cushioned victorias with silver-trimmed harness, the whole topped by a coachman on the box. The wives used these for afternoon shopping, for paying calls, for rather aimless drives east to the end of College Avenue, then west to where the Chute ended in the state road.

Appleton boasted its millionaires, but none of these was a Jew. The McNaughtons, the Van Nortwicks, the Pattens, the Peabodys—of Dutch, Scotch or New England descent—these were the really moneyed people of the town.

During the first year or two of our coming to Appleton my mother rather grandly established Friday afternoons At Home. Our hired girl of that day was of German descent: Tillie Schultz, a treasure of purest ray serene. Tillie was a naturally gifted cook. On Friday mornings the house was fragrant with the scent of baking dough; of sugar and spice, of fruits bubbling on the bosom of plum, apricot and apple kuchen. The cheese kuchen, made from a recipe in which cottage cheese was smartened by lemon juice and grated lemon peel, was a specialty of the house. At about four o'clock the tantalizing fragrance of coffee would be added to the rest. These Friday afternoons became something of a stampede.

My mother was rather a bombshell in this placid society. American-born, alert, original, she found she had little in common with these somewhat slow-thinking and sheltered wives. She gravitated toward two families in the Jewish community: one named Lyons who had come up to Wisconsin from the South; the other named Spitz. Mrs. Spitz, tiny, quick-witted, top-heavy with a magnificent crown of braided red hair, was, like my mother, married to a Hungarian.

Two reasons caused the discontinuance of the Fridays At Home. First, the lively Julia became bored with them; second, there was no staying sociably at home, surrounded by coffee, cake and feminine chatter, when the business needed her energies

[63]

and intelligence more and more. Curiously enough, for so advanced a town, there were very few business women in the Appleton of that day. But then, the woman in business had not yet taken her astonishing place in the American commercial, financial and professional world. Even fourteen years later, when I wrote the first of the Emma McChesney stories, a series whose chief character was a traveling saleswoman with a line of Featherloom petticoats, they were greeted as something completely fresh and novel in fiction.

I was busy having fun. I played, I read, I went to school, I rode my bicycle. With Esther or Belle or Frances I scoured the near-by country woods for wildflowers and came home laden (we'd know better now) with delicate hepaticas, with miniature lilies called trillium, with violets, Dutchman's-breeches, saucy little Johnny-jump-ups, mandrakes—evil somehow—and sunny clumps of cowslips. In the autumn these same woods yielded hickory nuts, black walnuts, thorn apples. We would crack the hard green nutshells between stones and pick out the half-ripe meats with fingers stained tobacco brown from the juices inside the shells. There were picnics along the lovely banks of the Fox; we watched the excursion boats going through the locks, a fascinating sight as they eerily sank, sank in the first lock, then rose majestically in the second.

In the winter there was superb skating on the Fox River. From November until March or even April the streets and sidewalks were covered with snow and ice. The bottom layer, formed by the first snows, became a steel-like sheet, and to this were added layer on layer, so that by February you walked on a solid glacier. Sometimes the temperature would go down to eighteen below zero. No one dreamed of staying indoors because of this. The cold cut your forehead like a knife. Your walk was a little trot, skillfully balanced so as not to slip on the tricky ice. On Saturdays and after school we went bobsled-catching, roving the streets like a horde of young Tartars. A farmer would come along on his bobsled. Out we rushed and flipped its broad runners, hanging on the side of the box-body as the horses plunged through the snow, our feet swishing against the roadway drifts, our mittened hands stiff with cold. You stayed on the bob until you espied another headed in the opposite direction. Then off you leaped and caught a ride home. I don't know why this was considered such a grand sport, but it was. Wisconsin spoiled me forever for one-season climates. Stinging cold white winters, hot golden summers, springtime brilliant as a sword thrust, autumns that were like a conflagration in every street and road and farm site—the seasons were not marked merely by December, April, July and September. They were spectacular events, varied and clearly defined as phenomena.

The battleship Maine blew up in Havana harbor; and down Oneida Street to the Northwestern depot trotted the boys of Company G in uniforms and leggings and big broad-brimmed army hats to die in Cuba of dysentery, typhoid and ptomaine caused by rotten army beef provided by American profiteers. And a toothy young man in a saucily cocked hat and glittering eyeglasses made a name for himself by scrambling up San Juan Hill. At school we kids collected lapel buttons on which was printed:

> *Remember the Maine.*
> *To hell with Spain!*

There were others which said, Dewey Did It. Then the silly war was over and Dewey was a national hero. He married, and you read column after column all about the intimate details of his bride's trousseau. A silk drop skirt to every dress. A petticoat of silk, actually not meant to show, but of silk nevertheless. Well! A violet taffeta shot-silk drop skirt under her going-away suit, we read. Our eyes popped. A grateful nation presented Admiral Dewey with a fine house, which he, love-befuddled, deeded over to his bride. The nation turned on him in rage and wounded pride, tore down the Dewey emblems, spat on his name, reviled him. It was the first time I had seen America turn on one of its heroes. I have seen it often since.

The Fox River Valley from Oshkosh to Green Bay hummed with commerce, yet it was serene and lovely with its ravines and woods and jewellike lakes. The ravines, characteristic of the region, were things of especially enchanting beauty. The town dipped and swooped into hollows that once had been Indian camping grounds. Little brooks tinkled through these green recesses. The monster falsely called Progress was presently to come along with his oily promises and counsel the filling of these natural parks, and soon they were used as dumping grounds, their lovely slopes were foul with ashes, tin cans and garbage. Solid now with buildings whose utility can never compensate for lost beauty, the vanished valleys should be haunted by the grim ghosts of Indian braves and squaws. Their revenge lies in the desecration that the white man has himself wrought.

The region abounded both in manufacturing and agriculture, but the huge paper and pulp mills were the valley's chief industry. The vast plants stretched for miles along the river; when you neared them your nostrils were pricked with the acid smells of the churning pulp tubs. Some of the mills made rag paper, others pulp paper. One saw a pair of ragged blue overalls made into a snowy sheet of writing paper or a great rugged tree emerge as wrapping or news paper. Many years later, in 1934, when I was writing the novel Come and Get It, I again made use, as always, of the old yellow-trunk method by fishing up out of my memory the paper-mill lore and knowledge acquired in the girlhood years spent in the Fox River Valley. I knew the mill hands, I knew the mill millionaires, first in my casual childhood, later as they came as customers to Ferber's store for one thing or another, still later when I became a reporter on the Appleton Crescent.

If the girls who worked in the rag-sorting rooms were a trifle pale and inclined to cough, no one paid any particular attention. Dust and lint poured out of the bins. Those were the good old days. On the other hand, if a mill owner wanted to chop down a thousand acres of forest, with never a thought of reforesting, or if his mill acids polluted a river, or if he found it convenient to divert a waterway, a complaisant world made no objection. A few years later, in the governor's chair at Madison, a fiery little man named La Follette was to stir up considerable dust of his own which got into the eyes and throats of the wealthy Wisconsonites. Their bellows could be heard for miles—as far as Washington, in fact.

My sister Fannie had entered the Ryan High School and was busy with beaux and parties. My mother and father had joined the Sunday-night card club, and my mother was a member of the Ladies' Aid Society. For the latter there were Meetings with a capital M once a month, on Sunday, at the home of a member. A mammoth supper was served. We, being not so well-to-do as some of the other Jewish families, naturally tried to outdo them in lavishness and variety. Huge platters of cold fowl, tongue, sausages hot and cold, baked dishes, salads, vast tortes and cakes, ice cream, all were set out. My sister and I were pressed into service as waitresses, as were the other daughters of members. Over all hung the rather wry odor of horses, in spite of ruddy shaved cheeks and fine broadcloth and fresh linen. I don't know exactly who benefited by the Aid, but I hope they fared half as well as the members of the Society itself.

At the card parties you saw Jacob Ferber seated behind the players at this table or that. They played whist, but not he. The red and black symbols and the pictures on the cards now were only little smeary spots to him. He hadn't even the doubtful diversion of kibitzing as he sat there, apart.

The kindly itinerant eye doctor of the Ottumwa days had been all too right. My father's eyes were growing steadily worse. My mother was in the store now almost all day. She had developed a rather surprisingly shrewd head for business—surprising because her direct heritage and background had taught her nothing of this. Perhaps one of the Berlin banking or business Neumanns were cropping up in this, their descendant. By now she realized that she must take the helm or the business would founder altogether.

There now appeared in the house as part of our daily lives a monster known as the Pain. The Pain was like a fifth person in the house—an evil prowling thing never absent, though often hidden; quick to pounce on its helpless victim as he sat, as he

lay sleeping, as he ate at table. As the Pain delivered its preliminary crashing blow, a low moan would be wrung from my
father. He would reel to the nearest chair. I early discovered that
my hands could help, or could give the effect of helping. I had,
even then, unusually long, strong fingers through which seemed
to flow, for this suffering man, an electric and soothing quality. I
would go to him as he lay groaning, his face scarlet, his eyes
glazed with agony, his breath coming in gasps. Standing behind
his chair I would take his head in my two hands, my fingers
pressing hard on his temples and forehead, tighter and tighter
until it seemed to me that the very pressure must crush the skull
that was bursting with pain. Then I would begin to stroke the
head with a firm deliberate motion from the center of the forehead to the temples and down to the neck. After five minutes of
torture the tense body would slowly relax, the twisted face
would become gray-white, a cold clammy sweat would break
out on his forehead. The Pain had had its way, and had retreated, glutted for the moment, to its dark corner. This would
occur perhaps a dozen or more times daily.

My father never had been much of a reader. My mother, my
sister and I read whenever we had a spare moment, and even
when we hadn't we stole it. On winter evenings in a little town
one reads and reads—or did in that day. The radio and the
motion picture, in cotton-back satin and tinsel, had not then
come along to seduce the mind from the strengthening purity of
the printed page. So there, after supper, lay my book, with the
slip of paper marking the place where I had left off. I longed
to return to it. But there sat the near-blind man in his chair,
looking straight ahead of him. Silence had fallen upon the room.
In the kitchen the hired girl was humming in her nasal whine
as she did the dishes. There on the table lay the Appleton Crescent. Its black type stared reproachfully up at me from the white
page. I would open my book, quietly, plunge into a chapter. But
it was no good. A worm leered up at me from the first bite of
stolen fruit. I would shut the book, pick up the paper, the patient
passive face would light up with eager attention. Personal and
Local:

Mr. and Mrs. Otto Brettschneider spent Sunday with Mrs. Brettschneider's parents, Mr. and Mrs. Gus Koehler, in Kaukauna.

It is a boy at the Ben Gurnee home, 937 Durkee Street. Mother and son are doing well.

Miss Belle Schutz and Miss Corinne Wurdeman drove to Neenah on Saturday.

The family of Aleck G. Foster will take up residence in Oconomowoc, leaving next week to join Mr. Foster, who has accepted a position with the Oconomowoc Grain & Feed Co. Oconomowoc's gain is our loss.

Miss Ella Malone, head of the silk goods department of the Pettibone-Peabody Company, has returned from an extensive buying trip in Chicago

There will be a Chicken Pie Supper at Odd Fellows Hall next Thursday. . . .

He couldn't have cared. Certainly I didn't. (Three or four years later I was a seventeen-year-old reporter garnering just such items for the Crescent.) But it was the sound of a human voice in his ear, it brought to him a ghostly echo of life. I rattled off the commonplace items, the everyday log of existence in a small Midwestern town. To this day I can't comfortably read a book sitting up in the middle of the day or in the early evening. I find myself glancing up nervously, looking about me. It was years before I realized why I could read in peace only after I had gone to bed at night. The feeling of guilt, the surge of pity for this stricken man were still too strongly present. Children are careless, they do not understand. I wonder what thoughts came into that fine long head as he sat so patiently there through the long Wisconsin winter evenings while the boards of the house cracked with the frost, and the rare passing of wagon or carriage wheels made a creaking sound on the snow-covered road. God bless Montague Glass in whatever heaven he now inhabits for the happiness and laughter that his Potash and Perlmutter stories brought my father as I read them aloud. They had just burst upon a delighted public from the pages of the Saturday Evening

Post, and an entire nation fell upon them eagerly. The tale of Jewish life in fiction had come to be looked upon as a lugubrious thing, full of weltschmertz. Here were fresh and sparkling stories of Jewish life in the New York cloak-and-suit world; dimensional, human, humorous. In The Perfect Thirty-Six and The Arverne Saque the business partners bickered, snarled, bargained, dragged their family affairs into the fray, made up again. My father, who so rarely smiled now, laughed until the tears came to the stricken eyes.

Usually, on summer evenings, he and I took a walk, but I was impatient to be off with my friends. Children have no curiosity about their parents as human beings. They are merely household necessities, like chairs and beds and food. I wish I had talked to him about his childhood and his youth in Hungary, and his high hopes as he crossed the ocean, a lad, to find fortune and happiness in this golden new land. But I didn't.

6

I<small>T'S</small> <small>NO</small> <small>GOOD</small> <small>PRETENDING</small> that the demon elocutionist had been exorcised. She was, in fact, raging more virulently than ever. No longer content with school programs and end-of-term fireworks and occasional appearances at church sociables, I now entered the Ladies' Temperance Society Silver Medal Contest. I don't know why it was held in Appleton, that contest. Certainly Demon Rum had a scant harvest in that community. I don't think I ever saw anyone intoxicated on the streets or in any household. But the white-ribbon sisterhood had arranged this public exhibition, and I mysteriously entered as a contestant. Not a shred remains in my memory of other contestants, their recitations or mine, for that matter, except one incredible line which has stuck in my mind through the years. I thought the whole affair was nonsense and must have entered in a purely commercial and vainglorious spirit of competition. I wanted to win. The contest was held in Company G Armory. The horrid line was:

. . . For the trail of the serpent is over all, from the humble home of the working man [gesture toward the floor with the left hand, palm open] to the Capital of the Nation! [Gesture toward the ceiling with the right hand, forefinger leading.]

You will get a rough idea of the other speeches when I say that I won the silver medal and still have it somewhere in a shabby leather-covered box.

At fourteen I was singing in the choir at Temple Emanu-El. Years before, the wealthy Jewish families of Appleton had built for themselves a place of worship. The temple was a neat and dignified building in a good residence section of the town. It was a frame building, double-porched, with stained-glass windows, a charmingly proportioned pulpit completed by the ark and its twin seven-branched candlesticks. The choir loft was at the back. In the pulpit presided Rabbi Emanuel Gerechter. In stature a miniature, this little Dr. Gerechter, his tiny figure lost in the embrace of the stately oak and crimson-velvet chair on which he sat enthroned as the choir held forth in the hymns. He was (I now belatedly realize) a definitely engaging little man, possessing charm and personality, smothered by the thick conventionality of his congregation. He walked with a slight scholarly stoop; his tiny high-arched feet were neatly shod in softest kid tipless shoes, square-toed. He wore trim little whiskers of the kind we called sideburns which were, I suppose, burnsides, after the fashion of the army general of that name. A high-bridged nose, very keen brown eyes behind two pairs of glasses, one white, one blue-lensed, which served almost to obliterate the fine-featured face. He wore, always, a suit of black broadcloth with a Prince Albert coat. As the years went on, the little figure became more stooped, the walk more deliberate. His sermons, delivered in English on Friday nights and on Saturdays in German, were exemplars of dullness. I recall not a word of hundreds I must have heard.

Now, at last, I learned something of the Jewish religion. Singing in the choir, attending Sabbath-school classes, the history and chronicles of a religious sect which persecution had solidified into a race penetrated my consciousness. The Old Testament and the Biblical history gave me the dramatic stories of Ruth, of Sarah, of Esther, of Hagar. I learned the stories of the Maccabees; I was appalled at the wickedness of Haman, and at the sufferings of the Jews as they wandered through the desert after the flight from Egypt. I accepted these tales of courage and hardship as a heritage and was inclined to be snobbish about them as those comparative parvenus the sniffy Daughters of the American Revolution boast about their footsore and ragged ancestors at Valley Forge, or New Englanders of their Pilgrim ancestry, or the Huguenots of their triumph over persecutions. I often have heard it said that one of the offensive traits of the Jew is his habit of setting himself up as something quite special. Yet again and again I've heard the descendants of the early Americans, of the Pilgrims, the Huguenots, the Scotch-Irish— all fine sturdy courageous stocks—refer with pride to their origins. It has seemed to me a very human and understandable and harmless vanity, as vanities go. Certainly I never have thought of persecuting a Huguenot because he was proud of his great-great-grandfather.

Right here I may as well break down and confess that even at that early day in my life I had rejected the belief of a God as portrayed in conventional terms of worship. I did not then, and I do not now, accept this God. I was too young, then, seriously to evolve a spiritual belief of any kind. But out of the years has grown the only form of spiritual guidance I have ever had. It is, simply, the belief that God is Good and that Good is God. It makes life at once easy and complicated. I do not recall that there ever was a time when I actually accepted a formal religion of any kind. But if I had to pick and choose among the religions I think I should choose the formal tenets of the Jewish faith. It is a simple, spiritual and uncomplicated belief in a single God. The Universalist has much the same form of worship. The Jew in his worship has no sub-Gods, no saints, no graven images, no elaborate ceremonial. As for dietary laws, if the early Jew was commanded rigorously to abstain from pork, lobster, oysters and the like it was because he was smart enough to learn that these were the first foods to decay in the hot climate he inhabited, and the quickest to cause a stomach-ache and, often, death.

At the Friday-night service attendance was likely to be rather sparse. Usually there was no sermon. On Saturday morning the families were well represented. The men who had been away on business—up in northern Wisconsin, in Michigan and even Minnesota on farm business or attending horse sales—were present in their Sabbath blacks. The women of the congregation were very dressy. They wore rich silks and satins, trimmed with jet and lace, topped by hats beplumed and beflowered. They made their way down the aisles to their pews in a susurrus of silk petticoats under silken gowns and a clash of beads on chains and dangling jewelry.

Seating was pretty well regulated by the wealth and prominence of the congregation. In the rows nearest the pulpit sat the rich old members, their sons and daughters and grandchildren. Then came the next richest and most substantial. Then the middling well-to-do, then the poorest. The last rows were reserved for strangers and for what were known idiotically enough as "Russians." The Ferbers sat about midway. Our pew was not much occupied. Saturday was the big business day in the town, when the farmers came in from miles around. My sister Fannie, free from school on Saturday morning, certainly had other fish to fry. I was up in the choir loft.

Curiously enough, the most dramatic entrance of the morning was that of old Jake Hammel, brother of David Hammel, the mayor. He was like an ancient tree that walked. Before he entered you could hear his great steps on the outer stairs, clump, clump, clump, like the gods of the mountain. His legs were stiff; he wasn't gross or fat but solid, like an oak. Entering, he would remove his hat, raising his great arm slowly, slowly, then gripping the hat and bringing it off and down with a jerk, robot fashion. Sometimes he was halfway down the aisle before he quite managed it. The congregation, holding its breath, now sighed with relief. He set each foot down with a finality which made the onlooker feel that he was going to take root in that spot. His cheeks were ruddy, his hair and beard wavy, luxuriant and iron-gray. His responses in the service were like his walk, deliberate and inflexible. Rabbi Gerechter would say: House of Jacob, come let us walk in the light of God.

A mumble of response from the congregation: From Zion shall go forth the law, the word of the Lord from Jerusalem.

It never came out even. The younger, more agile members were finished long before old Jake Hammel's rumble continued to the end, and emerged a solo.

We of the choir sang in English, in German, in Hebrew. I had German at high school and had taken to it naturally, being of German and Hungarian stock. Of Hebrew I knew nothing and sang the words phonetically as they were written in English letters by Rabbi Gerechter in the hymnbook. I didn't even know the meaning of most of them. Mine was a fair contralto voice, completely untrained. Solo songs and such solo bits as occurred in ensemble singing went to Esther or Eva, daughters both of more wealthy members. Esther, my schoolgirl friend, stood next to me. She had absolutely no ear for music and sang steadily off key, her voice going into a screech on the high notes. Of this she was blissfully unaware, but it annoyed me to the point of fury. Though I never was awarded a solitary yip I made up for it by singing very loud in the hymn numbers and the responses. Certain hymns I loved to sing. Why art—why art—thou cast down, my soul? Why disquieted by fear? In this hymn there was the line—ever loving, though He strike. On the word strike I turned very dramatic and came out with a tremendous operatic burst on the last word. Ever lo-o-o-oving though He—STRIKE!

Esther and I used to gossip in sibilant whispers behind the hymnbooks, especially during the desert wastes of the sermon. Sometimes our absorption in these earthly matters got the better of our discretion. A sudden silence would fall, we would emerge from behind our open hymnals to find that Rabbi Gerechter had stopped dead in his sermon and was glaring at us stonily from behind his two pairs of spectacles, and over the heads of his congregation. Those heads, as the silence grew and deepened, would turn slowly sidewise and then backward toward us as though on a single pivot. Scarlet, we would bend over our books under pretense of turning to the next hymn.

Friday night's service held an agony of suspense for Esther and me. By now we were Ryan High School students, and the high school literary and debating society, called the Forum, held its weekly meetings on that night. Though the purpose of the society was supposedly cultural, it had its less lofty aspects. It was at the Forum meetings that you met your current beau, it was after its session that he walked home with you. With Esther and me the burning question on Friday nights was: would Dr. Gerechter have a sermon or would he not? A sermon meant being hideously late for the Forum session. If, after the Mourners' Prayer, he came forward with that little shake-kneed step of his and planted his tiny high-arched feet firmly behind the pulpit, we looked at each other in dismay, rage, hopelessness. We then resigned ourselves in stony attitudes.

There was the final hymn to be sung. May the words of our lips and the meditations of our hearts be acceptable—be acceptable—in Thy si-ight, O Lord! Horrible little hypocrites that we were, the meditations of our hearts as we fumed to be off wouldn't have been acceptable to the most forgiving Power. Having galloped through the hymn we clapped the books shut, bowed our impatient heads for the benediction. Impious fraud though I was, the simplicity and repetitious cadence of that closing prayer never failed to hold my scatterbrained attention:

May the blessing of the Lord our God rest upon you all. God bless thee and keep thee. May God cause His countenance to shine upon thee and be gracious unto thee. May God lift up His countenance unto thee, and grant thee peace. Amen.

We turned and fled down the temple steps with a clatter of heels and sped toward the Ryan High School, temple of learning, fount of innocent flirtation.

Of course, there were those hideous Friday evenings when we were required to stay for choir practice after the service. Blackness, utter and complete, possessed our souls at such times.

As in Ottumwa, the store in Appleton always was closed on at least two midweek days in the year—Rosh Hashana, New Year; and Yom Kippur, the Day of Atonement. Both these holy days came in the autumn, ten days apart. On the Feast of Passover, in the spring, we were invited to have dinner with the Lyons family and saw the family ritual of the Sedar service, simple but impressive. There, on the glistening damask cloth, were no toothsome dishes; no savory scents greeted the nostrils. At the head of the table sat old Mark Lyons, bearded, massive, waiting to conduct the service and read the prayers. It was the day which commemorated the flight of the Jews out of Egypt into the desert with Moses. There was the table sparsely set forth with the dish of salt, the bare lamb bone, the unleavened bread, the bitter herbs —reminders all of the hardships of our forebears. There was the vacant place for the uninvited but welcome stranger, whoever he might be. After the stark simplicity of that service how marvelous were Mrs. Lyons' soup with matzoth balls, and the succulent stuffed squabs, and Millie Lyons' many-layered chocolate nut torte at the finish.

The New Year was a day of praise and rejoicing; the Day of Atonement a time of fasting and prayer. I sometimes wonder why the Jews do not pause for a time in the repenting of their sins to give their non-Jewish neighbors a chance at repentance. I've wondered, too, why that rather charming little Jewish church in Appleton, as well as all the others I have attended desultorily, so rarely have been entered by visitors of other religions. Considering the antagonism that exists toward those of the Jewish faith, it is remarkable that visitors if only out of curiosity rarely avail themselves of the opportunity to investigate the forms and ceremonies of this religion. Myself, I have attended religious services in churches of every denomination—Methodist, Episcopalian, Catholic, Baptist, Unitarian, Christian Science, Presbyterian, Greek Orthodox, Lutheran, Quaker; on board ocean liners, in a penitentiary, under a tent, in the catacombs, on a mountain top. People at worship are adults who want to be children again, who want to be good again; their faces are, for the moment, washed and clear like the faces of children.

At regular weekly services in Temple Emanu-El the scroll, which was the holy book of the law, dressed in crimson velvet, was taken from its place in the ark, but on special holy days its covering was gleaming white satin fringed in gold. When the time came to read from the scroll two men members of the congregation rose from their pews and mounted the pulpit steps, one on each side, and joined the waiting rabbi. Solemnly the three turned and ascended the steps of the ark, Rabbi Gerechter opened the sliding panel:

House of Jacob, come let us walk in the light of God. . . . Blessed be He who gave unto His people Israel the Law in His Holiness. It is a tree of life to all who lay hold of it; and those who lean on it are accounted blessed; its ways are lovely, and all its paths lead unto peace.

The lights from the seven-branched candlesticks gleamed on the white satin cover of the scroll, the tall candlesticks and their branches were twined with the glistening green tendrils of smilax; the ageless Hebrew words of hope and faith rolled forth:

A brutish man discerneth it not, neither can a fool understand this. When the wicked spring as the grass, and all the workers of iniquity do flourish, it is that they shall be destroyed forever.

The Torah is the book of the law regulating the conduct of the Jewish people from five hundred years before the birth of Christ. The priest Ezra first worked with indefatigable zeal to convince the Jews that the Torah was the law of life. It was the Bible of the Jewish people before the Bible as we know it today came into existence. Rules of conduct, of health, of law, of learning are contained in this book. It is kept in the ark or altar in the rear of every Jewish temple and synagogue, and from its scroll the rabbi reads at every service. It must be admitted that this same Ezra used much the same methods that the hated Hitler is using today. He actually allowed only those to return to Judah who could point to their birth registration as providing irrefutable proof that they were either of Judean extraction or members of the family of Aaron or the tribe of Levi. When he and his batch of returned exiles reached Jerusalem he was horrified at the prevalence of mixed marriages, which he said were forbidden by the law, and sinful. The people themselves, swayed by him, came forward in the Temple with the suggestion that such mixed marriages should be dissolved. And so they were.

The books of Jewish history speak in phrases startlingly like those you hear employed in the German Reich of today. It is interesting, for example, to learn how the Bible was put together through the centuries; how the writings of men such as Joshua, Samuel, Jeremiah, Ezekiel, Isaiah were accepted. They were teachers all, though no one had appointed them to teach. It was these men who set about establishing a code of conduct for the Jews. Thou shalt do this, thou shalt not do that. There were health laws, religious laws, laws of decency and conduct. It is by these laws that civilization has conducted itself in the past two thousand years. Curiously enough, when these basic laws are departed from—forgiveness of debts, kindness toward your neighbor, eating, drinking, loving, living, dying—civilization becomes first brutal, then collapses. These Scriptures formed the official constitution of the Jews, according to which they guided their lives and by which they were ruled; this at a time when the rest of the world was bowing down to idols—gods of any action —gods of love, of the hunt, of fire, of water, of the dance, of the storm, of war, of wine. In the midst of this the Jews alone worshiped one God, who was Good. And say what you will, it was pretty bright of them.

This is, of course, a matter of history. Certainly it was at this time that the Jew began that custom of hedging himself in and setting himself up as being better than his neighbor. It was probably at this very moment, over 450 years before Christ, that the world outside the Jewish group began to say, "Well, who do they think they are! Chosen people, eh! The nerve of them!" And to try to destroy them for setting themselves up.

I think it has very little, really, to do with religion, but with a certain resentment of aloofness. The Jews of that day withdrew from the rest of the world. They set up their own laws, civil, religious, physical. They assumed a holier-than-thou attitude. They punished any Jew who married outside his religion; or declared the marriage void.

None of this, I am sure, went through the minds of the Congregation Emanu-El as Rabbi Gerechter read the words of the Law.

It was just before the approaching Day of Atonement that

Esther and I decided to fast for our sins. It was before my choir-singing days. We were then about thirteen. The fast on that holy day is one of twenty-four hours—from sundown to sundown, a longish stretch for an earthy little girl of thirteen. We two made a solemn pact. The evening wasn't bad. I ate an early and vast supper, went with the family to the evening service, came home and rather dourly went to bed. My sister and I usually did a good deal of chocolate fudge-making, corn-popping and apple-crunching, evenings. As I went upstairs I heard Fannie bite into an apple with what seemed to me to be an unnecessary amount of gusto. I awoke next morning to the tantalizing smell of hot coffee, of brown breakfast rolls, of frying eggs. We children liked to use a system in the eating of a fried egg. The white frill went first. That left the yolk, jewellike, in the center of the plate. A dramatic pause, the fork broke the golden surface, the tiny flood was mopped up with warm buttery bits of roll. Fannie was engaged in this gustatory game as I came downstairs. I shut my eyes and went out to the front porch, breathing deeply.

It was an absurd performance, of course, and had in it nothing of religious feeling. It was a mere test of childish endurance. By noon I was ravenous, and Esther and I exchanged glances of mutual sympathy and deep understanding during the morning service. Instead of going home at midday I resolved to take no chances, and had a walk in the park, alone, feeling very spiritual and hollow. By three I felt rather weak and headachy. Esther tiptoed out, beckoning me to come with her.

In the first part of the novel Fanny Herself I used this episode of the fast day, and I am going to quote it now, using the fictional names as they stand, for having written it once I cannot write it again, and even if I could it would have none of the freshness of that first account written twenty-one years ago:

Fanny and Bella met, giggling, in the vestibule.

"Come on over to my house for a minute," Bella suggested. "I want to show you something." The Weinberg house, a great comfortable well-built home, with encircling veranda and a well-cared-for lawn, was just across the way. They skipped across the street and in at the back door. The big sunny kitchen was deserted. The house seemed very quiet and hushed. Over it hung the delicious fragrance of freshly baked pastry. Bella, a rather baleful look in her eyes, led the way to the butler's pantry that was as large as the average kitchen. And there, ranged on platters and baking boards and on snowy-white napkins, was that which made Tantalus's feast seem a dry and barren snack. The Weinbergs had baked.

It is the custom in the households of Atonement Day fasters of the old school to begin the evening meal, after twenty-four hours of abstinence, with coffee and freshly baked coffee cake of every variety. It was a lead-pipe blow at one's digestion, but delicious beyond imagining. Bella's mother was a famous cook, and her two maids followed in the ways of their mistress. There were to be sisters and brothers and out-of-town relatives as guests at the evening meal, and Mrs. Weinberg had outdone herself.

"Oh!" exclaimed Fanny in a sort of agony and delight.

"Take some," said Bella, the temptress.

The pantry was as fragrant as a garden with spices and fruit scents and the melting delectable perfume of brown, freshly baked dough, sugar-coated. There was one giant platter devoted wholly to round plump cakes with puffy edges, in the center of each a sunken pool that was pure plum, bearing on its bosom a snowy sifting of powdered sugar. There were others whose centers were apricot, molten gold in the sunlight. There were speckled expanses of cheese kuchen, the golden-brown surface showing rich cracks through which one caught glimpses of the lemon-yellow cheese beneath. There were cakes with jelly; cinnamon kuchen, and cunning cakes with almond slices nestling side by side. And there was freshly baked bread; twisted loaf with poppy seed freckling its braid, its sides glistening with the butter that had been swabbed on just before it had been thrust into the oven.

Fanny Brandeis gazed, hypnotized. As she gazed Bella selected a plum tart and bit into it—bit generously, so that her white little teeth met in the very middle of the oozing red-brown juice and one heard a little squish as they closed on the luscious fruit. At the sound Fanny quivered all through her plump and starved little body.

"Have one," said Bella, generously. "Go on. Nobody'll ever know. Anyway, we've fasted long enough for our age. I could fast till supper time if I wanted to, but I don't want to." She swallowed the last morsel of the plum tart and selected another—apricot this time—and opened her moist red lips. But just before she bit into it she selected its counterpart (the Inquisition could have used Bella's talents) and held it out to Fanny. Fanny shook her head slightly. Her hand came up involuntarily. Her eyes were fastened on Bella's face.

"Go on!" Bella urged. "Take it. They're grand! M-m-m-m!" The first bite of apricot vanished between her sharp white teeth. Fanny shut her eyes as if in pain. She was fighting the great fight of her life. She was to meet other temptations, and perhaps more glittering ones, in her lifetime, but to her dying day she was never to forget that first battle between the flesh and the spirit, there in the sugar-scented pantry—and the spirit won. As Bella's lips closed upon the second bite of apricot tart, the while her eye roved over the almond cakes and her hand still held the sweet out to Fanny, that young lady turned sharply and marched blindly out of the house, down the back steps, across the street and into the temple.

The evening lights had been turned on. The little congregation, relaxed, weary, weak from hunger, sat rapt and still except at those times when the prayer book demanded spoken responses. The voice of the little rabbi, rather weak now, had in it a timbre that made it startlingly sweet and clear and resonant. . . . The service marched on, a moving and harrowing thing. There seemed nothing comic now in the way old Ben Reitman, with his slower eyes, always came out five words behind the rest as they tumbled upon the responses and scurried briskly through them, so that his fine old voice, somewhat hoarse and quavering now, rolled out its "Amen!" in solitary majesty.

Over the little congregation hung a glorious atmosphere of detachment. These Jews, listening to the words that had come from the lips of the prophets in Israel, had been, on this day, thrown back thousands of years to the time when the destruction of the temple was as real as the shattered spires and dome of the cathedral at Rheims. Old Ben Reitman, faint with fasting, was far removed from his everyday thoughts of his horses, his lumber mills, his farms, his mortgages. Even Mrs. Nathan Pereles, in her black satin and bugles and jets, her cold hard face usually unlighted by sympathy or love, seemed to feel something of this emotional wave. The atmosphere seemed strangely wavering and luminous. The white satin of the ark curtain gleamed and shifted.

The long service swept on to its close. Suddenly organ and choir burst into a paean. The little rabbi raised his arms. The congregation swept to its feet with a mighty surge. Fanny rose with them, her face very white in its frame of black curls. She raised her face, instead of bowing her head, for the words of the ancient benediction;

"May the blessing of the Lord our God rest upon you all. God bless thee and keep thee. May God cause His countenance to shine upon thee and be gracious unto thee. May God lift up His countenance unto thee, and grant thee peace."

The Day of Atonement had come to an end.

It is Jewish temples and synagogues exactly like this that have been burned, plundered and completely destroyed by the hundreds in Germany and Austria only these past few weeks. And on the first page of the New York World-Telegram published in the city of New York in the United States of America in the month of December in the year 1938 I saw two separate news stories of New York Jewish temples defaced with painted Nazi swastikas and damaged with stones thrown into beautiful stained-glass windows.

A VAST COLLECTION of sentimental slosh has been written about dear old school days. Since I never had a college education I am in no position to speak for the Higher Learning. When I graduated from the Ryan High School of Appleton, Wisconsin, at the age of seventeen, my formal education was finished. But the ancient ramshackle firetrap was not merely the place in which I and my classmates had spent four years grubbing away at algebra, geometry, economics, English and physics. We had had four miraculous years of the most exhilarating and heartening fun. I have never seen a public school like it. It was, for us, a clubhouse, a forum, a social center, playground, a second home. We danced, flirted, played tennis there; learned to think and speak on our feet, learned a sense of honor and fair play, learned, in the best sense of the word, freedom of thought and conduct. On Saturday mornings I used to wake up with a sinking feeling because there was no school that day. By ten o'clock Saturday morning I and my crowd would be over at the high school playing tennis, roaming the dim echoing halls, so strangely quiet now in contrast to the clattering heels and din of talk on weekdays. We sprawled on the grass and talked; we had dates in the cool shade of the side porch, we rehearsed school plays, practised for contests.

There's no explaining the spirit that permeated that school. Its equipment was of the shabbiest and most archaic. It will seem fantastic to the point of madness when I say that when I visited Oxford many years later and saw the splendor of its spirit shining through its worn corridors and ancient rooms I was reminded of that little shabby dim high school in a small Wisconsin town.

Much of this quality of inner splendor must have been due to the influence of the school principal, Ralph Pringle. The man himself was a shy soft-spoken fellow, round-faced behind his spectacles. I don't know where he came by his modern ideas. Modern schools were not even in fashion then. No one ever told him or us that we were being educated in a strange departure from the usual school code. But I know that in those four years we were encouraged to think and act for ourselves; we were in an atmosphere where debate, oratory, theatricals and scholarships were considered more important than athletics. The system was almost purely one of honor. We were allowed to come and go almost at will. Pringle's little private office boasted the only decent mirror in the school—there was no proper coatroom or dressing room—and we used to drift into that office and airily primp before that mirror with as much freedom as though it were our own room. Public speaking was stressed. After four years at Ryan the shyest and awkwardest of boys and girls had learned a certain composure and ease on the platform.

Being a piece-speaking fool, this was, of course, just my cup of tea. In my sophomore year I entered the Wisconsin State Declamatory Contest held each May. The contest was a weeding-out process from which the survivors went to Madison, the state capital, for the final fray. The two local Appleton high schools chose three speakers each. Of these six, one was chosen to enter the district high school contest in which cities of a certain section of the state were represented. At this contest again one was chosen to represent the districts at the state contest. Wisconsin is a great state for public speakers; an articulate state, probably because its students are urged to express themselves in public. I selected as my recitation a short story entitled The Story of Patsy, by Kate Douglas Wiggin. It wasn't particularly suited to

[85]

declamation, and neither, it appeared, was I, for at Madison I came off second in the contest, to my fury. I am too vain to accept second-best.

My disappointment was assuaged by a visit to Chicago after school closed. World-rocking events may have been going on in Chicago that summer. I only know that I saw Henry Irving in The Bells, as a result of which it was years before I could hear a sleigh bell on the streets of Appleton without being shaken by remembrance of that terror-stricken face and those articulate hands; I was introduced to the enchantment of vaudeville at the Masonic Temple Roof Garden, where a slim Ophelia-like creature with haunting eyes and a lovely flexible voice gave uncanny impersonations. She was a newcomer billed as Cecilia Loftus. They liked her, and she was spoken of as Cissie. The Four Cohans performed there that summer, led by a nasal impudent fellow whose eccentric dancing and engaging trick of talking out of one corner of a crooked mouth endeared him to the audience. There was a miraculous troupe called the Agoust family, jugglers, whose act opened in a well-furnished room and ended with members of the family tossing (and catching) chairs, tables, couches, china, glass, curtains, drapes and lighted lamps in a crescendo of excitement.

The Ferber family hadn't neglected its love, the theater, in Appleton. A new theater had just been built in the progressive little town. You saw Rose Coghlan in the grisly Forget-Me-Not; Richard Carle in The Tenderfoot sang his enchanting song, I Met My Love in the Alamo; there was Blanche Walsh in Tolstoi's Resurrection; and, for music and merriment, Babes in Toyland, The Sultan of Sulu, The Burgomaster. There was an Appleton family of German parentage named Winninger, with a lot of boys who played all sorts of musical instruments and did acrobatic tricks and were generally entertaining cutups. It was said the father could play every brass or wind instrument ever devised, and the boys pretty well followed his example. Some of the boys married, and the boys and their wives started touring as a ten-twenty-thirty stock company. They played the Appleton theater for two weeks every year, giving the old melodramas and what they announced as comedy-dramas, with special numbers between the acts. The boys themselves played heavy, leads, character, second lead. There was a good deal of flicking of boots with riding whips and turning of innocence out into the snow. The Winningers doubled in brass—that is, they all turned out to play for dear life in the brass band in front of the theater before the opening hour, to attract the customers. Then, barely in time for the curtain, they would wrench their lips from the brass, rush into their dressing rooms, make up and go on to give the show. The leading man was the baby of the Winninger boys—a blue-eyed young fellow with golden curly hair and a winning warmth that caught the fancy of all the girls in town. His name was Charley Winninger. Almost twenty-five years later, at the first rehearsal of the musical play Show Boat, with Charles Winninger, the well-known musical comedy star, present in the part of Cap'n Andy of the Cotton Blossom Floating Palace Theater, the assembled company, together with Mr. Florenz Ziegfeld, the producer, Mr. Jerome Kern, the composer, and Mr. Oscar Hammerstein, the librettist, were mildly astonished to see Cap'n Andy and I rush into each other's arms with cries of, "Appleton! Oneida Street! Opera House! Ferber's store! Ten Nights in a Barroom!"

In my last year at Ryan High I again entered the state declamatory contest. My recitation was Richard Harding Davis's The Littlest Girl, a story about a stage child. I loved it, probably because it was of the theater. Its opening line: "It was at the end of the first act of the first night of the 'Sultana,' and there were over a dozen children in front of the footlights——" and I was off like a whippet.

I won first place at Madison. Curiously enough, this event always was given a great deal of publicity in the newspapers of the state. Appleton was delirious. I returned from Madison to find the entire high school and most of the town at the depot, together with the two complete fire-engine companies who had been called to control the gigantic blaze of the bonfire which had been lighted in the school athletic field just a block away. The Ryan High School boys had swiped dry-goods boxes and packing crates from the rear of every store on College Avenue, including Ferber's, where they definitely felt justified in helping themselves. The bonfire in celebration of the state-contest victory now threatened to become a conflagration. I was rather uncomfortably ridden to the bonfire on the shoulders of two husky football boys, and endeavored to appear shy and deprecating, but I was bursting with my own importance. My father and mother had stayed up until after midnight to hear the news the night before; the high school bell had been rung to waken all the local burghers out of their sleep. The school presented me with an inscribed loving cup, a dear possession which I still cherish. I was happy, elated, almost (but not quite) self-confident. The bristling resentful little girl of the Ottumwa, Iowa, days disappeared now for months at a time.

For the rest, I was not a good student except in the studies which came naturally to me—English, history, economics. algebra, geometry, physics were not difficult merely—they were impossible for me. I think I was given passing grades in these studies only because of a rather broad-minded tendency of the school faculty following my victory in the state contest. Otherwise I still would be a permanent member of the senior class at Appleton high school. The simplest problem in algebra today would floor me, and if I had to extract a square root or die, then death would have no sting.

Contests and high school Forum Debating Society appearances, together with leading-lady parts in school plays, gave me assurance. We presented A Scrap of Paper, and my role demanded that I faint in the second act. I set about learning how to faint with real limpness and dramatic effect. I had seen various leading ladies faint in professional performances, and few of them had convinced me. I wanted to go down with that crumpling of the muscles and joints which only the relaxed and unconscious body can achieve. The elocution teacher essayed to teach me the trick, but I wasn't satisfied. My mother, busy at the store, had a way of calling up the house on the telephone to learn how things were with the household, and how I was faring after school hours. My sister Fannie, three years my senior,

The High School Graduate. The Dress Was Sensational.

had graduated and was deep in other concerns, though by now she was managing the household as well.

The telephone rang. I had been busy rehearsing myself, and I resented the interruption, knowing that it was probably merely my mother.

"What are you doing?" this rather terrific lady demanded, it being a moment of pause in the business of the store.

"I'm fainting," I answered, tartly, impatient of the intrusion.

"What!" shouted my mother.

"I'm fainting!" I yelled, louder than ever, and hung up. The play had been discussed at home. I assumed she would understand. I didn't, as a matter of fact, give it a thought. I had a mattress spread on the floor of my bedroom, and I was flopping like a tenpin at three-minute intervals. It wasn't until my mother arrived, breathless, wild-eyed and generally frantic, that I realized the construction she had put on my two-word extra-curriculum report.

At that time I was a plump stocky and ugly girl in eyeglasses perched atop a high-bridged nose inherited from my father. It was a feature which gave his countenance dignity and strength. It was overpowering on my round-cheeked face. I was self-conscious about my plainness; this was aggravated by the fact that my sister Fannie was very handsome, with great lustrous dark eyes and a fine figure. She was exquisitely clever with fabrics and line and color. She could make dresses, make and trim hats, she had great feeling for the indefinable thing known as style. She was running the household and taking daily instruction in millinery in the workroom of a local milliner. I remember my awe and envy of a terrific piece of headgear she produced at this time, and which she wore perched modishly atop her pompadour. A pancake made of yards and yards and yards of pleated chiffon, a rose coquetting from beneath its brim. This, together with a form-hugging fawn broadcloth suit (homemade) caused the boys outside the Sherman House to sit up.

As my hair at that time was a black thick wiry bush, and as I played a good deal of bad tennis, I was accidentally given the nickname of Fluff. "Get the ball, Fluff!" someone on the side

lines yelled as I sped toward a trick serve on the Ryan High
School courts. And Fluff I remained for years, even into my
Milwaukee newspaper-reporter days, when my plumpness and
eyeglassed severity made the name quite out of character. Later,
in Milwaukee, that nickname was abandoned and I found myself known as Weber to my Journal office friends for a reason
which I'll later make clear. And Weber or Web I still am to certain Chicago and New York friends. I rather cherish these nicknames of my girlhood, my young womanhood, my later years.
Fluff—Boots—Weber. Nicknames are fond names. We do not
give them to people we dislike.

Curiously enough, plain though I was I never lacked a beau.
I must have been good company. When there was a dance, a hay-
rack ride, a picnic, an excursion, I was invited by the current
swain. His name never was Loeb or Hammel. The Jewish boys
of my age and Esther's didn't take us out. They yearned rather
toward the Gentile girls (though there was little enough distinction between us in Appleton). I was squired by Tom
Monaghan or Arnold Knuppel or Frank (Pat) Murphy. And I
had a fine time. As to health, I was sound and had endurance,
with muscular strength and a deep well of nervous energy. But
I was inclined toward anaemia, low blood pressure and low
thyroid. These should have served to retard me in anything re-
quiring energy or concentration, but ambition and a kind of fury
to succeed triumphed over them. I was able then, as now, to
sleep eight or nine hours without waking; to walk five or six
miles without tiring. I awoke alert and refreshed, I liked to drink
water and to eat three meals a day, and to dance. You can't be
ill on that unless you break your neck.

At home we had a maid of all work, supervised by Fannie,
but the omniscient Julia ruled the roost, though she was busy
now earning the living for all of us. We were encouraged to cook.
At Ryan I had joined the weekly cooking class, where I learned a
good deal about the principles of cookery. The dishes we
essayed were, however, a shade too smothered in cream sauce
for my taste. Goy cooking, we called it. Ours was richer, more
sophisticated food. My mother was fond of telling that when

she came, a bride, to Kalamazoo, she thought that the longer an egg boiled the softer it grew. She knew better than this now, but she had no real gift for cookery. She used to do a prodigious amount of preserving, pickling and canning, however, standing over the stove in the evening or early morning, before and after store hours, stirring, bottling, straining juices. The house would be fragrant with the delicious scent of boiling berries or peaches or quinces; or with the mouth-watering smell of vinegar and spice. In the cellar there were hundreds of mason jars, row on row along the shelves, showing scarlet and golden and purple and green; stone crocks of dill pickles, put up in brine with dill and grape leaves in layers; barrels of apples, bins of vegetables, besides such tantalizers as piccalilli, chowchow, corn relish, watermelon pickle, cucumber slices. But of cooking my mother did none except to make an occasional strudel. This famous Hungarian dainty she probably had learned early in her marriage, in deference to her husband's taste. I don't know how she conquered it, for it is a difficult dish, and no relation to the flabby heavy mass of dough encountered in restaurants under the name of strudel. She got out the baking board and the rolling pin only on very special occasions. The dough must be stretched so thin that it was transparent as tissue paper. A fraction of a fraction of an inch more and it must have split. Over this glaze of dough were sprinkled nuts, citron, raisins, cinnamon, brown sugar, lumps of butter. Then, ever so cautiously, it was rolled in a long papyrus, over and over, and coiled like a white snake into a well-greased pan. This delectable dessert emerged crisp and crackling on the outside, melting and toothsome on the inside. Eaten with whipped cream it was a Hungarian's dream.

We even baked homemade bread in our household of Appleton days. I am glad that I can remember the great yellow crock plump with white dough, covered over with a clean checked tablecloth and left to rise (or raise) overnight in a snug warm spot behind the kitchen stove or near the furnace radiator. In the morning the half-filled crock of the night before was running over at the top. Kneaded and shaped into plump loaves, butter-swabbed and slid into the hot oven, the bread emerged delicious

[91]

beyond description. The very scent of fresh-baked dough is one of the most tantalizing in the world, in a class with the aroma of hot coffee on a cold winter morning, or broiling bacon in the woods.

Fannie and I cooked the pot roasts, the potted chickens, the stuffed turkeys, the devil's-food cakes, the stuffed breast of veal. The back yard yielded refreshing desserts in the summertime— iced and sugared bowls of raspberries, currants, sweet cherries. Years later, after her marriage, my sister wrote Fannie Fox's Cook Book, published by Little, Brown & Company (Advt.), and I still think it is one of the best cookbooks of its day. I wrote a food-choked introduction to it, enviously.

Always I have felt sorry for boys and girls who haven't spent the first sixteen years of their lives in a small American town. There one finds a nice balance of leisure and society which makes for richness in living. Just to sit on the front porch and watch the town go by is something of an education. You knew the wives who were bad housekeepers, because their husbands went home to noonday dinner carrying a little moist brown paper packet that was the meat for the meal. We knew when a boy came courting and when he and his girl had quarreled, and he came no more, or only, perhaps, as a silent loping figure stealing past after dark for a hungry glimpse of his lost love through the unshaded small-town windows. The local drayman drove rattling home to dinner at twelve in his faded overalls and battered hat. On Sunday, in suave black, he ushered at the fashionable Congregational church, and passed the contribution box. The Congregational church boasted a choir of one hundred male voices, and the Sunday evening services were a dazzling success the year round. Every one of us had a beau in the choir. We would listen, entranced, to the shrill of his tenor or the rumble of his bass. Then we would dawdle a little on our way out after the service, in order to give him time to stampede his way out of the choir jam, dash through the Sunday-school room and out to the line-up at the front door. Two by two we paired off to stroll into the summer night or to walk, blissfully oblivious of the northern cold and ice, across town to our homes.

The swells of the town belonged to the Episcopalian church presided over by a pink-cheeked youthful rector named Selden P. Delany. I often attended evensong with my school friend Eva Hogue, because I loved the theatrical quality of the service; the white-robed choirboys, the very high-church goings-on, the incense, the ceremony. Then, one day, Mrs. Delany, the rector's mother, confided to my mother that they had noticed my visits to the church and that they did so hope that they would be able to convert me.

My attendance ceased.

By now the store was beginning to flourish under the active management of my mother. By active I mean to convey a kind of fury. She was up before seven. She wore shirtwaists and skirts, and she returned from a Chicago buying trip with the first short skirt that Appleton had ever seen on a grown woman. It just cleared the ground. The more conservative wives and mothers raised a disapproving eye at this, and our next-door neighbor took her aside to warn her that no nice woman would appear on the street thus with her ankles showing. But the determined feet under the ground-clearing gray cloth skirt marched their way down to the store and back twice a day, daily, just the same. And presently every woman in Appleton followed her initiative. Women did not use make-up in that day. My mother's skin was sallow. Rouge was considered definitely fast, but Julia kept in her dresser drawer a cotton rose leaf dyed a brilliant red, and this she used to brush on her cheek-bones to give the skin a faint flush of pink. Heaven knows for whom; just wholesome vanity. A touch of defiance, too, directed at life.

When first she had taken hold of the business there used to be a caller at the store whose appearance froze the blood in her veins. This grim visitor was the head of the First National Bank of Appleton; a shrewd, kindly-enough man with an eye to business. Affable though he was, he knew that my father's insurance had been mortgaged, that there were mounting doctor's bills, that money had been borrowed.

Into the store he would stroll, his greeting polite and even cheery. "Good morning, good morning, Mrs. Ferber!" He would stand a moment, balancing airily from toe to heel, taking a large speculative view of the shop and its shelves and bins of goods. Then he would begin to stroll ruminatively down one aisle and up the next, his shrewd little eyes seeing and appraising everything. He would hum a little absent-minded tune as he walked, picking up a piece of china to glance at its pattern, turning over a charming Limoges plate, all guileless rosebuds on creamy white, to note the maker's mark on the back; tapping a water pitcher with judicial knuckles, staring approvingly at a smart little toilet set of ebony brushes with silver ornaments. He would put each piece down carefully after his inspection, proceeding step by step to the lamps, the hardware, the stockings, the toys.

"Very pretty. Ve-ry pretty indeed. Hmm." And so, his hands behind his back, still humming, out the screen door into the sunshine of College Avenue, leaving desperation behind him.

But now those visits had ceased. I heard an endless amount of talk about business, and hated it. My mother was, I suppose, an unhappy woman at that time, and I must have heard something of this, too. Marriage seemed to me to be less than a desirable state of being. Perhaps it was then I decided that I would have none of it. Sometimes, when I have a nightmare, I dream that it is Christmas time at the store, the aisles are packed and feverish, drafts of icy Wisconsin December air stream through the constantly opening front door, and I am saying to a mill girl or to some townswoman, "What can I show you?"

At Christmas time we all helped. My school friends used to ask if they could clerk, for the fun of it. I loathed it—the rush, the noise, the rather senseless selecting of gifts. It must be accountable for my feeling about Christmas all these years. It depresses me, I don't enjoy it, I tell myself it is because I like making gifts when I feel inclined, or when the right object strikes me, and not when the calendar dictates.

Mill hands, farmers' wives, Lawrence University professors, East End society, middle-class householders—my mother talked to everyone. Rather, they talked to her. Sitting there, in a business lull, on a stool in a corner up front beneath the bookshelves,

Julia Ferber was a sort of small-town sibyl. She had pansy-like eyes, a sympathetic and compelling way. Practically everyone told her everything. To the slick young traveling men she was a sort of mother confessor. Theirs wasn't an easy life. These drummers, living in second-rate small-town hotels, unpacking and packing their samples, vying with one another for business, eating greasy hotel food, were lonely for their wives and children, or for their girls. In the evening, after the day's work, they would sit in the plate-glass windows of the Sherman House, or outside on benches in the summertime. The town girls would flounce by—good middle-class girls to whom these rather grubby little men from the world outside their home town represented who knows what of romance and adventure.

These would lean an elbow on the showcase in the store, push their smart saw-edged sailor hats back from their brows, open their hearts, show the picture in the front of their watch or wallet, and Tell All. Their love affairs, their business worries, their marital difficulties, their grievances against the firm back East.

"Why, that's terrible!" she would say. "If I were you . . ." Her advice usually was sound. Sometimes if they were broke she lent them a few dollars, but not much. She hadn't it to spare. They always paid her back.

I heard and saw a great deal of this, and absorbed its meaning and characters and atmosphere without being conscious of it. When she went to Chicago on her buying trips she visited the big German and French importing houses from whom she bought foreign china, glassware, toys. The salesmen often tried a flirtation or invited her to dinner and the theater, but she would have none of them. Dead tired at the end of a day spent in the wholesale district, making decisions on which depended the success or failure of the next six business months, she would go home and tumble into bed at the Neumanns'. Her three brothers and her sister, all unmarried, lived together in a comfortable house on the south side of Chicago. Of five children, my mother was the only one who married.

The margin between loss and gain was so slender in those

days of her first taking hold that there was something miraculous in her maintaining the balance at all. She tried little harmless tricks that represented the difference between a hundred dollars' gain or loss on the week. Two glass punch bowls that had cost a dollar each at wholesale in Chicago could be rented out, together with silver ladles that had been wedding presents to the Kalamazoo bride, every day in the week for college parties, club meetings, whist parties, dances and lodge shindigs. Nothing escaped her. Cracked or chipped dishes could be sold to the farmers' wives to be used in threshing or harvest time. Once, on a buying trip, she came across hundreds of discarded paperbound copies of Sappho. She bought the lot for almost nothing, had them dusted off, stacked them luridly in the window, from which they vanished like hot cakes for twenty-five cents apiece. Sappho was considered a very daring book indeed in those days. Rather pitiful little tricks, and touchingly desperate, but legitimate. She had an incredible eye for a bargain. At the famous importing house of Borgfeldt she happened upon a great bin with shelves full of dusty grimy china figures, evidently neglected and forgotten. They were from five inches to a foot high; religious figures, in colors, representing all the saints, the Pietà, the cradle in the manger.

"How much?" she demanded of the salesman.

"Those!" He stared, vaguely surprised. "Oh, you don't want those, Mrs. Ferber. That's a discarded lot of china stuff."

"How much for the lot?"

Shipped back to Appleton, dusty and shelfworn, in their bedding of straw and paper, they were given a bath in soap and water—hundreds of these small figures. Beneath the grime they emerged fine examples of foreign workmanship, their blue and gold and crimson and purple and white brilliant and fadeless as the colors found in the cathedrals of Europe. Saints, angels and cherubim gleamed fresh-cheeked and rosy in the window. Father Fitzmaurice's parishioners made a clean sweep of them in less than twenty-four hours. Only four hundred dollars. But no million-dollar Wall Street coup ever brought such a feeling of quiet triumph.

Some of this I used in the novel Fanny Herself. Much of the material used in the Emma McChesney stories stemmed from these days when my eyes and ears were wide open, and my mind as porous as a sponge.

The farm women and their husbands and their hard, often tragic lives emerged from the old yellow trunk when I started to write So Big, many years later. In those days there was no whirling into town in fifteen minutes in the Ford, to go to the movies and buy a Coca-Cola and the evening paper. The Wisconsin farmer started for town on Saturday before daybreak, the great farm horses, shaggy of mane and fetlock, clop-clopping down the dirt road or snow ruts, with the farmer, his wife, the day's market produce and such children as could be spared from the farm work piled into the buckboard. Calves, pigs, vegetables, chickens, corn, oats, children arrived in town half frozen in the winter, baked in the summer. At noon on Saturday you would see the farm wagons thick in the barnyard of the Farmers Rest Hotel on Morrison Street, and the smell of frying pork and potatoes and cabbage and pipe tobacco floated out from the open doors and windows. To the Ferber family it would have seemed very odd indeed to have to purchase at Appleton grocers' or butchers' in the ordinary way such supplies as chickens, ducks, butter, eggs, corn, peas, beets, beans, apples and the like. The farmers preferred to trade in these commodities for articles of wearing apparel and household necessity. Stockings, china, kitchenware, glassware made the exchange. A farm wagon would drive up to the door of the Ferber house on North Street and the kitchen table would immediately take on the look of a Hans Holbein still-life.

The farmers' wives were wrinkled and old long before their time. It was a bitter hard life. Such ready money as the farmers had went into farm machinery and livestock and repairs. There were no radios then, no washing machines, no electricity, no automobiles in the Wisconsin farmhouse. In winter the farmer's wife would be wrapped in a huge shapeless fringed shawl, but the husband would be snug in a sheepskin or even a buffalo-hide coat. Sometimes the women tried to furbish their mashed little hats with red cotton roses bobbing grotesquely atop them. Invariably the women had bad teeth, with great gaps where molars were missing. Often the comparatively well-to-do had new and improbable sets of gleaming blue-white china store teeth. The women, at thirty, looked like crones of sixty. Back-breaking work, childbearing and the monotony of farm life took their toll of young red-cheeked farm girls. Julia Ferber would talk to them as they waited in the store for their husbands to call for them.

"How many children?"

"Well, I had ten a'ready. And I never had no doctor, neither, time they was born."

"Who helped you?"

"Neighbor woman, she helped. We never had no doctor in our house, yet."

"How many of your children are living, Mrs. Koepke?"

"I got two boys and one girl, she ain't so strong, her back."

If the farmers came to Ferber's store for their threshing dishes and chamber pots, the social East End set soon learned that the whist prizes, the china, the glassware and novelties were distinctive. They were bought from importers, and had the foreign craftsman's touch. These, too, confided in Julia Ferber, strangely enough. My husband—my children—my gowns—my hopes—my fears. There was a little strain of mischief in her, and she sometimes used to guy these people gently; people who bragged too much. She called it "blowing."

"You don't say!" she would exclaim, murderously, as they recounted their importance or their social exploits. "That's perfectly LOVE-ly!"

Of the clerks in the store there were two who were more than employees; they were warmhearted friends and helpers. One was Martha Gresens. Martha not only clerked, but on dull days, or when the streets were locked in drifts of snow, you found her up in the broad balcony, where the sleds and tricycles and such heavy toys were kept, sewing on dresses for me or Fannie. Martha was an accomplished needlewoman. She actually made my high school graduation dress—a dream dress in my opinion, made of white point d'esprit with row after row of narrow white satin ribbon. A sensational dress.

Arthur Howe, an Irish boy, gangling, red-wristed and witty, was clerk, handyman and delivery. He was a born actor, with a devastating gift of mimicry. Fortunately, Appleton's dignitaries never heard or saw Arthur's miraculous imitations. Toward my father Arthur was patience itself. He took him on long walks—too long—when he delivered goods. Sometimes he made those deliveries trailing after him a child's size painted wooden cart, the blind man at his side. They must have made a touching and grimly comic picture. Mercifully, perhaps, it didn't strike us so, or the townspeople.

The eyes were very bad now. He could still see just a glimmering little. There never had come to him the compensation that the blind usually have—a heightening of the remaining senses as one sense grows weak and weaker. He never became reconciled to blindness, he fought it and bitterly resented it. He would start out alone when we weren't looking, and then would begin a rather wild hunt, with a clutching of fear at our vitals. For usually, when the Pain came upon him, he would grow dizzy and faint. Never, in those years, could I see a little crowd collected anywhere on the street that I failed to feel that clutch of sick apprehension. I would break into a little run, afraid to look but elbowing through the throng to look and peer until I saw whether what I feared was true or not.

He spent longer and longer hours on the front porch at home, and with this we were content. There was between us a mild joke. At an Elks convention in Appleton some years back the lodge members had gone up and down the streets shouting the Elks convention formula greeting of "Hello, Bill!" All that week I had greeted my father, facetiously, with the stock, "Hello, Bill!" and Bill he remained to me thereafter. He, from my early childhood, had called me Pete. I was, I suppose, a self-assertive and boyish little girl. So, then, there was this mild joke between us.

"Hello, Bill!" I would greet him.

"Hello, Pete! What you reading?"

"Dickens."

"Dickens! I thought you'd read that."

It was sad when he lost his taste for smoking. Ever since I could remember he had loved to smoke mild pale-brown dapper cigars. As sight slipped from him his enjoyment of this solace went with it. The smoker usually is unaware that he watches the smoke from cigar, cigarette or pipe, and is soothed by it as by the narcotic. It must have been so in his case. As he held his cigar between his teeth a little puzzled disappointed look would come into his face. He would take the cigar from his lips and look at it, sorrowfully, as one would survey a treacherous trusted friend. He would quietly put it down, the smoke would curl futilely for a while, then die. The fragrant weed would be a dead stinking thing, fit only for the ash can. When a friend or a chance traveling man offered him a cigar he would shake his head sadly. "No. I used to love to smoke. But now I can't see it. No sir, I don't enjoy smoking any more. I don't know why."

Now the four happy years at Ryan High School were over. Curiously enough, I not only had been happy—I had known I was happy. I used to say to myself, "Edna, you're having a wonderful time. You're having the time of your life."

Perhaps the bitter years of early childhood had taught me that. It is true that all my life (perhaps this was, unconsciously, the writer's double reaction) I have been able to have a sensation and to analyze myself while having it. It makes enjoyment doubly keen, and pain doubly sharp, and it is, incidentally, deathly hard on romance.

After winning the Wisconsin state declamatory contest just before graduation in June my mind was made up. I would go away to the Northwestern University School of Elocution, in Evanston, Illinois. I don't think my imagination leaped so far as to encompass the distance between this elocutionary course and the professional stage, but I must have had this stored away somewhere in the back of my mind.

My announcement of this resolution caused a family whirl-wind. I had no money of my own. I was seventeen. We, a family of four, were bound together in ties even closer than those of the average Jewish family. The blind man leaned on me, and I felt a great protective pity for him as he stumbled so clumsily through life. My mother was working like a man. My sister, pretty, gentle, talented in her own way, was too tied to the house and its duties. I tried to stand out against it all, but I was still too young and too tenderhearted and too weak. The matter of pocket money or some such matter came up, was threshed out, led to high words.

In a white-hot rage I, saying nothing to the family, marched down to the office of the Appleton Daily Crescent and had a blistering talk with Sam Ryan, its editor. He, owner of this well-run small-town paper, had heard of my work on the high school paper. Then, too, I had written a piece describing the confirmation service at Temple Emanu-El that year, and the Crescent had printed it. Too, the winning of the state contest had put me, so far as that small community was concerned, in something of the position of the college athlete who easily gets a job selling bonds in a broker's office.

My business with Sam Ryan concluded, I then marched home bursting with spite and announced that I had signed a contract with Sam Ryan to work for three dollars a week as a reporter on the Appleton Crescent. The fact that I was not of legal age, and that any contract must therefore be void, never occurred to any of us.

Well, there I was, a girl reporter. I didn't want to be a writer. I never had wanted to be a writer. I couldn't even use a typewriter, never having tried. The stage was my one love. To this moment I feel sure (but not so sure as I once did) that I would have been The Actress of my day. I go to the theater because I love it; I write plays for the theater because I love it. I am still wrapped in my childish dream, and I never see such gifted girls as Katharine Cornell, Helen Hayes, Ruth Gordon, Lynn Fontanne that I do not feel sure I could do much better than they if only I were up there playing the part. Perhaps one reason why I've never acted is the fear of showing myself up to myself as a fraud after all these resentful years.

At any rate, then, at seventeen my writing career accidentally began. It was brewed in a storm. I don't remember a day since then when I haven't been writing, in all sorts of circumstances, happy and wretched, ill or well, traveling or at home. Writing has brought me friends and fortune and happiness and world-wide interests.

But to this day I regard myself as a blighted Bernhardt.

8

THERE NEVER HAD BEEN a woman reporter in Appleton. The
town, broad-minded though it was, put me down as definitely
cuckoo. Not crazy, but strange. Big-town newspapers, such as
the Chicago Tribune and the Milwaukee Sentinel, employed
women on their editorial and reportorial staffs, but usually
these were what is known as special or feature writers, or they
conducted question-and-answer columns, advice to the lovelorn,
society columns or woman's pages. But at seventeen on the
Appleton Crescent I found myself covering a regular news beat
like any man reporter. I often was embarrassed, sometimes frightened, frequently offended and offensive, but I enjoyed it, and
knowing what I know today I wouldn't swap that year and a half
of small-town newspaper reporting for any four years of college
education. I'm a blank when it comes to Latin, I can't bound New
York State, and I count on my fingers, but in those eighteen
months I learned to read what lay behind the look that veiled
people's faces, I learned how to sketch in human beings with a
few rapid words, I learned to see, to observe, to remember;
learned, in short, the first rules of writing. And I was the town
scourge.

No wonder they found me a freak. In appearance I was short

and plump, my abundant hair tied at the back of the neck in a bunch of short black wiry curls held by a wide black taffeta bow. My coiffure was further enhanced by a large black ribbon *chou* nestling in one corner of a massive pompadour. My shirt-waist with its modish broad Gibson shoulder tuck was finished at the throat with a stiff white standing collar and a tie which should have been a four-in-hand but wasn't because I never could master that intricate knot. My Ryan High School class pin naïvely ornamented the tie. The whole effect was less that of a hard-boiled newspaper reporter than it is possible to convey. After six months of scouring the town it was suggested to me by Sam Ryan that perhaps I'd present a slightly more professional appearance if I'd put my hair up. I took the hint. The more sophisticated hairdress, together with my embonpoint, emphasized by the voluminous starched umbrella drawers, the petti-coats, the boned corsets and ruffled corset covers of the day changed me from a roly-poly schoolgirl into what seemed to be a plump Midwestern young matron. Dieting hadn't become a fad. I liked good food and ate what I liked. Besides, to know the fashionable figure of that time one need only dig up a photo-graph of that famous stage beauty, Lillian Russell, curved like a roller coaster.

Ten years of haphazard omnivorous reading served me well now. Year in, year out, I had read at least a book a day. In one long Wisconsin summer afternoon, stretched in the hammock under the cherry tree, I could gallop through The Three Musketeers. Now, when I needed it, I found myself equipped with a fair vocabulary. The deep reach within oneself for that right first word with which to start the paragraph miraculously brought the word to the surface.

O. Henry, the writer of short stories with the snapper ending, was the model after which every young writer patterned him-self. In the magazine room of the Appleton public library I always searched the periodicals for an O. Henry story. Now, unconsciously, I copied his style; but there was a strong dash of Dickens, too; and De Maupassant, Balzac, Mark Twain, The Duchess, and Robert W. Chambers were not slighted. Readers

The Reporter for the Appleton Crescent. The Pompadour Was a Success but Not the Four-in-hand.

A Senior at Ryan High School, Appleton, Wisconsin. The Blouse Seems to Be in Trouble, but the Hat (Whipped up at Home by Sister Fan) Makes up for Everything.

of the Appleton Crescent could not complain of faring meagerly at my hands. Much of it may have been hash—but it was good rich hash.

Those three dollars per week were earned. Eight in the morning found me at my desk. Lest that should have a rich and commanding sound I hasten to add that my desk was a shaky pine table in the darkest, smallest and dustiest corner of that dark, small and dusty room which constituted the Crescent editorial department. We worked underground, like moles. Why, in this sunny little Wisconsin town, Sam Ryan and his father James Ryan before him had chosen to install their newspaper plant in a basement, I can't imagine. Thrift, probably. There it was below the street level at the corner of College Avenue and Morrison Street. There were five little stone steps leading down to the front office. By the very way in which a reporter hurled himself down those steps you could sense whether he had a good story or not. As the windows, dust-dimmed, were on a level with the sidewalk, we in our little cave, as we sat at our typewriters, glimpsed the passing world only from the feet to the ribs. Though we saw no faces we learned to distinguish Banker Erb by his walk and his stomach; George Baldwin by his hands, always mysteriously gloved summer and winter; Mrs. Lawrence University Professor's wife Hotchkiss by her derrière; Earl Kenyon by the way he toed in.

Stuffed into the little room were five desks. We worked in a clattering heap. Sam Ryan, editor and proprietor, kinged it at a roll-top which was marked off from the rest of the room by a chicken-wire fence, heaven knows why, unless it was to prevent him from hurling paste pots at us, or infuriated reporters from throwing scissors at him. A difficult but distinctive fellow, Sam Ryan; an irascible bachelor, bald, sarcastic, fortyish. Fishing was his passion. He would let the presses wait to talk rods and flies with a chance visitor. The newspaper business irritated him. Outside the office he was kind, humorous, companionable. During working hours he lost his temper at the slightest provocation. It must have been indigestion or an inhibition or just rebellion at finding himself in a stuffy office instead of thigh deep in a trout

stream. He was a fluent curser. When he discovered a typo-
graphical error or when something went wrong in the back shop
the air crackled with his star-spangled profanity. Though a vast
wastebasket stood at his elbow he had a habit of throwing newspaper exchanges, old copy paper, letters and envelopes under his
desk, usually crushed into a vicious wad. When he began to
scuffle his feet among these papers, slam objects on his desk and
mutter imprecations we knew he was in a tantrum. He would
push back his chair with a squeaking of casters and make for
the back room, a sheet of galley proof streaming behind him
like the tail of a fiery comet. To me he was sweetness and gentle-
ness itself, under all his scathing irony and caustic comment. He
taught me much about newspaper work and writing. Through
those thick-lensed spectacles his myopic pale-blue eyes saw the
town stripped to the skin. His was a mordant but tangy comment. He knew writing when he saw it in others. He himself
couldn't write worth a cent.

At right angles with Sam's desk, her back to the street window,
sat his sister, Miss Ivy Ryan, a shrewd and witty spinster. She
was the office bookkeeper, she took want ads and all paid notices
for lodge and society meetings, death announcements and the
like. Short, plump, birdlike, Ivy Ryan was at once a pillar of
strength and a source of quiet entertainment in that fusty
little hive. She never lost her temper (God knows there wasn't
room for two tempers in that box); she had you classified before
you so much as turned the corner of the chicken-wire fence.
Her shirtwaists were always exquisitely crisp and fresh, she
wore armlets to protect her immaculate sleeves, her hair was
done in a psyche knot on top of her head. She taught me volumes. Lodge sisters were clay in her hands. It was before the day
of the Rotarians, and the town hummed with Foresters, Masons,
Odd Fellows, Knights of Pythias, Woodmen, Knights of Columbus, Elks. These were forever having suppers, dances, picnics,
initiations, parades, and many of them boasted a ladies' auxiliary.
One or another of these seemed constantly to be laboriously
descending the precarious stone steps into the basement office to
place an announcement or an ad. They called it "inserting a

squib." It is a phrase that infuriates all newspaper people. Nothing so offends a newspaper reporter as to hear his story spoken of as a "squib." "I saw your little squib in the paper today"— those are fighting words.

One ladies' auxiliary in particular was active beyond belief. No sooner had they finished with a Chicken-Pie Supper than they were waist deep in a Cake Sale. They were forever "inserting a squib." Deep-bosomed ample women in eyeglasses and sensible hats and durable coats, bent on relieving the tedium of child-rearing and housekeeping by these worthy social gatherings. This feminine adjunct of the male organization was called the Venus Lodge. Ivy Ryan took a wicked enjoyment in the name. She dubbed them Wenuses. In time we of the Crescent office designated as Wenuses all matrons of the big-bosomed, bustling and officious type. "She's a Wenus" meant a definite breed to us, no matter what her social standing. Ivy had a news nose keener than that of any reporter or editor in town. She knew the history, inside and out, of every household in Appleton, and no family skeleton so dry that she could not have ferreted out its bones if she had chosen. With all this she wasn't a gossip. Hers was a storehouse of knowledge which added just the proper soupçon of spice to her lively and sustaining conversation.

The remaining three desks were those of the city editor, Pomeroy; the reporter, Byron Beveridge; and myself. Pomeroy was an Appleton man. Very shortly after my coming to the paper he was replaced by a big-city importation, a shy nervous young fellow named John Meyer who had been a desk man on one of the Milwaukee papers. He was an easy blusher and we used to plot to make the scarlet rush up into his fine fair skin. He was too keenly trained for his job, really. He worked hard and well, but the whole setup irked him. He had a temper, too, and was of no mind to defer to Sam Ryan. The two would glare at each other, Sam would start to scuffle his feet among the papers under his desk, slam, mutter. There never was a cub reporter more blundering and naïve than I, but Meyer never lost his temper with me, and when he left to go back to Milwaukee some months later he made me heir to his job as Appleton correspondent of the Milwaukee Journal.

The reporter, Byron Beveridge, was a lanky cadaverous chap who had been a lieutenant in the Spanish-American War and was a great Company G boy and man-about-town. He wasn't a warm or even an engaging personality, but he knew everyone, everyone knew him, his lank stoop-shouldered figure ranged the town at a lope.

The printing shop and pressroom were separated from the front office only by a doorway, and the door never was closed. There were the type forms and tables, the linotype machine (a new and fearsome invention to me), the small press, the big newspaper press, the boiler plate, the trays of type, all the paraphernalia that goes to make up the heart of a small-town newspaper. The front room is its head, but without the back room it could not function or even live. The linotype and the small press went all day, for there the advertising was set up and printed, as well as handbills, programs, all the odds and ends classified as job printing. Mac, who ruled this domain, was the perfect example of the fictional printer. He had come in, a tramp printer, years before. He was given to periodic sprees, his brown hair curled over a mild brow, the corners of his drooping walrus mustache were stained with tobacco juice, his limp shirt seemed perennial. But his eye, though sometimes bleary, was infallible, and few if any shrdlus and etaoins marred the fair sequence of Mac's copy. His voice was soft, gentle, drawling, but he was boss of the print shop from the cat to the linotype operator. Mac seldom talked but sometimes—rarely—he appeared in the front office, a drooping figure, with a piece of news by which he had come in some devious way. Standing at the side of the city editor's desk he would deliver himself of this information, looking mild and limply romantic. It always proved to be a bombshell.

Such was the make-up of the Appleton, Wisconsin, Daily Crescent office.

In the past thirty years all sorts of ex-newspaper men from Richard Harding Davis to Vincent Sheean and John Gunther have written about the lure of the reporter's life, the smell of printer's ink, the adventure of reporting. It all sounds slightly sentimental and silly, but it's true—or it was, at least, in my newspaper experience. To this day I can't smell the scent of white paper, wet ink, oil, hot lead, mucilage, tobacco and cats that goes to make up the peculiar odor of any newspaper plant, be it Appleton, Wisconsin, or Cairo, Egypt, that I don't get a pang of nostalgia for the old reporting days. "I was once a newspaper man myself" has come to be a fun phrase. But practically everyone seems to have been, or to have wanted to be, a newspaper reporter.

My handwriting at that time was (and still is) that of a ten-year-old who is not quite bright. I never had used a typewriter. The city editor, the printers, the linotype operator rebelled at trying to decipher my penciled scrawls. Out of some back-room junk heap was retrieved a vintage Oliver typewriter which in appearance, sound and action resembled a broken-down lawn mower. On this I essayed painfully to pick my way with two forefingers and a thumb. After thirty years of typewriting daily for hours I still use this method, but necessity has taught me speed. As time went on it became impossible for me to think in writing terms unless my hands were on the typewriter keyboard. A pen or pencil is like a shovel in my fingers, and the signing of my name at the bottom of a letter or a check constitutes my longhand stint from one year's end to the other. On trains or shipboard I use a portable. A pencil spells creative paralysis for me, so strong is the habit of newspaper training.

The Appleton Crescent was my school and workshop from the time I turned seventeen until I was eighteen and a half. It was just long enough. The whole community may sift through a reporter's fingers in that time. It always has been my contention that when a newspaper man or woman has written that Christmas story three times for the same paper he should leave his job or reconcile himself to being a hack reporter forever. I may be flattering myself, but I think I can usually spot a man or woman who has been a newspaper reporter. I don't mean merely one who has dabbled in newspaper work, sending in vague "items," dreamy articles and amateurish out-of-town correspondence. I mean a reporter who has gone through the grind and tension of a year or more of actual leg work, getting the news, and getting it all, and getting it first if possible. The alumni of this school usually are alert, laconic, devastatingly observant, debunked and astringent. They are, too—paradoxically enough—likely to be at once hard-boiled and sentimental. The career of a newspaper reporter does not make for erudition, but through it one acquires a storehouse of practical and psychological knowledge, and a ghastly gift of telling the sham from the real, of being able to read and classify the human face, on or off guard.

It makes little difference whether the paper is large or small, the town one of fifteen thousand or a million five hundred thousand. There are—in the approximate words of the Harry Leon Wilson-Booth Tarkington play, The Man from Home —just as many kinds of people in Kokomo as there are in Paris.

Eight o'clock found me pounding down Morrison Street on my way to the office. Before eight-thirty the city editor had handed me my assignment sheet for the day. Dull-enough stuff, usually, for I was the least important cog in the Crescent office machine. When it came to news stories the city editor came first. He had his regular run—the juiciest one, of course. Next came Byron Beveridge. All the really succulent bits fell to them— the Elks Club up above Wharton's China Store on College Avenue, where the gay blades of the town assembled; Moriarty's pool shack, the Sherman House, the city jail, the fire-engine house, the Hub Clothing Store, the coroner's office, the mayor's office, Peter Thom's stationery and tobacco store, Little's Drug Store, the Sherman Barber Shop—these were the rich cupboards from which the real food of the day's news was dispensed. There you found the facts and gossip of business, politics, scandal, petty crime.

To me fell the crumbs. They gave me the daily courthouse run and I wondered why until I discovered that it was up in the Chute at the far end of town, a good mile and a half distant. You could take the bumpy little local street car, but that cost five cents one way, and the office furnished no carfare for daily scheduled runs. Sixty cents a week was too serious a bite out of a three-dollar weekly wage. I walked it. I walked miles and miles and miles, daily. At the end of that first year my plumpness had melted almost to streamline proportions.

At eight in the morning, then, I turned in any bits of news that I had accumulated since closing time the day before. I scanned my assignment sheet. I rewrote any out-of-town exchange clippings given me. Then I took up the run that I had dug up for myself. Ferber's Store (The My Store it had unfortunately been called by my father, who had fancied that as an original and distinguished name for his place of business, poor dear) furnished me with some meager odds and ends, what with Martha Gresens, the clerk who lived on the other side of the tracks, Arthur Howe from up in the Chute and Julia Ferber whose bright brown eyes saw everything. I paid a daily morning call on the Pettibone-Peabody department store, the biggest shop in town. Jo Steele, the general manager, didn't like a reporter nosing around, taking his clerks' time and making a sort of gossip center of his place of business. The other merchants didn't like my coming in for news, either. I always felt like a sneak thief when I entered Pettibone's or Peerenboom's or Ingold's. Fortunately, old man Peabody, our chief merchant and the town swell, never knew of my existence. He rarely favored Appleton with his presence. A widower and an Anglophile, he was the only man in our town who wore spats, a walking stick, and a pince-nez with a broad black ribbon. It is characteristic of the town's broadmindedness and tolerance that it neither ridiculed this affectation of his nor deferred to it. It was simply accepted as was my newspaper gallivanting and Doc Meeker's deafening red automobile—the first in Appleton—and the immoral goings-on of the town idiot, Minnie the Hatrack. Pettibone's was rather a rich vein. Irish witty Ella Malone in the woolens, Madonna-faced Tillie Whitman in the fancy goods and notions, the waspwaisted James girls in the silks-by-the-yard were utter darlings. They would pause in their early-morning stock arranging to give me such innocuous Personal and Local items as came to their

[111]

minds—a new sidewalk being built in front of St. Patrick's Catholic church, Mr. and Mrs. Ernie Wagner going to Madison for the graduation of their son Ernest at the University of Wisconsin. Then, with a swift glance around, they would hastily, and *sotto voce,* impart a smart bit of gossip that would send me off hotfoot on the scent of a real story. A man reporter wouldn't have been permitted to enter these places of business as part of his daily news run. They were too kindhearted to throw out a girl.

It was all to be grist for my mill in the years to come, but I didn't know it then. My first short story, entitled The Homely Heroine, starts with a brief description of the clerks in Pettibone's Dry Goods Store, and I used its atmosphere and that of Ferber's My Store for parts of any number of the Emma McChesney stories.

Another source of news, incredibly enough, was the gray stone monastery that nestled among the trees near the ravine next to the German Catholic church. My buddy was Father Basilius—Father Basil for short. He was the unofficial go-getter and publicity expert for the church. Such information as he gave me was church and parish stuff, and he was charming about it, with a real nose for news. I called at the monastery door twice a week. A plumpish brown-bearded man, Father Basil, peering with very nearsighted eyes through thick spectacles; his brown habit was tied with a stout brown rope-cord about his ample waist, and his bare feet were thrust into sandals. He and I would sit on the bench under the chestnut tree in the courtyard and have a good gossip, very cozy and comfortable. What do you know, Father Basil? Whaddyou know?

What do you know? What do you know? What do you know? It is the greeting of the reporter the world over. I sometimes find myself saying it still. When I hear it in greeting— whether from a senator, a millionaire or a tramp—I know that that one has been a newspaper man himself.

The courthouse, the county jail up in Chute at the other end of town, these weren't nourishing news sources, but I had to cover them. Such criminals as were housed in the tree-shaded county jail were there for crimes which already had been disposed of as news. Courthouse records were made up of dry bits such as real-estate transfers in the town and the near-by farm districts. There was nothing very exhilarating about jotting down items such as "State of Wisconsin, Winnebago County, Such-and-Such Township, sixty acres northeast section, etc." But having plodded the mile and a half up there I gleaned what I could. Bailiffs, clerks, courthouse hangers-on were a roughish tobacco-chewing crew with little enough to do. I was fair game for them. As I clattered up and down the long corridors paved with tiles, in and out of the land record office, the county clerk's office, here and there, making a lot of noise with my hurried determined step, one of the men in a group called out to me in greeting one morning, "Hi, Boots!" And Boots I remained as long as I worked on the Appleton Crescent.

I ranged the town, ferreting out corners too obscure or too obvious for the loftier glance of Meyer or Beveridge. Sometimes rich morsels repaid me for my pains. If space permitted I was allowed such feature or special stories as struck my fancy. This sort of half-imaginative writing turned out to be excellent practice for later fiction-writing use. I raked up tear-jerkers about the Poor Farm at the edge of town; when Barnum & Bailey's circus came to town I spent the day in the back tents with the performers. I ate dinner with the Living Skeleton, the Fat Lady, the clowns and the trapeze artists, and very good it was, too. The tents were miracles of cleanliness, the circus people friendly and warmhearted, my story was the trite and shopworn stuff about the bareback rider in the pink tights and spangles sitting in her tent just before the show sewing a fine seam on her baby's dress or mending her lion-tamer husband's socks, or some such matter. But it was all new to me, and true, so perhaps it had something of freshness, as well.

When notables came to town there was a race between Byron Beveridge and me, and that was where I usually won. Beveridge was a good reporter, but he wasn't a writer who could embellish a feature story or an interview with characterization, dialogue or humor. So, then, when any notable such as Lillian Russell came to town she was my dish. She was playing in Wildfire, and she was the first real beauty I had ever seen and the first stage star to whom I had ever talked. Lillian Russell was past her prime then, heavy even in that day of the round feminine figure. But hers was the beauty of conformation, of bone structure, of coloring which endures as long as the human body itself persists. Thirteen years later she and I spoke on the same platform at the Blackstone in Chicago during a World War Red Cross Drive. She must have been sixtyish; she was as beautiful, as radiant as ever. She had the unlined face of one whose character and disposition contain nothing of spite, meanness, jealousy or temper. Or perhaps fifty years of theatrical cold cream had something to do with it. As I talked to her in Appleton, a gauche, ugly, self-conscious girl reporter, she made me feel beautiful and important, heaven knows how. Perhaps it was because she herself had radiant beauty to spare. Her skin was poreless as—well, cream and roses will have to do—the eye lay in the socket like a sapphire pool, and it seemed to be cut out at the corners just that fraction of an inch beyond the average eye, so that it appeared larger and more lustrous than the ordinary. Her nose was the purest example I'd ever beheld of that vulgar feature, and the planes of her face from cheekbone to chin had the curve of a bird's wing. She wore a skin-tight striped tailor-made suit and a great picture hat.

I certainly spread myself on that story.

Celebrities didn't come our way often. When Houdini, the Handcuff King, arrived with his show he got shorter shrift than he deserved, being a home-town boy. Before my day he had been a local product, Harry Weiss, the son of a Russian Jewish rabbi. Failing to find him at his hotel or at the theater I encountered him by chance on College Avenue at the drugstore corner just across from the Crescent office. Outside the store was the usual slot machine containing chocolate and chewing gum. As he chatted affably with me Houdini leaned carelessly against this. At the end of the interview he dropped a cold metal object into my hand.

"There's the padlock to this slot machine," he said. "Better give it to the drugstore man. Somebody'll steal all his chewing gum."

I hadn't seen so much as a movement of his fingers. Tottering with admiration I went back to the office to write my story.

Just about this time there began to appear in the Saturday Evening Post a series of stories—I think by a new writer named Miriam Michelson—entitled A Yellow Journalist. That was a new phrase; those were fresh and racy newspaper stories all about a woman reporter and her dashing adventures on a big-town paper. There was the kind of newspaper woman I wanted to be. Immediately I dramatized myself as the Girl Reporter. Big news rarely broke in our well-conducted little town. I used to pray for a murder, but I never got an answer to prayer. In all the years of our life there not a single murder or even a robbery of anything more than a turnip field, an apple orchard or perhaps a trinket filched from a store counter ever marred the peace of the thriving Wisconsin town. The Appletonians worked, lived, were content, behaved as civilization does when it is not frightened and resentful.

I must have been quite obnoxious but I did bring in the news. As an amateur detective in a farce gets down on his knees to examine footprints in a cracker-barrel robbery, so I made much of small events and motivations. Housewives fled at my approach, clerks dodged behind counters, policemen turned their coats inside out and hid their badges, my best friends grew wary of confidences. Life for me narrowed down to this. It was news or it was nothing. I talked to everyone; the railroad-crossing gate-keeper, the farmers in town, the interurban-car motorman.

Ours was, of course, an afternoon paper. The rattle and clank of the linotype machine grew more feverish as noon passed. It had a fascination for me, that strange and talented contraption, and to this day I stand in awe of it. There was, for me, something human about the way in which it carried the leads, picked them up in its long skinny arm, brought them over, dropped them out of its metal fingers, deposited them neatly with a rattle and clank of relief, then stretched forth for more.

By two-thirty or three the paper was put to bed, the press was rolling. The chatter of the linotype, the locking of the forms, the thump-thump of the press were plain in our ears as we sat at our typewriters in the front office, for the open door between us and the back shop made one big room of the whole. Townspeople slammed and scuffed up and down the stone steps, in and out of the office, all day long. I early learned that the big story isn't the one that is brought to you. The things people want you to print in your paper usually are the things of interest to few besides themselves. One of the angles that make newspaper reporting so chancy, exhilarating and absorbing is the chase. The person you want most to talk to frequently doesn't want to talk to you, though it is an amazing fact that almost anyone, properly approached, will tell you almost anything. Half the people I encountered preferred not to have me discover the very thing I wanted most to know. It wasn't long before I learned, from that quick appraising look at my victim's face, to gauge his character and to shape my approach in accordance. If he didn't want to talk he must be made to talk by wheedling, bribing, cajoling, threatening, playing for sympathy. Roughly, the approach was one of these:

1. I understand your reluctance to talk about this. But I have to turn in some kind of story. I can't go back to the office without it. Don't you think we'd better get it straight from you?

2. It's going to be in the newspapers anyway. Take my advice. Talk.

3. I wish you'd help me out on this. If I come back without a story I'll lose my job.

4. I think—if you don't mind my saying so—that you've taken a wonderful stand in this matter. I'd like to be able to write it from your viewpoint, because it seems to me to be the only one worth while.

5. Perhaps if you'll tell me all about this, frankly, we can help you.

If all this sounds revolting, it is as nothing compared to coming into the office without your story.

During this year and a half of small-town cub reporting I formed the habit of trained observation and memory. A good reporter sees and remembers at a glance. It is called the camera eye. If it is a supercamera eye it not only sees, it gets a sort of X-ray impression. That kind of reporter gives vitality to bare incidents. Perhaps I was helped by the fact that we, as a family at home, were given to quick appraisal and decision. Perhaps it is a Jewish trait. People who must walk in the midst of crowded and dangerous traffic learn to see with the back of the head as well as the front. A sixth sense develops, for protection.

I learned to see and remember details without taking notes. If I had to take them it was done as surreptitiously as possible in the presence of the person being interviewed, or after I had left and was on my way back to the office. A trained reporter, in an interview, takes notes only if he must. It is only on the stage that a reporter whips out a notebook and begins to scribble feverishly. Most newspaper people do their note-taking on a little folded sheaf of yellow copy paper grabbed up on their way out of the office. If he must use this homemade pad he usually lets his pencil scrawl unguided, his gaze meeting the eye of the person speaking, and responding to it. To one being interviewed there is something disconcerting about the sight of that busy pencil traveling over the blank paper. His speech hesitates, falters, the flow of revelation ceases. People tell you more when you are looking at them with understanding or sympathy. It is a kind of hypnotism. After all, I was not yet eighteen, not even fully grown, my mind and body were elastic. I learned to remember whole speeches as I heard them, the phrases falling into the proper sequence. I saw and remembered the location of doors, windows, furniture, small objects. The eye recorded the look on a face, the turn of a hand, the style and set of clothing, the cadence of a voice. It wasn't done consciously. Necessity brought it about. Fortunately there was little nervous or physical strain connected with working on a paper in a town the size of Appleton. But the Milwaukee Journal did affect my general health for my lifetime.

The reporter's habit of hanging around the office after hours now insidiously began. I stayed at my typewriter or sat talking when the day's grist had long been on the press. In the evening I couldn't resist dropping into the little basement office if I came within a block of it. The yellow light glowed cozily through the grimy window level with the street. Someone was always at work down there, bent over a typewriter or a desk—Beveridge or Meyer or Ryan.

As for Mac, the boss printer, he seemed never to go home. No night hour so late, no morning hour so early that you wouldn't find Mac down among the type cases or sitting droopily on the back shop steps smoking a malodorous pipe and thinking vagrant thoughts. Perhaps he slept on the paper-stuffed burlap sacks, like the office cat. You knew that one day Mac would be missing—off down the road again, a few dollars in his pocket, the Appleton Crescent a memory, the next job awaiting his pleasure.

Meyer and Beveridge had out-of-town newspaper correspondence the less pressing stories of which they mailed out at night. I would busy myself somehow, just to hear the talk and be in on the atmosphere. It was more fun down in the Crescent office than any place in town. I loved it. Possessed of a strong inferiority complex (we didn't call it that, then) I liked the feeling that newspaper work gave me of power and inside knowledge. Whatever news there was, local or national or world-wide, you knew it first and truest. I was shy, brash, ambitious, funloving; and like a horrid little girl in a Victorian novel I gave my mother one out of every three dollars of my weekly wage.

Dazzling success (or so it seemed to me) now burst upon me. The Wisconsin State Federation of Women's Clubs met in Appleton for their annual gathering. Newspaper women from the Milwaukee and even the Chicago papers came to cover it. Women of the United States did not vote or hold office. Their civic and legislative powers had no united outlet other than through the women's clubs. These existed in practically every city and town and village, they were bound into State Federations and the State Federations united to form the National Federation. Thousands of women today owe to these clubs such legal, legislative, parliamentary, civic and national knowledge as they possess. Through these clubs they learned to think in terms of the world outside their homes; they learned to stand on their feet and speak in public, often extemporaneously. Their work was charitable, educational, intellectual, vicariously political. It is difficult to realize that at this time women had absolutely no rights in the government of the republic in which they had been born. But the politics, lobbying, high-powered goings-on and general devilment that went on in the national women's clubs almost made up for this underprivileged condition.

All the women writers from the big city dailies—the Milwaukee Sentinel, Free Press, News, Journal, Germania; the Chicago Tribune, Inter Ocean, Herald—were much older than I, they were deeply experienced, state club meetings were old stuff to them, they wore city clothes and talked a jargon strange to me, they cocked an eyebrow at each other, knew the Big Girlies and Madam Chairmen, had inside knowledge of secret programs and political surprises. I dashed from committee meetings to open sessions, feeling terribly out of it. They snooted me. No, it wasn't as definite as that. They utterly ignored me. I sat with them in the press section at the foot of the auditorium platform. I was enormously impressed with them—their city hats, their ease, their chit-chat among themselves. They would whisper together, laugh, write, there seemed to me an immense professionalism amongst them, they took so lightly the events which seemed to me to be world-rocking. Two or three of them would suddenly rise, then one or two more, leaving me to occupy the press section practically alone. Where had they gone? What were they up to? I was in a torment of fear, thinking that I was missing something vital. I worked, I slaved hand and foot, ears and eyes, like a Swiss bell ringer. It was my first big assignment. I was dramatizing it for all it was worth. I scurried between the Crescent office and the Congregational Church auditorium where the convention was in session. A stubby little girl, with black curls bunched and tied with a black ribbon bow, I must have appeared an odd newspaper reporter indeed.

The dear girls' united front proved their undoing. But of this, curiously enough, I was the last to know. I gathered my news, I injected such character stuff and interesting tidbits as the Crescent would permit, I wrote all this conventional to-do with enormous exhilaration, and some of this youthful spirit must have crept into the actual written account. At any rate, during an hour when I was absent from the auditorium, being down at the Crescent office turning in my morning's grist for the deadline, Miss Lutie Stearns, Wisconsin state librarian, leader of thousands of Wisconsin clubwomen, and a terrific and dimensional human being, announced from the platform that the best account of the week's convention was appearing in the Appleton Crescent; and she advised the delegates to send or take home the Crescent for their real report of the meetings, business, social programs, and the like. To Miss Stearns' amazement (this she told me years later) hell broke loose. One of the middle-aged and high-strung women reporters burst into tears and was led from the room by her sympathetic colleagues. She was scheduled to speak that very afternoon on The Press And Women's Clubs, but she refused to go on. At this auspicious moment I came rushing down the aisle from my newspaper office, fearful that I had missed something important. There was turned on me from the press section a battery of eyes so baleful that I could only return the stare, bewildered. At this, as one woman, the big newspaper girlies gathered their papers together, picked up their handbags and, beads clanking, marched up the aisle, out of the room and out of town on the first train.

They never forgave me, and I don't blame them. I must have seemed an insufferable little nobody and a complete outsider. When, a year later, I went to Milwaukee to work on the Journal they had their chance. They ganged up, and they rode me for the whole term of my three and a half years there.

Sam Ryan, in a burst of splendor and appreciation, raised my pay to eight dollars a week. I wasn't notified of this in advance. When I opened my envelope and saw the eight dollars I reported to Miss Ivy Ryan that there had been a mistake. But no, said Miss Ivy. I dashed home, reeling with my riches. In 1928 Mr. Russell Doubleday, of the Doubleday, Doran publishing company, brought to my New York apartment a single check for the first six months' book sale of the novel entitled Show Boat. It was the largest single check they had ever made out for a similar period in any book sale. It was a thrill, but not so deep a one as that five-dollar raise.

Appleton must have been divided into classes, as is any community. There was astonishingly little distinction between them. We had the millionaire paper-mill crowd; the Lawrence University set; the business and professional men and their families; the paper-mill hands. Yet I remembered seeing young Van Nortwick, of the rich Van Nortwicks, earning vacation money on a stifling July day working with the paving squad over the boiling tar kettle when the bricks were being laid for the new street paving on College Avenue. Barbara McNaughton, only daughter of one of the millionaire paper-mill widowers, married Professor Rosebush, a handsome and impecunious young teacher on the Lawrence University staff. The daughter of the janitor of the Ryan High School was voted the belle of her class. A young fellow whose mother took in washing to keep him at school, and who himself delivered papers, cut grass, tended the doctor's horse or ran errands after school hours, would beau to dances and picnics the daughter of one of the town bankers. At Ryan High School Rebecca Hollingsworth and I were great buddies because we two were alone in knowing and loving the novels of Charles Dickens. The Hollingsworths were one of the very few Negro families in the town. Creed, color, race, money— these mattered less in this civilized prosperous community than in any town I've ever encountered.

Of course there were snobs in the town. It wasn't heaven. The paper-mill aristocracy formed a little clique. Sometimes they aped city ways. Emma Patten tried driving horses tandem to a gleaming yellow cart. The town stared, amused, but there was nothing hostile in its glance. Occasionally one of the rich and social would come into the store and mistakenly patronize or offend that indomitable woman, Julia Ferber. These (they were few) she airily dubbed Stinkers, and she had her own quietly murderous way of knifing their inflated ego. One of these, married to money, had forgotten about the days when she used to be a waitress in the Briggs House dining room. Entering the store, she spent an hour picking up this piece of china and that, holding it up to the light, disparaging its pattern, disdaining the delicate Limoges.

[121]

"But haven't you something better? This seems so thick, so common."

Julia Ferber's patience snapped. "I don't dispute you. If anyone in Appleton ought to know about dining-room china it's you."

The town's population was predominately of German background. In the past five years I often have wondered if the foreign-distilled poison of Nazism has been allowed to seep into the wholesome flavor of this fine American town, tainting and crippling everything it touches. What a deep pity this would be.

One of my duties—a hated one—was the task of getting out the society column once a week, on Saturday. To this I had to write a chatty lead, done in the butterfly manner. A search of the old Crescent files would here reveal some of the worst writing in the history of the newspaper profession. Society in the formal sense bored me then as it does now. All the trite phrases of small-town society chatter of the day were tapped out on my old Oliver typewriter: ". . . leaning on the arm of her father, the bride was radiant in . . . delicate refreshments were served . . . weekly meeting of the West End Ladies Whist . . . green and white, the club colors, together with garlands of autumn flowers decorated Odd Fellows hall . . . music by Lehmann's orchestra . . . after dinner cards were played . . ."

Early in my career as society chronicler I pulled a boner. A dinner was given by Professor Plantz, president of Lawrence University, and Mrs. Plantz. I described the decorations, named the guests (mostly solemn faculty members and their wives) and then airily added, on my own, "Following dinner, cards were played."

Lawrence University was a Methodist institution, Dr. Plantz a regularly ordained minister of the Methodist church. I was confronted next day by a battalion of glittering eyeglasses and learned remonstrance. I suppose I looked so young and so bewildered that I was let off with a published correction. That taught me to make sure of my facts. Then, and later, on the Milwaukee Journal, the fundamental and unbreakable rule for reporters was the insistence on facts, and proven facts. "It is alleged" has saved many a publication from a libel suit, but when a statement was made it had to be a proved statement. A reporter who failed to verify was a reporter fired.

It was legitimate newspaper ethics to get your story by any means short of murder. But having got it, it must be proof against dispute or correction. That early training now leaves me gasping at the antics of today's newspaper columnists. People's personal lives, private plans, moral history, future hopes, dearest secrets, innermost thoughts are seized on, embellished or completely fabricated without the consent or even the knowledge of the victim. In the naïve prewar period such a fellow would have been fired; not only fired but no paper would have hired him. The one example of this type of garbage dispenser was a big-bellied whiskered dodo named Colonel Mann of New York. He ran a scandal sheet called Town Topics and lived on blackmail. How he came by his military title no one seems to know, but from all accounts horsewhips writhed about his head like black-snakes; and if all the outraged victims of his method who threatened to horsewhip him actually did so he must have been striped with welts like a zebra. Perhaps George Ade, Bert Leston Taylor, Ring Lardner, Eugene Field would make dull fare for column readers today.

Newspapers were not models of integrity; but certainly competition had caused no such havoc of journalistic disintegration as can be encountered today. You advertised in a newspaper or in a magazine. There was no radio, there were few motion pictures. The advertiser could withhold his patronage, but where could he go? Certainly he often influenced a paper's policy, but he rarely dictated it, as now.

What there was to see in Appleton I saw. A lively town, decent, literate. Automobiles were beginning to be seen on the streets, scaring the farmers' horses into fits. Appleton traveled, it went to Chicago for the opera (Grand Opera it always was called) at the Auditorium; it went to Milwaukee to do important shopping and to see a play, perhaps, at the Davidson Theater. It was chic to take the 7:52 morning train, eastbound. In its green velvet upholstered parlor car sat the well-to-do of the rich little paper-mill towns along the Fox River Valley. They knew the conductor by name, they knew the porter wasn't called George. They had had their good solid breakfasts, the men read the Milwaukee Sentinel. The women wore quiet well-made clothes and smart—but not too smart—hats. They knew what was fashionable and bought it. At home they prided themselves on knowing what was being served and served it; their linen and silver and glass and jewelry were good. They read; they educated their children at the University of Wisconsin or at eastern schools. They went to Europe if they could manage it, and that didn't in the least mean that they were wealthy. The streets of London, Paris, Rome, Dublin, Edinburgh and Munich were known to Appleton school-ma'ams who had achieved out of their earnings the five or six hundred dollars necessary for the trip in those days. Certainly no other nation, in the half-century before the World War, could produce a traveling cross section such as America showed; and the thriving little town of Appleton, Wisconsin, was representative of this urge to be on the move. Travel—even European travel out of America—was by no means confined to the wealthy or the middling well-to-do. School teachers, artisans, small merchants, laboring men—all the countless hundreds of thousands who later were to invest their earnings in new-model automobiles now lavishly laid them at the feet and thresholds of European statues, cathedrals, museums, ruins and hotelkeepers.

It was a comfortable way of life. Women—and most men—paid not the slightest attention to politics. As for European politics and the problems of the countries of Europe, Americans would no more have dreamed of interfering with these than they would have contemplated sinking the entire continent. Europe was simply something on the other side of the Atlantic. You visited it if you were lucky; you learned about it at school. Europe was history. Europeans were people who came to America because they didn't like it over there. Appleton was full of German, Bohemian and Irish parents whose children were thorough second-generation Americans. Europe was as remote to these children as to any American whose American ancestry went back two hundred years.

Our laundress (she was known as the washwoman) was Mrs. Schleppke, German-born, who with her husband had come to America some years before. They had three children. Two of the boys, rather furtive and sharp-eyed, called for the wash weekly and brought it back. Then, one day, Mrs. Schleppke herself appeared to announce that we'd have to find another washwoman. The Schleppke family, entire, was going back to Europe. Nothing here was as good as in Europe.

"In old country," announced Mrs. Schleppke, "is better. In old country meat is better, butter is better—everything. A piece of meat so big"—she made a gesture with her thumb that indicated the forefinger at the first knuckle—"is better than all the meat in America."

So they gathered together all the money they had thriftily saved in the country they despised; they packed the ice-cream freezer, the morning-glory phonograph, the sewing machine, the feather beds, the jars and glasses of plum, peach, grape and apple preserves; the pickles and relishes, the fine stuffed furniture; all the American things with which to dazzle the old-country neighbors. And off they went to spend their American money and the rest of their lives in Europe. The Ferbers found another washwoman. In less than a year Mrs. Schleppke and the two Schleppke boys, taller, thinner, more furtive than ever, appeared at the kitchen door.

"But what! Why? Where?"

Mrs. Schleppke, grim as ever, shook her head. "We didn't like."

"But you said everything was better there. You said the meat, even—why, you said just a bite of meat in the old country tasted better——"

A gleam of something like intelligence irradiated Mrs. Schleppke's face. "In old country a piece of meat like so"—again with the old gesture of the thumb and forefinger she indicated an inch—"tastes better than big piece of meat in America because in old country we got meat not more as once in a month. Here we got meat three times a day."

Though my reporting job took most of my time and energy I

had enough fun of the kind an eighteen-year-old girl should have. I was sad because I had quarreled with my beau of high-school senior days. He had gone off to the University of Wisconsin. Haughtily I had asked him to return my class pin (hoping he wouldn't). I think he felt rather embarrassed by a girl who scouted around town for news. Summer evenings, when young Appleton was harmonizing Sweet Adeline, I felt a pang of heartache. I used to sit on the front porch in the dark, feeling very sorry for myself (which emotion I later translated into my first short story, The Homely Heroine). That was something I was to learn by the time I turned twenty-two: that no matter what happened to me, good or bad, it was just so much velvet. Life really can't utterly defeat a writer who is in love with writing, for life itself is a writer's lover until death; fascinating, cruel, lavish, warm, cold, treacherous, constant; the more varied the moods the richer the experience. I've learned to be thankful for every stab of pain and disappointment.

But at that time I didn't in the least mean to be a writer of any form of fiction. I was a reporter. I wanted to go on being a reporter. In between times I went rowing on the Fox River with a beau, being careful not to get caught in the swift current above the big dam. We bathed and had picnic suppers at Brighton Beach resort on Lake Winnebago, between Appleton and Neenah, and danced to the music of the tinny mechanical piano in the pavilion. I belonged to a girls' club called (don't ask me why) the Lucky Twelve. We were very sociable. I went to dances at Odd Fellows Hall. I managed to get free railroad transportation (a recognized newspaper privilege) and took my sister Fannie to the St. Louis World's Fair. But best of all, my reporter's job entitled me to two free tickets to every theatrical performance presented in Appleton. The town had built a fine new theater on Oneida Street near the Sherman House. My tickets were two permanent thick blue pasteboards which had only to be shown at the box office. It was heavenly. Babes in Toyland. The Royal Chef with Raymond Hitchcock. Blanche Ring in Vivian's Papas. A sensational new comedy called The College Widow by that brilliant young playwright, George Ade. The

Wizard of Oz, that enchanting fantasy, during which I went backstage to get a feature story on the spectacular stage windstorm (feeling very worldly indeed); Blanche Walsh in The Kreutzer Sonata; Mabel Hite and Frank Moulan in a musical comedy called A Knight for a Day. I never had seen anyone in the theater like Mabel Hite. Hers was the same quiet relentless comedy method that is now used by the gifted Beatrice Lillie. It was the day of the pretty soubrette type but Mabel Hite was indifferent to looks so long as she made her point. Her dark vivid face was distinctive and impish. She appeared, very grand, as a Spanish señorita in a long wicked snakelike train. She then proceeded to get herself tangled up in the coils of this garment until she was practically climbing up her own legs. Her bewildered but grimly smiling face as she did this sent me off into such laughter as I've never known before or after in the theater. I'd give a hundred dollars for a laugh like that again. I never forgot her. In 1924 I wrote a rather grim short story called Mother Knows Best partly based on the life and character of Mabel Hite. With her mother she had left the little Ohio town of her birth and had climbed the heights of theatrical success. Death came early in her career. When the story was published it created a furore; and a lot of unpleasantness for me because it was construed as being founded on the life of Elsie Janis whose mother had been a tireless duenna. Elsie's many friends attacked me, but Elsie herself behaved really beautifully, in the circumstances.

We began to go to the motion-picture shows at the new Bijou Theater. They were crude films—policemen chasing tramps—that sort of thing. I rarely went. Once or twice my father tried sitting through these entertainments, but it was too painful. He would sit there, the lids closed over his almost sightless eyes. The silent thing flickered on. There would be a burst of laughter from the audience at some antic on the screen.

"What are they laughing at now, Pete?"

I would try to tell him.

The trick of seeing and recording simultaneously now became a habit. If I went to a party I found myself unconsciously checking on the people, their actions, the games we played, the conversation. Anything, everything was a possible news story. Faces, gestures, events were recorded. It was as though the camera never stopped clicking.

Now Meyer, the little blond city editor, left for his old job in Milwaukee, fed up with his small-town experience. He turned over to me his job as Appleton correspondent for the Milwaukee Journal. It became my duty to telegraph or telephone the briefest possible line on any local happening of consequence. This was called querying the paper. If they found the story of sufficient importance they would telephone or telegraph an order for the number of words they thought the story rated. Less immediate stuff I mailed in on the afternoon southbound train. Semi-feature stuff I pasted up and mailed in from time to time. I felt enormously important and professional. Among other things the Lawrence University football games had to be covered, as well as the Ryan High School games. This was a tough assignment for a girl. It had to be caught play by play. At first I was guilty of using such feminine adjectives as splendid and lovely, but after a bit I caught on to the sport writer's lingo, and I don't think that the Milwaukee Journal readers found the Appleton football correspondence too sissy.

Paul Hunter was the new city editor, imported from out of town. A moist, loose-hung man, eyeglassed, loquacious. He didn't like me. He didn't want a self-dramatizing Girl Reporter around the place. He began a systematic campaign. My run was cut down. My stories were slashed. My suggestions were ignored or pooh-poohed. I was in the doghouse. Midway through my summer vacation of two weeks I got word that I needn't return. I was fired. I can see why Hunter didn't want a girl around the place when a second man reporter could cover more varied ground. My rather embellished style of writing had no appeal for Hunter. He wanted the news and no nonsense.

The bottom had dropped right out of my world and I was left dangling in space.

The novel Cimarron, written in 1929, contains a vast amount of detailed description of a small-town newspaper office. The paper started by my hero, Yancey Cravat, in the land-rush village called Osage, following the famous run into the Indian Territory, was named the Oklahoma Wigwam. The paper and the town never existed except in my imagination, nor did Yancey Cravat and his wife, Sabra. But the newspaper stuff was newspaper stuff true of any small American town. I needed only to reach back into my mind and pull the Appleton, Wisconsin, Crescent days out of my memory. Mac is the Jesse Rickey of Cimarron. Sabra is partly (sorry) my own dramatizing of myself. The cases of pied type, the hand press, the little job press, the back room, the fusty little front office—all these bits of newspaper publishing description I gleaned during my Appleton reporter days.

I had been fired just in time, but I didn't know it then. My heart was broken.

That summer I tried to interest myself in Appleton life (as a layman. I! I who had once walked so proud as a newspaper reporter!). But the world was flat and flavorless.

In another six months I would be nineteen. Withered old age stared me in the face.

At the very nadir of this despair there appeared a message timed like a last-minute reprieve in a bad melodrama. It was from Henry Campbell, the managing editor of the Milwaukee Journal. He asked me to come to work on the Journal immediately at fifteen dollars a week, and to call him on the telephone in Milwaukee at once.

In order to telephone long-distance one had to go to the main office of the telephone company. I held the telegram in my hand. The family sat there, looking at me—my father, my mother, my sister. There is a curiously strong bond in Jewish families. They cling together. Jewish parents are possessive, Jewish sons and daughters are filial to the point of sentimentality. I wonder now how I ever had the courage to leave that blind invalid. It takes real courage to be selfish. Until now we had clung together, we four Ferbers. I am certain I never should have written if I had not gone. I was wrung by an agony of pity as I looked at my father's face.

"You go on, Pete," he said. "You go if you want to."

It is lucky that youth is ruthless, or the work of the world never would be done.

I walked down to the telephone company's office and put in my call for the Journal's managing editor. It took some minutes to get him. As I waited in the booth, my heart beating fast, a townsman who had come into the office stood chatting with the chief operator.

"That's Ferber's girl, isn't it?"

"Yeh."

"She the one is a reporter?"

"Yeh, she's calling up Milwaukee, the Journal there, she says they want her to go to work for them in Milwaukee."

The other man ruminated. "Wonder a girl like that wouldn't try to do something decent, like teaching school."

9

THEY PUT ME on the Schandein case there on the Milwaukee Journal. A good deal of the time I didn't know what they were talking about. But I sat in the courtroom with Cook, the Journal court and police reporter, taking it all down and telephoning it in, for it was hot stuff, and the Milwaukee papers were getting out special editions on it. The Schandein case had started, innocently enough, seemingly, as a private squabble about a will in one of the wealthy Milwaukee beer-brewing families. But in turning over these legal matters they were found to give off a frightful stench. Medical, clinical, sexual terms rose like a miasma from the witness stand. I was being initiated into big-town reporting with a vengeance. That was why they had so hurriedly sent for me. The regular woman reporter, who wrote under the name of Jean Airlie, was away on vacation when the Schandein case broke. Campbell, the managing editor, had liked my stuff as Appleton correspondent. I was put in as an emergency stopgap to get what was known as the woman's angle. If they were taken aback at the appearance of a wide-eyed kid they said nothing but hurled me into the nauseating mess and I waded through it. Milwaukee's aristocracy was made up of brewing families. They lived in vast stone or brick houses on Grand Avenue, the lawns decorated with iron deer, with pergolas, gazebos, and painted dwarfs patterned after those we now know in Snow White. The social gathering place for these clans was the old Germania Club. Names such as Pabst, Schlitz, Uhlein, Schandein were Milwaukee's Royal Family titles, and some of these were present in the courtroom or were pulled into the case. The Milwaukee papers were delirious with joy.

The Milwaukee of that time was as German as Germany. There actually were to be seen signs in the windows of shops on the almost solid German South Side which read, "Hier wird Englisch gesprochen." Of the four hundred thousand population, surely three fourths were German or Polish. There was a distinctly foreign flavor about the city—its architecture, its tempo, the faces of its people, its food, its solid dowdy matrons. Victor Berger, the Socialist, was a growing influence. When you were sent to interview him he was given to mild attempts at cheek-pinching, but then, mine was a plump pink cheek and politics is a dusty business. I didn't resent it.

Arrived, I made straight for a boarding house that had been recommended to me as cheap, clean, good. On fifteen dollars a week I couldn't be too luxurious. Kahlo's turned out to be a gold mine, for I used it, complete, in my first novel, Dawn O'Hara, written four years later. Kahlo's was a decent three-story brick house directly across from the pleasant Courthouse Square. I never have seen anyone work with such a fury of energy as the lean gaunt Mrs. Kahlo. She cooked, cleaned, showed rooms, managed the place. Her hair was skewered in a tight knob that seemed to pull the skin away from her eyes. She wore clean gingham, and I never saw her without an apron and rolled-up sleeves. Herr Kahlo, true to the tradition of boarding-house ladies' husbands, was the ornamental end of the partnership. I never saw him work, except that occasionally you might behold him setting a very special dish—an Apfel Pfann-kuchen or an extra Wiener Schnitzel—before a favored guest, with a flourish. He wore bright blue suits, sported a waxed Kaiser Wilhelm mustache, ushered the guests to their places in the dining room or sat chatting with them at table, a sociable glass of beer at his elbow. Perhaps he did the marketing. Certainly the food was excellent and plentiful enough to have been bought by one who liked good living and easy going.

Except for an occasional trip to Chicago I never had been away from home alone over a period of more than a few days. I wasn't lonely or apprehensive for a moment. I was enormously exhilarated. Every move was adventure. My first room at Kahlo's seemed fabulously luxurious, but my grandeur was only temporary. My permanent room, commensurate with my purse, was unavailable for the moment, and I was therefore regally lodged in temporary quarters. It turned out that my permanent bedroom, much lower-priced, could be reached only by passing through the kitchen. I didn't mind. It was a clean-scoured kitchen, full of fine smells. This room of mine boasted a fireplace in which I rather furtively took to burning bits of wood, old magazines and newspapers, lolling romantically before the brief blaze, until the fire-engine company dashed up and I discovered that I was about to burn the house down, the fireplace and chimney being intended more for ornament than use. I made up my mind that if ever I built a house I'd have a fireplace in practically every room. (The house is just built. And there they are. Life is truly a wonderful thing.) I never had had a bedroom to myself. This first one looked like a ballroom. My scant wardrobe was lost in the vast clothes closet with its forest of bristling hooks. This, I felt, was Life. This was the Girl Reporter in her proper setting.

At Kahlo's, as at home in Appleton, dinner was served at noon, supper at night. That held true in most Milwaukee households. Milwaukee businessmen, other than those owning the big department stores on Grand Avenue and Wisconsin Street, locked their shops at noon, went home to a huge hot dinner, then composed themselves for an hour's nap on the sofa, the open sheets of the day's Germania spread over their faces to keep the flies away.

Kahlo's dining room might have been a pension in Berlin or Munich. I put on a fresh shirtwaist and went down to supper. A roar of guttural conversation stopped as I entered the dining room. It was not that the Kahlo boarders were struck dumb by my beauty. It was their disconcerting way of taking stock of a newcomer. In silence Herr Kahlo ushered me to my solitary table. Forks were suspended in mid-air, spectacles turned like searchlights upon me, knobby foreheads glistened in my direction.

"Wer ist das?"

"Nichts schönes."

"Hm. Neues Mädchen. Hi, Karl! Etwas neues!"

I understand German. Not flattering.

They were, for the most part, engineers imported from Germany, employed in the huge works of the Allis Chalmers Company in South Milwaukee; in the Cutler-Hammer Company, or any of a dozen big steel works or engineering plants in and about Milwaukee. They had bulging foreheads, their hair was shaved or worn en brosse, many of them wore beards and thick spectacles, their neckties were echt Deutsch, they were brilliant technicians, they were the worst-mannered lot I'd ever encountered. An occasional engineering wife was meek, deferential and frumpy. Supper was buttery, German and good. Kalter Aufschnitt with Kartoffel Salat, or Wiener Schnitzel with German-fried. The floor was carpetless and clean, there was a stand of hardy potted plants in the bay window, the walls were ornamented with colored pictures showing plump bare-armed serving girls being chucked under the chin by mustached lieutenants in splendid uniforms. The men drank beer with their meals and read the Milwaukee Staats-Zeitung and the Germania.

One heard practically no English spoken. Herr Kahlo had assured me that, while he spoke English very well, still, in Milwaukee, "it gives meistens German." It did give mostly German, indeed.

After supper I went upstairs and wrote home a ten-page letter bursting with description.

That first glimpse of the Milwaukee Journal office was disillusioning. They were even then erecting a new building on Fourth Street, just off Grand Avenue. The present building was a ramshackle dirty brick affair on Michigan and Milwaukee streets. As at the Crescent office we were here jumbled together in a heap. The city room was dark, dusty, crowded. The city

A PECULIAR TREASURE

editor, the sporting editor, reporters, stenographers worked
amidst incredible racket and seeming confusion. I thought it was
wonderful.

At that time the Milwaukee Journal was a very yellow bulletin afternoon paper. Edition after edition rolled off the presses
from eleven in the morning until three in the afternoon. When
something enormous broke in the way of news there were later
editions. To this day my brain is freshest between the hours of
eight and three. After three it seems to click off as though ex-
tinguished by an electric switch. That comes of working during
my formative years on an afternoon paper. A fiction writer
trained on a morning paper usually finds his mind keenest at
night.

It was a good training course, that paper, but brutal. My
fifteen a week did not come unearned. Three or four of the
staff stood out as definite characters. Campbell, the managing
editor, turned out to be not only Scotch, but dour. His name was
Henry, but I always spoke of him as Haggis (behind his back).
Lou Simonds, the city editor, could have gone on in a play just
as he was, complete. He was young, massive, powerful; a slave-
driver. He wore a green eyeshade, a blue shirt with no collar, his
sleeves were rolled above his great elbows, his pink face was always smeared with ink or lead. In one mighty fist he usually
carried a wad of copy paper, his pants were inadequately sustained by a leather belt out of whose precarious clutch they appeared always on the verge of slipping. This, together with his
rather portly stomach, gave his costume a vaguely Egyptian
effect.

He swore fluently, but not offensively. Nothing he did was
offensive, for he was a really superb fellow and a great newspaperman. His method was nerve-racking. When you came in
with a hot story he would stand over your typewriter with a
huge pair of desk scissors in his hand, and as you wrote he
snipped the typed bits off your machine and thrust them at the
waiting copy boy to be rushed to the composing room. If you
delayed a split second he yelled, "Hell, what d'you think this is
—a weekly! Come on, now. Get it out!"

The paper was a miracle of condensation. It used the bulletin method. Most stories were worth a stick or two only. A stick is a printer's metal frame holding type. There was a saying in the Journal office that a murder rated one stick, a massacre two. By noon, when the city room was crackling with typewriters at which the reporters sat turning out their morning's grist, you would hear Simonds' bellow above the din: "Keep it down now, fellas! . . . Boil it! . . . Shave it! Na-a-a, Cook, don't get fancy. . . . Heh, waddy yuh think this is—a weekly!"

On the copy desk Distelhorst's blue pencil slashed like a Turk's scimitar. You learned to make one word do duty for ten. You began to search your very vitals for the right first word for that first paragraph. It was a city-room rule that the gist of your story must be packed into that first paragraph, and the paragraph must be brief. When I ceased to be a reporter and became a writer of fiction I found the habit of condensation so fixed that fifteen hundred or two thousand words covered any short-story idea I might have. The stories contained in my first book of short stories, Buttered Side Down, could only have been written by an ex-newspaper reporter.

By far the most picturesque and altogether engaging person about the Journal office was the little sporting editor, Wallie Rowland. Wallie was much more than sporting editor—he was a sort of unofficial general guiding spirit, though he would have denied this fact. He knew every inch of the newspaper business from the delivery alley to the office of Niemann, the proprietor of the Journal. He signed his stuff Brownie, and he was known all over Wisconsin. Thin, small-boned, swarthy, of Welsh descent, curly black hair, enormous black eyes in a sallow pointed face. His face was somber until he smiled his peculiarly winning smile, which transformed him. The women in the office all cooed over Wallie, but he played no favorites. Even Edith Crombie, the society editor, an old society gal herself, who came in daily at the elegant hour of eleven wafting a delicate scent into the gritty city room and wearing always the most immaculate of lemon chamois gloves, condescended to Wallie, though she spoke to no one else. Wallie called her Edie and slapped her

English tweed shoulders and she beamed frostily. At the age of six Wallie had sold papers on a downtown corner. Then he got a Journal job as office boy. Half the time he had slept at night on a pile of old papers and sacks in a warm corner of the pressroom. Occasionally he would be sent out with the photographer to carry the tripod and pretty soon he himself was staff photographer. He knew more ball players, fighters and horsemen than the sporting editor himself. He never went out of the building that he didn't come back with a story. He used to take a hand in the sports department on rush days. He became sporting editor. He could operate a linotype, he could act as managing editor in Campbell's absence, and did. His conversation was droll, wise, witty, laconic. He was partial to gaudy habiliments. His shirts, ties, socks and shoes bordered on the fantastic, but in the office he wore a disreputable out-at-elbows coat that was little more than a ragged bundle of tobacco burns, mucilage spots and ink. His office visitors were likely to be battered gentlemen with cauliflower ears, husky voices, brown derbies, and noses that swerved in odd directions, unexpectedly. Also ladies very bright as to hair and general color effect. He kept a revolver, loaded, in his desk drawer and had a disconcerting way of twirling it absent-mindedly on one forefinger as he sat back in his swivel chair, his feet propped high. No one knew what risky devious paths intersected little Wallie's life that he should have this grim weapon of defense; but it wasn't there for fun.

When we collected dimes and quarters for a devil's-food cake sent round from the Princess Restaurant it always was cut in Wallie's office, the portions firmly dissected with a piece of string held taut. He never drank. He smoked a virulent pipe whose bowl was shaped like a miniature automobile. There came to me more knowledge, warmth and companionship from my association with Wallie Rowland than from anyone I had ever known until that time. In my first novel, Dawn O'Hara, he appears in the romantic (I hope) character of Blackie. For purposes of fiction I killed him in the book, but he is alive as I write this and, from all accounts, as vital and winning as ever.

Fortunately the Journal office was within walking distance of

Kahlo's. By eight or eight-thirty I was at work. I stayed almost four years on the paper, doing a man-size job which, at the end, pretty well wrecked my health for a year, and which certainly has affected it in all the years thereafter. I loved every minute of it, and I'd do it all over again.

It was part of my duties to cover the morning nine-o'clock police court with Cook, when the dirt of the streets was swept in from the night before. In the foul-smelling room off the courtroom there always was huddled a motley pitiable crew of petty criminals, prostitutes, drunks, pickpockets, vagrants; all the flotsam and jetsam of the night streets in a town of four or five hundred thousand.

Thirty days. Thirty days. Thirty days. The judge rapped it out, monotonously. The bedraggled girls had the paint and mascara of the night before on their unwashed faces and stale cheap perfume emanated from their crushed finery. The faces of the men had the blank and secret look of those who have learned the prison lesson of keeping their mouths shut and their sensibilities from registering anything but sullen resentment. Outside corridors and courtroom benches were usually crowded with weeping or voluble relatives or hangers-on, or shyster lawyers. I was not yet nineteen, I had lived most of my life in the small-town atmosphere, mine was an intelligent middle-class family of taste. My year and a half on the Appleton Crescent had been a kindergarten. Now I was smack up against the real school of life.

That daily morning police court was—and is—a terrible indictment of civilized society. Vaguely I sensed this. Once, in the very beginning, when I spoke a word of pity or remonstrance a tobacco-chewing bailiff said, "Aw, don't worry yourself about them there. They earn it easy."

"They do not!" I snapped, feeling very superior. He laughed.

Juvenile court was another assignment. In these stories we were, humanely enough, forbidden to use the names of first-offense minors. The phrase "sob sister" to describe a newspaper woman feature writer had come in. Juvenile court stories were sob-sister stuff. About an old courtroom in daily use there is a distinctive smell that, to one accustomed to it, cannot be mistaken. It is an odor of unwashed bodies, unaired garments, tobacco juice, dust, and despair or fright. For the human body gives off certain odors under various emotions, as the glands function. Science may not agree with this, but then, science thus far knows very little about those mysterious organs called the glands. The courtroom smell is the smell of the underprivileged; the worried poor folks smell.

It was a fine breaking-in for me—the Schandein case. After that anything to which I was assigned seemed mild and fragrant. In those first days Cook and I covered the case turn and turn about; he would be out in the corridor telephoning his stuff into the waiting office while I held the fort. When he returned I dashed to the telephone to dictate my story to the waiting stenographer. I had to make a reasonably coherent and smooth-running story out of my hastily scribbled notes. I was blithely ignorant of the meaning of much of the testimony.

Today city newspapers pool their stories. There is practically no such thing as a scoop. The Richard Harding Davis days when reporters beat or scooped one another have vanished before a central news office from which a story is dealt out to each paper, all of one cut. But in my Journal days it was every man for himself. It made newspaper life exciting and newspaper jobs precarious. Underpaid, overworked, it was (and perhaps still is) one of the most exhilarating occupations in the world.

Strangely enough, though Milwaukee was full of beer gardens, ranging all the way from the famous Schlitz's Palm Garden to any little saloon backroom, none of these was the favorite rendezvous of Milwaukee's newspaper fraternity. After the Press Club (men only) it was Martini's that claimed their patronage. Though the name has a racy sound, Martini's was nothing more than a little German bakery and coffee house over on East Water Street. I described it at length in Dawn O'Hara. It was so much a part of the newspaper life of my Milwaukee that it should have a few lines here. The shop occupied the front, facing the street. The café was behind this. Before noon the pastry trays began to come up. No real meals were served. One could have only cakes and coffee or chocolate. The newspaper and theatrical people began to drop in at four in the afternoon or thereabouts. Milwaukee had clung to the old-country custom of coffee and cakes in midafternoon. Mr. and Mrs. Martini were Alsatians. That flaky confection, custard or cream-filled, known the world over as a Napoleon, was called a Bismarck at Martini's. There were acres of cakes and kuchens—coffee rings, bund-kuchen, apple, plum, apricot kuchens, cream-filled horns (hörnchen, in German; similar in shape to the French croissant, but richer). Practically every edible thing in Milwaukee was filled or ornamented with whipped cream. They put cream in the marinated herring, cream in the sauerkraut, in the soup. Their figures were frightful. In the back room were small marble-topped tables, a huge stove glowed in the middle of the room in winter, on the wall were racks holding German newspapers and magazines: Jugend, Die Woche, Fliegende Blätter. Chess games went on indefinitely. Oceans of coffee and rich chocolate topped with whipped cream were consumed, together with tons of buttery cakes. Here you found the afternoon newspapermen when their day's grist was in, and the morning newspapermen fortifying themselves for the night's work. The actors and actresses from the Pabst Theater German stock company had tables sacred to their use. These were a vivacious and picturesque crew, frumpy, voluble, self-absorbed.

Your coffee or chocolate was served you, but you armed yourself with plate and fork and foraged for your own pastries. Here at Martini's I spent many a late afternoon hour with Wallie. The reporters on the German newspapers seemed to live at Martini's. One of the dazzling sights of the place was Guido Enderis of the Germania. A tiny fellow, he compensated for his lack in stature by the sunset splendor of his costumes. His checks, plaids and stripes, his lavenders, greens, reds, blues and yellows made Wallie Rowland's lively garments seem almost funereal in comparison. Guido Enderis left Milwaukee for Berlin and it was there I last saw him in 1914, still a working newspaperman. I wonder what he thinks of that shell-shocked country now.

Martini's has gone grand. The massive crockery (you could just manage to get your lips over the thick cup edge) has become china, the old East Water Street stand (even that is now North Water) has been abandoned. Like many pleasant institutions, it went with the war.

Somehow, I made out on my fifteen a week. Free theater tickets often came my way through the office. My clothes were made in Appleton. My room with board came to about eight dollars a week. I simply did without most things. What I could not afford—and what could I not not afford!—I did without. About every two or three weeks I went home to Appleton by train, a distance of over one hundred miles. Sometimes I had enough money for this trip; sometimes I hadn't. But I had to see my invalid father; he counted on my coming. At such times I committed the only deliberately dishonest act of which I have been consciously guilty. I would buy a twenty-five-cent parlor-car ticket on the five-o'clock train and take my seat grandly in green plush luxury. When the conductor came round I would hand him the parlor-car ticket with a dollar bill neatly folded beneath. Years later I sent the Northwestern Railroad what I thought I owed them. But perhaps they still can put me in jail. It was pleasant to be with my father, my mother and sister for twenty-four hours, but it was good to be back at work on Monday. I liked my new independence. Appleton, outside my own family, had lost much interest for me.

Part of my job was interviewing well-known visitors or local Milwaukeeans. I enjoyed this. I tried to catch characterizations and to contrive lively dialogue all the way from Calvé, of grand opera fame, to Governor Robert La Follette, in Madison; or to May Irwin, in town with a play called Mrs. Wilson, That's All. I discovered that people rarely said anything noteworthy or even interesting and that these interviews had to be given strong injections of fancy writing and imagination before they showed signs of life.

The morning's assignment sheet usually necessitated endless telephoning before I started out for the day's leg work. The first edition demanded to be fed. A line of telephone booths stretched along one wall of the city room, and each cubicle reeked of the last occupant's pipe or cigarette or city-hall cigar.

"Hello! Is this Mrs. Stumpf? . . . This is Miss Ferber of the Journal."

"Who?"

"The Milwaukee Journal. Miss Ferber." (The personal touch.)

"Miss Weber?"

It always came back as Miss Weber. It got to be an office joke, and then an office nickname. Weber, they called me. Hi, Weber, Wallie would say. There are, to this day, certain friends who never call me anything but Weber, having heard the story— Franklin P. Adams is one, Lillian Adler another, Ralph Hayes another.

To some of my stories I was assigned; others I ferreted out for myself. Some of them were cheap and absurd. Yellow journalism was rampant. Even such exposé stories as I did were begun, not in a spirit of humanitarianism or a desire to set things right, but purely for sensationalism and dramatic effect. I spent a couple of uncomfortable nights in a Refuge for Girls because I had heard of unfairness and cruelty in practice there. To get out of the place I had to escape down a precarious fire escape, with a long drop to the sidewalk. I made it, skedaddled for home, had a bath, turned in my story and the place was cleaned out as a result, but I didn't really care about that. I merely had wanted to get a sensational exposure story. I closed up a Grand Avenue Arcade peep show. Passing this arcade countless times on my way to and from the office I noticed that it always had a line waiting to peer into the stereopticon pictures ranged in machines along the sides of the walls. Unsavory-looking men, and, after four in the afternoon and on Saturdays, scores of school children. This struck me as worthy, but slightly odd, as the pictures at which one peeped for a nickel a look were advertised in large letters on placards and banners as being educational views of Niagara Falls, the Grand Canyon, Yellowstone Park and the like. I dropped in for a smattering of education myself one afternoon and was treated to a line of such pornographic filth as would make Niagara Falls dry up in horror. My story, all about barterers in human souls and debasing the minds of the youth of our fair city, sent the Journal circulation up temporarily and shut the Educational Arcade as tight as a safe. I was pleased with myself for this and various other sensational exposé stories, and the managing editor, Campbell, expressed his meager Scotch approval. My fifteen-dollar wage remained the same. I didn't know I was being exploited by a wealthy little paper. The Girl Reporter was still dramatizing herself twelve hours a day. Niemann, the owner, worshiped the style and make-up of the Kansas City Star. We reporters were made to read it and follow its treatment of news and feature stories. Our editorial writers had the Star editorial page rubbed in their faces. This was fantastically paradoxical, for the Star make-up from front page to back was almost as conservative and small-type as the London Times.

Such fun as I had wasn't of the kind usually considered amusing by a girl of nineteen or twenty. But my substitute for conventional fun served me very well. My life was exciting, though not gay. My early years of newspaper work had given me a precociousness which made boys and girls of my own age seem rather flat to me. When I spent a week end in Appleton I found I had somehow grown away from my school friends. Their interests were no longer mine. The Lucky Twelve, the parties at Odd Fellows Hall, the picnics down river irked me. I preferred the story chase, the tension of the city room just before the paper went to press, the relaxation and banter after work hours in the local room; or in Wallie's little cubbyhole.

I ranged the town. I covered news, courts, features and interviews as they fell my way. When a gentleman shot his wife through the head while she slept I was assigned to ask him why he did it and what his sensations were while doing it. Astonishingly enough, he always told me. I had learned that if you asked a question or two, not insistently, and then were silent, waiting, almost anyone would tell you almost anything.

Milwaukee was a conservative town, prosperous and growing. Grand Avenue was becoming uncomfortable for dwelling purposes, with the rise of automobile traffic. Milwaukee's wealthy families were building out Whitefish Bay way, once considered the suburbs.

[143]

Occasionally I was sent on out-of-town assignments. This made me feel very important and professional. I went to get a story from old Ike Stephenson in Marinette. He was Senator from Wisconsin—a rugged and shrewd old buccaneer, true to the robber-baron pattern of his day. Lumber, land and railroads had made him a millionaire. A Wisconsin pioneer, he and his kind had slashed and cut their way to fortune, leaving bleeding tree stumps and thousands of miles of wasteland behind them. Reforestation never entered their heads. But already in certain quarters some agitation against this plundering and destruction of America's natural resources was being heard. Theodore Roosevelt put into use still another of his popular presidential phrases: conservation. Conservation of forests, of waterways, of wild-animal life. Wasteful careless America, killing, chopping, discarding, thought this a good joke. Conserve America's natural resources! Why, they were limitless. A lot of bunk. Teddy was just out to get some more publicity.

When I began to write Come and Get It, a novel of a Wisconsin millionaire lumber family, such knowledge as I had gathered then of Wisconsin forests and waterways and their rape at the hands of these old pioneer boys served me well.

In Madison, the state capital, I interviewed Robert La Follette on his way from the governorship to the United States Senate, and talked to that serene and tactful woman, Mrs. La Follette. Robert La Follette—"Fighting Bob"—always was good for a story. Spectacular, grim, dramatic, he was the real boss of Wisconsin, though he championed the common man and chased the railroad rich until the anti-railroad movement was known as a "prairie fire." Little Bob was a quarter of a century ahead of his day. Like many undersized men he wore his hair en brosse to give the effect of height. His eyes were fiery, his face seamed with the lines that emotion carves. It was said that he had dreamed of being a Shakespearean actor but, balked in this career by his lack of height, he had turned to his political rostrum and had poured his surging temperament into his political and sociological ideals. Chautauqua and lecture audiences knew and applauded him. Among other La Follette reforms, politicians, lobbyists, hangers-on, newspaper people—all the thousands who used to ride the railroads free—now were obliged to pay their fares like anyone else. It was an outrage, these said. Who ever heard of a newspaperman paying railroad fare!

Years before I came to work on the Journal there had been on the reportorial staff a woman whose name was now constantly held up to me as a model. I grew to hate the sound of it. From Milwaukee she had gone to work on a New York paper. From this she had graduated into a highly successful fiction writer. Her name was Zona Gale. It sounded to me made-up and affected. Then, one day, there was a great to-do down the hall. One heard the voice of Campbell, usually harsh and grating, now dulcet as the dove. He appeared, hovering calf-eyed over a fragile and lovely creature whose skirts rustled silkenly as she moved.

She had great dark tragic eyes in a little pointed face; the gentlest of voices; a hand so tiny that when one took it in one's grasp it felt like the crushing of a bird's wing. I was introduced and mumbled something inadequate. This was the first real writer I had ever met. I wasn't envious. I was impressed. I never had remotely thought of becoming a writer outside newspaper work. Some of the boys on the copy desks or in the local room used to talk about fiction writing, darkly. They must have had dog-eared manuscripts and rejection slips in their desk drawers and boarding-house bedrooms to account for the bitterness of their tone. Disty, on the copy desk, used to say, with terrible definiteness, "You can't earn a living writing short stories."

"Can't you?" I said. And believed it. I had never considered trying. I couldn't see why anyone wanted to, when it was so thrilling to be a reporter.

At the desk behind mine sat Jean Airlie, who conducted the People to the Journal column. She had known Zona Gale in her reporter days. They talked together now, the successful fiction writer and the weary-looking newspaper woman. Blandly I listened.

"Tell me the name of a good writer's agent," Jean Airlie pleaded. (So she was trying to write, was she!)

Zona Gale mentioned a name. It sounded highly floral and

faintly improbable. "Send your stories to her," Miss Gale said. "She placed my very first things, years ago."

Tidily I tucked the name away in my memory and closed the door on it.

Kahlo's boarding house shut up shop. I moved to Haley's— the famous "Ma" Haley's, on Cass Street. For twenty-five years I've tried to squeeze Ma Haley and Haley's boarding house into a book. They are too fanciful for fiction. My first room at Haley's was an attic room under the eaves, and right out of an O. Henry story. The kitchen smells came up to it through the smokestack; the bathroom was on the floor below; the furnishings, like everything else at Haley's, were decayed but reminiscent of past splendor; and for some psychological reason I can't remember the name of the lonely blond young engineer in the attic room across the hall.

Nothing could have been more unlike Kahlo's clean decent comfort. The house itself was an old Milwaukee mansion that had been a show place in its day. The rooms, aside from the attic, were vast, high-ceilinged and crammed to suffocation with ornate mahogany, hung with damask and tapestries, upholstered in velvet and satin, jangling with bric-à-brac. There were engineers here, too, among the Haley boarders, but no German ones. They were too thrifty and too fond of good food to patronize Haley's bizarre ménage.

Ma Haley herself comes well within the realm of the fantastic. Now long dead, she looked at that time like a distinguished and slightly mad corpse, particularly when she wore one of her yellow lace-flounced dresses. She may have been fifty, she may have been sixty. No one knew, and it was impossible to tell by her appearance. She had been a beauty in her day, but the face was ravaged by drugs and disease. Her eyes had the glazed and feverish brightness that yet is dull. She wore trailing silks and satins and laces, she glittered and clanked like a chandelier with gold chains, diamond-studded; with lorgnons and watches and chatelaines. Her maculate yellow fingers were a mosaic of gems in old-fashioned settings encrusted with dirt. Though the house was definitely rich and even luxurious there was about it something sinister, and this same grisly spirit hovered about the tall, white-haired, strangely smiling figure of the mistress of the house. The ruined face, the time-yellowed laces, the crumbling splendor always reminded me of Miss Havisham, that spectral bride in Dickens' Great Expectations. I wouldn't have been surprised to hear her say, "I have a sick fancy that I want to see someone play. There, there, play, play, play!"

Haley's boarding house was famous in Milwaukee, really solid and even distinguished people lived there for months and years on end, yet unsavoriness pervaded its every corner. My little room was eight dollars a week, with meals, probably because of my newspaper connections. I almost always was able to come home for lunch (which statement will send today's newspaper reporter into paroxysms). This left me seven dollars a week for general devilment. A dollar a day. I don't remember that I felt deprived. When I got free tickets or was invited I went to the theater. The office furnished street-car fare. On my Appleton visits I usually lugged home a suitcase bulging with laundry to be washed. With an occasional beau I rode horseback out to Whitefish Bay, or had dinner at Schlitz's or the Gargoyle, but my pulse never skipped a beat at his nearness. The boys at the Journal office, wise, witty, hard-bitten, informed, had spoiled my taste for any smug young engineer or lawyer who came my way.

An active newspaperman—or even one whose newspaper days lie behind him—rarely craves any formal social life. He doesn't need it. If he has covered his job capably he has seen every kind of human being under every possible human circumstance. The average social gathering is more than likely to be an anticlimax for him, after a day's work or a night's work crammed with drama. You usually will find him in his hour of ease at a little table in a quiet pub, his glass of beer or his whisky-and-water before him, talking, low-voiced, to one or two keen and undeceived ones like himself.

The food at Haley's was terrible. In selection and raw material it was sound and varied enough, but between the market and the kitchen stove something happened to it—everything happened to it that shouldn't overtake well-cooked food. The servants were Negroes, but of the lower type. Strange and evil rumors of drugs, of illicit relations between the servants and Ma Haley floated about among the boarders. The chef was said to go crazy when drunk, and he drank periodically. Every now and then, just before dinner in the evening, the house would be terrorized by screams, shouts, curses. The chef, gone mad, would be chasing Ma Haley or one of his helpers with a cleaver or a carving knife. He did carve up one or two, though not fatally. On these occasions the more finicking of us elected to eat out.

Ma Haley had a recognized routine for greeting every prospective guest or newcomer. We old hands used to listen, snickering. Her voice was drawling, bemused, like one talking in her sleep. She slurred her consonants. On the wall above the massive stairway landing, amidst potted palms, cut-glass bowls, jardinieres, lace curtains and chandeliers hung an oil painting of a mustachioed man with pink cheeks and a generally dashing though raffish air. Toward this likeness Ma Haley would wave one skinny claw, her glazed eyes half closed, her voice little more than a hum.

"Thas pishur of m husban," she would drone. "Whah hansome man he was! Evbody said he was hansomest man in the whole state Wisconsin."

The caller would murmur something appropriate.

Next day we would hear her again at the stair landing, a fresh victim in tow. "See tha pishur? M father, the Colonel. A gran good man—a wonnerful man, my father. Hansome, too. He wah said to be the hansomes man in the state of Wisconsin."

Though the guests numbered people of the utmost respectability there were some strange birds, too; and about it all there was a kind of whorehouse atmosphere. On Sunday evenings, after the heavy midday meal, Ma Haley used to like to invite some unattached woman guest to sup with her at eight or eight-thirty at the Pfister Hotel, the swank hostelry of those Milwaukee days. The trick was to get out of this grisly engagement. Ma Haley's behavior in public was likely to be erratic, her appearance was always bizarre, one was sure to be made vicariously con spicuous. In her gala silks, satins and plumes, loaded with jewelry, clanking with beads and chains, she would make a grand entrance into the main dining room of the Pfister. Once, unable to escape, I was forced to be her guest, and felt exactly like a girl out with the madame of the house. She always lavishly ordered the most expensive dishes.

The Haley cocoanut cake became historic in Milwaukee. Regularly at Sunday noon there appeared in the hall off the dining room a huge cocoanut cake. It reposed on the serving table there, a five-story edifice, vast, snowy, a Mount Everest of a cocoanut cake. The serving of it was a rite at which Ma Haley presided. The old-timers would as soon have eaten rat poison. They grimly watched while the innocent new boarders consumed their slices with cries of rapture. But once they glimpsed Ma Haley slicing it at the hall table, placing one bony unwashed hand against the piece, lifting it to the waiting plate, licking her fingers soundingly with a curiously blackened tongue before going on to the next slice, they never again ate Haley's famous cocoanut cake.

For three years, from the time I was eighteen and a half to almost twenty-two years of age, it was a strange life I led for a young girl. I worked like a man, dramatized myself and my work as usual, and the Journal took advantage of this unadult posturing. In rain and wind and bitter Wisconsin cold I sloshed about the town covering every sort of story that comes in the way of human behavior. I saw in a social way almost no girls or boys of my own age. I preferred the company of people who were ten, fifteen, twenty years older than I. I suppose my wandering background and my early newspaper experience had given me a rather hard-bitten viewpoint for one so young. But certainly pink-cheeked youths and coy misses bored me. The courthouse, the city hall, the prison, the Journal office, the theater, the city's streets and outlying districts, people's emotions and dramas— these were my occupation and my preoccupation. Nighttime found me usually weary, what with my own tense and emotional make-up and the stress of the day's assignments. I had to prepare the night before for next morning's rising. There always were those knitted union suits and the day's stockings to wash out

in the boarding-house bathroom. And I belonged to the vast
army of handkerchief-pasters. My dresser mirror was always
ornamented with a fresco of newly wet handkerchiefs which
next morning I neatly folded and tucked (slightly gray) into
my purse.

Sometimes there were unpleasant and even hair-raising experiences in the pursuit of the daily rounds. Or perhaps I, a
young girl of a simpler day, found them somewhat terrifying
when the nineteen-year-old girl of today would be merely
amused or bored. I remember being sent by Simonds, the city
editor, to interview a very fashionable (vandyked) doctor on
some silly subject; I forget what it was—Do You Think the
Woman of Today Is Something or Other—one of those bits of
nonsense. His office was just across the street from the Pfister
Hotel side entrance. I had seen him frequently at the Gargoyle
Restaurant and the theater and at like places. When I entered
his private office he had been taking a brief nap and he eyed me
malevolently.

"Wait a minute," he said, as I sat at his desk. He then locked
the door. I put my question, rather uneasily. He looked at me,
then he went to a locked drawer, took out a sheaf of pictures
and slapped them down on the desk before me. "Look at
these!" he said, and gripped my shoulder firmly as I sat there.
They were pornographic pictures such as dirty postcard vendors
on the Rue de Rivoli used to thrust at tourists, only these were
much larger and more detailed and altogether more splendid.
The doctor was laughing. He held the door key before my face.
"Now what are you going to do?"

I was very scared. We weren't so glib with our perverts and
our psychological knowledge then. I realized that screeching in a
doctor's office got you nowhere, so far as outside help went.
Some ancient and hitherto untapped knowledge told me to be
cool and to show no flicker of fear.

"Awfully interesting pictures," I said with what I fondly
hoped was a bored drawl, "but my city editor sent me over here
to get a story and told me I'd have to be back in fifteen minutes
to catch the first edition. If I don't get back in time he'll raise

the dickens—especially if I am delayed and have to tell him why."

He unlocked the door.

Perhaps he was just being malicious; teaching me, a cub reporter, not to disturb a man of science during his rest hour. Or perhaps his fashionable patients were less squeamish than I. Still, the key-brandishing had made my heart skip a beat.

At Haley's I met three gay companionable married couples. We became great friends. They were older than I by a considerable number of years, and they rather adopted me in an unselfish and unpossessive way. They were Will and Eva Rosewater, of Cleveland (he was an engineer with the Allis Chalmers Company); Lewis and Mary Tatum, he of old Philadelphia Quaker stock, an engineer with the Cutler-Hammer people; and Agnes and Isaiah Rosenthal, of New York (he was Western representative of a New York cigar company). Together we went to theaters, restaurants, beer gardens. Isaiah, witty and sardonic, would meet me for coffee at Martini's. When we all found indigestion staring us in the face through Haley's unedible fare— by this time I was dangerously anaemic, but didn't know it—we combined to rent a roomy furnished house up on the East Side while the owners went abroad. I came home to good steaks and chops and pot roasts and green vegetables. We all got on beautifully together. How sweet they were to me! The girls were superb housekeepers. I gathered strength enough to take me through the next few months. But back again at Haley's I turned away from the doubtful eggs, the unsavory meats; the whole atmosphere of the place revolted me. My appetite failed, I became listless, white, eternally weary. I had most of the luxuries but few of the necessities. I realized this, found it amusing, and, a year later, put the idea into the speech of the heroine in the novel Dawn O'Hara:

"Necessities! Pooh, who cares about the necessities! It's the luxuries that matter. What if the dishpan does leak!"

This was all very fine and romantic, but the truth was that I was pressing too hard; I ate meals improperly balanced and at irregular hours; I was doing man's work; the red corpuscles were losing in the fight against the white. I had no ambition toward a career as an independent writer. But I wanted, somehow, to get together ten thousand dollars. Ten thousand dollars seemed to me then to be the ultimate in wealth, and my reason for wanting it would sound like something out of the Elsie Dinsmore stories. How I planned to amass this sum at fifteen a week I don't know. But the little plan was temporarily sidetracked (and, curiously enough, eventually achieved) through the fact that I quietly fainted one morning when I was dressing to go to the office. We Ferbers and Neumanns are not fainting families. Certainly I had never before performed this Victorian gesture. A doctor was called in, my mother arrived from Appleton, and I was taken home and told to stay there for a month. The Journal office assured me that my job would be waiting for me at the end of the month, and paid me two weeks' salary. I don't recall having had a vacation in the years of my work there. The month in Appleton became six weeks, the six weeks lengthened into six months. I never returned to the Milwaukee Journal or to newspaper reporting.

10

LT IS A CURIOUS THING—that sort of illness unaccompanied by ɔain of any kind. At first I stayed in bed and stared at the wallpaper and cared nothing about living or dying. I had had five years of exciting and stimulating work, undertaken when I was still a growing girl. I had paid little or no attention to proper diet; wet feet and damp shoes were items about which one didn't mollycoddle oneself; overheated courtrooms, icy Wisconsin winter streets were all part of the day's work; winter, summer, rain, snow, you picked up your assignment sheet and hoofed it here and there; out to West Allis, over to the South Side, up to Whitefish Bay. I longed to be back in the midst of it. I couldn't imagine the Journal getting out an edition without me. I wept at the slightest provocation, or at none at all. Presently I began to sit on the front porch, propped up amongst pillows. The town went by. "Howyah today!" I croaked a dismal reply.

I would be well enough to go back next week—next week—next week. But walking two blocks left me exhausted. I drank gallons of milk, ate hundreds of eggs, my sister Fannie behaved like an angel, appearing at unexpected moments with frothy eggnogs, with tempting trays decorated with snarls of mayonnaise, curls of parsley, jewels of jelly. I gulped port wine, lay on the grass in the sun in the backyard and began to take a glimmering of interest. I would go back to the Journal in the autumn. Now, because for years I had had my hands on the typewriter keys for hours daily, I wobbled out one day like a sleepwalker and bought myself a second-hand typewriter for $17. This I lugged into a sort of lean-to off the dining room. The icebox was kept there (later I loftily transferred it to the back porch), bits of old rug, junk, odds and ends temporarily stored in a place whose door can be opened and shut hastily. This was my first solitary workroom. I don't know what I meant to do in this room, the broken-down old typewriter grinning up at me with all its time-stained teeth. But the sight of it and the feel of my fingers on the keys reassured me. A kind of strength seemed to flow from them to me.

In the Chicago Tribune there was started a contest with a prize of twenty-five dollars for the best article on something or other—Why I Lost My Job, or How I Kept My Job, or some such nonsense. I wrote two hundred words and sent the article in to the contest. I won. Then I bought a chunk of yellow copy paper and without in the least meaning or planning it—I had no fixed idea as to what I was going to write—I began my first piece of creative fictional writing. Curiously enough, it wasn't a short story. It was a novel entitled Dawn O'Hara; the story of a newspaper woman in Milwaukee, but it wasn't my story. The heroine was romantic, beautiful and Irish. There was an insane husband, a strong silent doctor-lover, a New York past. I did use Wallie Rowland, Martini's and Kahlo's, though; and the Journal office, certainly. I tried to work Haley's and Ma Haley into it, but it was like trying to introduce opium-smoking at a barn dance. It just didn't belong.

My sister Fannie and I were doing the housework, aided by a small girl who came in by the day. She was a chubby, rosy-cheeked child who drove me to distraction by singing nasally as she shucked peas or stoned cherries on the back porch:

We were so hap-py till fa-ather drank rum,
Then all our sorrows and troubles begun.

[154]

In my cobwebby little lean-to I worked at my typewriter all morning and part of the afternoon. My mother was at the store. Usually at about eleven in the morning my father would come home, brought by good Arthur Howe or blundering along by himself. He would spend an hour or two in the cool of the porch. I would emerge, disheveled.

"Hello, Bill!"

"Hello, Pete! What you doing?"

"Oh—typewriting."

He would have a glass of milk and a cookie. The dimmed eyes would look toward the quiet sunny street; the figure was beginning to look queerly shrunken within its clothes, the walk that once was marked by a characteristically Hungarian swing of the shoulders was quite shorn now of its little swagger.

Autumn came and went, and the hard Wisconsin winter was upon us. My hands were numb at the typewriter and I had to move out of the little spidery shed and into my bedroom which was almost as cold. I kept on writing. It is odd, but true, that I wasn't consciously writing a novel. At least I never admitted this, even to myself. I was, as I said when asked by my father, just typewriting. I wrote most of the day. I read and read. I walked a little with my father and read to him. We went to the theater: Cameo Kirby. The Gentleman from Mississippi. The Winninger Brothers' Stock Company. Eugene Walter's great success, Paid in Full. Bernstein's The Thief. Not bad theatrical fare for a small Midwestern town.

At this late date I decided that my meager education ought to be enriched. Casting about for something to learn I fixed on French. This was, I suppose, a groping toward elegance. A knowledge of the French language was, in my mind, associated with world travel and savoir-faire (which I didn't quite know how to pronounce, but could spell). I knew no one who spoke French. At Lawrence University I enrolled as a member of the beginners' French class which met at eight o'clock in the morning. That was a bitter winter with endless snow, so that the morning walk to Lawrence, a distance of about a mile, often meant plowing through virgin drifts to my knees. After class

I would trot over to the store on College Avenue to see my father; then home again through the snow or ice-laden streets. The morning's work took shape in my mind as I went. Quite unconsciously I was doing exactly the right thing in preparation for a day's sedentary writing. The brisk walk set the blood to circulating; the sharp Wisconsin air cleared the morning cobwebs from my brain; the little look-in at my ailing father and a moment's chat with him reassured me about him and assuaged my Jewish-Puritan conscience on the point of selfishly spending a morning at my own work. I had walked to work in Milwaukee; I walked back home to work now. The habit is fixed fortunately. Every morning, before sitting down at the typewriter, I still run out to walk somewhere, anywhere that approaches quiet and that boasts a bit of green. Of French learned that winter I recall not one single word except part of the familiar exercise:

"Un homme descendit de Jérusalem à Jéricho, et tomba parmi des brigands, qui le dépouillèrent . . ." Etc. All about the priest and the Levite and the good Samaritan. In after years, in my visits to France, I never found this paragraph of much help in conversation with waiters, taxi drivers, dressmakers and railroad conductors.

It seemed as if that winter never would end. Eight inches of snow fell late in April, as though in spite. Yet, in a trancelike way, I was happy. Spring came at last, the first exquisite palegreen almost liquid spears of the lilies of the valley showed above the earth beneath the lilac bush, and soon the lilac plumes dressed the shrub royally in purple. Now and then I took time off to make a pie from the cherries glistening dark red on the tree at the side of the house, for I was a good cook and liked a cooking spree occasionally. The early June apples were crisp and snowy white when your teeth went through the thin scarlet skin. Every morning I went out to see what had come up overnight, to pinch the withered blossoms off the pansy bed, to water the porch boxes and hanging baskets laden with salmon geraniums and vinca vines. It was good atmosphere for writing. The book grew and grew. Suddenly, in the late summer, the thing was finished. I sat staring at it. I didn't know what to do with it. You sent stories to magazines, that was it. They published them month by month. That ten thousand dollars. This was the way I should come by it. Instinct told me to send the story to a woman's magazine. I did. Back it came. Another. Another. By early autumn the manuscript of Dawn O'Hara, none too professional-looking when its travels first began, was a disheveled and dog-eared bundle of papers. The magazines would have none of it.

On a visit to Chicago in the late summer I gathered together all my courage and visited the Chicago Tribune office in search of a job. They wanted none of a small-town girl, even if she once had been a fifteen-dollar-a-week reporter on the Milwaukee Journal. Back to Appleton. Well, now what? The manuscript of Dawn O'Hara lay there, an untidy mass, to reproach me. The massive rackety old typewriter stared up at me. I began to do a short story—my first—entitled The Homely Heroine.

Jacob Ferber had grown feebler and feebler. Out alone he would fall and hurt himself. It is something about which I can't think now, after all these years. In September, after an illness in bed of only four days, he died. When in after years the money poured in I used to torture myself with neurotic thoughts of how much luxury, expert professional aid and even gaiety I could have given him if only he had lived to enjoy my writing success. A decent, kindly, peace-loving man, he didn't have much fun in his life, that little Hungarian Jewish boy who came to America with such courage and high hopes, all ending in pain, persecution and blindness.

My mother decided to sell the store, stock and good will, to sell the house and most of its furnishings, to move with her two young lady daughters to Chicago. In the midst of this turmoil I kept right on writing. A year went by before we left Appleton. During most of that time my sister Fannie and I were alone, for my mother was in Chicago for weeks on end, attending to business there. I would write, help with the housework, help in the store. Very active physical work seemed to stimulate the mental process. Clearing out the vegetable bins in the cellar seemed to clear out the cobwebs in the brain. A long walk out along the country roads, scuffling the piles of acrid autumn leaves, made the words leap the more readily from the typewriter keys. So I walked and read and baked cakes and cooked the pot roast and wrote. The Homely Heroine, finished, had been sent to Everybody's Magazine. The story was about a very fat girl named Pearlie Schultz who never had been kissed. "But Pearlie Schultz, in spite of her two hundred pounds, had the soul of a willow wand." She used to sit on the front porch summer evenings and watch the couples stroll by and stop in the black shadow of the big tree for a breathless moment and then go on, arm in arm, close. I enjoyed writing The Homely Heroine. It was good writing; astringent, economical. I now saw that Dawn O'Hara was sentimental and schoolgirly. This second piece of writing had a completely different attack. It was as though two distinct people had written these two pieces of fiction.

I never had seen a magazine editor or a book publisher. My imagination pictured them as white-bearded scholarly gentlemen with gold-headed canes; a pass between Longfellow and old James Ryan. Everybody's Magazine and the American Magazine were enormously popular. The vogue for muck-raking articles had been started by Ida Tarbell with McClure's publication of her exposure of the machinations of the Standard Oil Company. The circulation of Everybody's had leaped from 150,000 to 750,000. Exposé articles became more and more lurid. Thomas Lawson wrote a series entitled Frenzied Finance and spent a fortune publicizing his own articles. My decision to send The Homely Heroine to the editor of Everybody's was arrived at simply enough. It happened to be the one magazine on the living-room table. Its address was printed on the index page. Off went the story, badly typed and minus return postage.

In an unbelievably few days the answer came back. I can still see Julia Ferber as she appeared at the corner of Morrison and North streets. I was lolling on our front porch. "Yoo-hoo!" she called with a note of hysteria in her voice; and held an envelope high in the air. The letter was from Hall, the fiction editor of Everybody's. They had accepted The Homely Heroine, my first short story, and enclosed please find their check for $50.60.

I was furious. I'd never had so large a sum presented to me at one time. Of magazines and national magazine prices I knew nothing. I didn't feel elated over the fact that my first short story had been accepted by the most popular magazine of its kind in the United States. I only knew that $50.60 wasn't an adequate price for an acceptable short story; and more than anything, that sixty cents rankled.

"Isn't it wonderful!" said my family.

"No!" I snarled. "I'll never send them another story as long as I live. The old stingy-guts!" And I never did. (Well, maybe so. But they're out of business, aren't they?)

A second short story, entitled The Frog and the Puddle, had been started. By now the house was a shambles. We were selling off the furniture piece by piece. My typewriter table stood in the center of the bare sitting room. Fannie and I were the saleswomen, for Julia Ferber was busy downtown or absent in Chicago on business. In the midst of a paragraph an Appleton housewife or a farm woman who had heard of the house-goods sale or who had seen the want ad in the Crescent would appear at the front or back door.

"I see where you're selling your furniture. Have you got a good bed with mattress and springs?"

I'd leave my heroine suspended in mid-air. "Wonderful bed."

We'd stand surveying the old carved walnut bedstead that dated from Kalamazoo days. Fannie and I had been born in it. Or it might be the ramshackle icebox or an armchair or the old black leather couch on which Jacob Ferber had, for so many years, found momentary surcease in the nirvana of his afterdinner nap.

"Why don't you nap a little longer, Bill? It's only two o'clock." There had been so little for him to do.

"I don't want to sleep my life away."

As the furniture vanished the story grew. It was finished. With Everybody's banished from my presence the American Magazine now enjoyed my favors. The Frog and the Puddle was sent to the American Magazine, and I commenced work on a third short story, The Man Who Came Back.

On the editorial and writing staff of the American Magazine

at that time there were a number of people who had worked on McClure's Magazine in its heydey of sensational exposures. To the American had come Ida Tarbell of Standard Oil fame; John Phillips, who became editor-in-chief of the American; Bert Boyden, associate editor; Ray Stannard Baker, Lincoln Steffens, and a blue-eyed babe named John Reed, whom no one called anything but Jack. These people I was later to meet and know, and my life was to be enriched by their friendship. A quarter of a century or more afterward, on what seemed to be another planet, I stood before the grave of John Reed, national hero of Soviet Russia, now buried with the illustrious dead in Moscow's Kremlin Wall.

Two weeks went by after I had sent the story to the American Magazine. No word had come. Haughtily I typed what I later learned was an incredible letter to the editor—whose name I did not know. Roughly, it ran thus:

DEAR SIR:

Two weeks ago I sent you a short story called The Frog and the Puddle. I have heard nothing from you. It seems to me you have had plenty of time in which to make up your mind. Will you please return my story immediately. "If you don't want her, I want her."

This last line seemed to me to be a brilliant bit, quoted from David Warfield's speech in the popular play, The Music Master.

In reply to my stupid and arrogant letter there promptly arrived a courteous and charming response by the next New York mail (no airplanes whirled letters across the continent in a few hours in 1910). They wanted the story. Was $100 satisfactory? Had I other stories they could see? And when was I coming to New York? And the writer was mine sincerely, Albert A. Boyden.

Well, that was more like it! My first hundred-dollar check. In a glow I discussed its possibilities with the family. I had written the story in a few days. On the Milwaukee Journal, at fifteen dollars a week, it would have taken me almost seven weeks of hard work to earn one hundred dollars. Maybe after all, I thought cautiously, one could earn a living writing short stories. For temporary safekeeping (it was fun to take it out and look at it, with those two fat zeros after the one) I tucked it away in a little drawer of the old carved walnut writing desk in the sitting room. While I was absent from the house Fannie sold the desk. The purchasers loaded it onto their cart and drove off with it. By some miracle she remembered the name of the buyer. People are not difficult to locate in a town the size of Appleton. I dashed up to the house, breathing heavily, and said that a check of one hundred dollars had been absent-mindedly left in the desk drawer. The desk owners sat in an ominous circle, their faces blank. They knew nothing of a check. Besides, they had bought the desk. Anything it contained belonged, they said, to them. Some hidden spring of business knowledge welled up within me.

"That's all right," I said, airily. "It's no good to anyone but me. I've had payment on it stopped."

At which the woman of the house rose and blandly produced the check, slightly moist, from within her bosom.

I offered no reward.

It was now midsummer in Wisconsin (and, I presume, elsewhere). The little town drowsed under its canopy of green. The catalpa tree in our front yard shed its heavy sweet blossoms, and I celebrated July Fourth by coming down with an attack of mumps from which I very nearly died. Convalescent, I resumed writing, for by now it was part of my life, part of living, like breathing, eating, sleeping. Writing was not only a profession; it was a necessary function.

With early autumn our departure drew close. The house had been sold—the two-story frame house on North Street for which my mother had saved, and which she had bought with such pride. "If the worst comes to the worst—whatever that means," she always had said, "we'll have a roof over our heads, anyway." Her nightmare had been that she would die leaving her two girls with a blind invalid father. The Geenan Sisters Dry Goods Store had bought the My Store's remaining stock and had taken over the store lease. September, and we were burning those odds and ends and scraps that accumulate after a dozen years of living in a house. We were down in the cellar standing before the open furnace door—that balky smoky old coal furnace into whose maw my sister and I, having no active man in the household, had shoveled so many tons of coal. The scraps and papers made a fine, though ephemeral, flame. Some of the papers were first drafts of short stories I had written, and I grew philosophical about the way these flared up briefly, then vanished forever. In the basket was the battered manuscript of Dawn O'Hara. It had the limp look of the rejected. I held it in my hands a moment with considerable distaste and some regret. Julia Ferber turned a smudged face toward me to see what was causing the delay in the furnace-feeding.

"What's that?"

Suddenly I felt embarrassed. Failure always embarrasses the unsure. "Oh, just that—uh—book thing I was trying to write last winter. It isn't any——"

She took it out of my hands and put it to one side, neatly. "I wouldn't burn that if I were you. Keep it."

"Nobody wants it."

"You never can tell. Maybe you haven't sent it to the right person."

Inexplicably, out of that recess in my brain where it had lain stored popped the memory of that day when Jean Airlie had asked for the address of an agent and Zona Gale had given her that curiously floral name. What was it? Rose May Flower? Holly Rose May? Flora Holly—Flora May Holly. That was it. Search back, back . . . One Five Six Fifth Avenue New York.

Not even retyping the manuscript I again wrapped the wretched bundle and sent it on its Eastern journey. This woman with the curiously horticultural name had placed Zona Gale's first written things, had she? Well, I thought, proudly, I had placed my own first short stories, at least. But this was too much for me. Anyway, a new little voice said, deep inside me, it isn't good. It isn't as good as you are this minute.

So then, the Ladies' Aid Society presented the departing member, Mrs. Julia Ferber, with a silver mesh bag and a vote of regret. For the last time I walked out to the neat little Jewish cemetery, bright with autumn leaves and the yellow of golden-glow and the scarlet of salvia. I said good-by to the solitary mound at the foot of the big marble slab engraved with the name of Ferber.

We had spent thirteen years in Appleton, as a family. My Milwaukee interlude was now as much a thing of the past as Appleton was to be. The lovely little town had treated us well. Always I was to think of it with affection.

Ours had been a roving sort of life. It had had a curious rhythm, too. Kalamazoo—Chicago; Ottumwa—Chicago; Appleton—Chicago. Chicago had been a springboard, but now it was different. I never once thought of New York as a place that I was ever to see. I didn't even feel at all sure that I could make a living writing stories. A precarious business, that. Perhaps now I could get a Chicago newspaper job, as we were to live there. I set my face toward it. Another small-town girl, like hundreds of thousands, on her way to the Big City.

11

I<small>T WAS A CURIOUS</small> wandering life that now began for me. I, who
hated hotels, who loved my own bed, my own typewriter, my
own bureau drawers and bookshelves and homemade popovers,
spent the next thirteen years of my life in hotels and furnished
apartments. Chicago, New York, Chicago again; Vienna, Munich,
Paris, Florence, London, Berlin, California; Chicago, New York,
Chicago, New York. I was the Flying Dutchman, I was the
Wandering Jew. There were two reasons for this. First, I wrote
and wrote and wrote with a fury of concentration. Rather than
spend strength and emotional energy in other channels I accepted the discomfort of a roving life. Second, my mother, with
whom I spent much of those thirteen years, had no liking for
housekeeping. Doubtless she had had enough of it in the quarter-
century of her married life. Then, too, her business years in the
store had weaned her away from the petty details of a domestic
routine. Into my muddled head had come the fixation that, after
her years of hard work, disappointment and worry, it was my
duty to make her path rose-strewn, gay and carefree. Any com-
petent psychoanalyst could have set me right in six months, but
the whole school of psychoanalysis was unknown to the mass of
the world at that time. If you had an exaggerated sense of re-
sponsibility toward your parents it was considered an admirable

trait rather than an indication of repression elsewhere. Ignorant of all my own motivations I only knew that certain things irked me to the point of rage. As a great creature of fifteen or sixteen I had been presented to acquaintances of my mother: "And this is my baby, Edna."

"Well, quite a baby!"

I would glare.

The truth was (and still is at this writing) that Julia Ferber as a human being was so dimensional, sustaining, courageous and vital that my years of close companionship with her never were dull; irritating at times, and even infuriating, but dull—never! She had and has a gigantic capacity for enjoying life and for communicating that enjoyment to those about her; a humorous gay shrewd woman with an amazing sense of values. Astringent as grapefruit, her insight into human frailties often makes her judgments seem harsh. She belongs definitely to that race of iron women which seems to be facing extinction in today's America. They braved the Atlantic in the sixteenth and seventeenth centuries; they crossed a wilderness of plain and prairie in the eighteenth; they plunged into business and the professions in the nineteenth through a storm of horrified disapproval. Hardy, indomitable, of the earth and its fullness. We shall not see their like again.

Julia, Fannie and I moved into a three-room apartment at the Vincennes, on Chicago's South Side. It was then a middle-class family apartment hotel facing a small park with fountains, neat flower beds and cool trees shading gravel paths. In today's Chicago the Vincennes is in the very heart of the Negro belt.

Out came Everybody's Magazine with my short story, The Homely Heroine. I had the thrill of seeing my name under a story title for the first time. Pearlie Schultz was purely a creature of my imagination, but when, a year later, I returned to Appleton for a few days there wasn't a fat girl in the town who would speak to me. It was then I learned that a writer who creates lifelike characters in fiction exposes himself or herself to resentment and even libel. The average reader seems incapable of realizing the existence of the imagination in writers. A purely fictional character that moves, breathes, talks, reacts like an everyday human being must, to them, have been copied from life, like a bad painting. Through the years I have had countless letters from strangers saying, "How dare you use me [or my cousin or my Aunt Mehitabel or my mother or father] in your book!" Other readers express their coy pleasure at finding themselves characterized, and want to know where you got your information about them. Then there are, of course, those mad people who go about the world representing themselves as being the authors of other people's books. They sign letters and autographs and even fill lecture engagements under your name. Every writer of any success is haunted by at least one of these odd birds.

Now, however, these success troubles had not arrived to pester me in any great numbers. I settled down as best I could to write a certain number of hours daily in a bedroom with the family life swirling about me. Here there was no convenient spidery little lean-to off the dining room into which I could creep. I made no elaborate arrangements for my daily stint of writing because I didn't regard myself as a writer. I just wrote. I worked in a bedroom because I didn't dream of affording a separate workroom. Sometimes I thought vaguely that it would be marvelous to work without interruption, but that this actually could be achieved was beyond my imagination. It is a curious thing about writers. Some of us work heartbreakingly hard, like stevedores, like truck drivers, like slaves, and we get a few hundred dollars a year for our pains. Some of us work heartbreakingly hard, like stevedores, like truck drivers, like slaves, and we get a quarter of a million a year (some years). But the difficulty in getting a room and decent privacy in which to accomplish the earning of our living is almost unsurmountable. People don't understand. One's family mysteriously doesn't understand. It all seems so easy—a typewriter, or a pencil and a piece of paper. Nothing to be so fussy about. For years my mother spoke of my work as "Edna's typewriting." The fact that creative writing is a good deal like having a baby every day for so many hours daily doesn't occur to the layman, and he wouldn't believe it if you told him.

Somewhere in the midst of a difficult paragraph the bedroom door would be thrown open. My mother would sail in, rummage about in the clothes closet, select her costume for the day to the accompaniment of a running stream of comment and instruction.

"I'm going over to the stores on the North Side. That drugstore man is two months overdue with his rent. I'm nearly crazy. . . . That agent is no good. . . . I thought on my way back I'd stop at Field's and match your green . . . There's plenty in the icebox for you girls so Fan needn't do any marketing. . . . Don't forget to drink your blood, it's all squeezed out."

This last wasn't as cannibalistic as it sounds. Still rather alarmingly anaemic I had been ordered by the doctor to eat an unbelievable number of eggs daily and to drink the sanguine juice of a pound of raw steak squeezed through a meat press. With a pinch of salt to make it palatable, my eyes shut and holding my breath I managed to gulp this down daily. It did no good. Minot hadn't then been given the Nobel Prize for telling the anaemic world about liver. Grandma Neumann a half-century earlier had given her anaemic young daughter Julia a daily glass of port wine from a brown jug in which a handful of rusty nails had been thrown and left to stay.

With Julia off to do battle about her Northwest Side property (she had invested her money in Chicago business real estate) and Fan engaged in trimming a hat or cutting out a dress I would go on mumbling my story. On the Milwaukee Journal I had formed the habit of talking aloud to myself as I wrote. Cook, the police reporter whose desk had been next to mine, had had the same habit; only he, in a transport of creative ecstasy about some particularly dramatic police story, had gone the whole way. He would push back his chair and stand up, putting one foot on the chair seat, smiling idiotically, his china-blue eyes fixed on some imaginary audience. Oblivious of annoyed or derisive glances he would declaim a paragraph or half a column, fitting gestures to dialogue, tossing his head, stamping his great feet. I discovered that talking aloud while writing made the thing more real to me and to the reader. The words came alive. The two of us in that corner of the Journal city room mumbling and gesturing must have given the effect of actors in a madhouse drama.

Though I had sold all the short stories I had written I still was afraid that this golden gift would be snatched from me. It didn't seem possible that one could earn a living just by sitting home cozily in front of a typewriter and bringing people to life on paper. As soon as I could summon the courage I paid a visit to the Chicago Tribune office in search of a steady job. It was Burns Mantle who talked with me on the Tribune.

"I'd like to work on the Tribune," I said, flat.

"Doing what?"

"Reporting."

"We don't use women reporters."

"But I can do man's work. I did on the Milwaukee Journal."

"How much did they pay you on the Journal?"

I wanted to say twenty but thought I'd better not. "Fifteen dollars."

"We pay forty." I waited. "But we don't want any women reporters. We'd rather have men do men's work."

I wanted to say, But look, I'm good—really good. I can write. But one doesn't. Perhaps, I suggested, they'd let me submit feature stories for the Sunday supplement. Mr. Mantle said he thought not, but if I wanted to try, why, there was nothing to stop me. I then took my crushed leave. In the next week or two I did submit two feature articles, both of which the Tribune accepted. They were trite things—a Sunday afternoon at the Chicago Art Institute . . . Italian families with their babies . . . young lovers hand in hand before the Something or Other that was symbolic. These two articles constituted my entire Chicago newspaper career. Various articles and statistical books have stated that I was a reporter on the Chicago Tribune. I wasn't. They wouldn't have me.

With the most beautiful dramatic timing there now arrived a letter from the Frederick A. Stokes publishing company, and a letter and a contract from Miss Flora May Holly who sternly concealed her sex under the signature of F. M. Holly. Stokes wanted to publish Dawn O'Hara in the early spring of 1911.

I was an Author. I was a Novelist. Chicago Tribune me eye! With no more than one hasty bedazzled glance I signed my name to the book contract. Read now, it would freeze the blood in the veins of any member of the Authors League of America. Any writer in doubt of that organization's benefit to authors during the past quarter-century is invited to see my Dawn O'Hara contract. This is no reflection on the Stokes company. It was the usual form contract of that day. In accordance with its terms I gave away practically everything but my virtue. All form contracts for book publication were more or less in the same pattern. Motion-picture rights did not then exist, but I certainly would have thrown those in if I'd ever heard of them. The Stokes company now wrote to say that they'd like to publish the book with a subtitle. Dawn O'Hara, The Girl Who Laughed.

This seemed to me terrible, but if, at the moment, Stokes had suggested Dawn O'Hara, or, Up in a Balloon Boys, I'd have said yes.

The book was dedicated:

To
My Dear Mother
who frequently interrupts
And To
My Sister Fannie
who says "Sh-sh-sh!" outside my
door.

It was well reviewed and sold ten thousand in its regular edition, which wasn't by any means spectacular but which wasn't, on the other hand, bad for a first novel and a mushy novel at that. In some inexplicable way it still sells, twenty-seven years after its publication. Much of its contents and all of its title still have the power to make me slightly ill on sight.

Chicago opened up before my eager receptive eyes. The slightest stimulus sent the imagination racing. Just to be out on the Chicago streets, with their smoke-blackened apartment houses and their bedlam of Loop traffic; their misty green lakeside parks and windswept skyscrapers—strange mixture of provincial town and cosmopolitan city, with the stink of the stockyards from the west side, and the fresh tang of Lake Michigan from the east side—this was to know adventure.

A mail carrier, his sack laden, an errand girl, sallow and shabby, a morose man with a split in his shoe standing gazing at a luxury fruiterer's window on Randolph Street, across from Marshall Field's. Chicago at its winter worst—wet, slushy, penetrating to the marrow. In the window pineapples, peaches in cotton wool, great dusky grapes, alligator pears, and a strange exotic thing so foreign that it had to have a little printed sign all its own: Maymeys from Cuba. The eyes of the window gazers stared at this, fascinated. Their lips moved a little in silent pronunciation of the strange word. Peaches, grapes, pineapples in January—yes. But there was something wanton, something devilish in this sending all the way to Cuba for a fruit so rare to jaded palates that one didn't even know how to pronounce it. I went home and wrote Maymeys from Cuba. It wasn't at all a noteworthy story. It is mentioned merely as an example of the casual thing that sent me off on a story scent. That story, by the way, contained a certain note of rebellion against the idle luxurious world. I should say that everything I have written, from that time to this, with the exception of the novel Show Boat, which is frankly romance and melodrama, has had a sound sociological basis. Few people—certainly no professional critics—have recognized this. The basic theme was partly hidden by the stories' readability. Your real tub-thumper is a bore; and if a bore is windy enough and repetitious enough he usually is mistaken for a brainy fellow.

Chicago short stories tumbled, one after another, out of my typewriter. New Year's Eve in a Chicago Loop hotel—the story of a kitchen checker; it was called The Kitchen Side of the Door. A woman buyer in a Chicago department store, One of the Old Girls. A clerk in a cut-price shoe store—What She Wore. They were stories of working people, of the Little People, of those who got the tough end of life. I never have written what used to be called shirt-front stories, stories of the rich and successful. Society in the small sense bores me more than any other single thing in the world except people who try to tell the plot of the movie they saw last night. The stories were quickly sold with the exception of two. Editors were afraid of the theme of each. One was called Where the Car Turns at Eighteenth. The sight of a U. S. Navy poster popped that story into my head. The poster ornamented a huge billboard just where the street car rounded the curve at Indiana and Eighteenth. It showed a virile six-foot sun-tanned god in a uniform of the U. S. Navy standing amidst coral strands, sapphire-blue ocean, palm trees and exotic flowers. He was having a splendid time, and his invitation was to join the navy and do likewise. But I remembered a boy I had known back in Appleton who had joined the navy and then killed himself to get out of it. The story wasn't pretty. The second hard-seller was The Woman Who Tried to Be Good. It told of a madame in a house of prostitution who sold her place, bought a cottage in a decent middle-class neighborhood in a small town and tried to spend her life in peace. That story bounced from magazine to magazine, and always came back with little reproving notes from the editors. I was terribly eager to have it published. I knew it was good. I wrote George Horace Lorimer of the Saturday Evening Post. "I want this story to be published and read. It's good. It isn't the Post's kind of story. I'll take whatever you'll pay for it, or I'll let you have it for nothing."

Curiously enough, Mr. Lorimer took it, paid $400 for it (much less than I was getting at that time) and published it. I still hear from that story.

In 1912 the Stokes company published my second book, a volume of collected short stories entitled Buttered Side Down. In a day when the happy ending was practically obligatory in published short stories, these had, almost without exception, an ending which came inevitably out of the story's march. Hence the title. In that day, and for a girl in her early twenties, they were rather hard tough stories. They showed the O. Henry influence. They could only have been written by an ex-newspaper reporter. The book got good reviews. I was startled and grimly pleased when some of the reviewers said that obviously these stories had been written by a man who had taken a feminine nom de plume as a hoax. I always have thought that a writing style should be impossible of sex determination; I don't think the reader should be able to say whether a book has been written by a man or a woman. Certainly many of my short stories as well as the novels Cimarron, Show Boat, The Girls, Come and Get It, and the book entitled Nobody's in Town could never be designated as feminine writing in theme, characterization, style or attack. They were written by a cerebral human being who had a knowledge of the technique of writing and of the human race. That is as it should be. When the writer obtrudes in a work of fiction it is bad writing.

Now I began work on a short story about a traveling saleswoman. I never had seen a woman drummer, but I once had heard my mother in Appleton tell of a brisk woman who had come to the store selling—it sounds fantastic—mouse traps. I never heard about her again. I knew nothing of the life of traveling salesmen or of the wholesale houses they represented except for such talk as I had heard between my mother and father in connection with the store. I suppose that I actually had absorbed, in those years of small-town life, a good deal of information about buying and selling and the lives of commercial travelers. This story was called Representing T. A. Buck. The traveling saleswoman was the story's chief character. I called her Mrs. Emma McChesney. I don't know why. The name popped onto the white paper as I wrote. I never changed it. She sold underskirts for a firm which I named the T. A. Buck Featherloom Petticoat Company. Off went the story to Bert Boyden of the American Magazine and immediately I started a short story about a scrubwoman in a Chicago office building. I never wrote it.

An excited letter arrived from the American Magazine. In Emma McChesney, it said, I had created a new character in fiction. The American business woman never had been done. Emma was novel and refreshing. There had been a special staff meeting to discuss her. Would I do a series of stories about Mrs. Emma McChesney? And when could they count on the second story?

It never had entered my head to write a series of stories about this or any other character. I wrote Mr. Boyden that I couldn't possibly do another story about Emma McChesney. I knew nothing about business, or selling goods on the road, or the life of a female drummer, I assured him. I never had seen a traveling saleswoman. But immediately after having sent him this refusal I thought of a story which named itself Roast Beef Medium. I wrote it, with Emma McChesney as a mouthpiece for its philosophy. The story was a turning point in my writing life. Roast Beef Medium, published, became the most-talked-about story of the month. Emma McChesney caught the public's fancy. She had a son, charming but rather weak, called Jock McChesney, still at college. Every successful fiction magazine in the country wrote me asking for a McChesney story. The Saturday Evening Post sent a representative who offered me a thousand dollars a story as a starter. I never had received a price such as this. The American Magazine paid me $600. I felt (rather sentimentally) that the stories, if I were to continue to write them, belonged in the American Magazine. The first two had appeared there. The editors of that publication had discovered in Emma a fresh and novel character and had urged me to go on with the series. The stories belonged there. I wrote about thirty McChesney stories, most of which were published in the American Magazine. Curiously enough, the editors of that magazine never raised my price until I myself protested. By that time I had discovered that I could transact my business, to my own satisfaction at least, better than an agent. I do not think that money or talk of money in business is vulgar, and I am not among the artist souls who shrink therefrom. I gladly, however, use the services of an agent in all motion-picture business transactions. There are limits to my business hardihood.

After two years or more of the McChesney stories in the American I did a half-dozen or more for the Cosmopolitan Magazine. Then a curious thing happened. The stories, after magazine publication, had been published by the Stokes company in three volumes, the first in 1913, the second in 1914, the third in 1915. One day I picked up a review of the third McChesney volume entitled Emma McChesney & Co. I don't remember the magazine, though I think it was Vanity Fair, and the name of the reviewer is beyond me. Perhaps I wanted to forget both. But whatever the magazine and whoever the reviewer, God bless it and him.

"Edna Ferber," the review said sagely, "in her latest volume of the saga of the traveling saleswoman is evidently keeping Emma McChesney alive with injections of black ink."

I stared at that line for a long time. It had brought me to my senses like a blow to one half asleep. I had been sliding to oblivion on a path greased by Emma McChesney.

Again at the most dramatic moment, and with the same un-believable timing, there appeared a letter. It was from the editor of the Cosmopolitan Magazine. They wanted more McChesney stories. They would take as many as I was willing to write. How about twenty? With the letter was enclosed a contract. I never have heard of one like it. A blank space had been left for the number of stories, and a blank actually had been left in the space where price ordinarily is indicated. I was to fill out both as I saw fit.

I did get a kind of oily satisfaction in looking at that contract, but I was shocked by it, too. There was no struggle in my mind, because my mind was made up. I hadn't much money at the time, but I virtuously tucked the contract into an envelope and sent it back to the Cosmopolitan editor naked as the day it was born. I had resolved never to write another McChesney story as long as I lived. I know now that if I had signed that contract I never should have advanced as a writer and probably never would have written a fresh line again in all my life. The truth was—though I hadn't realized it—that I didn't really enjoy writ-ing the McChesney stories any more. I could do them with my eyes shut and one hand tied behind me. I and my readers were sick of the old girl. But she had been a good friend to me.

Through these stories I had begun to get a steady stream of fan mail (they were called mash notes then). There are writers who profess indifference to, or contempt of, those people who write them or even accost them, saying that they have enjoyed this or that book, short story, play, poem. Now, undoubtedly some of these people are bores, **some** slightly mad, many self-seeking. But the mass of them are moved by a generous emotional impulse. In letters, even in telegrams, or on shipboard, in trains, on the streets, strangers write or say, "You must be tired of hearing people say they like your books, but I just want to tell you . . ."

A writer doesn't tire of hearing people say they like his book or play. He loves hearing it. But the difficulty is this: by the time the reader has read it or the playgoer has seen it, the writer has laid it away in lavender. To him it is a ghost. If his response to flattery or appreciation seems absent-minded, forced and even churlish it is because he scarcely knows what you're talking about. The thing is remote, finished, beyond his reach. His mind, imagination, emotions, creative powers are concentrated on the new thing he is trying to write. Still unconquered, that fresh work is tugging at him, deviling him, eluding him when he tries to pin it down. It grins up at him from his dinner plate; it walks with him on the street; it prods and pinches him when he tries to sleep, it leers at him from the pages of other people's books or the scenes of other people's plays; it insinuates itself slyly between him and the person to whom he is talking; it jabbers at him when he himself is talking. Only that interests him, claims all his attention. If the last book was good the next one must be as good, or better. To relax is fatal. To bask in the warm glow of praise makes for flabby muscles. A trapeze performer might as well say, contentedly, "I made the leap yesterday, and very good it was, too. How they applauded! If I try to make it today, and miss, it really won't matter."

All's to do again. There is a poem of A. E. Housman's that sometimes comes to me when I'm weary or discouraged or depressed, sitting there a wooden woman in front of the typewriter, staring at its taunting keys.

> *Yonder see the morning blink.*
> *The sun is up, and up must I,*
> *To wash and dress and eat and drink*
> *And look at things, and talk, and think*
> *And work—and God knows why.*

Oh, often have I washed and dressed,
And what's to show for all my pain?
Let me lie abed and rest.
Ten thousand times I've done my best,
And all's to do again.[1]

Just the same, when those letters stop coming my way—those letters beginning, "You probably will be surprised to get a letter from one who is a total stranger . . ." or, "It is now three in the morning and I have just finished your book, but I can't go to sleep without telling you how . . ."—when those letters, as I say, stop appearing in my mail, or when strangers no longer approach me on ocean liners or in train diners I shall know then that I am through, through, through. It will be a tragic day for me. God bless them, even if they're occasionally maddening. For, though I write as I please, it is pleasant to know that I please others as I write.

More than a year had gone by in Chicago, and still a visit to New York was as remote from my plans as a trip to Europe or Asia. Under Chicago's vast smoky dome I felt protected and curiously at peace. The city's pace was that of a ponderous giant; it sprawled, sooty, powerful, over miles of the Illinois prairie. Its eyes were full of cinders from the I.C. trains, it sweated, and odors none too ambrosial rose from its Gargantuan body. Its feet were in the prairie muck, but its head was Jovian, its brow godlike, it was at once of the earth and of the sky.

It was packed with stories for the indefatigable mole, E. Ferber. On Chicago's west side was the largest Polish population known to any city in the world—including Warsaw. And there, too, was Halsted Street, said to be the longest street in the world. And on Halsted Street was Hull House, that noble brain child of the spinster, Jane Addams. A tough lusty unformed city. There were times when the humid summer heat off the lake made your body a sponge; there were other times when you gasped for breath as the icy January blasts struck you, and the cops had ropes strung across Michigan Boulevard to keep you from being blown

[1]Printed by permission of Pinker & Morrison, Inc., agents.

off your feet. I ice-skated on the lagoon in Jackson Park; I picnicked on the lake front; I walked miles and miles and miles along the lake, buffeting the winds and finding it exhilarating. I wrote, I read, I prowled Chicago's streets and byways, I ranged the town from the stockyards to the Art Institute, from Evanston on the north to South Chicago. I found it then, and I find it now, one of the most vital, unformed, fascinating, horrible, brutal, civilized and beautiful cities in the world. I spent at least half of each year for the next twelve years in Chicago. I saw what there was to see, and there was a lot. Certain sights I never shall forget. The pigsticking at the Yards; the men working at the open hearth in the steel mills; Pavlowa exquisite, unreal, dancing in the open air while one dined at the Midway Gardens; Lake Michigan in a storm when its waves were white chargers thundering down the piers; symphony concerts at Ravinia; Maxwell Street in the heart of the Jewish district on a Saturday night; the Black Belt around Thirty-first Street and the time of the unspeakable race riots; the Loop at national convention time.

I'd always thought I would like to do a novel about the Chicago stockyards, but I never did. Nothing came of it except a short story called Blue Blood which is used, I am glad to say, in the University of Chicago English course. Besides, Upton Sinclair's The Jungle had rather finished the Yards for fictional purposes. You couldn't top that fragrant bit. Still I went to see for myself. One stood on a balcony runway overlooking a great open pit the size of a large cellar. Across this pit there ran a wire pulley and along this pulley there moved endlessly a line of pigs suspended by their feet, securely tied, and they were squealing in abject terror as they came. In the center of the pit stood a Negro. I described him in Blue Blood. I can't do better now.

You now saw a giant Negro, stripped to the waist, a magnificent ebony creature with great prehensile arms and a round head, a flat stomach, flat hips, an amazing breadth between the shoulders. From chest to ankles he narrowed down like an inverted pyramid. He raised those arms that were like flexible bronze and effortlessly, almost languidly, as you would cut through a pat of soft butter, they descended in a splendid arc.

[177]

The floor of the pit was smeared with a rich and stunning Gauguin scarlet and the same vivid color ran in rivulets down the upraised black arm and the splendid torso. In the right hand he held a knife with a long thin blade that measured surely eighteen inches. The procession of pigs moved along just over his head, the arm came back, up, down. Back, up, squeal. Down. The squeal ceased. Knife, floor, walls, man ran red. You could not bear it, you could not take your eyes from it. You saw them kill the steers, you saw them kill the little lambs, it was weeks before you could eat a lamb chop. You had lunch, then, at the Saddle and Sirloin Club in the Yards. The menu was thrust before you.

"Uh, no, thanks," you said. "I'll have just a salad and a cup of coffee."

South Chicago was red, too; orange by day and crimson by night. The great furnaces never were cold. The steel-mill workers lived in smoke-blackened shanties. Some of them slept by day, some of them slept by night, but the glare of the chimneys seared their eyes, waking or sleeping, and bathed the houses, inside and out, with the torturing reflection of the flames. Tiny figures that were six-foot men crept like gnats about the vast steel girders, they stepped between the giant ladles that held molten death, they stood beside the white-hot rivers of liquid steel. They were bare to the waist, their faces ran sweat so that they were striped grotesquely black and white, like zebras. The open hearth, it was called. A cozy, comfortable, slipper-and-pipe name for that inferno. When the war came their wages were sixteen, twenty-five, thirty-two dollars a day. They struck for shorter hours and higher wages and the world condemned them. No money can pay a man for that work. For those few years they wore silk shirts, smoked black cigars, rode in good automobiles. You couldn't get near the park in which the strikers' meeting was held, for their cars blocked the streets. They and their kind, striking round the world, could stop war forever. But to the man at the top the millions are sweet; and to the man at the bottom the thirty-two dollars a day is sweet.

There were writers of distinction in Chicago; I met some of

them, but I saw them rarely. Carl Sandburg was writing his powerful lusty Chicago poems. Ben Hecht was living there, trying hard to be Rabelaisian, sliding his eyes around in a leer, thinking to hide his warmhearted conventional soul; Charlie MacArthur, brought up as a missionary's son, showing his rebellion by a series of puckish pranks; Floyd Dell, living his moon-calf days; Susan Glaspell, Llewellyn Jones, Sherwood Anderson; and the poet Harriet Monroe with the face of a New England school teacher; Maxwell Bodenheim, striding along Michigan Avenue in beret and smock, looking like a Weber and Fields version of an artist. They were sometimes referred to as the Chicago School of Writing as one would say the Barbizon School of Painting. I don't know that they ever resented this or found it comic. Over in Evanston Henry Kitchell Webster wrote with a promise which he never fulfilled. Some of these were older than I, some my own age. Bert Leston Taylor, signing B.L.T. to his Chicago Tribune column, was a journalistic fad that threatened to become a fetish. A Tribune sport-page column by a chap named Ring Lardner didn't get a tenth the attention. These I met as acquaintances. We never became friends. Chicago distances were vast. Many of these writers had newspaper affiliations or associations. They met a good deal in the refined artistic atmosphere of the Fine Arts Building on what they called the Boule' Miche, or in a smoke-filled Clark Street beer room. Some sound instinct told me that a writer could learn little from writers' talk; that that talk might be gay and even amusing, but practically never sustaining or enriching to the listener. After working hours I wanted to see all kinds of people in all walks of life; or I wanted to walk alone.

I did encounter all kinds of people, deliberately and out of curiosity. My interest in all that went on about me in that great city functioned like a network of electric antennae reaching out and striking a spark from anything it touched. Many of my Chicago friends were Jews like myself. Usually Jews are more exhilarating as companions, individually. Collectively I find them almost too heady. A whole roomful of Jews is like a charged battery. The vitality sparks seem to fly, and frequently the result is a short circuit.

On Sunday mornings the thing to do was to go to the Jewish Temple on Grand Boulevard to hear Rabbi Emil Hirsch hold forth. Finding the Saturday-morning congregation too largely feminine he had arbitrarily switched to the Christian Sabbath for his main service. Crowds packed the place. Aquiline, acid, vituperative, brilliant, bold—all these words crowd the mind when one tries to describe this great Jewish scholar. Courageous, too, and wise with a terrible wisdom, like the prophets. I am glad that this great Jew of German ancestry did not live to see the German nation degenerate into the savagery of the Dark Ages. Yet I should have liked to hear his tongue lashing their brutality from the pulpit; I should have liked to feel that his leadership, unafraid, was helping more timid Jews in their ageless battle against world ignorance and intolerance.

It is a curious fact that, with one or two exceptions, the handful of people on whose friendship I know I can count to the last drop are men. Perhaps training, background, experience have given me their viewpoint. Certainly they are sympathetic to mine. I know four men to whom I could say, "Look. I have leprosy, I have just murdered my grandmother, I haven't a penny in the world, the police are after me," and I know they would meet this with, "Come on in. Don't worry. We'll fix it up in no time. Have you had dinner?"

To be able truthfully to say that is to be rich. Among the women of whom I can say it is Lillian Adler. She is now functioning superbly as one of the chiefs in the United Charities of Chicago, a social service organization. In my early Chicago days she was a plump golden-haired blue-eyed girl, daughter of wealthy German-born Jewish parents. She, in her twenties, was reaching out to find something beyond the conventionally comfortable life of her prosperous family. She started by taking a dancing class at the Maxwell Street Settlement House. She always had been interested in dancing. She infected me with it. She was, like many rather heavily built people, very light, graceful and quick. In gym bloomers and ballet slippers she taught the intricacies of the ballet and brought gaiety, beauty, rhythm and the relief of self-expression to the girls of the crowded Chicago immigrant section. The old Maxwell Settlement, at that time, was a grubby red brick building. Municipal playgrounds were just beginning to come into being. Though wretchedly housed, the Maxwell House neighborhood people were not so badly off as those of New York's teeming East Side. They were less aggressive in consequence and less deferential, too. Though you saw the fish markets, the bearded men, the bewigged married women, the chaffering and bickering of the Russian and Polish immigrant Jew here as in New York, there was, at least, not the almost complete lack of civilized living accommodations that later I saw prevailing on New York's lower East Side. Chicago could afford to be more generous of space with miles of prairie for elbow room.

Watching Lillian Adler's dancing class I learned to be glib with dancing terms; first position, second position—tourné—tour jeté—coupé—sauté—and ONE and TWO and THREE and STOP! The eager glowing little faces. The ragged pathetic undergarments beneath the ballet skirts or bloomers. Lillian drove a luxurious electric brougham that looked like a jewel case. In this glass-enclosed bijou we rumbled all over Chicago, absurdly grand. It is astonishing that no one resented it or that even our undeveloped social sense wasn't embarrassed by it. But then no one seeing Lillian's merry benevolent face could resent the electric. She had the gift of understanding, a most exquisite humor sense, and a social sense which grew and developed through the years. Much of her I used later in the novel called The Girls, though I might be the first to deny it, and she the second. I dedicated the book to her. It is, perhaps, the best novel I have written.

Chicago writers talked a great deal about The Russians. By The Russians they meant Tolstoy, Dostoievsky, Chekhov and the lesser school of powerful gloomy chroniclers who sat behind the porcelain stove pulling the legs off flies. American writers emulated the Russian writers' style, they adopted their pessimistic philosophy. This seemed to me as absurd as to exchange caviar and vodka for cider and pumpkin pie. They were foreign to our habits and tradition. Here in America, I thought, there was lightness, buoyance, and an electric quality in the air. Here everything was still to be done. We took life, if anything, too lightly, like children. Between us and the Russian way of thinking—or, for that matter, the English, the French or the German—there lay three thousand miles of cleansing salt water; and, still more effectually separating us, a bulwark of freedom of speech, of thought, of conduct. Here was a new fresh country. Why not write in American? All this I said none too tactfully. Ben Hecht particularly looked at me pityingly.

It wasn't that I was swollen by self-confidence or that I was satisfied with my writing style. On the contrary I was obsessed by a fear that the gift of writing might be snatched from me any day, leaving me ragged and shivering like Cinderella when her sudden splendor vanished. Also I was suffering under a terrific inferiority complex which made me feel that all other writers were superior to me. But beneath this veneer of self-deprecation was (as usually is the case) a solid granite foundation of belief in myself and my work. The modesty was purely protective and false as hell. Deep down I thought I was very good indeed, but I seemed constantly to need bolstering up. Perhaps this could have been attributed to my early Ottumwa days. It caused me a great deal of wretchedness and must have bored my friends stiff.

Someone would say, with sincerity, "I like your McChesney stories. They're great!"

Immediately I'd belittle them. "Oh, do you really! I thought that last one was quite bad. I don't know anything about traveling salesmen, anyway. It wasn't about anything, really."

It was a sickening attitude that went for everything. "What a pretty dress!"

"This old thing! Last year's—and it cost almost nothing."

"That blue's becoming to you."

"Don't you think it makes me look sort of sallow?"

Harmless to others, but not to me. Dishonest and irksome. I was writing in all honesty, working indefatigably. Yet when praise came my way I immediately set about tearing it down. The fact that I had success in spite of years of this neurotic simpering and mock modesty speaks well for my work. I do believe, however, that this attitude of mine had some effect on the reception of my writing in various quarters. The world judges for itself, and usually, in the long, long run, fairly. But the termite of self-deprecation can undermine even a solid structure—or at least weaken it. Sometimes, even now, I catch myself at my old trick. Once I heard myself say of my new mink coat which had cost me my life's blood, "Oh, this is last year's m——" I led the howl that went up. Perhaps all this was just a superstitious fear that the bad fairies would hear and, jealous, snatch my golden gift away.

The little three-group of mother and two daughters was broken up. My sister Fannie married Jacob Fox. I took my first real traveling holiday up into Canada and decided, never having been abroad, that no European city could be quainter than Quebec. It was before the Canadian Pacific had built that nice new shiny railroad station just below Dufferin Terrace. From the Château Frontenac you could look down on the market-place stalls with their gay umbrellas only half hiding the scarlet and green and gold of fruits and vegetables and flowers. Up the Saguenay River to Chicoutimi, through the shrine of St. Anne de Beaupré with its grisly festoons of crutches, braces, trusses, canes, wheel chairs. It seemed that if you wrote you earned quite a lot of money, and if you earned quite a lot of money you could travel and see the world, and the world was quite a place to see.

There were letters from Frederick Stokes and William Morrow of the Stokes company; from John Phillips and Bert Boyden and Ida Tarbell of the American Magazine; from George Horace Lorimer of the Saturday Evening Post. When was I coming East? If you were a writer you came to New York.

It was the New York of 1912 that I first saw. It was just that trembling moment when the last of the Victorian age simpered its way out and the first of the prewar period whooped and jazzed and fox-trotted its way in. A great stroke of luck for me —for all those of us who have seen two worlds (and probably will see three) in one lifetime.

Whether it was the Liberty Bell or George Horace Lorimer that caused me to stop over in Philadelphia on my way East I can't remember, but I entered New York via the Pennsylvania

road and rode uptown in a cab from Thirty-third Street by way
of Broadway (by request). I was disillusioned to the point of
gloom by this first glimpse of what I had thought to be a dazzling
splendid thoroughfare. The obliging driver, knowing a Midwesterner when he saw one, pointed out the Metropolitan Opera
House. I had pictured it a magnificent edifice out of whose gold-
studded doors ladies in diamond tiaras and Van Bibbers in In-
verness capes and top hats would be strolling any hour of the
day or night. It looked like a cold-storage warehouse, and still
does. Broadway itself in the winter's afternoon was a grubby
crooked street lined with one- and two-story shacks. I was bitter
about the Flatiron Building. New York on that glum January
afternoon in 1912 affected me much as a child is upset who dis-
covers that Santa Claus is only Uncle Elmer in cotton whiskers.
Yet here, I sensed, was something different. Here was something
older, harder, more brilliant than the conglomerate mass of
Chicago. This city had crystallized, had set itself. The sky was
different; the people were etched with a sharper acid. The accent,
the intonation of the newsboys sounded queer in my ears. The
newsboy's call in a strange town always rings a new chime to the
traveler. Joinal! they called. Woild! The cab driver had been
friendly instead of surly, as in Chicago. And that night, at dinner,
when the hovering waiter suggested ersters I was thrilled as a
tourist at first sight of the Taj Mahal.

Next day, rested and refreshed, I looked at New York with
new eyes. Now a quarter of a century has gone by. I've seen the
inside of its slum tenements and of its French and Italian Renais-
sance palaces (they're both coming down now, thank God,
masses of brick and stone and rubble). I've had pain and disappointment and happiness and success and fun and friends and
gaiety and hard work and sickness and health in my New York
years. I love it. Though I leave it, I love it—from afar.

Inured to tough Wisconsin winters where to stand still on a
December street meant frostbite; and to the Chicago brand of
cold which was, at best, like wading through icy water, and at
worst like an arctic night, what with fog, wind, blizzard and soft
coal, New York in January seemed to me a tropical heaven. I

marveled at the people sitting comfortably on benches in parks
and squares. Women stepped daintily along in midwinter dressed
in silk suits and high-heeled fragile slippers ornamented with
cut-steel buckles; people rode on top the open buses. These I
loved. Chicago had had no buses. I clambered up the precarious
steps and viewed New York delightedly from the obliging backs
of these swaying Fifth Avenue elephants. Though New York's
streets were filled with motorcars there were plenty of horse-
drawn vehicles. You saw broughams lined in plum color broadcloth, drawn by matched chestnuts, a coachman and a footman
on the box. Drays lumbered along pulled by huge draught horses.
The breath-taking skyscrapers of the postwar period had not yet
been built. The Singer Building was to give way to the Woolworth Building, the Woolworth to the Chrysler, the Chrysler to
the Empire State, the Empire State to the Arabian Nights
labyrinth called Rockefeller Center.

Someone had recommended the Belleclaire Hotel at the corner
of Broadway and 77th Street. It was more formal than the Chicago hotel in which I had lived. There were palms, red carpets, a
doorman in uniform. From the sitting-room windows I had a
typical New York dweller's view of other people's windows. I
never had been confronted with this and hated it. From that time
on I always tried, when in New York, to live where the outlook
is high and free and the sun may enter boldly. It is a most costly
habit of living. The average New Yorker's indifference to sun
and light in his daily life and his complete unawareness of the
sky have always amazed me. Cloud formations, the intense blue
of the city's sky on a clear winter's day, a sunset across Central
Park or the Hudson, moon and stars when the night is lavish are
phenomena neglected and unnoticed. In a thoughtless moment I
have said, "Did you see the sky this morning at about eleven!"
to be met with a sourly suspicious, "What sky!"

The Belleclaire proved pleasant enough, though nondescript.
We ate the Belleclaire steaks and apple pies, very good and not
too costly, and in between for the next twelve years in various
hotels did a lot of cooking over spirit lamps or on little electric
plates, evolving lunches of eggs, salad, hot canned tomato soup

or even an occasional surreptitious lamb chop. It wasn't economy so much as my hatred of a steady fare of restaurant food. I infinitely preferred to stop work for a scrambled egg and a cup of tea done over the Sterno than to order up the food that had become tasteless to my palate. In and out of the hotel I sometimes paused to coo over a red-cheeked chubby baby who was being wheeled to or from the park by his nurse or his parents. The mother was a pretty pink-and-white woman, the father dark and springily muscular. I learned that their name was Mr. and Mrs. Douglas Fairbanks and that he was an actor. I discovered there were other actors in the hotel; I was impressed with the British accent and appearance of a tall man with a curiously seamed actor's mask named Aubrey Smith.

Now began a most exciting and breathless time. In the vastness of Chicago no one had paid any particular attention to me. Writing, working, walking, snooping, playing a little—that had been my life. Now I found myself in a distracting whirl of engagements, telephones, interviews, offers. It was all very strange. I didn't quite like it, breath-taking though it was. Newspaper reporters, men and women, came to interview me. This made me feel very shy because the shoe always had been on the other foot. For years I had interviewed people. To this day I can't accustom myself to being interviewed, I can't forget that I am at heart a newspaper reporter with an imagination, and so I stumble and am tongue-tied under questioning. This has, I am afraid, given me among newspaper people a reputation for being arrogant. I was immensely pleased and astonished to learn that they all had read the McChesney stories. They asked questions about writing, about future plans, about my impressions of New York. I didn't make very good copy. A man from the New York Sun asked the time-worn question: To what do you attribute your success? I hadn't, as a matter of fact, had anything solid enough to be called success. Two books had been published, the McChesney stories now appearing in the American Magazine had caught on like a house afire, I was in my middle twenties, so I fumbled this question, thought a moment, then blurted what I felt to be the truth:

"We-e-e-ell, I think if I've had any success it's because I was born a Jew."

The young man jumped as though he'd been shot. "Oh, I couldn't say that!" he objected.

"Couldn't you? Why?"

He stammered, "I couldn't," as though I'd said something obscene.

Frederick Stokes and William Morrow and Mr. Dominick, my publishers, came calling. Mr. Stokes turned out to be even more impressive than I had expected. A kindly, rather shy man, he talked with a curiously English drawling accent, he wore drooping Dundreary mustaches, he invited me to stately dinners where I found I was to talk to the man on my left for five minutes, then the man at my right for five minutes. Two kinds of wine. Hm! I was impressed but fidgety.

The American Magazine crowd turned out to be birds of gayer plumage. John Phillips, the editor-in-chief, was a complete darling; quiet, gentle, droll, wise. But Bert Boyden, the white-bearded old dodo with the gold-headed cane, as pictured in my pre-New York imagination, turned out to be a gay handsome young fellow—even young enough not to seem middle-aged to my twenties. He had brilliant white teeth and deep blue eyes and an overpowering zest for life and curiosity about it, as though he must quickly cram as much fun and experience and lavish generosity and friendship into it as he possibly could. He was right, or he was psychic, for the war killed him. I never have known anyone who was so genuinely and wholeheartedly interested in others. He never talked of himself; it was you, you, you. What are you doing? What are your plans? Where do you want to go? Do you like the theater? Have you ever seen Coney Island? Will you come to dinner? Whom do you want to meet? What do you like to eat? We went dancing at Reisenweber's in the Circle, and at the McAlpin and Castles in the Air. It was Bert who taught me the fox trot and the Castle Walk, those new strange dances introduced by the dance team of Vernon and Irene Castle. All New York—all America—was mad about them. Bert could hypnotize you into writing a story on schedule. He could make you feel that your next short story was the most important single thing that civilization could hope to evolve. He was a superb editor. He was a superb human being. When I last saw him he lay dying. He no longer had the strength or the will to raise his eyelids. They were closed over the sunken sockets. He spoke, though, in a whisper that was little more than a ghostly breath. I leaned closer. "What are you writing? When . . . finished? Good? Good."

I went to dinner at the Knickerbocker Hotel, and wished I could peek at the men's grill and bar famous for its Old King Cole picture (among others). But women didn't enter bars. No one ever heard of such a thing. Supper at Martin's, which was, I learned, pronounced Mar-TANS with the n slid over, French fashion. No relation to the homely American Martins. The New York tearoom was mushrooming into favor, but its fare was of the lettuce-leaf, chopped-apple, marshmallow or cream-sauce school, too anaemic for my Jewish palate, trained to a richer tangier taste. I was introduced to a golden innocuous-looking drink called a Bronx cocktail, in appearance very much like orange juice but with a bitter potent addition which turned out to be gin. From years of acquaintance with Dickens I had thought that gin was something only charwomen imbibed. I felt a new respect for their good judgment. The Midwestern Great Lakes whitefish, broiled and served with parsley butter, had seemed to me the king of aquatic foods until I tasted the sweet white meat of Maine coast lobster, and the soft-shell crabs, the oysters and the crab flakes of the Eastern waters. They had the tang of novelty for a Midwesterner, unused to the appetite-inducing salt-water flavor.

It was only a dozen years after the turn of the century, and Greenwich Village was one of the city's sights, it was New York's Latin Quarter. Hick that I was, it is strange that it did not attract me. Perhaps I was innately conventional and middle-class; or perhaps my childhood and young girlhood had been sufficiently varied and chancy to satisfy my craving for the bizarre. I occasionally went down to Washington Square, I had friends there, I now and then ate in the Village restaurants, and loved to dine in the Brevoort basement or at the Lafayette near by. But I discounted the Village with its rather unadult posturings, its pumped-up camaraderie, its imitation Domes and Reserves. I never longed, Iowan, Wisconsinite, Michigander and Illinoisan though I was, to live in its red brick attics. I admired its Early American façades but I wasn't intrigued by what lay behind them. Greenwich Village was something to look at, not to live in.

Of course, dinner down there with Jack Reed was another matter. Jack, the blue-eyed babe of the American Magazine crowd, had money enough for a spaghetti-and-red-wine table-d'hôte dinner, but even if he hadn't it wouldn't have mattered, because you paid no attention to mere food when Jack sat across the table, laughing, talking, eager, young, just mad enough to infect you with madness. You rode home on top of the Washington Square bus if he had bus fare left in his pockets. If he hadn't you paid it. I was immensely flattered when he wrote the lyrics for one of the Dutch Treat Club shows and put me into a song. I still prize that score, autographed by Jack Reed. Five years ago, a tourist in Russia, I saw the Moscow papers full of announcements of meetings of John Reed Clubs—organizations with branches all over the Republic and named after a national hero. Wherever he is, he's getting the joke. I feel sure that the historic Kremlin Wall in which he lies buried must show a slight crack where he has shaken it with his boyish zany laughter.

To a Midwesterner New York was like a brilliant play upon which the curtain never went down. When I had left Chicago that winter its factories and six-family apartment houses and its I.C. trains were belching soft-coal smoke over streets that already were a mire of dirty snow, ooze and grease. The roar of the L trains maddened the shopper in the Loop. The icy winds searched your very backbone. Here in New York the winter sky was a heartbreaking blue, the bluer in contrast with the white shaft of an office building's tower. The air had a salt tang, the sunshine was piercingly brilliant. At sunset as you looked toward Riverside Drive there was, as Christopher Morley has said, "a bonfire at the foot of every street." When you rode home on top of a lurching bus the breeze whipped the color into your cheeks, the people along Fifth Avenue, across Fifty-seventh and up the Drive walked with a spring as though an electric force poured out of the concrete pavements into the soles of their feet. You were going to the theater to see Ina Claire in The Quaker Girl, with supper afterward at Rector's. Life was wonderful. I felt gay, important, alive.

Between the very formal Stokes dinners and the scampering table d'hôte of the Jack Reed evenings was dinner at Bert Boyden's apartment in Stuyvesant Square; and that was best of all. I never had seen a bachelor apartment until I came to New York, and I was naïvely astonished to find that a man could live in such comfort, unwed. Here were tasteful charming rooms; delicate china and glass; candles, cocktails, wine, delicious food beautifully served; gay, witty, friendly dinner companions. Bert the boy from Illinois, soigné in those smart dinner clothes of his, sat down at the piano and played and sang that song we wanted to hear from the new musical play. Here I met Ray Stannard Baker and Lincoln Steffens, Kathleen and Charles Norris, Rube Goldberg, Fontaine Fox, Charley Towne, Kate and Grantland Rice— scores of people who were writing or acting or editing or publishing. There was good talk. I didn't try to meet Names. But I found, when I did encounter those people about whom I had heard and read for years, that they were friendly, warm and generous as any neighbor back in Appleton, Wisconsin. Perhaps if I'd ever been among the down-and-out in New York I could tell a different story. But certainly that New York coldness and remoteness of which I've so often heard has never come under this eye. Luck has sometimes gone against me in the years I've spent in New York (though the world mercifully remembers only one's successes and forgets the failures); I've known illness there, and discouragement, too. I never have lacked the friendly hand, the encouraging word to sustain me.

I wrote every day; there was so much to see, crammed into that first short bewildering New York visit; the telephone rang, rang, it never stopped ringing. There was Ellis Island to visit, I couldn't believe New Yorkers who had lived in the city all their lives and never had dreamed of seeing this modern Babel. The gates of America were wide open, they were pouring in from the Old World, anyone could enter who had a few dollars in his pocket and who wasn't actually afflicted with bubonic plague, trachoma or tuberculosis, and doubtless even many of these managed it in those free-and-easy days. Irish, Lithuanians, Bohemians, Turks, Greeks, Russians, Poles. The vast majority of them stayed in New York, for America was heedless of the warning of the sage Carl Schurz who had called New York the bottleneck, and who had urged America to distribute its millions of immigrants over the hundreds of thousands of miles of Midwestern and Western prairie and plain. They huddled now in wretched tenements on the narrow strip of land called Manhattan Island, already groaning with its burden of population. There was Chinatown to see, with its strange smells and stranger food; Wall Street, Trinity Churchyard, Coney Island, the Battery, the Bowery (disappointment!), Grand Street, upper Broadway, and the ocean, a thrilling sight to a Midwesterner, though it seemed to me that Lake Michigan did very well by comparison. I saw an ocean liner for the first time as it inched its way out into the Bay, headed toward the open ocean, and I wondered if I'd ever be a passenger on one of these; and knew well that I would.

Writing McChesney stories, writing, writing, all the morning and part of the afternoon. Quite a lot of money by now, or so it seemed to me. Some of it I spent, some of it I gave away, some of it I thriftily put by, and this I have tried always to do. Mercifully, the government now saves me the trouble of trying to accomplish the third gesture. But in my childhood I had seen what worry and illness and money shortage and fear for the future could do to a human being, and I had made up my mind that I would not be caught that way if I could help it, nor any of those whom I loved.

Editors of various magazines offered me more money for the McChesney stories, but I sentimentally stuck to the American where they had originated. Business was unimportant to me then. Sometimes the odd young man who was publicity writer for the Stokes company used to talk to me about it, whenever he managed to talk seriously at all, which was practically never. He was a gangling, redheaded popeyed fellow; shambling, untidy, up-roariously funny. Together we would go gesticulating and jab-bering along the New York streets, leaving a procession of startled or shocked faces turned toward us as we went. The cuckoo young man's name was Sinclair Lewis, but everyone called him Red. He and I had built up two characters which we always assumed when together. Red was Gus, the janitor of a mythical office building, and I was Tillie, the scrubwoman. We talked in a bad German dialect, faintly Weber-and-Fieldsian, and not very funny except to us.

"Tillie, you vas earning goot money on new chob, ain't?"

"Ja, only for my knees, them new kind stone floors."

This would go on for hours. Red was better than I at it—more outrageous. His linen was the grubbiest, he had no money, he would escort me to the door of one of those literary parties to which I had been bidden, but nothing could induce him to come in.

"Naw, I'd be trun out of there. They wouldn't want me in there." In a year or two I, too, learned that literary parties got you nowhere and were very dull stuff indeed.

One encountered in New York for the first time a certain mas-culine type of woman, enormously efficient and pretty over-whelming in a business way. There was the formidable agent, Elisabeth Marbury, all chins and marble-blue eye and massive gold chains. There was Jeannette Gilder, very tall, with a round white moonface behind thick spectacles; a superb mind, the kindest of souls. She strode in wearing the first really mannish tailor suit I had ever seen. She was enthusiastic about my stories and books, she had written splendid reviews about them, she gave me sage advice. She came to tea one day, a towering broad-shouldered woman with a scholarly stoop; enormous hands and feet; she was wearing a rough tweed skirt, plain and narrow, and a mannish jacket. We sat down at the tea table.

"Won't you take off your coat?" I said, politely, the hostess.

"My coat off! What for! You wouldn't ask a man to take his coat off, would you!"

It was all a new world, this New York. The Night Court.

One of James Montgomery Flagg's McChesney Drawings. Emma Is Evidently Getting the Best of It Over Her Shrinking Boss, T. A. Buck.

Adams' Trained Seals at the Republican and Democratic National Conventions of 1912. Standing: William Allen White, Edna Ferber, Jay (Ding) Darling, Harry Webster. Seated: George Fitch, George Matthew Adams.

Emma Goldman lecturing about things that seemed too daring for words (they teach them in the grade schools now). Lunch at the Colony Club with Ida Tarbell. Dinner at the Lafayette with Bill Morrow or Bert Boyden. Elsie Ferguson playing The First Lady of the Land. Charley Towne giving his brilliant imitations after dinner. Young, healthy, on the way to success, I found myself saying again, as I had said to myself during my happy Ryan High School years, "Edna, my girl, you're having a fine time. You're having the time of your life!"

And again I was right.

Yet when early spring came I wanted to be back in Chicago. The sap was stirring in the trees. Chicago was far from sylvan, but out on the South Side you had the feeling of being in a small Midwestern town, you could go out to Seventy-fifth Street and find yourself in the daisy-strewn prairie for miles. This turning my face westward was the unconscious urge to get nearer the earth. New York's stone and cement and steel were beginning to pall on me. I wanted to picnic in the woods south of Chicago; I wanted to see the kids in Lillian Adler's dancing class at Maxwell Settlement; I wanted to bathe in Lake Michigan which seemed to lie so accommodatingly at the foot of every west-east Chicago street.

June in Chicago that year turned out to be less than completely pastoral. I covered the Democratic and Republican national conventions for the George Matthew Adams Newspaper Syndicate; a ferocious attack of tonsillitis with a high fever laid me low in the midst of this; my sister Fannie bore her first baby, a girl whom they named Janet. Janet Fox turned out to have blue eyes, which astonished me because her mother, her grandmother and her aunt had dark brown eyes. Being a matriarch by nature and inheritance I refused to consider the fact that Janet's father was blue-eyed. I then recalled that Grandpa Neumann's eyes had been blue, and relaxed. I wished they had called her something more distinctive than Janet, but I was glad they hadn't named her anything as commonplace as Edna.

Janet's birth coincided with the week of the Democratic National Convention in Chicago, in consequence of which I was considerably less the hovering auntie than I otherwise might have been. Covering a national political convention is a full-time job. This was the first newspaper assignment I had taken since I left the Milwaukee Journal. I was excited and scared. George Adams was paying me a thousand dollars a week for the two weeks and all expenses. He was familiar with my stories; I was to do what he called human-interest articles with a feminine sort of angle and on the crisp side, in the style of the Emma McChesney stories. He had engaged William Allen White to cover the straight political news; George Fitch to do humor; Jay Darling and Harold Webster as cartoonists. We were known as Adams' Trained Seals.

Chicago was a bedlam of bands, parades, badges, banners. Delegates milled like cattle in and out of hotel headquarters. It was a steaming hot Chicago June. We five were supposed to do a preconvention story or cartoon. We met for dinner the night before the first day. It was then that William Allen White walked into my life. His friendship, his wisdom, his philosophy, his gorgeous humor have enriched it ever since. I saw a rotund broad-shouldered man in a pale gray suit and astonishing pale gray kid shoes that he displayed with pride as having been snared from a shoe drummer in Emporia, Kansas. And how did we like them? He had the smile of a roguish little boy, with dimples complete; the broad noble brow of a philosopher and statesman; the eyes of a poet and the shrewd determined mouth of the politician, businessman, newspaper editor. The eyes dominated. I noticed that ordinarily they were a rather washed-out blue as though the color had drained out of them when he relaxed. When he was stirred, emotionalized, they would darken and deepen and widen until they were blue-black pools in his round pink face. He saw everything; he knew everyone; his wit was pungent, salty, homely and sophisticated at the same time. There was a difference of perhaps twenty years in our ages. We were friends and comrades from the start. Jay Darling ("Ding" to you), George Fitch and Harold Webster turned out to be gay charming companions. George Matthew Adams watched over us like a hen guarding her chicks. He treated us as if we were visiting royalty. I was one woman in a group of five men, all clever, all amusing and friendly. It looked like a gala two weeks.

The gods decided it was too much plush for one girl, and humbled me with as nasty an attack of tonsillitis as can be summoned. For two days I couldn't leave my bed. I couldn't write a word. In those two days Bill White and George Fitch, after turning in their own stint, wrote my piece as well, signing it with my name. It was faintly Rabelaisian, highly mischievous and terrifically readable stuff. For weeks afterward I had letters from far-off readers of newspapers included in George Adams' nationwide syndicate.

There never was such a national political convention. No newspaper training was adequate for this. In that week the Progressive Party was born. The Republican convention hall was never for one minute anything but a mass of screaming, shouting, stamping, hooting maniacs. Little Victor Rosewater, editor of the Omaha Bee and chairman of the Republican National Committee, standing on the platform, diminutive, gentle, trying to make himself heard above the roar and yammer, was as effective as the rustle of a leaf above Niagara's torrent. Screaming women in the galleries of the old Wabash Avenue Armory hall; howling men on the delegation floor; shouts of "Liars! Thieves!" directed at Elihu Root, at Governor Hadley of Missouri, at anyone who attempted to raise his voice from the speakers' platform. Ten thousand men during one solid week made noises such as animals fighting for their lives in the jungle would have considered unjustified. As the Roman aristocracy from the vantage point of their garlanded loges looked down upon bloody gladiatorial combats, so Chicago society and its out-of-town Social Register guests in chiffons, flower-laden hats and Palm Beach suits surveyed the hoarse-voiced gesticulating frenzied mob rampaging on the Republican convention called to nominate a man for President of the United States of America. In my Journal days I had learned one rule for effective reporting of any fantastic or seemingly indescribable event: simple short words, economy of adjectives, boil it down. I remembered Lou Simonds' cautioning shout on the Milwaukee Journal, "Keep it down now, fellows!

Boil it! Waddy yuh think this is—a weekly!" I boiled what I had to say until there remained only the strong clear essence. But feature stories were no good in that convention. The bare news stories were too bizarre, too incredible.

At the Congress Hotel I met Theodore Roosevelt for the first time. Bill White introduced us. Roosevelt's first remark to me was characteristic. Here he was, in the midst of the fight of his fighting life.

"What are you going to do about Emma McChesney?"

Of course I was stunned and immensely flattered, as he had meant me to be. "Why—uh—I don't know, Mr. Roosevelt."

Briskly he took charge. "Well now, I'll tell you. I think she ought to marry again. What became of her first husband? Die? Or did she divorce him? You never said. Anyway, she's got to marry T. A. Buck. An immensely vital woman. She could manage business and marriage all right. Now, in that last story you had her . . ."

I knew this was a trick of his, but I was completely disarmed nevertheless. He hadn't just skimmed the stories; he had read them all. He knew the character as well as I did.

A breathing spell, all too brief after that week of turmoil, and Adams' Trained Seals were off to Baltimore for the Democratic National Convention. There George Matthew Adams had performed a miracle for his expensive pets. Baltimore was inadequately equipped for the thousands who now poured into the city. Hotels were swamped. Restaurants had to close their doors against the crowds. Delegates and newspaper correspondents were sleeping in bathrooms, in hotel corridors, in barber shops. Even the most luxurious hotel suites were uncomfortable in the humid Baltimore summer weather. Somehow divining this weeks before, George Adams had rented furnished for one week the private house of a Baltimore family who were fleeing the city before the convention. It was a fine old brick mansion just two or three houses back of the Belvedere Hotel, on Charles Street. Four stories high, cool, ample, well furnished, and equipped with a vast amiable colored cook who looked as if she had just made up for a Southern sketch, apron, bandana, plump cheeks, white-toothed smile complete, that Charles Street house became an oasis in the desert for the favored correspondents who were lucky enough to be the friends of Adams' Trained Seals.

I had what was known as the bridal suite on the third floor, front. I've never had a happier week. We all felt carefree, though we covered our jobs decently enough. But the Democratic convention provided dull fare after the insane shenanigans of the Chicago fiesta. We paid little enough attention to it, for there was little enough to see and hear. Most of the sessions turned out to be star-chamber stuff. The day's meeting would be called, there would be the opening prayer, piously droned by a local divine, then a brisk squabble and a surprising adjournment until late afternoon or evening. The delegates and the Big Bosses were in difficulties, but, unlike the Republican convention which had preceded this, their floundering, squabbling and clubbing one another over the head were, for the most part, done in private committee meetings from which reporters were excluded.

We drove about Baltimore's lovely outlying countryside, we lunched at country clubs, laughed, worked a little. Then Bill White and I, pitying the starving high-powered newspaper correspondents less lucky than we as we lolled in our luxury, decided to give a Baltimore breakfast. William Allen White knows and loves good food. Anyone who has ever stopped for a meal at the Whites' house in Emporia, Kansas, knows that Bill and Sallie White are epicures. Will shares my distrust of those people who say, dreamily, "I forgot all about lunch." Or, "I really never pay any attention to food. I hardly ever know what I'm eating." I've never seen a really dimensional or important human being who was indifferent to good food and its preparation.

We interviewed the good-natured Negro cook. She was not only willing to cook the breakfast, she was rolling-eyed about it. We volunteered to do the marketing. With a glitter in our eyes and huge Baltimore market baskets on our arms Bill White and I headed toward the big open Lexington Market.

There we went mad. We bought everything in sight—fish, flesh, fowl, fruit, vegetables. As we drove home our eyes could just be seen above the stacked baskets, bundles and boxes.

We had invited as many as the big mahogany dining table could manage, with squeezing, and, as it turned out, a dozen or so humbly stood up or squatted on the floor, plate in hand. I still remember Henry Beach Needham hanging around sniffing and dreamily closing his eyes while the meal was cooking.

There was no session at the convention hall that morning. There had been an adjournment until half past eight in the evening, according to the strange workings of that political group. We all gathered at about one o'clock. No one in history, including Henry the Eighth at the height of his gustatory powers, ever sat down to such a breakfast. There were no courses and no particular routine. It was all there in Gargantuan profusion. A kind of awe crept into the faces of the visiting correspondents. There were oranges, peaches, grapefruit. There were bacon and eggs for the unimaginative; soft-shell crabs, succulent and sweet; fried chicken, lamb chops, stewed fresh huckleberries (no one knows why. We merely had seen them in the market, bursting black giant huckleberries, and Bill had breathed something about their being elegant with hot popovers). There were waffles with syrup or preserves, little hot biscuits and big hot popovers. Steaming coffee in urns and pitchers of cream. The fat cook kept bringing in fresh supplies. A kind of glaze came into the eyes of the breakfasters. Presently even the cook saw that the famished scribes were replete. At a piled-up platter they only shook their heads, groaning, speechless.

For the rest of the day we sat about blinking and staring at each other like overstuffed pythons who have just swallowed too many rabbits. It was very hot. Finally we gathered ourselves languidly together for the stroll over to the convention hall, where the night meeting was about to begin. All except George Fitch. He said that nothing would happen in that old Dorcas society, anyway. It never had, all through the week. He was going to write his piece just where he was, in comfort. He had it all in his mind, and very funny, too. Also, he added, reflectively, perhaps he shouldn't have eaten that fourth soft-shell crab after all that chicken and waffles and coffee and this and that.

We left him hunched over his typewriter, whether in the throes of composition or a stomach-ache we weren't quite sure. Still languid and logy we entered the convention hall and took our seats boredly in the press section. At that moment William Jennings Bryan, the old war horse, came to the front of the platform, shook back his mane, thinning now at the top, raised his arms high in their heat-wrinkled alpaca sleeves, and shot the speech that nominated Woodrow Wilson and that really made him President of the United States.

There followed one of those spectacular and spontaneous riots that run the gamut from exhilaration to exhaustion. There was nothing of the usual pumped-up political-convention demonstration about this. We dashed off our stories, hot, filed them on the spot and staggered home, weary, but with the feeling of triumph that follows the writing of a good piece at white heat. We had forgotten all about George Fitch. He had finished his article and was awaiting our home-coming like a loving father who wants all the chicks to be in bed before locking up. In his stockinged feet, coatless, he was relaxed in an easy chair, reading. We told him. He picked up his typed sheets and slowly tore them into ribbons. They made quite a nice little feathery sheaf which he handed to me with a low bow:

"Curl papers, Miss F."

On the way back to Chicago I stopped in New York for a few days. A man named Adams telephoned me at my hotel and I talked to him for five minutes on the telephone, thinking it was George Matthew, until I discovered that it was Franklin P. Adams, the famed F.P.A. of the New York Evening Mail column, the Conning Tower. This was our first meeting. Had I seen his sister Amy, in Chicago? And how about coming out to dinner? We dined at a strange, rather tough and interesting place—the Metropole Hotel dining room. Great place for gamblers and race-track men, Frank said. We played a little game, picking out the diners who looked the part. Shortly after that night they called Herman Rosenthal out to the street and shot him on the doorstep of the Metropole. There followed the worst civic scandal that New York had ever known. The revelation of police corruption that attended the trial of Police Lieutenant Charles

Becker and his gang resulted in the conviction and electrocution of Becker.

Back in Chicago I began to get insistent inquiries about the dramatization of the Emma McChesney stories. My handling of these offers was a triumph of mismanagement. I paid very little attention to them, but the little I did about them was almost dazzlingly inept. I went on writing. I sent letters to New York saying that I'd be there in the winter, and what was the hurry about a McChesney play, anyway! Woodrow Wilson was elected and the world marched calmly on its way toward twenty-five years of unimaginable horror. Pictures and posters of the scholarly Wilson looked frostily down upon the American voter, in direct contrast to the smiles of his predecessors, the billowy Taft and the vociferous Teddy.

As usual now when midwinter came I yearned for the gaiety and the brilliant winter sunshine of New York. The murk and gloom of Chicago depressed me. I didn't laugh enough in Chicago. Still I didn't think of New York as a city in which to live. It was a place in which to have a sort of working holiday for a few weeks or months. It turned out to be a bad winter, even in New York. I rented a tiny furnished apartment in East Thirty-second Street, taking it on sight late one dark afternoon. It taught me a lesson, at least. The place turned out to be just back of the old Colony Club where a stentorian doorman bellowed carriage numbers all night, for they seemed to give endless soirées, those social Colonists. A stable, in active use, nestled just across the narrow courtyard and a whiff of my clothes as I entered a room placed me immediately as one of the less ablutionary members of the ridin' set or a hostler's daughter. Not a glint of sunshine penetrated the rooms. I battled colds and flu all the winter and did less work than I had accomplished in many winters. As a graceful finish I handed the McChesney dramatic rights to a bewildered press agent named Lee Kugel, the least of the theatrical folk who had been battling for them. The one bright spot in the winter was the theater—Fanny's First Play; Maude Adams in Peter Pan; Laurette Taylor in Peg o' My Heart; The Poor Little Rich Girl. I looked forward to coming back to Chicago in February—the skating in Jackson Park, the clean gale tearing along the lake front.

Though I didn't know it, I was a little stale. I had gone on writing short story after short story. The steaming Chicago summer seemed to be good for work. With my mother I moved into a furnished apartment in a row of brick apartments facing directly on Lake Michigan. The little parklike place, green and shady, was a sort of Chicago Pomander Walk. On the front of each apartment was stuck one of those glass carbuncles known to Chicagoans as sun parlors. In these transparent nooks Chicago disported itself, goldfish fashion, sewing, reading, napping, playing bridge in full view of an uninterested world that was busy doing the same. One could put on a bathing suit and cross the little patch of lawn into the icy waters of Lake Michigan with only a few floating orange peels and watermelon rinds to mar their northern purity. On thick nights the great foghorn mooed like a cow seeking its lost calf. I drove a Buick through the tangle of Loop traffic and out to the open prairie. Chicago, in many ways, was still like a frontier town. You drove and drove through close-built streets—and suddenly there you were on the open prairie amidst the black-eyed Susans and the fireweed. The heat was tropical. That July my sister Fannie's second child was born, another girl, just thirteen months younger than her sister Janet. They named her Mina. My family feelings were now somewhat hurt.

Early in 1914 the second volume of the Emma McChesney stories was brought out by Stokes. It was called Personality Plus, which I then considered a very apt title indeed. The stories featured Emma's son Jock who was now in business. The title sprang from the fact that Jock had so much personality and charm that his customers forgot all about the goods he was selling. The stories in this second book weren't as good as those contained in the first.

New York that winter was literally dance mad. Stenographers tangoed and fox-trotted at lunch. The moment anyone entered your house he tore up the rugs, turned on the phonograph and began to dip, swoop and jiggle. You danced at teatime, at lunch, at dinner, at supper, in hotels, restaurants, tearooms. Buxom elderly matrons, school boys and girls, dignified professional men rushed to the nearest dance space—and a dancing floor was any clear area over five feet square. Diners ordered food, then left it to congeal on their plates uneaten. I danced with the rest of the world. I'd always loved dancing since before my Ryan High School days. It was—though we did not sense it then—a prelude to world madness.

That winter the Authors League of America was born, a rather puny and unwanted child; no one dreamed it would grow up to be the support and comfort of its parents' old age. There was a dinner at the Biltmore Hotel to celebrate the accouchement, with all the Name writers out in their stiffest shirt fronts and lowest dresses. Pet authors sat at tables with their watchful publishers. I was in the Stokes corral. There were speeches and visiting about among the tables, all pretty dull. At about ten-thirty, with the appearance of the biscuit Tortoni and the coffee, Jack London appeared dramatically in the big doorway. Scorning such trappings as starched shirts, tails and patent leathers, he had gone to a good deal of trouble to get himself up in corduroys, open-throated shirt and belt. He didn't come in. He merely stood there—he-man, Socialist, open-spaces stuff. The effect was superb. He made a ballroom full of people feel slightly resentful and silly.

By now the McChesney dramatic rights were in the hands of a producer named Joseph Brooks, and a playwright named Charlotte Thompson was trying to fashion a play from the stories. It didn't occur to me to try to do the thing myself. Or perhaps I was timid about taking such a plunge. I evaded the whole business by sailing for Europe early in 1914.

12

WHAT A SIMPLE COZY little world it was! You wanted to go to
Europe. There it was. You boarded a ship with practically no
formality. Passports were things they used in Russia, land of
Siberian barbarism, czars and pogroms. You worked, you saved
your money, you spent it on travel or what you pleased. Income
tax! Who ever heard of such a thing! Hard enough to earn
money without paying a penalty for earning it. Italy, Austria-
Hungary, France, Germany, England, there they sat, hospitably
waiting for me and my kind. Everything polite and cordial and
friendly. Policemen, waiters, shopkeepers, bank managers, coach-
men, stewards, guides—Küss' die Hand . . . c'est rien, mademoiselle . . . zu befehl . . . grazia . . . 'k-you! Of course you
had to tip them all (including the bank managers) but their
manners certainly were lovely. Except when you chanced to
scratch the veneer.

The boat was the Hamburg, of the Hamburg-American Line,
only eleven thousand tons, which seemed gigantic to me. She
was to sail from Hoboken, headed for the Mediterranean and
Italy. The trip would take sixteen days. I couldn't believe my
luck. The day before our sailing there descended upon New York
a blizzard such as I had never seen even in the days of Wiscon-

sin's lavish snows. By morning the New York streets were blocked. No vehicles were moving. Paths burrowed through were walled on either side by snowbanks as high as a man's head. New York looked like a Currier & Ives winter print.

But in the next twenty-four hours all this was forgotten. Every day was a dream day. There was precious little deck space, but I didn't know that. Every morning at eleven the ship's German band struck up a horrible cacophony. The food was rich, varied and excellently cooked. I spent a lot of time up in the wireless room of this free-and-easy boat, getting the wireless news first-hand, talking and laughing with the two wireless operators, blue-eyed German boys who spoke English precisely, out of a book, with a German accent. Landing in Naples I was startled to find that one of the young men had followed me to the Grand Hotel and was making a solemn offer of marriage. In our conversations up in the wireless room he had talked a good deal about how wonderful it was at a voyage's end to have a few days in one's own cottage reading and talking in the lamplight. I had thought it sounded awfully dull, but if that was what he liked I was too polite to argue. Besides, it was his life, not mine. Now, it seemed, I was to be the lamp-sitter opposite. I learned then that the senti-mental Germans are not to be trifled with.

On the voyage I had met a marvelous woman of middle age. We struck up a real friendship in spite of the difference in our ages—a friendship which the years and the war failed to destroy. She was Frau Clara Ewald, a portrait painter returning from her first American trip. I promised to spend a fortnight at her cot-tage near the foot of the Bavarian Alps, some distance from Munich. That visit is one of my happiest memories of a prewar Germany.

We had stopped on the way to Italy to visit Funchal, Madeira, briefly. It had been incredibly lovely rising out of the sunrise sea. Algiers, too, and Gibraltar. Looking back on it now it seems unbelievably naïve of the obliging British Tommies to have guided us tourists through the fortress of the mighty rock. They showed us where the guns were hidden, how they worked, the enormous caches of food stored in tunnels. We took it all for granted. You were sight-seeing, that was all. War was something that belonged to the Dark Ages.

All the conventional tourist sights—Naples, Capri, Sorrento, Amalfi, Pompeii. Driving along the winding mountain roads (carriage and horses) you heard the blue of the Mediterranean below likened to sapphires and heaven and opals and delphinium but privately I thought it was exactly the color of the washday water after the bluing had been dropped into it back in Appleton.

Rome. Florence. Scarlet-robed priests crossing the greensward on the Pincian Hill. Dazzling mustached officers in pale blue capes and silver helmets slyly snapping your garters as you passed them on the narrow ledgelike sidewalks of Roman or Florentine streets. Michelangelo's statue of the young David standing out in the open market square with the peasants and townspeople lounging and chaffering beneath it as though it were any piece of common clay.

Florence was a maze of terrible tearooms patronized by British and American spinsters in amber beads and silk shawls, decaying among the Caesars. Italy of those pre-Mussolini days was dirty and utterly delightful. When next I saw it it had been scrubbed —but not behind the ears. Though Rome and Florence had been dictator-slicked the villages which the average tourist never penetrated had been left encrusted in their accustomed mold. No one then could foresee that the socialist-minded newspaper editor Mussolini, burning to modernize and stabilize the business and political life of Italy, would travel the path of all dictators— reformer, oppressor, dictator, tyrant, megalomaniac.

In Florence I rented a typewriter (American) whose keys were dotted with strange marks and symbols for the Italian trade, and got to work. I had contracts which must be filled. I was to be in Europe for six or seven months. It was hard to face the typewriter with the Florentine kaleidoscope whirling all about and the Arno flowing just outside the window.

It took all one's strength of character to get to work mornings at the Hotel D'Italie, in Florence, right enough. Just to glance out of the bedroom window was fatal. There'd be the Prince of Italy reviewing troops; or a funeral procession, all swaying plumes and mysterious hooded black-robed attendants, their eyes glittering through holes in their masks; or a passing garbage wagon with a plume of acacia in the horse's ear, the driver singing Rigoletto at the top of a surprising tenor voice.

All through Europe during those months of winter, spring and summer of 1914 I dutifully Saw the Sights. Cathedrals, statues, galleries, ruins, historical monuments, mountains, cemeteries, views. Like a child who has eaten its spinach and lamb chop in order to earn the ice cream and cake I then turned to the pastime I loved best—sitting out on Main Street, watching the town go by. It might be called the Via This or the Rue That, or Somethingstrasse; any outdoor café or restaurant suited my purpose. The habit of watching Ottumwa, Iowa, stroll by on a Saturday night was still with me.

Night train for Budapest. By morning I would be in the city of which I had so often heard my Hungarian father speak. It is rarely that life is so accommodating as to let you find something exactly as you had hoped it might look. Budapest in the spring of 1914 was like that. It was a picture postcard come true. The fairy lights on the high hill at night, the strange Moorish architecture, the vivacious arrogant Hungarians themselves, mixture of half a dozen races. There was the theater (not as good as I had hoped); but the great gray-white globules of caviar eaten with black bread and little crocks of sweet butter made up for that; and the Tokay wine and the wild passionate music of the czigany orchestra. I saw the dark narrow streets of the factory workers' district lined by rows of damp gloomy-looking houses. Best of all was to walk or sit in the Corso between noon and one o'clock and watch the world stroll by. It was a musical-comedy 1914 world so soon to vanish. At that hour the wide thoroughfare that ran along the Danube (which is yellow instead of blue, but no matter now) was closed to all vehicles. The broad pavement became a promenade for pedestrians. Carriages and motorcars of every description drove up to the rope boundaries, and out stepped the world and the half-world and even the underworld of Budapest. The 1914 women of Budapest were beautiful and voluptuous and they all dressed as Marlene

Dietrich (then probably an infant) now gets herself up in her femme-fatale films—all skin-tight satin, slashed skirts, paradise aigrettes in their hats. Among the men only the officers in their scarlet and blue and gold were dashing. The civilian men were the frumpiest males I'd ever seen, not excluding those of Ottumwa, Iowa. One heard no word of German spoken. To accost a Hungarian in German was to offend him. He pretended not to understand.

The name of Ferber seemed to be not uncommon in Budapest, spelled with two e's exactly as we spelled it. There was a vast to-do of bowing and bending and hand-kissing. By half past one a Hungarian version of the fairy godmother waved a wand and the grand world was whisked away. The Corso became just a street in Budapest with fiacres and horses clop-clopping along, and nursemaids in their wide manifold petticoats and laced bodices and peasant caps took over with their charges.

At four, miraculously, the aigrettes and the army uniforms all appeared again at Heinrich Kugler's or at Gerbeaud's for tea. The orchestra played, the air was thick with smoke and perfume and the sweet scent of rich cakes. There was tea with plenty of rum in it and platters and trays of cakes like flowers in a garden. At about half past four a crimson carpet was spread from the door to the street, a carriage and splendid pair drove up and out stepped a tall plain woman in black, the Grand Duchess, and with her a young man with curious vacant eyes and an open loose-hung mouth, her idiot son of sixteen or thereabouts. Everyone in the café stood up, their mouths full of cake, and remained thus until royalty was seated. I thought I had come a long, long way from the Vincennes Hotel in Chicago, the Appleton, Wisconsin, Daily Crescent, and Ferber's Bazaar in Ottumwa. As things turned out, it wasn't so far, after all. It was the end of all that, though I didn't know it then.

Sometimes I think Vienna was best of all. Six weeks or more there. The rented typewriter, American-made for the Austrians, was full of umlauts. We settled down at the Pension Atlanta for a stay of five or six weeks. Every morning the indefatigable Julia Ferber started out as briskly as though she were headed toward the store in Appleton. In those seven months she saw more of Europe than most people who have lived there for years. Side streets, boulevards, antique shops, cafés, fairs—she scoured them all. At noon she would return in triumph, her big black handbag heavy with swag.

"What's that, for heaven's sake!"

"A petit-point chair cover . . . an eighteenth-century pewter dessert service . . . a Dresden figurine . . . a tooled-leather desk set . . . a lace luncheon set . . ."

"Yes, they're lovely, but what'll I do with them? I haven't even a house."

"You will have, someday."

(And she was right, and here they are, each one glowing richly in its proper place, pleasing to the soul and the senses.)

I worked all morning in my room except when I was hanging halfway out of the window watching the construction of the new hospital across the way. Women did all the rough work. In their short full skirts, little three-cornered headshawls tied under their chins, peasant fashion (American girls wear these now with their shorts and slacks), they toiled like animals. It was the women who carried the weighted buckets of mortar, the laden hods of brick and stone, up and down the ladders and scaffolding. It was amazing to watch how they bent to pick up the dead weight of the buckets or the brick loads. They braced the ankles, the knees, the hips, the back, they would hoist the loads to their heads in one splendid unbroken gesture. Then, necks set like stone pillars, they would turn and march up the ladders. At the top the men waited for the burden bearers.

Every noon at the lunch hour one particular girl would wipe the crumbs off her lips, stand up before the rest, and sing or recite. I couldn't catch the words, but I heard enough to know she sang in the Viennese dialect; she was a superb comedienne, her audience roared and slapped its thighs. This woman hod carrier with her merry impudent face singing at the noon hour for her delighted fellow workers I later used in the short story You've Got to Be Selfish. All through Europe that trip I impaled a short story here or there, and wrote it in the city in which I found it. Writing hot off the griddle like that is no good for me. A story must simmer in its own juice for months or even years before it is ready to serve. But things were new and fresh to me, I was excited and enormously entertained, I wanted to put some of it down just as I found it. So in Italy I had done The Guiding Miss Gowd. In Vienna the girl hod carrier (I turned her into a great musical-comedy star at the story's finish); in Paris, Sophy as She Might Have Been. They were surface stories. America, American men and women, these are the only materials with which I can fashion a first-rate story or novel. I don't know why this is true, but it is.

That Vienna of April 1914 was the Vienna of the nostalgic songs, of the Strauss waltzes. The orchestras played:

> *Wien, Wien, nur du allein*
> *Wirst stets die Stadt meiner Träume sein.*

You drove and walked in the Ringstrasse, you took a droshky with two fleet neat little horses driven by an unbelievably musical-comedy Kutscher in a glazed hat and cockade. He talked a Viennese patois all his own, pungent, impudent, philosophical. The Austrians seemed to me to be the most enchanting people I had ever seen. They had the Frenchman's love of beauty without his avarice; the Italian's passion without his temper; the German's sentiment and music worship without his arrogance and sheeplike sentimentality.

The shops in the Koerntnerstrasse were full of exquisitely fashioned leather and linen and enamel and jewelry. The Austrian officers were snugly corseted, their shoulders sloped down to slim waists and flat hips, their heads were held haughtily above the tight velvet collars of their uniforms, their swords clanked at their spurred heels, their boots glittered like glass, their heels clicked like castanets as they bowed in the eternal hand-kissing. It was the day of the Merry Widow sailor and the skin-tight fawn broadcloth tailleur for women. Every pretty Viennese seemed to wear a pair of diamond eardrops the size of hazelnuts screwed into the lobes of her ears.

Dinner at Sachers' was a rite. Frau Sacher herself, in tight black silk and gold chain, her hair pulled straight back from her round unsmiling face, knew all the secrets and all the scandals of Austrian royalty. There was opera; the changing of the guard at the Emperor's Palace; the theater. Rosa Rücker made me my first real tailor suit, amidst much hand-kissing. It was a navy-blue Eton with the tightest possible hobble skirt, slashed up the back so that I could walk without stumbling. As it was I had to place one foot directly in front of the other, like a tightrope walker. There was a sort of bustle-peplum at the back, so that the effect of the figure was that of an inverted pyramid. With this was a soft creamy-white crepe blouse and a tiny blue hat with a single pink rose in the front, and a veil. Very chic. I thought I looked every inch a Viennese.

Any city but Munich would have been an anticlimax after Vienna, but the Bavarian metropolis had a charm and personality all its own. There was an unforgettable week spent with Frau Ewald while she painted my portrait in her cottage at the foot of the Bavarian Alps. The country people passing by in their little short pants, bare-kneed, with embroidered suspenders over their shirts and a Tyrolean brush in their Robin Hood hats, said "Grüsz Gott!" amiably and gravely. "Grüsz Gott!" you said, in return. Grüsz Gott—God's greeting—through the fresh pungent pine woods. Heil Hitler must sound very odd in its place.

Berlin was full of relations living beautifully in their luxurious houses. They had lived thus for centuries in Germany. We, the American cousins, dined with them. The silver, the glass, the china were impressive, there was salmon on a silver platter, there were delicate birds, wines, sweets. My little fifteen-year-old third cousin in a white dress and pigtail smoked a cigarette after dinner to my astonishment. I never had seen a young girl smoke.

We were having coffee one afternoon at the Bristol Hotel, we talked of the family and I mentioned the name of Uncle Isidore, my mother's oldest brother. Instantly the cousins hissed, "Sh-sh-sh!" I looked over my shoulder, expecting I don't know what. There was nothing. I went on: ". . . and Uncle Isidore said that . . ."

"Sh-sh-sh! Don't say that!"

Unbelievably, it turned out that in Berlin the name of Isidore had some sort of Jewish connotation, it was low comedy or worse, these people shrank from hearing it; seemed frightened, even, at hearing it. Well, I thought, you're queer Jews. Why do you care a whoop if it sounds Jewish or not? It is Jewish. What of it?

The German way of living seemed the height of physical comfort, of Gemütlichkeit. But the Prussian way of thinking infuriated me. I wasn't happy or comfortable there. I didn't know why, but there was for me something poisonous about the whole Prussian atmosphere; it was as though something treacherous, foul and brutal lurked beneath that thick-necked, well-fed sentimental Germany of 1914. I was revolted by the foppish Berlin officers trying to ape the British with the monocles stuck in their hard blue eyes; the round shaven heads; the everlasting eating and drinking; the constant sneering at America and Americans. It was the one European country (other than England) whose language I spoke with considerable fluency; my maternal grandmother and grandfather had sprung from there, and all their ancestors. I was ill at ease. Perhaps it was the staunch revolutionary spirit of Grandpa Neumann warning us. Come Edna, come Julchen, get out of here, get out.

I wanted to be in Paris in June, and June was almost here.

Glad to be out of it and on the way to Paris. Paris was crammed with American tourists, including Chicago friends and a New York beau. At the very thought of all that I managed to do in those first brief Paris weeks I bow to a vanished youth. I revolved like a top from Versailles to Maxim's, from Fontainebleau to the Dome, from the Butte to the Moulin Rouge, from Pré Catelan to the Louvre.

The blood of kings is so remote in my veins that horse races—any horse races—bore me. Still, the Grand Prix races were held the last Sunday in June, and this was something one had to see. Horses or no horses, you simply had to go to the Grand Prix races if you were in Paris June 28th. There were the mannequins parading the last word in 1914 summer costumes; there were stage beauties in pearl necklaces and hobble skirts. Poincaré,

President of France, entered his box with his guests. The races began. An attendant entered the President's box, leaned over, spoke to him privately. President Poincaré turned sharply, he stood up, the entire box party rose with him. A moment later the box was empty. The races went on, but there was a buzz of conjecture. By Sunday evening the streets of Paris were full of the news. Archduke Francis Ferdinand, heir to the throne of Austria, and his morganatic wife, the Duchess of Hohenberg, had been shot and killed by a young Servian student, Gavro Princip, while the royal pair were driving to the Sarajevo palace from the city hall in the province of Bosnia, newly acquired by Austria-Hungary.

Well, what of it? After all, you can't break down and cry about a grand duke. What's all the fuss about!

"Where's Bosnia?"

"Ask *me!*"

"I'll bet that's why the President and his crowd left the box."

"Diplomatic stuff—he was the nephew of the Austrian Emperor —Franz Josef."

"The paper says old Franz said, 'Is nothing spared me!' "

"Well, he's had it tough, you know—old Franz Josef."

"I'd rather be me than king. . . . Look, where'll we go for dinner?"

After months in Italy, Austria, Germany, France, London was, somehow, drab. Or perhaps it was just my impatience to be home again. I had had enough, seen enough. I had tourist's mental, visual, emotional and physical indigestion. Now I was sullen about the Tower, St. Paul's, the Houses of Parliament, Madame Tussaud's Wax Works and the Cheshire Cheese. All my life London had meant Dickens to me, and it didn't quite look as I had planned.

I did perk up a bit at the suffrage riots, though, with the Pankhursts being pushed all over the place. Patriotically I went to see Elsie Janis who was playing in a London revue and singing (in beautiful smooth English tails and top hat) I'm Gilbert the Filbert. There was a week end spent in Sussex with Neil Lyons

whose short stories I so loved and admired. I had read and reread
Sixpenny Pieces, Arthur's Coffee Stall, Love in a Mist, Clara.

One thing more I recall with considerable delight. From a
London theater box I saw a play called My Lady's Dress, by Edward Knoblock. In the cast was a tall gawky girl, very thin, all
elbows and angles, but with a memorable face and a lovely unforgettable voice. She played in one scene only, the part of a
cockney pickle-factory girl; but she did the bit so magnificently
that when the lights went up I scurried about in my program to
find out who she was. But the name meant nothing to me. I'd
never heard of the girl. Lynn Fontanne, the program said.

For no reason at all I decided I'd had enough and changed
our sailing to the North German Lloyd ship, the George Washington, a good boat sailing the end of July. I've no idea what
impelled me to do this. I felt a surge of happiness at the thought
of facing toward the western world. It had been wonderful, but
I had had enough. Since then I never have failed to know that
feeling after weeks or months in Europe, no matter how gay or
restful the holiday. Always there is that lifting and soaring of
the spirit at sight of the great hulk of an ocean liner with its out-
size funnels and its outflung gangplank waiting to take me back
to my own land. Even the boat train is fun. All those American
women in their new Paris hats and new French suits and those
little dabs of jewelry or gewgaws picked up in the Rue de Rivoli
or the Rue St. Honoré, wherewith to dazzle the home folks.
Their hair, too, done a new tortuous way. I first saw gleaming
red-lacquered fingernails on a tender at Havre and thought for
one shocked second that the crimson-tipped hands had been
dipped in blood. All the fun and all the weariness of foreign
travel is over; uniformed men pawing your most personal be-
longings; the strange tongues, the unaccustomed sights, the
foreign foods, the hostile or curious glances. Here was the mov-
able bridge that led toward home and the American language,
and strong coffee with plenty of cream, and peaches in bushel
baskets instead of being wrapped like jewels in cotton wool;
and the New York Times, and thick steak with fried onions, and
the sun on New York Harbor, and the independent cocky

American way of talking and walking and thinking. No hand-kissing. No tipping the bus or street-car conductor or the bank manager. Dollar-mad Americans, eh! I had found that the European street-car conductor wouldn't stop at your corner unless you had tipped him a heller or a pfennig when you paid your fare. I wondered what would happen to you if you were to try to give a penny tip to a Broadway street-car conductor. Throw you off the car, probably, and spit for good measure. Lavish, sloppy, noisy, careless, friendly, unsuspicious polyglot America. Naïve, generous, slangy, colorful, electric *schnuckle* America.

The voyage home began pleasantly enough. The ship was twice the size of the little Hamburg on which I had sailed East. On board I met Newman Levy, the Flaccus of F.P.A.'s column, we became good friends, and six years later we collaborated on the play $1200 a Year which opened (and closed) in Baltimore, in one week.

At dinner that August evening the dining-room stewards suddenly began to behave like maniacs. Up to now the service had been smooth, efficient, in the well-known German manner. But now our steward, heretofore so capable, so quick, so ready with suggestions, was bewilderingly inept. Dinner simply didn't appear. Passengers at near-by tables were turning, muttering, casting black looks toward the kitchen service doors. Our steward was a man in his thirties; he had told us about his wife and his two children at home in Germany. Now his manner was strange, his eyes were wild, when we gave an order he seemed not to hear. If we ordered soup we got caviar; roast beef instead of lamb.

"What's the matter, Otto? Are you ill? What's wrong in the kitchen?"

"Nothing. Nothing. What will the Herrschaften have? I am sorry. What will the Herrschaft——" But then he was off again, staring into space.

Up in the smoking room after dinner it was the same. Suddenly, at about half past ten, when the early birds and the elderly were thinking of turning in for the night there rushed through the room two ship's officers, their faces ashen. It was impossible not to be alarmed by their aspect and manner. Immediately the stewards went about dimming lights, closing portholes, muffling windows. An order went out. No passenger must light a cigar or cigarette on deck. No portholes or windows or doors must be allowed to reveal a ray of light. The George Washington of the North German Lloyd Line was being pursued by a French gunboat.

War had been declared.

Through the night we huddled out on deck in the mist and rain, our shoulders hunched in greatcoats and slickers. It was a foggy thick night, the black boat cut full speed through the darkness. With the dawn we stumbled to bed. All those white-faced stewards had known that the ship, once in New York Harbor, never would return to Germany. It was interned there, and the crew with it. They did not see their families for years.

Well, it was all very exciting and dreadful, but it was their war and none of our business. It would all be over in a couple of months. I regretted having missed the chance to see a Europe plunged suddenly into war. Tourists abroad were scrambling wildly for American-bound boats—any boats, any sort of passage, second-class, third-class, steerage. I told myself I'd have stayed on to see the sights. The ex-newspaper reporter. My friends congratulated me on getting in just under the wire.

How grateful I am to have seen that Europe of 1914 just before it vanished, never to return. Gay, brilliant, beautiful, richly historic. The vain and silly old dodo now skulking in Doorn had not given the word—the word that had been withheld for forty years while a vast army was nurtured and trained to wreak destruction. And the madman who was to follow after—he of the Charlie Chaplin mustache and the hysterical woman's voice—had not even been thought of. That prewar Europe is something to take out of one's memory, to look at fondly but with a twist of pain at one's vitals, as when we look at the photograph of someone dear but dead.

Back in New York it was joyous, it was hilarious to see the new Ziegfeld Follies, so fresh and lavish and beautiful; to drive in Central Park; to walk up Fifth Avenue; to see the alert American faces.

There was astonishing news about the McChesney dramatization. Ethel Barrymore wanted to play Mrs. Emma McChesney. Charles Frohman, her manager, would produce it. The Frohman name was magic in the theater. They wanted me to dramatize my own stories in collaboration with some experienced playwright. It was any young writer's dream come true. I shocked the world of the theater by saying that I didn't think the part was right for Miss Barrymore; Emma McChesney was crisp, alert, businesslike, magnetic. Ethel Barrymore was glamorous, beautiful, the aristocrat, the star who was just right in English drawing-room plays. My family, my friends, my publishers, my editors combined to try to convince me that I not only was wrong—I was stark staring mad. Any sane writer would be down on her knees offering up prayers of thanks.

That autumn I began the dramatization in collaboration with George V. Hobart. I knew nothing of playwriting other than my instinctive dramatic sense. George Hobart had written a number of successful plays, mostly farces, and one so-called miracle play entitled Everywoman. He was wise in the ways of the commercial theater, he was a gentle, amusing and able man, and I agreed with practically nothing he said about playwriting. His idea of stage dialogue offended my ear. I said, over and over, not very politely, "But people don't talk like that."

"It'll sound all right when it's spoken on the stage."

I didn't believe that.

We never once quarreled or had what is known as "words," but the thing wasn't right. We were working at cross purposes. I was living at the old Majestic Hotel in Central Park West. I would work on dialogue and characterization until about two o'clock. Then George Hobart would appear. Together we'd go over my morning's grist. He would suggest a scene or situation.

"But they wouldn't do that," I'd object. "The audience never would believe it."

"They'll believe it if they see it before their eyes, on the stage."

We floundered along, the play was finished in the spring. In May 1915 the Lusitania was torpedoed and sunk by a German submarine, killing 1,198 people, among them Charles Frohman,

America's foremost theatrical producer. I like to think of the thing he said to the actress Rita Jolivet who stood next to him at the ship's rail as the huge liner sank: "Don't be afraid of death. It's the most wonderful experience in life." So the little rotund Frohman, with his kindly puckish face—the little Jewish boy from Sandusky, Ohio, whose name became a synonym for all that was fine in the theater—went to his death at the hands of the German nation as so many were to do after him.

Well, I thought, that ends Emma McChesney. But the structure that Charles Frohman had built with his own efforts and his own talent for the theater was too solid for such quick destruction. The Frohman staff, with Alf Hayman at its head, carried on. And Ethel Barrymore, punctual, radiant, generous, was there, eager to begin rehearsals on that first day in September. We rehearsed and opened at the Lyceum Theater, a Frohman house. In point of importance it was, at that time, the second theater in New York. Frohman's Empire Theater was the aristocrat. I had dreamed of our having it for McChesney. With its red plush and gold, its massive boxes, its portraits of famous stars lining the foyer, it seemed to me to be everything that was rich and glamorous in a theater. William Boyd played T. A. Buck to Miss Barrymore's Emma McChesney. Lola Fisher, that deft and exquisite comedienne, was miscast as Jock McChesney's sweetheart. The play was called Our Mrs. McChesney and I thought (and still think) it was terrible. I not only was, as always, stage-struck; I really loved the theater. Yet I wasn't happy about this, my first theatrical experience, with America's First Lady of the Theater as the star, and America's foremost management as producers. This was because I knew the play itself was clumsy, inept and spiritless. And the brisk character of Emma was wrong for the elegant Ethel.

It was directed by Augustus Thomas, himself one of the most brilliant and successful playwrights of his day. George Hobart was assistant director. I was the bundle of misery known as the negligible author. I didn't mind. I wanted to learn about the theater. I wanted to see these people in rehearsal, to watch Augustus Thomas direct.

[217]

It must have been that Augustus Thomas was ill without actually being aware of it. He died a few years later. I had admired him enormously; his accomplishment in the theater made him one of the outstanding theatrical figures of the Nineteen Hundreds. From the very outset his manner and conduct shocked me beyond belief. I couldn't recognize this man as the gifted and successful playwright of whom I had heard so much. He began by insulting everyone except Miss Barrymore. I suppose he knew that that witty and intrepid lady would be more than a match for him.

One evening, after a week or two of rehearsals, I was leaving the theater rather late, when most of the company had gone. George Hobart and I had had some changes to discuss. Thomas was still there. Near the door I called out across the stage, "Good night, Mr. Thomas."

He glanced up. "Ah—good night, Miss—uh—uh—mmmm ——"

"Ferber," I prompted him, icily. He had seen me every day for weeks.

"Yes, yes, of course. Ferber. Ferber. I never can remember these Jewish names."

"That must have been difficult for you when Mr. Frohman was producing your plays," I retorted, by some lucky stroke; and slammed the door. Nothing slams more satisfactorily than a good heavy metal stage door.

It is considered worse than bad taste to speak against the defenseless dead. I hereby have made my contribution to the army of the tasteless, and I do it in the name of all work-loving theater-loving people like Charles Frohman and myself.

At rehearsals Ethel Barrymore behaved like an angel. She was tireless, uncomplaining, never demanding. She never tried to steal a line or a scene. She never tried to play upstage. Everyone in the company adored her. I had heard stories of her brilliant wit, and they were true. She took direction gratefully. George Hobart turned out to be a much more gifted director than Thomas. He could get inside a part; he himself would have been a fine actor. I watched the play as it built. It was a fascinating process. Certain scenes in it I hated because they were false and unconvincing. When the time for these approached I always left the theater—I'd stroll out into the empty lobby or stand in the alley outside the stage door until such time as I thought the scene would be over. I suggested rewriting those scenes; but the entire play would have had to be taken apart.

I loved the smell of the theater; the bare stage, the single naked light before rehearsal began, the plain pine chairs and kitchen table in temporary use, the rows of steam pipes against the bare brick of the back wall, the little groups of actors standing about talking quietly before work began, or rehearsing themselves in a corner, oblivious of everyone else. There was born in me then the most enormous respect and admiration for actors. I still have that feeling, after repeated experiences in the theater. I admire their courage and their love of their work; their vanity and their humility and their angelic hopefulness. When they work they work harder than any craft, trade or profession I've ever known, under the most maddening and idiotic circumstances, and they almost never complain. In the worst organized and most badly managed of the professions they have for centuries survived insult, precarious living, disappointment, unfair treatment, inadequate working conditions, sudden failure, almost complete insecurity. Actors are changing now in some superficial respects, but fundamentally they remain much the same. The old-time actors—even the recognized and successful ones—used to feel that they must be sprightly, well dressed always, they must present a prosperous front. This is still largely true of them, but the younger school is contemptuous of "front." They are not curled, rouged, corseted, shiny, pressed, barbered. The hard reality of the past ten or fifteen years has debunked these. Flat-heeled, carelessly got together, hatless, the men quite likely to be unshaven, the girls waveless even for an important interview, they are holding aloft a new flag of defiance in the face of a difficult world. They no longer try to impress you with their exterior elegance. The shine is off the surface, but their young faces— eager, intelligent, hard-bitten, mobile—reflect an inner glow that is more dazzling and more convincing than the old shiny veneer.

From Ethel Barrymore I learned how a star may conduct herself in the theater. I say may because I never have encountered anyone like her since. Certainly many a lesser lady of the stage has brought the potential murderess in me to the fore. I learned a good deal about her. A fine musician, she had wanted to be a concert pianist. On the road tryout she would play Sibelius to us on a smeary hotel piano, she had the pianist's strong almost masculine hands with blunt fingers. She carried a large flat scarlet box of Pall Mall cigarettes wherever she went; she was a very beautiful and exhilarating person indeed with that amazingly fine poreless skin, the enormous blue eyes, the classic Barrymore nose, the biting Barrymore wit.

We opened in Atlantic City for a tryout. The Apollo Theater on the boardwalk was a favorite tryout house. The opening day was an eye opener for the young lady from Wisconsin. We were stopping at the old Shelburne, a rather ramshackle frame affair in that day and famous for its excellent food. Late in the morning I went round to Miss Barrymore's apartment to see how she was getting on. She had asked not to be left alone. She was nervous and frightened on opening days, even in a tryout town. There were one or two others in her sitting room. Miss Barrymore was just dressing, she stuck her head out of the bathroom door to greet us. She had rehearsed very late the night before, her face was dripping with water, she had a towel clutched in her hand, her hair was all about her shoulders, she was a triumph of sheer beauty over adversity. I put that impression thriftily away in my memory. Twenty years later, when I tried to describe the fresh girlish beauty of Lotta Bostrom in the novel Come and Get It as she was washing up in a train compartment after a night's journey I remembered Ethel Barrymore's face like a morning glory with the dew on it. And I just described that.

Miss Barrymore spent the rest of that day buying hats and vomiting.

She couldn't sit still. She couldn't digest anything. We went up and down the Atlantic City boardwalk, that dreary stretch of wood and sand and false-front shacks, and she bought hats and hats and hats, none of which she ever wore afterward. One,

I recall, had a vast bird on it, and another was a fuzzy white knitted thing of the pussy-cat type such as young girls wear in Currier & Ives prints when shown skating on the old millpond.

We opened in New York at the Lyceum Theater October 19th, 1915. I went round to see Miss Barrymore in her dressing room. She was terribly nauseated. Between seizures she went on carefully making up. The call boy made his rounds. Half-hour, Miss Barrymore! . . . Mr. Frank, the house manager, came round to report on the Names in the house. . . . Fifteen minutes, Miss Barrymore! . . . She looked like one waiting for the tumbrel to take her to the guillotine. . . . Overture, Miss Barrymore! (I used this later in the play called The Royal Family.) . . . First-act curtain, Miss Barrymore.

She stood up, gave herself that last searching look in the brilliantly lighted make-up mirror, made a last futile dab with the rabbit's foot and powder puff, stood in the wings a moment, set herself, threw over her shoulder at us that gay desperate self-amused look and walked on with the string of traveling men who were registering at the small-town hotel of the first scene, her little drummer's suitcase in her hand.

I hung around the theater, evenings, for a few nights. Then I realized this was sheer vanity and quit it. I haven't done that sort of thing since. I buckled down to work again after all those weeks lost (yet gained) in rehearsals. I caught up on sleep, went skating at St. Nicholas Rink. I went to a number of nice little after-theater parties and found I wasn't working very well next day. A little private stock-taking convinced me that I was getting nowhere. I didn't like the play itself. But it had been great fun, I had learned a lot.

Now what? Short stories seemed a deadly anticlimax. I felt I wanted now to attempt something more sustained. Rather spiritlessly I worked and read and played and went to the theater. A little group of stage-struck amateurs had started a theater in the East Fifties. It was called the Bandbox Theater and they were known as the Washington Square Players. They did mostly one-act plays, fresh and amusing and certainly a change from the old-fashioned fare provided by the playwrights of the George

Hobart–Augustus Thomas–Charles Klein school. After the play you went to the back room of the little saloon next door and had a glass of beer. The first play presented by the Washington Square Players was a little gem on birth control written by Lawrence Langner, a member of the group. This was considered breathlessly daring. Birth control was something mentioned only in the confines of a physician's consulting room, and then in whispers. Theresa Helburn was to play the heroine's mother, but her conventional family got wind of the play's subject and snatched her out of the cast. The play dealt with an unwed mother whose lover was killed just as he was hastening to her house to marry her. On the opening night the curtain went up too soon and the audience was treated to an unexpected view of the corpse sitting up and talking to someone in the wings. Then there was a dandy one-act number—pantomime—called Another Interior, all the action of which took place within the human stomach. Philip Moeller played The Emetic. They did The Sea Gull, with Helen Westley as a rather glum and forthright Irina and Roland Young as her son. Then Theresa Helburn dashed off a play in which Edna St. Vincent Millay was starred. But at the final dress rehearsal they decided to close the whole thing; it being conceded that the play and the star were terrible. It was all considered pretty daring. In one play the star actually appeared in scant pink silk lingerie. After the curtain practically everyone in the audience rushed backstage, including Otto Kahn. A girl named Katharine Cornell played briefly in the company. It was in the little back room next door that I first met two New York newspaper dramatic critics, both vast of girth and of wit, but Heywood Broun's was a drawling, humane, philosophical wit, while Alexander Woollcott's was caustic, scarring. A cheerful and enormously amusing company, there in the little back room, with actors and audience and critics all mingling affably like the animals in the ark. The Washington Square Players babbled of branching out, building themselves a theater right in the midst of the theatrical district, and calling themselves the New York Theatre Guild. But everyone knew that was just the windy talk of a lot of stage-struck, though talented, amateurs.

Now I settled down for the long pull of novel-writing. I had put it off as long as I could, dreading it. It was January 1916. Dawn O'Hara had been published in 1911. In between I had published a volume of unrelated short stories, three volumes of McChesney stories, and had written the McChesney play in collaboration. This seemed to me a pretty poor performance. Aside from the creating of the character of Emma McChesney I had done no solid thing.

I started Fanny Herself, the story of a Jewish family in a small Wisconsin town, which I called Winnebago, Wisconsin. A good deal of it was imaginary, a good deal of it was real. Certainly my mother, idealized, went to make up Molly Brandeis. Bits and pieces of myself crept into the character of Fanny Brandeis. Appleton undoubtedly was the book's background; and little Rabbi Gerechter and Arthur Howe and Father Fitzmaurice and a dozen others formed the real basis of the book's people. Before book publication the story ran serially in the American Magazine. The first half is good. I recall having written it with zest and even enjoyment. But the second half is weak and floundering. The trouble was that in the middle of the book I killed Molly Brandeis because she was walking off with the story under the heroine's very eyes. When Molly Brandeis died the story died with her. She was too sustaining and vital to dismiss. Twenty years later, in the writing of the novel Come and Get It, I was guilty of exactly the same stupid blunder. I killed Barney Glasgow in the middle of that book because he was dominating the story. The book gave a gasp right there, and the murder was doubled. Book characters must have their way or they take a terrible revenge.

The start of a novel always is a terrifying and thrilling experience, and the months that follow are harrowing and exhausting, with just an occasional moment of exhilaration to keep one from being too suicidal.

The book's idea or theme or meaning has been stirring about in your consciousness for months and probably years. When the idea first hits you you feel enormously stimulated and heightened. Then you wish you could get away from it, but now nothing but death can separate you from it. It's no use. The thing must have its way. Now everything else in your life takes second place or fades out of your consciousness altogether. Clothes are unimportant, letters go unanswered for days or even weeks, parties you regard with a lackluster eye, travel is a lure to be avoided like death, for it is ruin to the sustained rhythm of your work day. Teeth go unfilled, bodily ills run unchecked, your idea of bliss is to wake up on Monday morning knowing that you haven't a single engagement for the entire week. You are cradled in a white paper cocoon tied up with typewriter ribbon. Awake and asleep the novel is with you, haunting you, dogging your footsteps. Strange formless bits of material float out from the ether about you and attach themselves to the main body of your story as though they had hung suspended in air for years, waiting.

Three pages if possible—a thousand words a day—a thousand words a day—a thousand words a day—day after day, week after week, month after month. Talking, walking, eating, sleeping, the thing is with you always. Some days you cannot manage more than fifty or a hundred words. Other days, in a spurt, you write three or even four thousand; but that is too rare to be counted. Sometimes you feel a surge of joy in the thing—a sentence, a paragraph—sometimes the burden of it is unbearable, the monotony endless, you'd give anything to be rid of it. It is as inevitable within you as the forces of nature. You have been making notes probably for years. There is a mass of these notes, collected now, sorted and ticketed in loose-leaf notebooks. Your first draft is made from these notes. It is slipshod, a mere skeleton loosely tied together by the theme or background. Plot is something that doesn't interest me. Character I find absorbing. My novels usually are character-strong and plot-weak. I'd be sorry to have it the other way round. Then comes the second draft in which the characters move and breathe and live. Usually there is a third. By that time I am heartily sick of the whole thing.

Bath, breakfast, the morning paper, you give the news a terrific reading from front to back. Hm! Cotton market stronger, eh? Nothing could interest you less than the cotton market. But your eye clings to it as an excuse to stay away a little longer from work. A short walk, with the day's work as you walk taking shape from where it left off yesterday. You dread to begin, yet you want to let nothing stop you. Well, nothing to do about it, you go into your workroom, you say, "Don't call me unless someone in the family is murdered. Don't call me to the telephone until one-thirty, no matter what." You shut the door, firmly. You sit down and take the cover off the typewriter. You have made up your mind not to read the morning mail until afternoon. Too distracting. But there's a blue envelope in a familiar hand or a big square white envelope with a well-known letterhead or an envelope with a British or French postmark. Well, just one, like a drunkard. Then you read them all, the whole sheaf.

Perhaps you answer one letter, just to get up steam for the day's run, or as a ball player warms up before the game. You read what you wrote yesterday. Not so terrible. With a soft lead pencil you make some changes, tightening a line there, crossing out a word here, inserting a margin note for the next draft.

I have learned not to tear up my stuff until I've slept on it. I have sometimes written page after page through the workday in a kind of agony of ineffectualness, feeling weary, limp and unvital, only to discover on reading it bright and fresh next morning that the stuff has, somehow miraculously, pace and meaning.

You put a fresh sheet in the typewriter roll and stare at it bleakly. You sigh deeply and your fishy eye roams the room. Anything to escape. Help! Help! A thread on the floor. You get up, walk over to it, stoop, pick it up. You know it's idiotic; you can't help it. . . . Cigarette. . . . Nope, smoking no good in the morning. Makes you dopey. The typewriter keys grin up at you, like teeth bared. Well, let's see. Uh—page one seventy-three . . . uh. . . . Far off the telephone rings. Wonder who it is. May be something very important. Tiptoe to the door and listen. . . . "She's in her studio." (Must tell her not to say studio. Sounds arty and pretentious but can't seem to break her of it. Workroom. She's in her workroom. Or say she's out and back at one-thirty. Simpler.) . . . Glass of water. Doctors say you ought to drink at least eight glasses a day. . . . Take a peek at the New Yorker or this week's Nation. No, mustn't. If only there were something tangible to drive you to work; a boss, a time clock, a waiting secretary, a client, a customer. But there is only your conscience, the necessity to earn a living, and the desire to get the thing out of your system before it kills you. Finally you can evade it no longer. With an inner groan and a setting of the jaw and a piece of gum in your mouth you pull the typewriter toward you, settle unhealthily down on the middle of your spine and begin the day's grind. . . . One seventy-four, one seventy-five, one seventy-six, one seventy s . . .

Lunch. Lunch on a tray in your workroom, very light and digestible and dull. That cigarette for which you've been longing all morning. Eager now to get to the typewriter. You're in the swing of it. Two o'clock, three, four. Everyone else in the world, you feel, is out playing golf or lunching or driving or having fun. Let 'em, the poor things. A slave, that's what. But hugging your chains.

At the middle or end of the afternoon there stumbles out of the room a witch, a disheveled crone with wild hair and haggard face, her stockings rolled at the knee, her fingernails broken, her skin putty-colored, her eyes dull.

Who telephoned? Who sent those books? Why didn't you say I'd call back?

In between, you walk if possible where it is green and quiet because the motion of walking somehow helps the writing process in your mind; if you read it is so that you may be stimulated or taken out of yourself; you eat carefully so as not to upset the digestion; you listen to music because it emotionalizes you and helps to clear your story; you will yourself to sleep so that you may feel refreshed next day. Pregnant women will recognize the technique.

The layman, interested, puts his question. "Now tell me. You writers just work when the inspiration comes to you, don't you?"

So Fanny Herself, the novel of Jewish family life in Midwest America, was slowly and painfully written.

It was a curious thing about the war in Europe. It had been going on for over two years now. I read the daily Schrecklich-keit; had become hardened to it, my senses were dulled by horror. First, thousands dead, then hundreds of thousands, then a million. Then figures ceased to mean anything. American men I knew were beginning to go over to France to drive ambulances or to work in the hospitals of France. America was muttering and stirring. People were saying Too Proud to Fight or Save Civilization or Let's Keep Out of It or Let's Go Over and Clean Up Those Boches. They were having what they called Prepared-ness Parades. There was a tightening all down the line. The United States had had two years or more in which to see what modern warfare meant. You needed only to look over the edge of the bloody mess to realize that once you got into it nothing but horror awaited you.

The book Fanny Herself was finished, lamely enough, in February 1917 and I wanted only to get away from Chicago, from New York, from a year of concentrated work. I never had crossed the entire country from coast to coast. I was off now for California.

On the way I stopped for a day with the William Allen Whites at Emporia, Kansas. When your world is awry and hope dead and vitality low and the appetite gone there is no ocean trip, no month in the country, no known drug equal to the reviving quality of twenty-four hours spent on the front porch or in the sitting room of the Whites' house in Emporia. Practically every-one of any importance in America has at one time or another stopped at the White home on their way East or West. Myself, I've even been known to take a sneaking trip to Colorado or California just as an excuse for stopping over. There are a hun-dred stories about the Whites' hospitality, and they're all true. The Whites' hired girls are famous. So is their fried chicken. So is the Emporia Gazette. Theodore Roosevelt, after being shot by a would-be assassin in Milwaukee, stopped at Emporia on his way West. At dinner at the Whites' there was served platter after platter of fried chicken. The bones were stacked like cordwood about Roosevelt's plate. Bringing in the final relay the hired girl squared herself and observed, distinctly, "The bullet was never made could kill a man that can eat as much fried chicken as that and live."

I saw for the first time the flat little town of Emporia, squatting on the prairie. Just straight little streets, the one like the other, lined with plain frame houses. The Whites' house, of red brick, later done over from plans by Frank Lloyd Wright, was full—but not too full—of lovely fabrics and china and glass and embroidery and paintings brought from every corner of the world in their travels.

I suppose it is not too much to say that a town like Emporia, Kansas, is the pulse and temperature chart of the United States of America. The Big Town people are in the habit of thinking the Emporias of this country something of a mild joke. They're wrong and, what is more serious, they're silly. Emporia, Kansas —and there are hundreds of American towns like it—is a town of about ten thousand whose living depends on the intersecting railroads and railroad shops, on agriculture and on cattle. There is the prairie with its sea of corn and wheat; there is the plain, with its browsing cattle (and the huge Kansas City stockyards near by); there are the railroads, running east, running west, through the town. When Emporia is poor, you are poor; when Emporia is content, you are content; when Emporia is bigoted, or sulky or frightened or resentful or bewildered, then so are you. In the trek westward it was settled by people from Connecticut, Massachusetts, Indiana, Ohio. Walk down Emporia's main business street with Editor William Allen White and you will see a cross section of America complete.

Cheered and refreshed I went on to California. I was a tourist in America. There was the Grand Canyon to see. Down the Bright Angel trail on muleback, a magnificent and terrifying experience. Tourists in riding clothes and smart boots; people in red sweaters and corduroy pants. The trail was glassy with snow and ice. A guide, very Western, assured us in a soft drawl that there was nothing to fear—there never had been an accident. Whenever my tiny mule turned a sharp corner on a ledge so

narrow that his rear quarters stuck out into the wide world over
a sheer drop of two thousand feet I tried hard to believe him.
Then, at a hairpin turn, one of the mules lightly tossed a clumsy
rider over his head. By a miracle of luck the turn was a double
one, with the second footpath just below it and the sheer drop
just below that. The victim just rolled down the little slope, onto
the path just beneath, and stayed there. The guide was a poor
frail human being like ourselves, then! There was no turning
back. We went on. I reached Riverside, California, next day crippled with fatigue and tight nerves.

After the bitter Chicago January and the precarious slopes of
the Canyon; after girlhood years of Iowa and Wisconsin winters,
California in February was a dream world of palms, acacia, pepper trees, flowers and sunshine. At Pasadena there was Upton
Sinclair, feverish of eye, grim of purpose, but with the Gartz
millions seeming to hover too much in the background. Santa
Barbara seemed almost as lovely as Italy, but something was missing. The mountains were there against the blue of the Pacific;
the exotic flowers, the birds, the pink plaster houses. Perhaps it
was spoiled by the Grand Rapids Spanish furniture, the pipe-
organ mansions, the people who seemed to typify the Spirit of
American Country Clubs. Hollywood was just a straggling town,
nothing of the glamorous metropolis about it then. Tourists
streamed through the motion-picture lots as they might through
the Chicago Stockyards or the Metropolitan Museum. Carl
Laemmle was considered a glittering example of film mogul, and
Universal City was the thing to see.

But San Francisco! There was a city! It seemed to me then, and
it seems to me now, one of the half-dozen great cities of America;
a city of distinction, of flavor, of the quality which excites the
visitor. Perhaps the people who had built it had had much to do
with this intangible spirit of the place. Certainly not all of these
had been admirable or worthy or heroic. Among them had been
rogues and harlots and rascals and criminals. But the first of them
had come thousands of miles by oxcart or by wretched boat.
They had come seeking adventure or gold or land or freedom,

but whatever their reason that journey had demanded courage and endurance and ambition of sorts. One saw this in the faces of these pioneers' descendants.

A boat that smelled sickeningly of brown sugar in the hold took me to Honolulu. It struck a Pacific swell and wallowed in it, then ran into a real hurricane that smashed everything except the hull of the ship itself and we bounced into Honolulu Harbor practically on our funnels. But there were the flower leis and the white-clad natives and the American officers from the fort in uniform. And that pretty Mrs. Whosis, who had talked so much about her beautiful home in Honolulu and her marvelous husband and the pineapple plantation all the way coming over from San Francisco, turned out to be very like a woman in a Somerset Maugham story when she was met at the dock by a very black gentleman who kissed her.

There in Honolulu I received the number of the American Magazine containing the first installment of Fanny Herself. That was exciting at first, but the stuff, as I ran a quick eye over it, seemed choppy and inadequate. The Hawaiian Islands probably weren't quite the ideal background for the reading of one's second novel. Hawaii was more nearly the tropics than anything I'd ever seen. It was another world; and seeing other worlds is very refreshing after one has had one's face in a typewriter for a year. The vast tourist traffic that swarmed on Honolulu in later years was unknown to the Islands then. The boats were smallish, the passage likely to be choppy, the best hotel on Waikiki Beach was the Moana, a rather tottery frame structure. Every day, out of a seemingly clear sky, there fell for an hour or so a little golden rain which the inhabitants had been trained to call liquid sunshine, a phrase which the enraged tourists rejected.

It was pleasant to drive to Diamond Head, to the Pali; to eat the honey-colored pineapple, sweet and melting and fragrant, no relation to the hard green-white fruit of the American market. The Hawaiians seemed a beautiful race with their fine slim bodies and regular features. It was hard to believe that disease was rampant among them, brought by the white man. Tiny Japanese women in kimonos pattered about the streets; the scarlet hibiscus, the floral Sadie Thompson of the tropics, flamed and flaunted its petals from every hedge. I ate poi, native fashion, with my fingers and thought it looked and tasted like billposter's glue. At the same feast I politely ate raw fish and pig roasted in a pit (and recollected Charles Lamb's essay). It was arranged to meet old ex-Queen Liliuokalani, tragic and dignified. On Waikiki Beach Duke, the champion native Hawaiian swimmer, disported himself for the benefit of the tourists. Standing like a bronze god, his arms widespread, he would ride the waves on a surf board, looking like something come down from mythological company. The white girls lolling on the beach eyed him adoringly and touched his beautiful body. The American women living on the Islands seemed rather faded and frumpy in their damp muslins and ruffles and sunshades, but the officers from the fort were trim and crisp in their white ducks. They danced in the moon-light on the veranda of the Moana Hotel while the Hawaiian orchestra played On the Beach at Waikiki, over and over and over, until I felt an insane urge to brain them with their own ukuleles.

The volcano of Mauna Loa near Hilo, which I reached by taking a largish boat, was performing nicely but not dangerously. I'd always had the schoolgirl idea that a volcano was a cone-shaped thing, something like a mountain with a hole in the top. Not Mauna Loa. The Kilauea crater was a vast yawning canyon in the earth itself, like the Grand Canyon, except that this thing was alive and writhing and hissing, while the Canyon was dead —ten thousand years dead. Driving up the suave road from the port through giant ferns and tropical forests, it was startling, it was terrifying and utterly fascinating to come upon this yawning chasm in whose depths a lake of molten fire heaved and tossed and sent up occasional fountains of scarlet and gold and orange and blue. It was impossible to take one's eyes from it. I begrudged the time spent over a hastily snatched dinner at the near-by Vol-cano House (the affable Mr. Demosthenes, Prop.) and scurried back to sit at the crater's edge again staring down into the hell which so accommodatingly kept its place and that was so much more fantastically beautiful by night than it had been by day.

It was a very short time afterward that the volcano gathered itself together in a mighty boiling rage and, seething over the crater's rim, swept down upon the road, the forest, the town of Hilo nestled at the foot of the volcano, destroying with its fiery fingers everything it touched.

The fates seemed to protect me a shade too jealously. I thought, resentfully, that protection had reached a point where it might be called coddling. I had missed the war by a couple of days; and the Rosenthal murder; and the only volcanic eruption I'd be likely to encounter in a lifetime. But the fates had even a more infuriating gesture than that in store for me.

By the time I reached Chicago in April America had entered the war. All through that summer and the winter and the summer and autumn that followed there could be heard through that South Side section of Chicago which is cut by the Illinois Central tracks the sound of boys' voices, high and clear. Often the sound woke me out of my sleep at night. By day the trainloads rumbled by, car after car, packed with lads on their way to the training camps. Their gay or impudent or scared young faces were stuck out of the car windows. Sometimes the baseball caps of their home-town club were stuck rakishly on their heads.

E-e-e-e-YOW! they shouted as the trains bumbled through the heart of the vast sprawling city. Wow! Yee-ay-ay-ay-ay!

Berlin or Bust was scrawled in chalk on the sides of the cars. Kill the Kaiser. Boys from the Midwest and the far West—farm boys from Nebraska and Iowa and Kansas and Illinois—on their way to France to make the world safe for democracy. Thousands of them knew France only as a pink place on the map and certainly they never counted on staying there draped in grotesque and improbable attitudes on barbed-wire fences, carrion for crows.

I tried to write war propaganda. I did write it for all sorts of war organizations and it never was any good. I can't write to order. Yet I turned out articles for the Red Cross, for the Y.M.C.A., for the Liberty Loan drives, for the Salvation Army, but they seemed to me absurd and ineffectual. In between I tried to work as before. Directly after the California-Honolulu trip I did succeed in writing one short story which was, I knew, the best short story I had ever written and which, I think, may still stand as a fine example of the American short story. It is called The Gay Old Dog and appears in the volume of collected short stories entitled Cheerful—By Request. I gave my consent to have this story published in the O'Brien Best Short Story volume for 1917. I did this so that I might legitimately protest against the title and publication of these volumes. I didn't want anyone to cry sour grapes. Since that time I never have allowed Mr. O'Brien to use a short story of mine in any of his collections. The O'Brien books are published yearly under the title of The Best Short Stories of that year. Sometimes the stories are the worst short stories, not only of that particular year, but of any year in the history of writing.

The Frederick A. Stokes Company brought out the novel Fanny Herself late in the winter of 1917. It sold only mildly. I always have wished that I might rewrite the second half of that book. This, my second try at novel-writing, was not good enough; much better than the juvenile sickly-sweet Dawn O'Hara, certainly— but still not a well-sustained effort. I wondered if my newspaper training was, after all, a liability rather than an asset.

America was a world of parades, of flying flags, of trumpet calls and speeches and "drives." From England we borrowed the phrase "do your bit." The knitting needles bristled like a forest. No army ever went into battle so completely swaddled in olive-drab sweaters, mufflers, wristlets, socks, chest protectors and bellybands. A million miles of gauze bandages were rolled by hundreds of thousands of women in Red Cross aprons and caps. Spellbinders talked themselves hoarse. Give Until It Hurts. . . . Business as Usual. . . . Keep the Home Fires Burning. . . . Do Your Bit. Now and then a voice was raised against the hysteria of war, against the whole bloody sickening mess, but such unpatriotic fellows were thrown into prison, where they intelligently remained for the duration of the war which was being fought to make the world safe for democracy.

I went up and down the land, speaking in churches, town halls, armories, ballrooms, street corners, theaters, auditoriums. I talked myself into a horrible laryngitis and could talk no more for weeks.

I had now left my twenties behind me and was a woman in the early thirties. I hadn't married. I thought marriage was fine —but not for me. Perhaps this was because there was no one I really wanted to marry. Perhaps because marriage as I had viewed it had seemed far from a desirable state. Maybe it was for the reason given by Alice-Sit-by-the-Fire in the play of that name. She said, "I've met the man I'd marry, and the man who'd marry me—but he was never the same." Dancing in Chicago at the lovely Midway Gardens or the Edgewater Beach, or in New York dining at the Brevoort or out along the Hudson at Longvue, under the influence of the music and a moon and a highball poured from a Prohibition-time hip flask I became engaged a number of times (I am a little ashamed to admit) and hastily wrote to break it off next morning before I started the day's grist of writing. That sounds cold-blooded. It was, I suppose, only unadult. I wanted perfection. All old maids are perfectionists. That's why they're old maids. When, at ninety, friends are bending close to catch my last words I know I shall point a bony accusing finger and say, "Hi, wait a minute! Where's that white-plumed prince you promised me!" Male perfection, heart in hand, doesn't come to plain thirtyish women who are too keen and analytical for their own (or anybody's) comfort. This will be no chronicle of amours. I do not think love is sacred. I think it is a very moving and personal and private matter between two people. Respectability must stalk by my side, for the men who have cared for me have wanted to marry me, and I think that was dear and sweet of them. Julia Ferber, who was with me much of the time during those years, unconsciously did what she could to discourage the swains. Hers had not been a very happy marital experience; she thought, doubtless, that no one was good enough for her typewriting daughter. Hers certainly were grim looks directed at the boys.

I wish I could be tactful enough to say that I regret not having married. I must confess that I know no woman with whom I should want to exchange places.

As the war went on, my writing became worse and worse and I longed more and more to do something really constructive in war work. In New York, the winter of 1917–1918, I looked about for a chance to be of definite service. I went on writing as best I could. That year I changed publishers, going over from Stokes to the firm of Doubleday, Page & Company, with whom I have published for the past twenty years.

New York that winter of 1918 was a dazzling kaleidoscopic world center. Just to walk on the streets—practically any street—was an emotional experience. Fifth Avenue had a look of perpetual carnival with the flags of all the Allies flying brilliant in the winter sunshine. The pavements, the theaters, the restaurants were clanking with officers booted, spurred and belted—French officers trim and slim in their pale blue; six-foot Britishers in beautiful London tailored uniforms and the shiniest of boots; Italians in an odd sallow-making green with red doodads; Australians in big Anzac hats like cowboys gone fancy. Anything and everything but German uniforms.

Women and girls I knew were going to France, some as nurses, some to drive ambulances, some as entertainers, as dancing partners, as canteen workers. Others had a different reason. They said, "All the men are over there. I'm not going to stay here with Grampaw. I'm going where the fun and the boys are."

I had a magazine offer to go over to write a series of articles on the humorous side of the war. William Allen White happened to be in New York at the time. He gave me, with great finality, one of the few bad pieces of advice in our long friendship:

"There's nothing humorous about war. War is a dirty, deadly, brutal stinking business. Don't go."

I declined the offer, feeling very high-minded. A few months later William Allen White and Henry Allen (later governor and later still senator from Kansas) went abroad on a mission and shortly afterwards there appeared a series of gay humorous magazine articles which subsequently were published in book form under the title of The Martial Adventures of Henry and Me. He had written them quite innocently, but I sometimes hold that little incident over Bill White's head when he shows signs of becoming pontifical, which is rarely.

I made up my mind that if I couldn't go over legitimately I'd stay in America and do what grubby war work I could. The whole thing was a colossal nightmare. To write anything seemed futile, absurd. The war stories—fictional—that came out were particularly stomach-turning, hot off the griddle as they were. I thought that writing them was like grave-snatching. I may say that while I did what I could with no great grace I never rolled a bandage or knitted a stitch.

The thing I had hoped for was dropped into my lap. The American Red Cross asked me to go to Europe. I was to go as a perfectly free agent, associated with no unit, subject to no superior officer. I was to travel where I pleased in England, France, Italy, or elsewhere in the Allied countries. That which I saw and heard and felt and thought I was to incorporate into a series of articles which were to be published in practically all the thousands of daily newspapers in the United States. People were giving millions of dollars to the Red Cross. If they could be shown, in a series of graphic and true word pictures, exactly what happened to these hard-earned dollars which they so freely gave, perhaps they'd give even more freely. The lists of wounded were piling up, piling up. The war was in its fourth year; it might go on four years longer. Who knew?

Well! That was more like it! Now I could go. Now I could go with a clear conscience; with eagerness. My pass was to take me anywhere, at any time. It was a bit—just a little bit—frightening. But when Julia Ferber mentioned this, I said she ought to be ashamed of herself and looked very martial and patriotic.

It was a lovely uniform. The boots were nice, too, and the little cap, and the whole effect wasn't bad. Trim was the word, I thought. Now and then I wondered if, once over there, I'd be able to write the sort of thing that actually would pull the additional dollars out of the already deflated American pockets. The newspapers announced the appointment. As the time approached, my mother sometimes emerged from her room looking slightly red-eyed, but we didn't mention it.

Friends began sending me wartime going-away gifts. Enumerated, they seem very strange now. Sweaters, hand-knitted of course; mufflers, wristlets, stockings. Boxes of white loaf sugar, a war delicacy. Boxes of candy. My uniform arrived, was pronounced perfect, was hung in the clothes closet. My trunk was packed. I went to Washington for sundry necessary papers and to be vaccinated and inoculated for smallpox and typhoid. Washington treated me to a knee-deep snowstorm and a quite tough two-day attack of typhoid, but I returned to New York prepared with everything but my passport visa. The passport itself I had. My ship was to sail in two days. Henry Allen of Kansas was going on my boat. That gave me a nice homey feeling. He had a fine memory and a gift of oratory and I had a last line all prepared in case we should be torpedoed in midocean.

We were to land in France. I went down to the French consul's office to have my passport visaed. The place was a bedlam; I waited my turn amidst an unbelievable clamor of English and French exclamations and expostulations. My time came. I handed over my passport. The young clerk looked at it, disappeared with it, there then appeared a tall harassed and haggard-looking man of middle age, grayish, with a grizzled mustache. Vice-consul, or something official like that. He regarded me with a lackluster eye.

"Madame, you cannot go to France."

I said, "What?"

He repeated it, very precisely, with a French accent: "Madame, you cannot go to France."

My heart stopped beating, but I didn't die. I spoke, trying to be as precise and distinct as he had been: "I'm afraid there has been a mistake. This is my passport. I am sailing tomorrow. My name is Edna Ferber. I am a writer. I have been chosen by the American Red Cross to go to Europe to write a series of articles. There has been some mistake."

He only repeated it in a fatigued way; and I suppose he really was fatigued, poor overworked man. "Madame, you cannot go to France."

Well, then all my fine calm was swept away, my heart began

to beat again, it hammered, it pounded, it thundered, it shook me with its terrible blows.

"But why?" I shouted. "Why! Why! Why!" Faces began to turn toward me.

He turned. He conferred a moment with another weary face behind the enclosure. He turned back to me. "There has been found to be many spies in France working under the guise of the Red Cross and other similar organizations. The French government has just this week made a rule that no one may go to the zone of war except under strict surveillance and as part of a unit under command. This passport allows you to go anywhere you please. The government will not allow it. It will not allow you to go to France. Your father was born in Hungary."

The room whirled and whirled and whirled. I thought it never would come right again, but I clung to the edge of the counter and it did stop revolving. "My father! My father came to America when he was a boy. He lived here all his life after that. He never left it. He has been dead ten years. My mother was born in Milwaukee. I was born in Kalamazoo, Michigan [his right eyebrow went up, ever so slightly], I am an American. You can't do a thing like this to me. You can't! You can't!" It must have sounded comic. He seemed hardly to hear.

He bowed a little, in finality. "Madame, I am sorry. You cannot go to France." He turned away.

Home, somehow. The telephone. People were wonderful. Theodore Roosevelt, on his way to the hospital for an ear operation, paused long enough to cable France, to wire Wilson, to telephone Ambassador Jusserand in Washington. Kindly Henry Allen allowed his boat to sail without him, waiting over in the hope that I would somehow be allowed to take the next one. William Allen White moved heaven and earth. John Finley did everything possible to clear the fantastic situation. The rule was an ironbound one, and brand-new. There was nothing to be done. I did not go to France.

Before the wretched news appeared in the papers friends continued to send belated bon-voyage gifts. I was living at the Majestic Hotel. Every few minutes the doorbell would ring, it would be a bellboy with a corsage of violets or orchids; a bottle of wine; candy, gloves, sweaters, books, baskets. Whenever I heard the doorbell I wanted to crawl under the bed like a sick puppy.

I never have dreamed about that half-hour in the French consul's office. I know if I ever do I shall die in my sleep of rage, horror and chagrin.

13

A<small>NY EQUESTRIAN OR AVIATOR</small> knows that, having fallen off a horse or out of an airplane, the thing to do is to pick oneself up and ride again. So I bounced around the country making impassioned speeches in behalf of the Red Cross and the Liberty Loan all the way from Minneapolis to New York, from Peoria to Duluth. A group of speakers was called a team. War makes strange platform companions. You might see Harold Ickes and Lillian Russell and Clarence Darrow and me all trying our best to charm, wheedle, scare or reason the money out of the pockets of an audience and stuff Liberty Bonds or Red Cross pledges into them. Though I hadn't seen Lillian Russell since my teens in the days of the Appleton Crescent there she was on the platform of the Blackstone Hotel ballroom, plumper perhaps but otherwise miraculously unchanged; lovely as ever, her skin unblemished, her eyes clear and lustrous, her costume actually still a tailored suit, tight-fitting, and a big black hat. It was a reassuring sight; a vision to fortify one's faith in a tottering world. As she stood speaking in her firm clear voice I forgot for a moment war and its horrors and wondered, idly, why I could name no authentic and dazzling beauty of my own day and age. Ugly and frumpy females are astonishingly rare; pretty girls and chic attractive women one sees by the hundreds of thousands; but the raving tearing howling beauty of the '90s, the Maxine Elliotts, the Lillian Russells, the Lily Langtrys, seem to have vanished as completely as Helen of Troy. Perhaps the machine age, the finger wave, sun tan, dieting, exercise, cigarettes, cocktails and freedom have molded the women of today into a pattern of combined neatness, passable prettiness and utility that makes them as undramatic as a flock of Ford cars. Perversely enough it is the rather ugly and striking woman who is the beauty of today.

As I look back on the four years of the World War and forward to the war which threatens today's world, incredibly, twenty years later, I try to recall one single benefit, however infinitesimal, reaped as a result of that holocaust. Only this tiny and absurd item comes to my mind: a blessed and rather touching war measure known as Gasless Sundays when for one day in the week no motor vehicle except that used in emergencies or for the wholesale transportation of passengers could travel the streets or roads. Planned as a means of gas conservation it was, to the nerve-racked city dweller, peace, bliss, heaven.

When my speaking voice became ragged and my vitality sagged there was one spot which even the World War scarcely had touched. The top of the Colorado Rocky Mountains seemed successfully to defy Mars. Old Longs Peak in Estes National Park looked down from its height of more than fourteen thousand feet upon a writhing tortured bloody world.

"I've seen all this so many times," it seemed to say. "Greed and envy, threats and reprisals, blood and death, exhaustion and recuperation, greed and envy, threats and reprisals, blood . . . Silly little ants down there. Never learn. Never learn. Well, one day they'll destroy themselves completely. Then I'll be left in peace as I was in the beginning. Ants are only a nuisance anyway."

Enos Mills, the naturalist, coming to Estes years before in search of health, had stayed to become the father of the Rocky Mountain National Park. He had built a unique inn in a lovely valley nine thousand feet high, with Longs Peak to the east, wreathed in clouds, and Twin Sisters to the west, pine-clad. The inn had been built ranch fashion of many log cabins, but they were log cabins de luxe hiding beneath their rough exterior hearts of gold in the form of steam heat, bathrooms with hot and cold water, log-burning fireplaces and comfortable mattresses. This altitude, I had discovered, was just right for my low blood-pressure make-up. At nine thousand feet I was normal. Or perhaps I merely thought I was normal because at that altitude I felt lighthearted and carefree. Many guests were troubled by insomnia; and by day their hearts were likely to pound, their lungs protested, their heads sometimes swam. But I could bound about like a mountain goat; I felt gay and a little tête-exaltée, as though I'd had a good cocktail on an empty stomach.

Though the inn patriotically of course served brown sugar, wheatless bread and all the rest of it still up there it was possible for ten days at a time almost to forget what was going on down below. For a fortnight I could selfishly pretend to be an Olympian high above the war-torn world. Year after year I came back for a long or a short stay. Usually I did not work up there. Then I made an interesting (to me) discovery. Any writing done in that altitude or directly after having been in that altitude was completely different in tone and treatment from my work done at sea level. It had a fey quality; was gay and lighthearted as I was myself; had a lighter touch. The short story entitled The Afternoon of a Faun exemplifies this, and so does the long short story called Nobody's in Town. I think writers who drink alcohol for stimulation must get much the same effect that the Peak gives me. My fingers seem to fly over the typewriter keys, the words come with ease, the characters leap into life. Writing, ordinarily such a slow and painful process, became a merry occupation. I've wondered if this could last over a period of months and if I shouldn't put it to the test. Perhaps I'd turn out to be a female Mark Twain instead of an old saga sister. At any rate it is an interesting bit of data on metabolism.

I put Estes Park and Longs Peak into the second half of the novel Fanny Herself but they fitted badly into that environment.

But, good or bad, it was the best I could do at the time. That, I should like to add, is true of everything I have written. Those critics or well-wishers who think that I could have written better than I have are flattering me. Always I have written at the top of my bent at that particular time. It may be that this or that, written five years later or one year earlier, or under different circumstances, might have been the better for it. But one writes as the opportunity and the material and the inclination shape themselves. This is certain: I never have written a line except to please myself. I never have written with an eye to what is called the public or the market or the trend or the editor or the reviewer. Good or bad, popular or unpopular, lasting or ephemeral, the words I have put down on paper were the best words I could summon at the time to express the thing I wanted more than anything else to say. No doubt in stating this I have given away the measure of myself as a creative craftsman.

In my visits to Estes I had been fascinated by the Peak, had been really hypnotized by it, as is almost every visitor to that region. There it towers, taunting you as you gaze up at its jagged cliffs. Scaling it made a tough climb of perhaps twelve hours, there and back. The last three or four hours of the climb meant crawling, sliding, slipping; hand over hand; sometimes a sheer drop of two thousand feet below you, and you on a shelflike ledge. I hated the thought of it. That kind of adventure repels me. But climb it I had to, once and for all. Get it over with. It wasn't until 1921 that I made it with the aid of Shep Husted. Shep, mountain guide and perfect gentle knight, may be sixty now, maybe seventy; he's changeless and seemingly indestructible as Longs Peak itself. Shep is made of iron and gold and granite in pleasing proportions, like the Rockies. He is tireless, dependable, cautious and wise in the ways of mountains. His feet, in their fine riding boots, are slim, neat, high-arched as a girl's. His voice is gentle, slightly drawling. He ought to be in a book but he's too fanciful for fiction. I tried to sneak him into Fanny Herself but he wouldn't fit. Too perfect. He left the imagination nothing to work on.

That climb taught me what I already suspected: that there's

nothing like the top of a sizable mountain peak to give you a clear idea of your own importance. Perhaps that's why mountain folk are quiet, soft-spoken and quizzical of eye, with no trace of arrogance in their make-up. Seafaring people have much the same look. It is the look of all people who live exposed to the elemental forces of nature and who know how powerless man is against them.

At that time the drive from Denver up to the Inn at Estes was an all-day journey over a narrow rough mountain road with only an occasional cut-out for the passing of two vehicles. Now one can do it in a couple of hours over the new oiled hard roads. It is all changed, tourist-ridden, just another National Park.

My return from Colorado this trip was nicely timed to meet the ghastly influenza epidemic which swept America in the summer of 1918. A foul breath from the sodden fields of the dead in France, it struck down thousands and killed them, another by-product of the many scourges that accompanied the war and followed it.

It was in Chicago that I saw the false peace celebration of November 7th, that gigantic hoax perpetrated upon a war-sick world. When the real Armistice Day arrived on November 11th one would have thought that there could be no tears, no shouts, no joy, hysteria or laughter left. But perhaps no city outside Paris, London and New York produced a more spectacular demonstration of mob hysteria than Chicago provided. It was something to see. I mingled with the crowd on Michigan Boulevard, I was buffeted by the screaming howling throngs on Wabash and on State. For a day, at least, one saw the democracy of a common emotion—that of overwhelming relief after strain. There was no distinction of race, creed, color, position. Strangers hugged one another, stenographers perched on the tops of North Shore limousines, mobs milled in and out of hotels, drank, and paid or left as they pleased, people who never had seen each other before cried and laughed together. Staid men and women cut grotesque and foolhardy capers. It was a mob without hate, revenge, lust or greed in its heart. Pure joy motivated it and cast a kind of radiance over it.

The millions of dead men, once strong joyful lusty fellows like these in the streets, must have wondered at this spectacle as they groped their troubled way through misty space.

It is the lot of the imaginative creative writer always to look on, never to participate. Or perhaps it is nothing like this, so highfalutin, but merely the reporter in me who sees and mentally notes and senses the dramatic overtones—and trudges back to the office with her story. Still one must be either a spectator or a participant. One can't march in a parade and see it too. I may be, and often am, in deep sympathy with a cause, a movement, a belief, but I can rarely voice it in terms of creative or imaginative writing. I can sometimes manage it in a straightaway article, written factually. The moment I hear of a well-known male writer running for political office to save his country, or a female writer heading committees and sponsoring Causes, I know that the creative fount is beginning to dry up. When the average writer of novels, short stories or plays feels that he must leap into the brew of today's headlines—political, racial, national, inter-national—he should leave behind him the realm of the imagination and write in terms of the factual. Perhaps this accounts for the preponderance of biography, autobiography, sociology, science, politics, essays, philosophy and personal observation contained in the book lists published in the past five years. A world which hid its head in the sand for twenty years in order to avoid seeing what was going on about it seems tardily to realize that it may as well face facts. Of course propaganda, so dangerous in the hands of the average fiction writer or dramatist, is a tremendous weapon when wielded by a genius. A Tolstoy or a Dickens may breathe life into a mass movement or a cause or a belief. A theme which is dull, windy and unconvincing when presented by a run-of-the-mill writer may become a glowing moving thing under the magic of genius. For genius is capable of creating flesh and blood out of star dust; and the dimensional men and women thus born live long, long after the cause through which they were conceived is dead or forgotten. That is why imaginative writers should think in terms of human beings first and Cause afterward. The public schools of England are no longer places of brutality, greed and ignorant neglect, but Nicholas Nickleby lives on. Women are free as men to come and go and live their lives, but Nora, in Ibsen's A Doll's House, is a living breathing woman, though her problems are long since solved. There is yet to come the genius who will interpret the strife and horror and bloodshed and brutality of today's bewilderment in terms of human beings. When this miracle happens the men and women thus created on the printed page will survive long after the Hitlers, the Mussolinis and the Francos are mere nightmare bogies like the wolf in Red Riding Hood.

That year following the war—1919—found me writing short stories rather grumpily. Doubledays brought out the collection of short stories called Half Portions, as well it might be, for only half the stories were good. I hadn't yet written a novel under the Doubleday imprint. How was a novel possible, I asked myself, when wherever one looked, forward or back, the war reared its hideous head? But the short stories were growing longer and longer, their content was not short-story material, but the stuff of which novels are made. In such brief pieces as The Gay Old Dog, The Maternal Feminine, You've Got to Be Selfish, Farmer in the Dell, Old Man Minick and Perfectly Independent, there was crowded a lifetime of this character or that. The short story should be an episode or an acid-etched characterization; these were really novelettes done in the space of six or seven thousand words. It was like crowding a trunkful of clothes into a suitcase. The cover bulged and threatened to burst open, the contents emerged wrinkled. It was incredibly stupid of me not to realize that I was crazily throwing away novel material. It was the most idiotic wastefulness. There is nothing more precious to the writer than a fresh idea. Yet each fresh idea as it welled up into my consciousness was mashed into a short-story condensation. They were riches squandered in my foolish youth and exuberance, as a radiant spoiled woman is lavish of beauty, jewels, money, love, thinking they will, somehow, last always.

Of the stories born of the war perhaps The Gay Old Dog, The Tough Guy and The Maternal Feminine were the only ones worth consideration. But one chance short story in that rather shabby collection was to be the most important single influence in my writing life.

In itself it wasn't much of a story. It was called Farmer in the Dell and was all about a horny-handed old tiller of the soil whose second wife nagged him into selling the farm and moving to the city. Walking or driving about Chicago's streets I had seen many of these transplanted farmers withering and dying under a life of ease in the big city. The down-state prairies yielded up hundreds of these forlorn creatures. You saw them clumping along the asphalt or sitting, vacant-eyed, in the porch swings of their bungalows on the far South or West Side of Chicago, their great hands lying inert and open on their knees. One of these lonely frustrated souls I depicted as prowling around South Water Street, at that time the produce market which fed Chicago's millions. What I really encountered in that world of market gardeners, produce men, wholesale grocers and commission men was a woman whose face so impressed me that it made an indelible picture in my mind. She was a small quiet neat woman in blue serge. Her face had something of the cameo quality of the exquisite Mrs. William Allen White. I don't know what she was doing there among the boxes, barrels and crates of potatoes, chickens, tomatoes, beans, turnips, squash. I never talked to her, I never saw her again. But somehow I connected her with that truck-garden region south of Chicago where families of Dutch descent worked their little plots of ground and drove daily to market with their laden wagons. I had seen the loads, horse-drawn, plodding toward the city in the evening twilight.

So truck gardens and wagons, South Water Street and little wrenlike woman were tucked away in my mind in 1919 to grow and ferment and twist and turn until finally they emerged five years later in the form of the novel So Big. The unknown woman of the soft brown eyes and the shabby blue-serge suit emerged as Selina Peake.

Floundering thus between the devil of the short story and the deep sea of the unwritten novel I had a letter from Newman Levy, the New York lawyer whom I had met during that war-chased voyage between England and America in August 1914.

He had won considerable recognition in the writing world through his light verse, his satirical essays and revue sketches. He had, he wrote, a fine idea for a play, and what did I think of it and would I collaborate with him in the writing of it.

I never had written in this way, using someone else's idea. I shrank from it. The play was to be about a university professor who was paid $1200 a year while the steel-mill workers in the town got $25 a day. Brawn over brain was what it amounted to. I thought then that the idea was fairly amusing and timely and I said so in a letter. I then went on with the writing of the short story on which I happened to be engaged. Two days later a short stocky handsome young man lugging a heavy suitcase appeared around the corner of East View Park, in which I lived. The maid tapped at my door, a thing which was strictly forbidden during working hours.

"What is it?"

"There's a young man to see you."

"Tell him to go away."

"But I can't tell him to go away. I did tell him, and he says he's come to stay. He's come to work, too."

So there we were, writing $1200 a Year. We had, really, quite a fine time as we worked. We roared with laughter at our own witty lines and amusing situations, which turned out to be a good thing because nobody else ever did. While we were working on this play George M. Cohan happened to be in Chicago playing in something or other whose name I've forgotten. He was at that time still associated with Sam H. Harris in the play-producing firm of Cohan & Harris. Airily I telephoned him (never having met him) at the Blackstone Hotel to ask him how he'd like to produce a play called $1200 a Year. I then told him the plot of the play as dramatically as possible, considering that I was handicapped by the telephone.

"I like it, I like it!" said the incredibly brash Mr. Cohan. "Send it to me when it's finished and if I like it as well as I think I do I'll produce it."

Though I have been canny enough about the marketing of other forms of writing I almost always have shown very little sense in my behavior toward the business of the theater. My feeling about the theater is so strong, I am so completely happy to be working in it that I am befuddled, I think and act foolishly, without caution, like a person in love.

Incredibly enough, we did finish the play, though toward the last Newman Levy had to desert it, for his father Abe Levy, the famous criminal lawyer, died; and very soon afterward Newman married and went off on a honeymoon. Then the firm of Cohan & Harris dissolved partnership. But the feeble little play managed briefly to survive even all this. Sam Harris took it over and we actually blundered through some weeks of rehearsal, opened in Baltimore and played there through one dreary week.

The play wasn't really bad. It just wasn't good enough. I regret nothing about it because, first, it was the theater, good or bad; and second, it brought into my life that dear, shrewd and misleadingly soft-spoken man of the theater—Sam Harris.

He had come to none of the rehearsals, which in itself was a bad sign. Now, on the opening night in Baltimore, he appeared. I can see him now, dapper, neat, his good kind face with its somewhat battered features turned toward the scene of the catastrophe. He was standing up at the back of the house following the fatal first night.

"Well, Mr. Harris?" I said in what I meant to be a chirp but which emerged as a croak.

"Needs a lot of work." In the years to come I was to recognize that phrase and learn to expect it. Anyone who has ever produced a play with the canny Sam will chant it in exact time with him as a first-night tryout curtain descends. "Needs a lot of work, boys and girls."

But at this time it meant nothing to me. "What's the matter with it?" I demanded.

Sam Harris is a man of few words, his voice is husky and very low. He is slightly deaf, and perhaps his manner of speaking is his unconscious way of making others realize the annoyance of this handicap. He spoke tersely enough now: "No evening clothes."

"What!"

"No evening clothes. All about poor college professors and mill workers. No evening clothes. People won't like it."

I replied, with considerable hauteur (lost on the gentle Sam), that there had been no intention of writing a play in which evening clothes could figure. This was a play for thoughtful people —done in terms of entertainment. But Sam only shook his head and hunched his shoulders a little and that punishing jaw of his came forward just a trifle. "No evening clothes. They won't like it." Still in that gentle maddening voice.

How right he was! What sound sense! I didn't know it then. I was pretty bitter about the whole business. The theater, my love, had let me down. There was some talk of calling in Roi Cooper Megrue to rewrite, but nothing came of it. A world fatigued by war and its horrors didn't want to hear about the class struggle between a group of college professors and their neighbors, the mill workers. The little play was published by Doubledays and, surprisingly enough, did quite well in amateur and little-theater performances.

A diminished soul, I returned to Chicago and the lake front. It was spring, 1920. For the second time I had contracted to cover the Republican and Democratic national conventions, the first scheduled for Chicago, the second for San Francisco. It was the ex-reporter sniffing the battle smoke again. There could be no other reason for my doing it. I argued that it was a good thing for me to mingle in this turbulent gathering; to keep abreast of the life stream. That was, of course, nonsense. I simply enjoyed an occasional reportorial job, as I always shall. This time the United Press Association was my boss; and William Allen White as the political writer and Jay (Ding) Darling as the cartoonist again formed part of the team.

June found me seated at the rough pine-board table which constituted the press section of the old cobwebby Wabash Avenue Armory. There I saw the brewing of as poisonous a political mess as any party ever stirred up in the history of the United States government.

Again Chicago was insufferably hot with the humid sticky heat of that lake region. Through the high windows the sun beat

down on the bald heads and the heat-suffused faces of the delegates. As before, I idly wondered why we were known as the
white race when we really were pink. The men sat in their shirt
sleeves and as the sweltering week wore on they shed collars,
ties, even shoes in some cases. It was the American male politician
reduced to the most common denominator.

Just behind me in the press section sat Arthur Brisbane who
did a column for the Hearst papers. The narrow pinched face,
the domelike brow, the egg-shaped head and the thick-lensed
glasses gave him the goggly look of a Martian creature. He was
doing a running story for his papers; it consisted of putting down
literally everything he saw. It wasn't writing, it was a sort of
verbal dysentery. He dictated everything. Beside him sat a secretary who wrote on a small noiseless typewriter, taking down
everything that Brisbane said. As I sat down Brisbane leaned
forward.

"Are your pearls real?"

"Certainly," I replied, with dignity. "I paid five dollars for
them at Mandel's."

His voice droned on as the typewriter keys chattered softly,
"Edna Ferber has just come into the press section she is wearing
a blue dress with a scarlet hat and pearls the pearls look real but
she says they cost five dollars . . ."

I wondered what the people in Portland, Oregon, and in
Tampa, Florida, made of that as they searched the papers for
news of one of the two most important political gatherings that
the United States would see in four years.

In the course of the nominating speeches there came up the
names of men known for their achievement and their integrity:
Leonard Wood, Herbert Hoover, Frank Lowden of Illinois,
Hiram Johnson, Nicholas Murray Butler, Senator Robert La Follette of Wisconsin. Able, courageous and wise men. And this
was the first national political convention in which women had
an active and conspicuous part.

In a smoke-filled room of the Blackstone Hotel a little group
of shirt-sleeved men chose as their candidate a figure stuffed with
straw and this figure they stood up and he was nominated next

day under the name of Warren Gamaliel Harding. The convention went through the form of taking ballots. The vote was taken, the roll was called, state by state, an empty farce. It happened that I had met Warren G. Harding a few years before in Cleveland. He and I had been speakers at a large convention. I had sat listening to his speech and as I listened I had thought, then, "Here is a living cartoon of the American Fourth of July stuffed-shirt orator."

And now they had nominated this man for the office of President of the United States on the Republican ticket.

Men began to march up and down the aisles of the armory now. Red-faced, sweating, they marched with banners and shouted as they marched. Round and round they went like witless children. They timed their cheers like machines. They knew they must cheer just so long, according to instructions from headquarters. Sometimes in their weariness and moist discomfort they looked piteously toward their leaders as a dog gazes with pleading eyes at his master as though to say, "Don't make me run after that ball any more. I'm tired."

I had gone into that convention firm in the belief that the World War had taught us something. I had thought that the Peace of 1918 and the Wilsonian plan that followed it would bring a measure of new dignity, of universal humanity into a war-torn world. It now sounds incredibly naïve but nevertheless I did believe this then.

Now, in the trumped-up fanfare that followed the nomination of Harding I felt these beliefs being torn from me as a child, helpless, is bereft of her toys. I knew that I was going to cry. I tried hard not to. Perhaps I was weary, nervous, a little hysterical from the noise and the heat and the excitement. But I knew deep down that it was the horrible pain of disillusionment in my country and my people that was making me weep. I stared steadily at a small round window high up near the ceiling of the vast room. If you stare very hard with your eyes wide open you sometimes can hold back the tears. So I stared. The window was very dirty and festooned with cobwebs. The clamor went on outside and inside me. The stony-eyed effort was not going to work.

Two tears slid down my cheeks and plopped onto the front of the blue dress; two more, two more.

Bill McNutt, just beside me, put his great hand over mine. "Don't bother," he said. "Doesn't matter . . . hundred years from now."

Then they nominated Calvin Coolidge for Vice-President. At that a very strange thing happened. That same William Slavens McNutt made a prediction and it came true. McNutt was a war correspondent and special writer; a gigantic fellow, hard-boiled, tenderhearted; wise with the terrible wisdom of the experienced and intuitive newspaperman. He had a great fist that looked as if it could fell an ox with a blow. This massive member he now brought down on the pine table with such force that we thought he had splintered the boards. The combined press section jumped as though pulled by one string.

"There goes Harding!" bawled McNutt.

"What do you mean?" I asked, rather waspishly.

"Harding'll never serve his term out. He'll die and Coolidge will be President."

"Don't be silly. What makes you say a thing like that?"

"Wait. You'll see. Coolidge luck. He's shot with it."

If the convention was fantastic it was nothing compared to the hurried reception given afterward at a local hotel. I forget whether it was the Congress or the LaSalle, but there I was with the throng of special writers and there, dazed and groggy, were Mr. and Mrs. Warren G. Harding. Tall, handsome, commanding of figure, he seemed the very model of a statesman—until you looked into his eyes. Lambent, deep-set, meaningless, there was nothing behind them. They were just eyes; features with which he saw objects and people. They were not windows of the soul because the façade on which they were fastened was nothing but a false front. I never have seen a less happy man.

Mrs. Harding made up for his strange silent reserve. Her dress had a net yoke and a high-boned net collar such as I hadn't seen since my girlhood days in Appleton. She carried a large cluster of pink roses and all about her twittered and chirped a group of females in what looked like starched muslin. These Mrs. Harding

addressed as "girls." Her eyeglasses were attached by a slender
gold chain to the pince-nez clip on her bodice. I discredited the
whole scene as an optical illusion or an anachronism cleverly
faked. But it wasn't. The "girls" had been brought all the way
from Marion, Ohio.

And, "Oh, girls," cried Mrs. Harding, "if only Pa was here!
If only Pa could of lived to see this day!" She turned to the rows
of correspondents facing her, their countenances impassive, like
intelligent cameras. "Pa didn't want me to marry Warren. Pa
was a banker, you know, and Warren just ran the paper in
Marion. Well, I guess he knows now he was wrong, only I wish
he could of lived to see it. . . . President! . . . Oh, girls, think!"

You could see Pa, the small-town banker, purse-proud, with
his heavy gold watch chain and his square-toed boots, balancing
judiciously from heel to toe, weighing his prospective son-in-
law, the handsome young newspaperman, and finding him not
good enough for his plain but highly solvent daughter.

The Chicago farce finished, we started for San Francisco and
the Democratic convention. I planned to spend the summer in
California and I took the redoubtable Julia Ferber with me. A
pity they didn't make her chairman of the Democratic convention. She could have hammered some semblance of sanity and
order into the zany assemblage.

The great trains that pulled us across the continent of prairie
and plain and mountain were not air-conditioned in 1920. It
was a perishing trip in midsummer when you struck the desert.
We did a good deal of whimpering about dust and heat as we
sipped our iced tea or orange juice and sluiced our wrists with
cold water from the faucets of our drawing-room lavatories.
Kansas and Nebraska were stifling, the heat was like the breath
from a steel-mill furnace, the dust ground itself into your hair,
your eyes, your teeth.

I had a fine time. Of all forms of locomotion I like train-riding
best. Nothing but admiration amounting to awe fills me as I
contemplate the hardships and the bravery of the covered-wagon
pioneers, but I myself hate roughing it when I travel. I like to
make use, on an American (or any other) train, of every luxury

it can offer. Perhaps I had enough of roughing it in the days when I had to make a small bundle of myself so that my mother need not pay full fare for me.

Boats bore me. I am depressed by the flat monotonous reaches of the sea, gray, blue or night-black. I have no kinship with it. The rows of rug-wrapped mummies stretched out on deck chairs, the walkers, the shuffle-board players, the lady passengers who bounce out, bright-eyed and smelling of Guerlain, in those lace evening dresses at eight—these plunge me into gloom. I love the coziness and the freedom of a train compartment. My idea of the ultimate in exciting luxury is to lie stretched out among pillows in an air-conditioned crack American streamliner watching the United States of America slide by, a living panorama. It is not only a panorama, it is a cross section of a continent, as neatly cut as though sliced with a cheese knife. By the look of the wheat in Kansas, by the freshness of the permanent waves in the hair of the girls at the Nebraska railway station, by the degree of glitter on the paint of the automobiles spinning down the Arizona highways, by the very neatness or slovenliness of the little flat prairie towns as you flash by their pavements and back yards and Main Street neon signs, you can sense whether the country is in the doldrums or on the crest. Certainly the doldrums have had it these past ten years, but 1920 told a different story. Once the train passes Kansas City my face is pressed to the window. And where, by the way, is the Whitman to sing of the Kansas City railway station? Your Eastern traveler, or visiting European, with an hour to spare between stops, steps off his westbound train to find himself wandering among the pillars of a sort of Aladdin's palace. There you can buy everything from a dress shirt to a camera. In it the amazed tourist is confronted with a bookshop more complete than those of most cities of a million. On its shelves and counters may be found anything from James Joyce's Ulysses to this week's Variety. The Middle West, the Far West stimulates and excites me more than any other section of America. There is about it a naïve and unfinished quality that appeals to the imagination. I don't think it's nobler or better or more moral or desirable. It seems to me to be fresher, more vital, an integral part of the American way of life. In the West and Midwest you find little of the cosmopolitan European influence, of the aping of foreign manners and ways. Necessity, hardship, vast distances of prairie and range have served to mold the manners and customs as well as the bodies, the faces, the speech of the West. It is pleasing to my ear, it is refreshing to my eye. Being a hundred or so years younger than its Eastern twin, the West is less sophisticated. The historian tells us that little of the so-called American aristocracy was in the westward movement. Brawn and muscle settled the West.

So, then, I am fascinated by the hundreds and hundreds of miles of prairie and plain and mountain land; of desert and sagebrush. I have seen it in all seasons; when the dust and drought have seared it as though flames had swept it, so that it looks for all the world like the stricken battlefields of France: dead, ashen, rigid. Yet so enormous is the vitality of the region that a year later the gray fields are green again and fertile. I like to see the Midwest farm boy shading his eyes to watch the streamliner flash by like a silver comet. His face has a look different from that worn by his father in boyhood. For this lad has been to town every day in the Ford, he has seen the world through the movies, his father has been to France in 1917. Likely as not there is a radio attached to the plow, and as he sits perched on the plow seat with furrow after furrow of rich brown loam turning toward the sun he hears the news of the world: wars, music, politics, crops, theater. Perhaps the song of the meadow lark, the yearly almanac and the Sears, Roebuck catalogue were richer, more sustaining after all. Tomorrow's world will know.

There is something impressive about setting your watch ahead three hours as you travel east from coast to coast, or three hours back as you span the continent westbound. That is a country for you! you think, as you whirl from the Atlantic to the Pacific.

Nowhere is the wastefulness of this vast land better exemplified than on one of these luxurious transcontinental trains. I ask for coffee with hot milk; no cream. They bring me a pitcher of hot milk and a great pitcher of rich cream. Another pitcher of cream with the baked apple. Another pitcher of cream with breakfast food. There is enough cream on the single table to supply a family for a week. Butter. More butter, though you don't want it. Twelve clean hand towels on the rack above my bedroom washbowl. They are renewed in the morning, at mid-day, at night. I remember the one thin gray wisp of gritty linen called a towel on any European luxury train. I am given bars of good soap. I have a separate closet for my clothes. An order of toast is a formidable stack. There never was such a nation for sheer wanton waste.

Now, as I travel here and there across the land I see the names of the hamlets, the little towns, the cities and they have a new meaning for me, a more poignant significance. The whole history and spirit and purpose of America can be read in the names of these towns. I love the sound of them, the purport of them: Casa Piedra, Kansas, and Las Flores, California, and Cimarron, Oklahoma—those were Spanish settlers, I say to myself. Schomberg, New Mexico—a German group must have settled there. Joliet, Lafitte—these were the courageous Frenchmen. Manchester, Hyde Park—the English, nostalgic perhaps for the land they had forever left, had thought to keep its memory thus, and to give that memory an inheritance to their descendants. Moscow, Kansas, a strange wedding of the Russian and the Midwest American. Comanche and Medicine Mound, Texas. No American Indians now ranging those once unbroken horizons. Wagon Mound; Skull Valley; you can hear the grind of the covered-wagon wheels on desert sand. German, English, French, Spanish, Dutch, Indian, Swedish, Russian, Italian names for the towns scattered from the Atlantic to the Pacific. Four hundred and fifty years of planting these towns by the shores of lakes and rivers, along the foothills of magnificent mountains, through the forests, in the valleys, on the vast plateaus. Protestants, Catholics, Jews who were being persecuted in European lands; French Huguenots, English Puritans, German liberals. With their hands and their hearts and their spirits and their blood they built these towns. And now, when the brave fight has been fought, and the house solidly built, were the termites to be permitted to bore and crawl and pry their secret way through the sound timbers, making them rotten with Nazism and Communism and Fascism until they fall!

I sometimes wonder, as I cross this enormous land, if a sort of grisly game is not going on; if the land is not destroying the people who inhabit it as the people who inhabit it are destroying the land. A magic continent, a peculiar treasure, stuffed with riches, millions in it are starving in the midst of plenty. Slash down the forests, drain the rivers, till the land and let it lie there turning to destructive dust. Perhaps that still small voice that could be heard above the song of the meadow lark is drowned out now by the iron-throated machines. Or perhaps in this quivering electric continent no one listens now. Yet the words are there, so clear if we will pause to hear. Now, therefore, if ye will obey my voice indeed, and keep my covenant, then ye shall be a peculiar treasure unto me above all people; for all the earth is mine; and ye shall be unto me a kingdom of priests and an holy nation.

14

Liar! . . . Coward! Come outside and I'll . . . Mr. Chairman, I demand that you take a roll-call . . . Bless this gathering, O Lord, and bring wisdom to those who . . . I will be heard, I stand on my constitutional rights as an American cit . . . Shut up! . . . One whose name is known to every intelligent . . ."

That gigantic circus, the 1920 Democratic National Convention, was in progress. Again William Jennings Bryan, in his wrinkled habiliments of the Nebraska spellbinder, tried to dominate it, but the fire was quenched in the old eagle's eye, the gold was drained out of the voice.

It was, in its way, almost as saddening a sight as the Republican convention had been. Usually, once the opening prayer had piously died on the air, there broke out from two to a half-dozen actual fist fights on the floor of the assemblage—battles that raged up and down the aisles until guards separated the contestants. The meeting droned on. Nothing seemed to be accomplished. The special writers and the reporters turned in their stories as quickly as might be and leaped joyfully into the refreshing sea of San Francisco hospitality. Of the convention itself I recall practically nothing, but pleasant memories linger of dinners up at the Woods house perched so high on Russian Hill that the motorcar had to tack from one side of the road to the other as we ascended; of other dinners with Frederick O'Brien as host, he who had written White Shadows in the South Seas, which everyone was reading; hot clams spicily marinated and eaten out of a soup dish; Solari's restaurant, and the sweet white meat of the crawfish eaten with mayonnaise. Red wine and champagne always with dinner, for though Prohibition's blighting breath hung over all the rest of America, San Francisco was superbly unaware of it. Bill White and I strolling down Post or Market Street eating enormous ripe cherries out of paper bags and flipping the slippery stones into the gutter. And the talk at the Woods' about the state being more important than the individual. And I, who knew nothing about it, shouting, "That's not true! The individual is more important. What's the state but the individual multiplied by a million! There can be the individual without the state. There can be no state without the individual."

A lot I knew about it then. A lot less do I (or does anyone else) know now.

I had made up my mind that as soon as the convention week was past I would take a small house somewhere in California and try to begin a first draft of a novel which had been simmering for a year or more. I had already named it—The Girls. Its background was to be Chicago, its chief characters three old maids of three generations in one family, all alive and each representing the American woman of her day. Charlotte, Lottie and Charley; great-aunt, aunt and niece.

In between I thriftily decided that I'd try to sell the novel Fanny Herself in pictures. Very little motion-picture money had come my way. If I was to spend a year or more writing The Girls, it would be fine to have a little movie money tucked away to tide me over the lean period.

I went, in my youth and ignorance, to Hollywood, and there I rented a furnished house in Lanewood Drive, with Jean McPherson living across the street and Leo Carrillo next door; and roses red and white that bloomed enormous at midday and fell in a shower of petals at night, and that had no scent at all, like ghosts. The whole city appeared ghostlike to me. It seemed literally that, glancing out of my bedroom window in the morning, my amazed eye would behold a white stucco house, palm-encircled, where no house had been the night before.

But before the Hollywood house there had been a strange few days at the Alexandria Hotel in Los Angeles, at that time the best hotel the city boasted. At about nine o'clock on the second morning here, after I'd had my bath and was reaching for my dress the floor of my hotel bedroom began to dip and sway like the deck of a boat in a swell. As I staggered there came a roaring sound. It was a little like thunder and a little like the sound wild animals make in a zoo just before feeding time. Then came the crash of breaking glass followed by shouts and the screams of women.

It was my first earthquake. Not nice. As I was dashing for the lobby ten floors below, a fresh series of tremors came up with the lift and a gray-faced elevator boy seemed none too sure of the controls. The lobby was filled with pale and frightened people. The morning train from San Francisco had just arrived. Prospective guests were lined up at the desk, waiting to register. A flock of bellboys streamed in from the street, laden with luggage. Another sickening shock surged through the building. The man first in line at the hotel register dropped the pen with which he was signing his name, turned an ashen face toward his bellboy, beckoned him and fled, followed by the whole line like a musical-comedy chorus, headed for the next train out. The effect was hilarious—or would have been if the earth had subsided and if the sound of falling bricks and mortar hadn't dulled the sense of humor.

The wide open spaces of Hollywood seemed safer after this, for that city had not then become the glittering capital which it now claims to be; and as for Beverly Hills, that was a suburb in the wilds of which Mary Pickford and Douglas Fairbanks chose to live in royal isolation.

I did succeed in selling Fanny Herself for an unimposing sum to a very, very young and very, very bright lad named Irving Thalberg. Until then I had fancied motion-picture producers as large gentlemen smoking oversized cigars. But this young man whose word seemed to be final at Universal City turned out to be a wisp of a boy, twenty-one, so slight as to appear actually frail. Something about this boy impressed me deeply. When he became the most important and the most intelligent man in the motion-picture industry, I was not surprised, nor am I surprised that since his untimely death no one has come along to take his place. High intelligence, taste and intuition combine rarely in Hollywood or elsewhere.

In the bizarre background of Hollywood, but no part of it, I began the first draft of The Girls. All the varied aspects of the Chicago I had seen in the past ten years and all the dramatic and absurd stories I had heard and read about its brief past came flooding back to my mind now. The old Fort Dearborn days; the Civil War; the Chicago Fire; the shocking performance of The Black Crook, with women actually wearing tights; Potter Palmer, the dry-goods merchant, and his wife who became queen of Midwest society; the high rickety wooden sidewalks above the mud wallow of the streets of 1875; picnicking in the groves around Twenty-ninth Street.

As these bits and pieces combined to form a pattern I led a curious life in Hollywood. Yet slowly I had come to realize that this was the only life for a writer while in the process of producing a novel. Work, walk, read; work, walk, read. I worked, I walked, I read. Sometimes, briefly, strange figures floated into my ken, then disappeared. They scarcely had the feel of reality. Carl Laemmle, gnomelike little Oshkosh storekeeper who, like a figure in a fairy tale, had become a millionaire overnight because he had seen the possibilities of a thing called the nickelodeon; Nazimova, Claire Adams, Louise, Glaum, Carmel Myers, shining their brief moment in the Hollywood firmament; Elmer Rice, biting the hand that fed him; Rupert Hughes, delivering dinner speeches about the glory of the motion-picture industry.

About the town, its life and its people there was in 1920 a crude lavishness that had in it nothing of gusto. It wasn't American, it had no virility, it sprang from almost pure vulgarity. There was about it none of the lusty native quality of the old gold-rush camp days. Offended by it, and bored, too, after the first glance or two needed for complete comprehension, I retreated gratefully into the work-walk-read routine of escape. I read a history of France in the Tauchnitz edition, very nice and horrifying; I reread Thoreau's Walden as one takes a drink of pure cold spring water to slake a champagne fever. Reading it gave me a feeling of guilt. I always have had a weakness for shoes. Book in hand I opened my clothes-closet door to look at the array I had brought with me. There they were staring reproachfully up at me, all the way from riding boots to pink satin slippers. Walden Pond indeed! I shut the door on them, hastily, feeling like Bluebeard.

I discovered that when I walked in the deserted sunny town, people peered from windows as at some strange animal loose in the streets. I learned that no one walked in Hollywood. This is still true, almost twenty years later. Just a few months ago people passing in motorcars stared and pointed at this strange biped walking along the palm-lined avenues of Beverly Hills. I had offers, of course, to write for the pictures. I never have written a line or a word for motion pictures, though numbers of my books have been filmed.

In this atmosphere The Girls did not go too well. The sun came up, day after day, day after day. None of the clouds, none of the storms, none of the summer caprices of the temperate climate to which I was accustomed. It was like seeing someone in red satin daily. What a grateful change to see them in clean gray gingham for a change. I visualized the lake front in Chicago on a rainy evening, with the lake a gray mist and the water sloshing in my shoes as I trudged.

With relief I left Hollywood for the San Francisco I loved. There was a quick run out to the ranch where Charles and Kathleen Norris lived with the riches of the Peninsula spread lavishly all about them. The ripe prunes of the late summer crop made a royal purple carpet. As they dropped, dropped, dropped with a juicy plunk Charles, the spiritual, said, "Hear that! Every plunk means five cents in my pocket."

There was research to be done in the Chicago Historical Society Library. As I found myself, months later, approaching the end of the book, I thought it would be a fine thing if I could serialize it in a magazine whose circulation would not interfere with the book's sale. The autumn and winter of that year would not see the book's publication. It was too late for that. While waiting for late spring the novel could appear serially if I could sell it. But two or three editors were already too fully booked ahead or they objected to the ending of The Girls. They'd publish it, they said, if I would change the ending. This I refused to do. I wanted to serialize in a woman's magazine because this type of periodical could, at that time, use as much as twenty-five thousand words in a single installment, thus releasing a novel in three or four installments. For some reason one's book sales were not affected by serialization in this medium; and they paid a whopping price for serials, being highly solvent, with enormous advertising contracts.

Prudish editors of the 1920 period seemed, however, to block my clever little plan. I never had met Gertrude Lane, editor-in-chief of the Woman's Home Companion. I wrote her, saying that I was on the last lap of a novel about three generations of Chicago old maids. It might do for a serial; and would she care to look at it.

We met for lunch at the Cosmopolitan Club. It was the beginning of a friendship that has lasted eighteen years. I saw a sturdy quiet alert woman. You sensed here power and intuitive understanding. She looked New England—with a glint in the eye. Dressed very quietly as she was, it was only after you had talked with her for half an hour or so that you began to note certain details. As you talked, you thought with one corner of your mind, "H'm, those look like real sables." Then, a moment later, "Moses! They are!" A single fine emerald on her right hand. Line and fabric had been cunningly contrived in that sedate blue dress. She ordered lunch, and there obviously was a woman who knew and appreciated good food. Here was a grand combination of Maine saltiness and Latin temperament. Somewhere, surely, far, far back, a great-great-great-grandma or -grandpa in the Lane line must have stepped out to have produced a Gertrude in this century.

Briefly I outlined the story. "And—uh—look, I have something to say that you may not—that is—at the end, Lottie, the middle one you know, has a baby."

Miss Lane sipped her coffee black. "Does she? That's interesting."

"But she isn't married. She goes to France, and she comes back to Chicago and she brings this baby and it's her baby."

"Have a mint," said Miss Lane. "After all, mints aren't really candy. Waiter, some more hot coffee. . . . Well, now, just what is your deadline for the book-publishing date?"

"You don't object to the ending? I mean, the magazine won't insist on changing—because I won't change——"

"Certainly not," said the brisk Gertrude. "I'm the editor. The baby stays."

It may sound prim now, but it took some doing in 1920 in a woman's magazine.

I had a feeling of smooth pleasure and anticipation about The Girls. It was as though I had come out of a smallish room that was Fanny Herself through a long, long passage that became rather dim and sunless toward the end (the McChesney stories, that passage was) into a bigger, brighter, airier room that was The Girls. Fanny Herself had been rather groping and juvenile, especially in the second half; the McChesney stories, though fresh in characterization and attack, had been a shade pert and consciously brisk. But The Girls was a mature novel. I felt it marked a definite advance and that it was by a large margin the best piece of writing I had done up to now. I had left Emma McChesney behind me.

My horror, then, cannot be expressed (postal regulations) when my eye fell upon Doubleday's first newspaper advertisement of The Girls. I saw it in the Chicago Tribune. I began to send blistering telegrams in all directions. This triumph of maladroit publicity said:

IF YOU LIKED THE EMMA McCHESNEY STORIES
YOU'LL LIKE EDNA FERBER'S
NEW BOOK
THE GIRLS

Nevertheless, the novel received really superb reviews. It didn't sell particularly well, and though it continued to sell a little through the years it has never, I think, reached more than a total of about fifty thousand. I still judge my readers by the standard of whether or not they like The Girls. I had hoped it would sell tremendously. It didn't. I should have been depressed. I wasn't. Rather pleased with myself, if anything. I had proved I could write a novel.

After the long pull of a novel it was almost a holiday change to go back to short stories. It is a writing pattern I've followed through the years. A novel—short stories; a novel—a play; a novel—short stories; a novel—a play, like the swinging of a pendulum. Of course, one could take a complete vacation and write nothing. But why, when writing's so much more exhilarating! It will sound smug, but I must say it: I feel sorry for women who can lunch out when they please; buy a new hat in the morning; sleep late as they like; have a swim at eleven; come and go, eat and sleep, play or idle as they feel inclined. I've never been able to do that since I was seventeen. Fun is still a treat. There's no sauce for play like work. Lunch in a restaurant is an adventure; to be up after midnight gives me a delicious feeling of guilt. Achieving a new dress means five-o'clock fittings.

All those gay industrious people with whom I spent more and more time in New York worked like that. But when they played they went at it as blithely, as wholeheartedly as children. New York had become a six-months' home to me. I think I loved it because it brought me laughter and gaiety and stimulating companionship. There was now for me something heavy and brooding about Chicago's murky skies, its winter streets ankle deep in sooty snow. The air of New York was brilliant, revivifying. My friends there worked like horses all morning and part of the afternoon, as I did. If you were busy they understood. You never had to explain if you were late, or absent, or if you vanished altogether for days at a time. You merely said, "I'm working," and they understood. A merry, brilliant, gifted crew, and they are, with one or two exceptions, still with me, thank God, in friendship and warm understanding, through the years.

In the three years following the war I had not visited Europe. For the next thirteen or fourteen years I was to make the crossing yearly—frequently twice a year—and it was a fearful thing to see a continent—a civilization—crumbling before one's eyes. It was a rapid and seemingly inevitable process to which no one paid any particular attention. An occasional voice, raised in shrill warning, was greeted with a "Hush, hush! Everything will be all right. Economic consequence of war. Nothing to be alarmed about. Hush!"

I wanted to go abroad in the winter of 1922 to see Germany, Austria, England, France. November 1921 found me in New York hard at work on short stories. I hoped to be able to bring out a book of short stories sometime in 1922. I worked very hard, played very hard, skated at St. Nicholas Rink, so convenient to the Majestic Hotel in which I lived; went to the theater, stage-struck as ever. I had got into the way of filling a few public speaking engagements each winter, under the management of a lecture bureau or on my own. I usually spoke briefly on some innocuous topic—books, or writing or some such subject—and then read a short story or two. It was, I suppose, pure exhibitionism. I loved it. Usually, before the time arrived to fill these engagements I would heartily wish that I could get out of them. Cleveland—Detroit—Columbus—Chicago—Pittsburgh—Davenport; I saw the American towns and cities, I talked to the people. It took a tremendous amount of nervous energy. But once up on the platform, launched, I was happy, I loved making an audience laugh and cry, I loved the sound of my own voice. The blighted Bernhardt of Appleton, Wisconsin, days lost, for the moment at least, her feeling of dramatic frustration. The piece-speaking fool was in her element.

I liked coming into a town I'd never seen. I would take one quick look at my hotel room in order to assure myself that the room was as quiet as anything available. (Some day I should like to be rich just so that I might found a city hotel whose rooms are not built around railroad tracks, street-car lines, cab ranks, newspaper stands, phonograph salesrooms and college reunions.)

Then, as the telephone began its first shrill clamor I would be off down the elevator to investigate the town.

I had made some speaking engagements for February 1922. Early in February my mother came to visit me in New York. I was to leave for the West on Monday, the 13th. A curious thing then happened which I should like to record, though it sounds slightly mad.

On Sunday night at about ten o'clock we were seated in the living room of our hotel apartment, I at one side of the room, doing a bit of last-minute mending before closing my suitcases, my mother reading at a table opposite. We had left the apartment at about three that afternoon, had dined later with our dear friends Mannie and Flora Rosenthal, and had returned early because I had a lot of eleventh-hour odds and ends to tie up before my journey. The room was quiet and cozy.

I glanced up from my sewing. There on the carpet directly in front of my mother's chair was what looked like a scrawled chalk mark or paint mark about the size of one's hand. It was white on the beige carpet. In shape it was interwoven and meaningless—rather like the Masonic charms men sometimes wear dangling from a watch chain.

"What's that on the carpet?"

My mother looked down. She stretched forth a foot and rubbed the mark with her shoe. It didn't come off. "The maid must have had something or other stuck into her carpet sweeper. No one else has been in the room all day."

I crossed over to it, knelt down. "But why didn't we see it when we came in and sat down?" I stooped and rubbed it hard with my hand. It did not change. I went to the windows, pulled down the shades, pulled them up again. I moved the objects in the room—the lamps, any bright ornaments, turned out the lights, turned them on. There it was.

My mother rose and went into the next room. Over her shoulder, as she went, she said, "It's nothing. The maid probably had something stuck to her broom. We'll call the housekeeper in the morning."

I glanced down at the mark again.

It was gone.

A curious prickle set my hair on end.

Next day I took the train for the West. Blanche Lait, Lola Fisher's sister, and Edith Rosenthal Brown, who was a doctor, took me down to the train. My mother had developed a slight cold and stayed home.

At midnight on the train I awoke with a feeling of alarm. But in the morning I told myself that this was neurotic and silly. I spoke in Detroit. I couldn't shake off the feeling of apprehension. I sent a wire and went on to Chicago. A reply said my mother still had a cold, but it wasn't serious. I spoke there; then, with complete lack of reason and, for that matter, integrity, I canceled the remaining engagements and took the Century for New York. I knew I was facing a crisis. Arriving in New York early in the morning I went directly to my apartment at the Majestic Hotel, turned the doorknob, inserted my key, but the door was locked from the inside. I rang the bell. A complete stranger opened the door. She was dressed in white.

"Who're you!"

"I'm the nurse."

"Who's nurse?"

"Mrs. Ferber's."

My mother had pneumonia. She had passed the crisis the night before.

Well, there it is. It sounds silly. But there it is. If anyone told me that story I'd say a neurologist might possibly help her, in time.

In March I went abroad, taking my mother with me and using the southern route so that she might have the benefit of the sunshine and the sea voyage. Again Madeira, Gibraltar, Algiers. But this time there was no showing the tourists around the hidden caches of the mammoth rock.

As I set foot in Italy I saw the beginning of the change. The Europe I had seen during those seven months in 1914 was gone, never to return. On the surface there was little to note. Of course, women in black everywhere—Florence, Rome, London, Paris. In Paris one saw only black. American tourists said, "Oh well,

French women always wear black, you know, on the street. Thrifty." They said, too, that it was marvelous to see Europe gay once more, after those four years of gloom. Look, everybody's dancing.

And so they were. All Europe was dancing, a mad St. Vitus' death dance. Jiggle, hop, slide, whirl. I took tango lessons of a slim blond youth in Lake Como. An Austrian, he said; a lieutenant in the war. He didn't go into it very much. He didn't seem to care for the subject. He was very young indeed. As we slithered, loose-kneed, across the ballroom floor at Villa D'Este he would say, sharply, in German, "Kopf—rechts!" Like a drill sergeant. The head, in the tango, is supposed to be held parallel with one's partner's head. This I would sometimes forget. "Kopf —rechts!"

Nice, Cannes, Paris, Budapest, Vienna, Berlin writhed and twisted in the dance. In the side-street dance rooms of Florence, in the great boulevard restaurants of Paris they were performing exactly the same gyrations. Over all the American jazz music boomed and whanged. Saxophones, drums, cymbals, castanets, sandpaper.

"Who are those young boys? Why do they dance with those old women all the time?"

"They're gigolos."

"They're—what?" I had never heard the word before; didn't know what it meant.

"They're paid to dance. You pay them five francs, or more or less. The old gals are all crazy about dancing. They hire these gigolos to dance with them."

The gigolo, born of the war, was something to watch. He too was a symbol. But no one was interested in symbols. These slim sleek silent boys, at the first note of the music, would cross the floor, bow before some buxom Midwest American matron or her daughter, they would take correct position. They were French, Italian, Austrian, Hungarian. Their faces were old as the Pharaohs. They were terribly young. They had been in the war at sixteen, seventeen, eighteen. Now they were old men of

twenty, twenty-one, twenty-two. They danced beautifully, effortlessly, like dream machines. Through the long dance number,
through the encore. Unsmiling, with dreadful politeness, they
would bring their plump middle-aged partners or their slim
gauche girl partners back to the tables at which the American
husbands and fathers sat, pleased that their womenfolk were
having such a merry whirl.

"Having a good time, Mother? That young fella certainly
shakes a mean foot."

The boy would bow stiffly from the waist, his heels clicking
smartly, once. He would turn and walk away without a word.

The American girls touring with their good middle-class
mamas and papas were enormously taken with these ghostly
boys. They confided to me (and anyone) that they thought them
so romantic-looking. Kind of sad and stern and everything, and
so different from the boys back home in Detroit. And their
manners simply lovely, only they hardly ever talked to you unless you kept talking to them.

"Were you in the war? . . . Honest! . . . Were you hurt?
. . . Oh, my goodness! Well, I don't think anybody could tell—
anyway, this side of your face is all right and you look just like
anybody else. They say everybody's face is different one side from
the other. . . . My sister—she's older than me—had a friend in
the war, he was in the American Personnel Bureau in Paris, he
said the war was simply awful. . . . Do you speak French? . . .
Je pense que—um—que France est le plus belle—uh—pays de
France—I mean—de Euro—de l'Europe."

The reply in clipped contemptuous English: "That is most
kind of you, mademoiselle."

It seemed to me that all America was swarming on Europe in
1922. Their money had been bursting their pants pockets now
for five years. And look! the tourists said, you can get hundreds
of marks for a dollar. A whole fistful! Why, you can live practically anywhere in Europe on the fat of the land for a dollar a day.
Isn't it marvelous! Try as hard as you please, they gurgled, shak-
ing with laughter, you simply couldn't spend five dollars a day
unless you went in for Rue de la Paix jewelry. Hotelkeepers in

Munich, Berlin, Paris, Vienna breathlessly demanded hundreds of marks or kronen a day, but next day their arithmetic was all wrong again, and you were occupying a bedroom, sitting room and bath for practically nothing. In the banks haggard men behind the metal grilles counted out great bundles of paper money which the well-dressed well-fed tourist grabbed gleefully.

"You can get a manicure for three francs and a facial for two and a wave for practically nothing! I have the whole works every day," the women tourists said jubilantly. Tortoise-shell combs, fringed shawls, bead bags, coral and amber chains, jade earrings. You saw the pale-blue and lavender tweed tailleurs of America's wives and daughters flashing gaily amongst the black crepe of feminine Europe. What do you mean—buzzards! We give them our good American money in exchange for this junk, don't we! Well then! They can be darned glad to get it.

I wrote a short story called Gigolo. I read it today, after sixteen years. It is not a first-rate short story. The ending is inexcusably false and sentimental. But as a picture, concise and slightly bitter, of a certain phase of 1922 postwar Europe it is still good. I made the mistake (over the protests of my publishers) of calling the 1922 volume of short stories Gigolo, after this story. As practically no one in the United States had ever heard the word, or knew what it meant, or how to pronounce it, the book's sale was seriously affected by the strange title. This was a pity, for that volume held Old Man Minick and The Afternoon of a Faun and Home Girl and The Sudden Sixties.

In Paris that June I found Aleck Woollcott and Neysa McMein and Donald Ogden Stewart and Deems Taylor and Jane Grant. We whirled around together, we ate ices or drank apéritifs outside the Café Nationale, we saw the Russian Ballet at the Opera in that first tour which gave Scheherazade and Petrouschka to a bedazzled world. Woollcott, Don Stewart, Jane and I did a tour of the battlefields in a very smart town car (rented) and driven by a mustached French chauffeur who misunderstood the nature of the expedition. His name was François. François, at the start of the trip, put his own Gallic interpretation upon it. Two young (or young enough) couples ringless, traveling by motorcar into the countryside, meant, to François, amour. As the first day wore on, surprise, bewilderment, unbelief and hurt succeeded one another across his face like clouds across an erstwhile sunny sky.

The car accommodated two passengers in the upholstered back seat and two in the small collapsible chairs in front of this. The two chairs turned out to be Inquisition relics. Our courtly cavaliers stood this just so long and then it became a race to see which of us would gain the car first in order to grab the comfortable back seat. From time to time we descended, of course, to look at old Roman ruins, at newish battlefields and at very new cemeteries indeed. That accomplished, the two fleetest runners and most agile wrestlers won. No holds were barred. The top being down, Don once made it by a neat dive over the back. François, the erstwhile beaming Eros, became a cross and baffled Phoebus. Crazy Americans, his face said plainer than words. And he was right.

This romping was, as a matter of fact, our protection against the dismal sights we saw. For we saw that while the war hadn't exactly made the world safe for democracy as an institution still it had provided curiously democratic safety for an astonishing number of young men. Hundreds and thousands of little white crosses, the neatest imaginable, row on row, marked the new cemeteries of the French countryside. You had only to read the names to realize that really nothing could be more democratic.

Karl Bauers. Tony Mazzetti. Sam Johnson. Leo Cohn. Joyce Kilmer. William Caldwell. Ignace Prybzbyzski. Nick Popoudopoulas. No arrangement could have been fairer.

Berlin was prophetic enough for anyone who cared to read the writing on the wall. But we played craps with Woollcott and Frazier Hunt and the American newspaper correspondents in Berlin at the little scarlet bar at the Adlon Hotel and the wads of paper money lost or won were so enormous in size (though not in value) that Woollcott, massing together a peck or so of it, said he was going out to find a horse to choke. Dinner at the Bristol Hotel in Unter den Linden brought forth a rather grisly little occurrence one night. We sat, a half-dozen Americans, eating our meal quietly enough. I don't remember what the con-

versation happened to be. It was all in English. Perhaps we spoke
of America. Suddenly our waiter burst out in fury. He was a man
in his thirties, not bad-looking; a small dark mustache. Somehow
one always thinks of a German waiter or a Swiss waiter as having
been born into the world with a tray deftly balanced in his hands,
so expert, so unobtrusive are they. This is what he said in a
shout; in German:

"God damn you Americans! If it hadn't been for you we'd
have won the war. But wait. You'll see. We'll soon be strong
again and then we'll fight again, and we'll tear France to pieces.
But to pieces! This time we won't lose. This time we will conquer
the world, and you damned Americans too."

I tell this story simply because, if that waiter knew it, then
all Germany knew. And 1933–1938 isn't, perhaps, as much of a
surprise to them as it was, say, to Viscount Halifax.

They killed Rathenau. We went to the theater to see Ernst
Toller's play Die Maschinenstürmer. Prophetic events, both.
Toller's play pictured the attack of the workingmen on the vast
machine that was taking the bread out of the workman's mouth.

Munich was worse. They stood in long queues outside the
pawnshops. In their hands were precious bits of jewelry or
household treasure; a silver spoon; a wedding ring; a lace hand-
kerchief.

In Vienna the streets were full of children—girls of twelve
or thirteen—soliciting men. In the Ring or on the Koerntnerstrasse you would see a woman, gray-haired, ivory of face,
dressed in a shabby frock whose line and fabric and style were
unmistakably the work of a haute couturière. At the look in her
face we would stuff a wad of kronen into her hands. And she
would take it. Vienna was full of old and middle-aged people
who had put by ten, twenty, thirty, fifty thousand kronen against
old age. Now you could buy one loaf of bread for fifty thousand
kronen. Their money was worthless.

No one with human sensibilities could eat a meal in a restaurant when the streets were filled with starving men and women
and children. A waiter in the Stadt-Park restaurant turned the
tablecloth, hopefully, on the other side as we seated ourselves.

He stepped back to survey its soiled surface, shook his head dolefully and changed it back to its original side. Yet it was in that Vienna of 1922 that I saw Onkelchen Hat Getraumpt under Reinhardt's direction at the Josefstadt Theater with the Thimmigs playing in it. It was one of the most superb performances I've ever seen in the theater in any country. I cabled American managers in all directions and next night, taking John Emerson and Anita Loos in tow, went again to see it. And then they, though they understood not a word of German, began in turn to cable American producers. No one, so far as I know, has ever done the play in this country. Perhaps it was the production and the performance that so dazzled us.

Europe, an entire continent, was doomed. It was plain. One could read it in the faces of the people. This I shouted at the top of my voice when I returned to my country. I was the bore of that entire winter. . . . Well, what if Europe is sick! It's none of our affair. Let 'm get well. . . . But listen, you don't understand. If they're sick we'll be, too. We're living on the same planet. You might as well say of your body that you have a cancer in one arm, but otherwise you're sound as can be. . . . Oh, stop croaking.

It is always, for me, a glorious feeling—that of coming down the Bay into New York Harbor. Sunlight, hard and brilliant, snorting tugs, sky line, the Old Girl with the Torch, the waiting crowd massed at the dockhead. But this time I saw these things with something like hysteria. I had spent six months on the crippled continent of Europe. Back in the United States I stared with unbelieving eyes, like an immigrant, at the fruit and vegetable stalls; at the grocers' lavish windows. Fifth Avenue in October shimmered with the thick rich enamel of powerful motorcars flowing five abreast, a torrent of wealth. Everyone in silk stockings, and no runs. I remembered the shreds that vainly tried to clothe the thin legs of Vienna, Berlin, Munich, even Paris. After an absence of half a year there was about America an incredible gaiety, lightheartedness and brilliance. Women in green, red, blue, gray, brown, beige, pink, wine. Anything but black. I thought, they are wearing black in Europe not only for their dead but thriftily and prophetically for the future so plainly before them.

The youth of America was especially gay. It was more (or less) than gaiety. It was an hysteria which was to mount and mount and mount until the bubble burst in 1929. Money. Everyone had money. Furs. Jewels. Automobiles. Radios. Palm Beach. California. Europe. No generation of American boys and girls ever had so much money and received so little in return for it. They called themselves the Lost Generation, but they really were only playing hide-and-seek with life.

And then the story of So Big that had lain so long dormant in my mind floated, released, to the surface. And I sat down to write the story of a material young man, son of his earth-grubbing idealistic mother. Hundreds of thousands of people later read it. I'm not sure that many ever knew what the story was about. But I did.

It was a queer sort of book to start at the beginning of a New York winter, in a furnished apartment overlooking Central Park. I kept at it, day after day, for a year. In New York that winter I went to parties, I went to the theater, I had fun. I had, for that matter, ten years of fun ahead of me; of work and fun and friends and health. I had thought The Girls would be a success. I never dreamed that So Big would be. I wrote it against my judgment; I wanted to write it. It was the story of a middle-aged woman living on a little truck farm just outside Chicago. Nothing ever really happened in the book. It had no plot at all, as book plots go. It had a theme, but you had to read that for yourself between the lines. It was a story of the triumph of failure. There was in it practically no action. The book's high dramatic point came when Selina drove to town with a load of cabbages, turnips and beets. If I had confided this to any publisher, editor, reviewer or reader he would have laughed in my face. But I didn't. I wrote my book because I wanted to write it more than anything else in the world. Occasionally I had a moment of happiness about it—a line, a paragraph, a page, even. I wrote and rewrote it. I knew literally nothing about farming or truck gardening. The entire background was farm. The South Water Street night market chapter was written purely out of my imagination. I meant to visit the market at midnight, or at two, three, five or six in the morning. But I never did.

I shall now make a statement which I expect no one to believe. But believable or not it's true, of me.

I can project myself into any age, environment, condition, situation, character or emotion that interests me deeply. I need never have experienced it or seen it or, to my knowledge, heard or read about it. I never have been on the Mississippi or in the deep South. I wrote Show Boat. I know nothing of farms or farming, which forms the background of So Big. I wrote Cimarron after spending exactly ten days in Oklahoma. I gave three days to the part of Connecticut which forms American Beauty. I had less than a week up in the Michigan lumber country about which Come and Get It centers. People have liked or disliked these books; quarreled with their themes, resented their characters, rebelled against their endings, disputed their meanings. But only once have I had a criticism of their veracity and soundness of background. A book reviewer on the New York Herald Tribune worked herself up into a fury against Cimarron for some obscure reason, probably psychological (frustration at not having written it herself), and announced, among other things, that of course anyone knew that cowboys never wore their neckerchiefs loose-hung in the front and knotted in the back. I had made rather a point of this. If she's right then Frederick Remington and all the cowboys I've seen in Colorado and Wyoming and Arizona have just been living in a fool's paradise.

The title So Big had been only a tentative working one. It helps to have a title of some sort during the process of writing. While the title exactly expressed the book's theme it seemed in itself to be pretty stomach-turning and I didn't for a moment mean to keep it. When the novel was serialized by Gertrude Lane in the Woman's Home Companion she so fully agreed with me about the impossibility of that title as to discard it entirely. In the magazine the novel was titled Selina. But when the book was finished I had found no title more fitting than So Big. I still didn't like it, but it had stuck somehow. I now think that those two short words, their familiar ring, and all the fat round curves in the S, the O, the B and the G helped to make the book a selling success.

Through the autumn, winter, summer and into the autumn again I wrote and rewrote So Big. It was to be serialized before book publication, and I wanted the book published in the late spring of 1924. The summer of 1923 found me back in Chicago. That winter I had had a large bright comfortable furnished apartment at Fifty Central Park West, overlooking Central Park. I had been happier there than ever before in New York. It had been wonderful to be able to run out into the Park before settling down to work. Sometimes a squirrel's tiny tracks in the early-morning snow were the only footprints to dispute my claim to being the first. It was balm to my small-town spirit to see spring tiptoeing over the treetops just beneath my windows and into the green-walled living room itself. I'd have stayed there, I think, through the summer if the people who owned it hadn't returned. To change environment in the midst of writing a novel is too upsetting.

With my mother I took an apartment at the Windermere Hotel on Chicago's South Side, across from Jackson Park and a block from the lake; spread out my typed sheets, pulled my type-writer toward me and settled down to work just where I'd left off in New York the day before. I knew exactly where I was going though I was having a terrible time getting there. The last page of So Big had been written before the first page was started. This same thing, later, was true of Show Boat and Cimarron. It usually is true of any first-rate piece of work which I do. If that last page writes itself before the story is well begun then the story itself will have inevitability. It may waver in the middle, it may be weaker halfway than at either end. But if the beginning is here and the end inevitably there, then the march between must at least have the soundness and convincing firmness of any traveling thing which knows its destination.

What a summer that was in Chicago! For sheer devastating steaming heat I've never seen its equal. The thermometer hit ninety-six and hung there for days. The Illinois Central suburban trains had not then been electrified. The curved front of the hotel made a sounding board that recorded and exaggerated every toot, rumble, roar and clatter. My being there at all was absurd, but I had followed the writer's instinct to seek out a familiar place in which to give birth to a novel. The lake front, the tree-shaded park with its lagoons, the vast distances of the great sprawling city, the few people I knew there, all were conducive to work. I need make no fresh effort, I need feel no shock of fresh contact. The cocoon of work-walk-read-sleep was woven tightly about me. I did not want to stir from it.

I worked in a single garment, a plain silk jersey step-in, for clothing was unthinkable in that humid heat. I was what Mr. Mantalini called a demd moist unpleasant body. Nine to four, nine to four. A walk. Home, dripping. A bath.

I am told that there are people who try to write best sellers as a matter of business. They write them, I am told, deliberately and mathematically, using a formula as a cook uses a recipe. I don't know how they do it. I don't want to know. I suppose they have some peculiar thermometer or mechanism by which they gauge that fickle phenomenon known as the Public Pulse. But occasionally someone comes along who commits a best seller in all innocence. Of such was I.

Not only did I not plan to write a best seller when I wrote So Big but I thought, when I had finished it, that I had written the world's worst seller. Not that alone, I thought I had written a complete Non-Seller. I didn't think anyone would read it. And that's the literal truth.

I had worked on it, day after day, for months and months. I knew where I was going and why I wanted to get there, but after a time I became like a patient plodder who must travel weary miles along a lonely road before he arrives at the city of his destination. Mile after mile I covered the distance, sometimes traveling swiftly, sometimes scarcely able to lift one tired foot after the other.

As the work of final correction began and progressed I doled out sheaves of copy to a typist. She would call for the typed pages and take them home with her, returning with four fresh copies so that I might have enough for editor, illustrator, publisher and myself. Always she appeared at about four in the afternoon when I had finished for the day and when I was at my limpest, dampest and lowest. I remember her as a nice fresh-looking red-haired girl in a cool crisp orchid organdie. She was the only other person who had read a word of the story. No other soul except myself had seen so much as a line. Each time she called I waited eagerly, hopefully, for some comment. I wanted her to say she liked Selina; I wanted her to say she didn't care for Dirk, I wanted her to say she thought the story should end this way or that way. I wanted her to betray some interest in the novel; to show some liking for it, or even to show dislike. She never did.

"Well," said I to my dispirited self, "that settles it, Miss F. I told you so! Don't say I didn't warn you. Who—I ask you—WHO would be interested in a novel about a middle-aged woman in a calico dress, and with wispy hair and bad teeth, grubbing on a little truck farm south of Chicago? Nobody! Who cares about cabbages? Nobody! Who would read such a thing if it came out as a novel? A dull plodding book written because you were interested; because you had carried the thought of it around in your head for five years. Who cares? It might go well enough as a serial. Besides, that's contracted for. But as a book? Never!"

I wrote to Mr. Russell Doubleday of my publishing firm, and this is a copy of the letter:

DEAR RUSSELL DOUBLEDAY:

I have promised to send you the manuscript of So Big, and here it is. I feel very strongly that I should not publish it as a novel. It will, as you know, appear serially in the Woman's Home Companion. I think its publication as a book would hurt you, as publishers, and me as an author. No one would read it. It is the story of a middle-aged woman in a Chicago truck garden. Nothing happens. The high spot is where she drives in to Chicago with a load of vegetables. I wish you'd discuss the thing with the other members of the firm. If you decide that it will be better not to publish I shall be entirely satisfied.

Russell Doubleday answered immediately. I might be right, he said, but perhaps I should let someone besides myself have a

About 1923. So Big *Was Being Written.*

chance to judge it. He suggested that perhaps I had been too close to it too long.

He read it. He wrote me again. He had wept as he read it. The entire staff had read it. The entire staff had wept. I pictured the offices, damp with tears, the water mounting, mounting, like a scene out of Alice in Wonderland. Not only, he said, did they want to publish it, but they would be proud to publish it.

Well, nobody could ask fairer than that. Maybe I had been wrong.

There was on the Doubleday staff a chap named Dan Longwell. I knew him as a shy quiet-spoken young fellow who seemed to have an unusual understanding of books and writing and writers. Unlike most publishers and publishers' young men, he knew books not only as merchandise but as a form of creative art. He was sympathetic, intuitive and shrewd—a rare combination. He mapped out a campaign for the selling of So Big. Like most of the firm, he believed in the book, but everyone thought his faith in it went much too far. He actually made a substantial bet that the book would sell fifty thousand copies.

So Big was published in the spring of 1924. The reviews were mixed; good and pretty good. It began to sell rather surprisingly well. Burton Rascoe, at that time book editor of, I think, the New York Tribune, came to interview me. His interview said that while So Big certainly was meeting with an exceptional sale, considering its content, he was willing to go on record as saying that one year from that day the novel would be as dead and forgotten as the interview he was writing about it.

That June I went to Europe. The first day out and every day of the voyage thereafter the decks, port and starboard, showed an unbroken line of orange color which was the blazing dust jacket of So Big. I knew then that I had, astonishingly enough, a best seller on my hands.

So Big sold three hundred and twenty-three thousand copies. This was before the day of the book clubs and the book guilds, to whose members books are sold at reduced prices. Automatically this skyrockets a book's sale figures. The figures on So Big, Show Boat, Cimarron, etc., represent actual retail bookstore sales.

Today, fourteen years after publication, it still sells a comfortable amount yearly and it is required reading in the literature and English courses of most of the American public schools and colleges. I hope (but not too fervently) that the same may be said of Mr. Rascoe's interview. Two motion pictures—a silent one and a talkie—were made of the novel. Both seemed to me very bad indeed. It received the Pulitzer Prize for the American novel of 1924. It was published in Germany, England, Holland, Finland, Sweden, Norway, Hungary, Poland, Russia, Denmark.

Back in New York I knew that I couldn't live in hotels any longer. I wanted my own things about me—though I possessed exactly none. The building at Fifty Central Park West in which I had lived so happily in a furnished apartment the preceding winter now had a similar apartment vacant on the eighth floor, with eight huge windows facing the green of Central Park. I signed a five-year lease, planted my typewriter in one corner of the living room, turned my back to the view and began to work again from nine to three. At three I closed up shop for the day and bought furniture. As a start I bought a thick-pile carpet, a Steinway grand piano and an enchanting set of living-room curtains made to order of French glazed chintz in lemon yellow, patterned in delicate birds and flowers and finished off with the most exhilarating pleated ruffles of flame taffeta with enormous pinwheel tiebacks. Oh, but it was wonderful to be rid of the imitation mahogany and plush of hotel rooms. I bought everything, and bought it all myself and paid for it as I bought it, like an Appleton farm woman. Linen, silver, beds, china, curtains, kitchenware. The living-room walls were a soft Adam green. Even without furniture—I had got the carpet down and the ravishing curtains up and the piano in place before I had bought so much as a chair—the room was glowing and livable. I felt settled and at peace for the first time in fifteen years. No bellboys, no bogus palms, no uniforms, no hotel clerks, no printed menus. The green of the Park seemed to come into the room. There was a fireplace at one end, and it worked. I could go into the kitchen and bake a cake. I had my own mattress, unhaunted by the ghosts of unknown sleepers, my own pillows, linen; coffee brewed for me as I like it quickly in the morning, hot and strong after bathing and dressing. My own friends in my own home.

Short stories again; Consider the Lilies; Our Very Best People; Classified; Holiday; Mother Knows Best. In the volume of short stories entitled Cheerful—By Request, published by Doubleday in 1918, there had been included a short story called The Eldest which originally had appeared in McClure's Magazine. Now, years later, I picked up a copy of the New York Times to see the announcement of a one-act play called The Eldest to be given the following week at the Provincetown Theater, which wasn't in Provincetown at all, but in downtown New York, around Eighth, near Greenwich Village. I called James Light, the director, and asked him to tell me something of the story of the one-act play called The Eldest. It was my story. Quite innocently he had accepted it as an original play which had been submitted to him by a young lady who posed as a promising playwright. Regretful as I was at causing the company any inconvenience I couldn't allow this to go on. I refused in a fury to read her play and dashed off my own dramatic version of the story which the Provincetown Players put into rehearsal at once and produced the following week. I was rather surprised to find myself again in the theater, even so briefly, and wistfully pleased, too. At this dramatically pat moment (Ah, here comes the Duke now!) I had a letter from George Kaufman whom I knew slightly. He had a number of successful plays to his credit, written, for the most part, in collaboration with Marc Connelly. He had read my short story Old Man Minick. He thought there was a play in it. Would I care to collaborate with him in writing it?

I didn't think there was a play in Minick, and I don't to this day, though the play was successfully produced and played in New York and Chicago. But if George had approached me with the idea of dramatizing McGuffey's First Reader I'd have been enchanted to talk about it. We met in the apartment up in 86th Street in which he and his wife Beatrice were living. George was still dramatic editor of the New York Times, a job he clung to long after he became spectacularly successful. That meeting between George, Beatrice and me has been followed by fourteen years of friendship full of ups and downs, with the ups definitely predominating. We've quarreled once—the three of us—in all that time, and that once we all were in the wrong, share and share alike.

"Minick's a play," George said now.

"No. I don't think audiences would be interested in a play about an old man who comes to live with his son and daughter-in-law. But The Gay Old Dog—there's a story that would make a marvelous play."

Old Man Minick won. And I still think George was wrong and I was right. Old Man Minick is a really good short story—one of the best of the dozen or so first-rate short stories I've done. Into its five or six thousand words I compressed the lives of three people. Its theme is touching and universally recognizable. But it seemed to me to lack the dramatic importance necessary to proper play construction.

Once started, though, the play went quickly—too quickly. George was, as usual, busy with a second play which was scheduled for the autumn. This was a musical called Strike Up the Band. The last act of Minick was written in three or four days in the secluded discomfort of a pretty bad American-plan hotel in White Plains to which we had fled to escape the telephone and New York in general.

Before we began to write George had outlined our play plan to Winthrop Ames, the producer and manager de luxe. I had never met Mr. Ames. George knew him well through the fact that he had produced Beggar on Horseback, the touching and beautiful fantasy adapted from the German by George Kaufman and Marc Connelly. If Minick had brought me nothing more than the friendship of Winthrop Ames I'd have been overpaid for any work, time, energy or creative effort spent on it.

No one could have been more completely unlike the accepted type of theatrical producer than Winthrop Ames. A figure of elegance; tall, slim; the long sensitive hands of an artist, the fine dolichocephalic head of creative intelligence. Boston-born and -bred, descendant of the first Massachusetts settlers, all of whom seemed to become governors on attaining their majority; it is difficult to describe him without using the words culture, wit, whimsy, taste, all of which are trite and none of which is good enough for him. Stage-struck. Perhaps that will have to do. Winthrop Ames, the millionaire, charming, highly intelligent, was hopelessly stage-struck. He cared as deeply about the theater as George Kaufman and I did. Nobody could be more love-bemused than that. The Massachusetts Ameses had made their millions in the manufacture of hand-turned tools. His bluenosed governor ancestors must have turned purple in their tombs to behold Winthrop pouring a goodly portion of the Ames millions into the vast ravenous maw of the theater. Or perhaps they weren't bluenoses after all, but free spirits who had fled England because they thought that Shakespeare was more important than either Cromwell or Charles. The amazing thing about Winthrop Ames was that in some inexplicable way he had shed all the absurdity and stuffiness of his Boston background, and so too had that deceptively wrenlike little woman, Lucy Ames, his wife. In their romantic and rather spectacular marriage they had defied all the laws of their social group. He had retained his fine standards and his beautiful manners and innate charm; and shed all the bunk. There was nothing of the parlor socialist about him. He made none of the sweater-and-soapbox gestures of the present-day rich boy rebelling against his heritage. He didn't speak of The Worker, a sickening phrase. He had inherited lots of money, and he gave beauty, vitality, enthusiasm and money to the theater. I wish there were a thousand like him and like Lucy Ames.

He had been one of the founders of the Century Theater, that circus-sized playhouse in Central Park West, planned with such high hopes, so magnificently conceived, so lavishly fostered, and so inevitably destined for failure.

In reaction Ames had built the Little Theater in West 44th Street, New York's smallest playhouse. He had offices at the top of this building to which you ascended in an elevator reached through an alley door. The offices were ordinary enough, and businesslike, fronting on 44th Street. But behind them, and known only to Winthrop's friends and theater associates, was a cozy apartment made up of living room, bedroom, kitchen, bathroom. It was here that play plots were discussed, productions planned, post-mortems held. The sitting room was hung with terrific tapestries left over from some gigantic Century flop. Hanging in somber folds they gave the room its name of The Materializing Cabinet. There always was a man in a white house-coat, and drinks and sandwiches and good conversation, but when it came to producing there was nothing of the dilettante about Winthrop. He knew his theater. No one in America has remotely approached his Gilbert and Sullivan productions. It was he who brought Ruth Gordon, June Walker, Winifred Lenihan, Katharine Cornell to stage success.

When Minick was finished George and I made an evening engagement with Winthrop for the reading of the script. George was to read it aloud. He's very good at this. Certainly he made Minick sound much better than it was. At any rate, Winthrop Ames liked it, the play was tentatively cast and rehearsals were scheduled for the following August. I was enormously exhila-rated at the prospect of an autumn spent in the theater. Off I scampered to Europe, from which I emerged in August, bright-eyed after three weeks spent walking in the pine woods, drinking the fearsome-tasting waters and being belabored in the massage rooms of Carlsbad. Also I stepped off the boat smug in the possession of a Reboux hat and a Premet gown. George, haggard from a New York summer spent wrestling with Strike Up the Band, met me at the dock and together we drove to the Booth Theater to see the set for Minick. I recall being especially pleased because the steampipes showed up the side of the wall in the sitting room (which was the set) from floor to ceiling, just as they would appear in an actual Chicago small cheap apartment of that day. I know now that realistic steampipes don't make a play.

That cast of Minick was good, but not quite good enough. I like to think, at least, that we would have had a more genuinely touching and dimensional play if the lead had been ideally cast. Old Man Minick was valiantly played by that excellent actor, O. P. Heggie. But Minick was an old man hailing from a little down-state Illinois town, bewildered, out of place, unwelcome in the little flat of his Chicago son and daughter-in-law. O. P. Heggie was English or Canadian, he spoke with an English accent, he was a man of about forty playing a gaffer of seventy. The cast, by the way, called for a colored maid, and we thought ourselves rather daring to use a Harlem actress rather than a white girl in blackface. White and colored actors did not then ordinarily mingle. The stage has grown in that direction, at least.

Rehearsals at the Booth were pleasant and even gay. Winthrop Ames carried things off with a generous hand. Every day at one o'clock the Ames chauffeur and the Ames butler appeared with white-covered baskets of sandwiches, salads, fruit and hot coffee. The entire company was invited to lunch off this or not, as they pleased. This, I hastily add, is so far from usual in the theater that anyone not having known Mr. Ames is likely to dispute it.

Mr. Ames conducted rehearsals for the most part. George rarely was present, being off on the road with Strike Up the Band, which was in trouble. There was rewriting to be done, and daily there came up those baffling problems which confront any play in rehearsal. As I look back on it now I'm afraid I wasn't the ideal author in these matters, for though I'd had some stage experience with our Mrs. McChesney and with the unfortunate $1200 a Year, I wasn't yet wise enough in the ways of the practical theater to be of any great help. Still I did the best I could and certainly Winthrop was never anything but gay, friendly, patient and painstaking. The whole atmosphere of rehearsals was completely different from that which had poisoned the air when Augustus Thomas and Alf Hayman had held forth during the McChesney play. And certainly, in that month, I learned a lot about the theater.

We tried out in New Haven, in Hartford and (strangely enough) in New London—strange because this was rarely used as a tryout town. We were to learn why. George was still absent with Strike Up the Band. New Haven and Hartford were not very good. New London was awful.

The theater there is, I believe, a Shubert house, or was; and evidently it hadn't been opened since the days of Edwin Booth.

On the opening night the house was half filled. I skulked in a second box, which proved an unfortunate choice. My idea was to see without being seen. I doubt, however, that the audience was sweeping the house with its opera glasses hoping for a glimpse of the winsome authoress. When the lights went up it was discovered that the gallery, dome and chandeliers had been a rendezvous for bats for years and that bats are prolific and long-lived. With the opening scene they began to dip, swoop, circle and dive all about the auditorium and on the stage itself. Women in the audience covered their heads with programs, with hand-kerchiefs, with scarves. Many of them fled. That the company went on with the performance and actually finished it was nothing short of heroic.

The post-mortem that night was held, as usual, in Mr. Ames' hotel sitting room. We were a dispirited crew, after the laughing hysterics of the bat invasion. We lolled about, our faces sagging. Even the rosy-cheeked high-spirited Phyllis Povah (whose name, I always thought, sounded vaguely like a Jewish religious holi-day), who was playing the woman lead, seemed wan and hag-gard. The highballs and sandwiches of after-work hours were ashes and hemlock brew in our mouths.

"Never mind, boys and girls!" Winthrop said. "Next time I'll tell you what we'll do. We won't bother with tryouts. We'll all charter a show boat and we'll just drift down the rivers, playing the towns as we come to them, and we'll never get off the boat. It'll be wonderful!"

"What's a show boat?" I asked, sourly. I'd never heard of them.

Winthrop explained. "A show boat's a floating theater. They used to play up and down the Southern rivers, especially the Mississippi and the Missouri. They'd come downstream, calliope tooting, and stop at the town landing to give their show. The actors lived and slept and ate and worked right there on the boat. The country people for miles around would hear the calliope screeching and they'd know the show-boat folks were in town."

I had been slumped, a disconsolate heap, on a cushion on the floor. Now I sat up and up and up like a cobra uncoiling. I forgot

[288]

all about New London and Minick and bats. Here was news of a romantic and dramatic aspect of America of which I'd never heard or dreamed. "How long has this been going on?"

"Oh, years," Winthrop said. "In the '60s and '70s and '80s. But I don't think they play the rivers any more. At least you never hear of them nowadays."

Minick opened at the Booth Theater September 24th and received a mildly approving press, except for the New York Times review in which Woollcott loosed vials of vitriol out of all proportion to the gentle little play's importance.

At any other time I might have been sunk in depression, but now Minick ceased to exist for me except when a neat little check appeared once a week. My soul didn't quite soar so high as to ignore that. But no sooner had the play opened than I was hot on the trail of show boats. Here, I thought, was one of the most melodramatic and gorgeous bits of Americana that had ever come my way. It was not only the theater—it was the theater plus the glamour of the wandering drifting life, the drama of the river towns, the mystery and terror of the Mississippi itself. At the very thought of the Mississippi there welled up in me from some hidden treasure-trove in my memory or imagination a torrent of visualized pictures, people, incidents. I don't to this day know where that river knowledge came from. Perhaps, centuries and centuries ago, I was a little Jewish slave girl on the Nile.

I didn't spend the time dreaming river dreams. I spent a year hunting down every available scrap of show-boat material; reading, interviewing, taking notes and making outlines. I had discovered that a few show boats were actually still playing the Southern river towns—the Mississippi, the Missouri, the rivers of North Carolina and Ohio and the Louisiana bayous. I was as excited and happy as if I had come upon a diamond mine. Early in my chase I heard of a show boat that was headed for a little village in North Carolina. The James Adams Floating Palace Theater, it was called. It was now October and the show-boat season was closing, but I, in my ignorance, didn't know this. I dashed down to Carolina, arrived at a town called Washington and engaged a colored boy with a Ford to drive me the thirty miles out to the little landing where the show boat lay. I learned then that these floating theaters almost always play the towns that are remote from the railroads. Certain glittering and gorgeous memories may slip from my mind as the years go by, but I'll never forget that Ford. Its original structure probably derived from the well-known brand after which it was named. But its owner had, perforce, supplemented it with bits and pieces of old metal, wire, canvas and wood, held together, seemingly, by chewing gum, spit and faith. Every bolt, joint, hinge and curtain shook, rattled, squeaked and flapped. I, in the back seat, was busy trying to hold the thing together. As a door swung spectrally open and I sprang to shut it a curtain would strain and threaten to tear loose from the cotton thread that held it to the body of the car.

By some miracle that worked in defiance of the laws of nature we drew up at the river's edge. In my feverish haste to reach the boat I hadn't notified the owners of my coming. Perhaps, to be truthful, that had not been the real reason for my remissness. I knew nothing of them. They might resent me. They might even refuse to see me. I was prepared for anything, but in spite of what might happen I was going to use every possible means to get what I'd come after. I remembered my old Appleton Crescent and Milwaukee Journal days of get-your-story-no-matter-how.

There was a great deal of activity about the boat as we drew up alongside. The gangplank was still down but there was every indication that it wouldn't be there long. A little tugboat was fussing in the offing. People were coming and going with the haste that denoted departure. I crossed the gangplank, stepped on the deck of the long flat-bottomed ship with its upper and lower decks more like verandas than any ship decks I'd ever seen. There on the lower deck near the gangplank stood a tall thin young man in eyeglasses.

I thought he might do as a starter. "I'd like to speak to someone who is in charge of this boat," I said lamely.

He made a little bow. "Well, I am, sort of."

"My name is Edna Ferber. I'm a writer. I am trying to write about show boats. I've come all the way from New York to talk to the owner of this one."

"Well, my God!" said the tall young man, and put out his hand to meet mine. "Emma McChesney!" He raised his gentle tones to a shout: "Beulah! Beulah! Emma McChesney's here."

I found I didn't need my old newspaper tricks and wiles, after all.

Charles Hunter and his wife Beulah Adams hadn't only read the McChesney stories; they'd read So Big and Fanny Herself and Dawn O'Hara and all the short stories and they'd even swiped a good deal of the McChesney play for use on the show boat, God bless them, and welcome. Charles Hunter was the leading man. Beulah Adams was the sister of the James Adams who owned the show boat. And I've never known two more understanding, sympathetic and heart-warming souls in all my life. Beulah was known as the Mary Pickford of the rivers. I was made welcome, but the boat was even then leaving; and not only leaving, but putting up for the winter. The season was ended. I had come, if not too late altogether, then just early enough by half an hour. There was nothing to do but leave for New York with a warm invitation to join the boat the following April at their very first stop, which was Bath, North Carolina. Back in New York I spent the winter doing an occasional short story and boning up on show boats. I discovered some people who had actually played on show boats. One of these turned out to be the actor Wallace Ford. Another was an editor on the Billboard. Curiously enough there was almost no literature of any kind—fiction, articles or reminiscences—on the show boats themselves. David Graham Phillips, in his novel Susan Lenox: Her Fall and Rise, briefly mentioned a show boat, but it played a small part in the story. It was unbelievable that this rich and colorful aspect of American life had been almost completely overlooked. I could find no mention of similar theatrical craft to be found in European countries.

I waited for April. It was a gay enough New York that winter of 1925. The people I played about with were, for the most part, as hard-working as myself. In that year, and for ten years to come, I had the most hilarious, gay, rowdy charming laughing time. They were a hard-boiled crew; brilliant, wise, witty, generous and debunked. With them I went to parties and to the theater, walked, played in the country. Many of them were just getting a firm footing on the spectacular success which was to become established in the ten or twelve years that followed. About their own work hours they were hard as nails. But when work was finished they had more fun than any other group I've ever seen. They played like children. But their talk was fresh, original and stimulating.

A number of them used often to gather for lunch at the Algonquin Hotel in West 44th Street. For a quarter of a century it has been (thanks to Frank Case, its owner) not only a hotel, but to hundreds of writers and actors, a free clubhouse, a refuge, a bank (for taking out, not putting in, as Lew Fields used to say), a New York pied-à-terre, a forum, a rendezvous. There always was reserved for a certain group a table called the Round Table. There, almost daily, you saw Robert Sherwood, Marc Connelly, George Kaufman, Brock Pemberton, Alexander Woollcott, Heywood Broun, Harold Ross, or any combination of fifty others. No one outside the mythical order was permitted to sit at the Round Table without invitation. The talk actually was witty, frequently biting and brutal, sometimes merry with a refreshing spontaneity that I do not remember encountering anywhere else in the world. Small wonder. Out of that group emerged some of the most brilliant and successful playwrights, novelists and actors in America.

As lunching out was something of an event for me (I made it perhaps three or four times in an entire year) I rarely had the fun of a Round Table luncheon session. Outsiders took a kind of resentful dislike to the group. They called them the Algonquin crowd. I was astonished to find myself included in this designation. The contention was that this gifted group engaged in log-rolling; that they gave one another good notices, praise-filled reviews and the like. I can't imagine how any belief so erroneous ever was born. Far from boosting one another they actually were merciless if they disapproved. I never have encountered a more hard-bitten crew. But if they liked what you had done they did say so, publicly and wholeheartedly. Their standards were high, their vocabulary fluent, fresh, astringent and very, very tough. Theirs was a tonic influence, one on the other, and all on the world of American letters. The people they could not and would not stand were the bores, hypocrites, sentimentalists and the socially pretentious. They were ruthless toward charlatans, toward the pompous and the mentally and artistically dishonest. Casual, incisive, they had a terrible integrity about their work and a boundless ambition.

Woollcott, Harold Ross, later editor of the New Yorker, and Jane Grant, then his wife, had taken an oldish house in West 47th Street and in this, together with two or three other friends, they lived community fashion. The house was reconstructed so that each had his own apartment. There was a garden at the back. Meals were served in the common dining room. The house itself was situated in what was practically a slum, but certainly the cream of New York drew up at that door. That house in 47th; the Swopes' apartment in West 58th or their big rambling Victorian house at Great Neck, Long Island; and Neysa McMein's studio in the ramshackle old red brick studio building at the corner of Sixth Avenue and West 57th Street were the gathering places for the clan. It was a big, floating, kaleidoscopic group—too large, probably, to be called a group. We were, loosely defined, just a hard-working lot of men and women who took our work seriously, but not ourselves. Neysa I had deliberately used (idealized, I may add) as Dallas O'Mara in So Big. At her untidy hospitable studio you might encounter, any day between three and six, anyone from Irving Berlin to the reigning Vanderbilt; from Father Duffy to H. G. Wells. And in the midst of the talk, and the music made by someone at the piano, and the roar of the L train on Sixth there was Neysa working calmly away at her canvas in the middle of the room, her hair wrung into a careless knot at her neck, her smock smeared with paint, her face smudged but wreathed in lovely smiles.

It was at this time that there walked into my life (via the Lincoln Industrial Exchange) that amazing and dimensional human being, Mrs. Rebecca Henry. Hailing from Maryland, she was—and is—a superb example of the Negro race. For almost fifteen years she has been a working member of my household. I think no one in my life has brought me more comfort and happiness. Anyone who has known me during these past fourteen or fifteen years has known Rebecca. A person of taste and distinction—and what a hand with chicken and lobster and banana cake and meringue and lemon chiffon pie and clear soup (simmered two days). My friends, seeing me after an absence, always say, "How are you? How's your mother, how're the Foxes, how's Rebecca?" Her people in Maryland and Washington are physicians, teachers, civil-service employees. When Rebecca says of a new hat or dress, "Oh, Miss Edna, that's good-looking!" I know it's right. A widow, she has a son, Waters Turpin, by her first marriage, whose first novel got reviews that would have made me jealous if I hadn't been so pleased, and whose second novel bids fair to rival the first. Novels of American Negro life, they are; but none of this Sambo stuff. Rebecca has taken a quiet pride in this achievement, but she never refers to it, and on the Sunday morning that brought us the New York Times' superb review of her son's book, These Low Grounds, my waffles and maple syrup were as crisp, as golden, as toothsome as though no undue excitement marked the day.

15

I<small>T</small> <small>DOESN'T SEEM POSSIBLE</small> that anyone ever had so much sheer fun, gaiety, novelty, satisfaction and money out of the writing of any one piece of work as I have had out of Show Boat. From the moment when Winthrop Ames first said Show Boat to me until this very hour it has been a source of happiness to me, like a child who has grown up to be gifted, gay, generous. Of course there were grim bits too. Lawsuits, for example, with which they pelted me as with a shower of stones.

When April came I went as eagerly as a lover to meet the show boat. I went primed with stories of Mississippi River boating; of stern-wheeler days, side-wheelers, keel boats, anything and everything I could lay my hands on. In connection with the publication of novels which have required enormous research, such as Show Boat, So Big, Cimarron, American Beauty, Come and Get It, I never have thought of listing a research bibliography. There seems to me something so pompous and disillusioningly authentic about a printed bibliography in a work of fiction. Any reader, confronted with it, might well be disconcerted to the point of giving up the whole idea of reading so laborious a book. At any rate I've made it a rule to do the dusty drudgery of my research and keep the dreary record to myself. Though I never yet have been on the Mississippi I know and feel that mighty river. I know my descriptions of the South I've never seen, of the river and its people, are sound and true. They never have been disputed. And in America, thank God, it isn't possible to make the most minute of writing errors without being inundated by a flood of remonstrance, criticism or hilarious hooting derision.

Bath, North Carolina, turned out to be a lovely decayed hamlet on the broad Pamlico River. In the days of the Colonies Bath had been the governor's seat. Elms and live oaks arched over the deserted streets. Ancient houses, built by men who knew dignity of architectural design and purity of line, were now moldering into the dust from which they had come. The one hotel or boarding house in the town was a fine old brick mansion which had been the home of the governor of the North Carolina colony in the days before 1776. Its rooms were large, gracious and beautifully proportioned. In the main room was a fireplace so huge that a room was built inside it. A message awaited me from the Hunters. The show boat had been delayed and would be a day or two late. I could expect them at the landing next day, or the day after.

My heart sank as I ascended the broken stairway behind my large and puffing landlady. In the heel of each stocking, above the open-back flat slippers, was a hole the size of a silver dollar. She opened the door of my room. In contrast with the fresh April air outside the room smelled of mice, mold and mankind. My eye leaped to the bed. Then, boldly, I crossed to it and turned down the dingy covers. My worst fears realized, I turned an accusing glare upon my landlady.

"What's the matter?" she demanded.

"The sheets."

"D'ye mean you want them changed?" she asked, with that touch of irritation one might show if a guest were to demand why her own monogram did not appear on the hotel bed linen.

"I do," I replied with dignity and finality. "It is, I believe, customary."

Grudgingly she began to strip the bed under my stern eye. She muttered as she worked. "Only been slept in by my own daughter, and she only used 'em once. She teaches school and comes home, sometimes. Saturdays. Only slept in 'em last Saturday night, fresh."

"Nevertheless——" I said, firmly.

That night I slept practically suspended in midair, defying the law of gravity, a good deal like the spangled lady who used to be put to sleep in Brettschneider's Furniture Store window, stiff between two chair backs and under the fell influence of her magician husband who was giving a show in Appleton that week. Little icy-footed mice skipped back and forth and chattered vixenishly in the wainscotings. I was up, haggard, to greet the April dawn. Breakfast was a grisly meal. A slab of indefinable blue meat floated in a platter of greenish grease. The black liquid mud in my cup was flanked by a tin can labeled Klim. My dulled senses finally conveyed to me the realization that this word was really milk spelled backwards. Leaving this lethal collation virgin as it had been set before me I wandered off to the little crossroads store a quarter of a mile distant that I had noted on my arrival. The musty little shop, as its doorbell dingled, assailed your nostrils with the mingled odors of kerosene, mice, broomstraw, tobacco juice and dampness. But I bought a slab of milk chocolate, well covered, a box of dampish crackers and a bag of last winter's apples. I surveyed the cheese and decided quickly against it. Fortified with this provender I made out very well for that day and part of the next.

And next morning the James Adams Floating Palace Theater came floating majestically down the Pamlico and tied up alongside the rickety dock. There began, for me, four of the most enchanting days I've ever known.

There, on the lower deck near the ticket window, stood Charles Hunter, his eyeglasses glittering, his kind face beaming, and there stood Beulah Adams Hunter, the Mary Pickford of the rivers, with her fresh gingham dress and her tight little curls and her good and guileless face, for all the world like a little girl in a clean pinafore. Show folks. My heart leaped toward them; like Tiny Tim I loved them every one, from Jo, the colored cook, to the pilot of the tugboat.

Those four days comprised the only show-boat experience I
ever had. In those days I lived, played, worked, rehearsed, ate
with the company. I sold tickets at the little box-office window,
I watched the Carolina countryside straggle in, white and colored.
I learned what Winthrop Ames had meant, and why, in that
dreary hour after the New London performance of Minick, he
had brought the show boat forth as a vague nostalgic memory.

Charles and Beulah Hunter gave me their own bedroom and
found quarters elsewhere for themselves. I didn't know this at
the time or I'd have made a protest—but perhaps not a very
wholehearted protest. It was such a dear room. Maybe I only
pretended not to know it was really theirs. A large square bright
room, with four windows looking out upon the placid river and
the green shores. Crisp dimity curtains flirted their pert ruffles.
There was a big square wooden bed, a washbowl and pitcher, a
low rocking chair, a little shining black iron wood stove. If wishing were transportation I'd be back there now.

The playing company numbered ten, including the Hunters.
Charles Hunter and Beulah were, of course, the star leads. Then
there was an ingénue and a juvenile lead. In show-boat terms
the juvenile lead was known as a raver and his acting method was
called spitting scenery. There was a character team, and a general
business team, a heavy and a general utility man. Then there
were, of course, certain members of the tugboat crew who played
in the band. It was the feminine half of the general business team
(a middle-aged married couple) who gave me the story of the
snuffing at childbirth which I used in Show Boat to describe
Magnolia's labor when Kim was born at floodtime on the river.
It was this actress's lot to play haughty dowagers, old Kentucky
crones, widows, mothers and such rather withered females. Her
husband (bronchial, and the rivers didn't help by any means)
did bankers, Scrooges, old hunters and trappers, elderly comics
and the like. It seemed to me a lovely life as we floated down the
river. Sometimes, the Hunters said, they played a new town every
night; sometimes, if the countryside was a populous one and the
crops good, they stayed a week.

I was delighted with the dining-room entrance which turned

out to be the little door under the orchestra pit. In my Ottumwa
and Appleton days I had seen numberless orchestra players
crouch through this little half-hidden opening and disappear into
the world of enchantment backstage. And now I was doing it
three times a day, delightedly. The dining room was just beneath
the stage. The food on the James Adams Floating Palace Theater
was abundant, well cooked, clean. The female members of the
troupe came to breakfast in kid curlers, wave combs, boudoir
caps and spectacles, disillusioning but sensible. We all sat at one
long table. The Negro cook and waiter, man and wife, placed the
food, sizzling hot, on the table all at once. Hot biscuits in the
morning, platters of ham and eggs, coffee, jam, pancakes. If you
were punctual you got the best and got it hot. Late, you took it as
it was, hot or cold. There was no mollycoddling.

The low dining-room ceiling formed the floor of the stage
above. Leading off this, at the rear, were the dressing rooms
which, after the show, formed the sleeping rooms of the troupe,
as well—except the Hunters' room which I now was snugly
occupying. Out front was the auditorium; and above this the
balcony for the colored people of the South. There, at the entrance, was the little box office. Outside, the deck and the gangplank up which the audience streamed. New York was another
planet.

They rehearsed in the daytime, they played at night. That first
night's performance was a bastard resulting from the combination of East Is West and The Shanghai Gesture, pleasingly mated
by Hunter. I sold tickets at the box office; I watched rehearsals
and performances; I played a walk-on; I chatted with the audience. Sometimes, after the show, they pulled anchor and went
down river that night; sometimes they waited until early morning. I slept in the cool airy bedroom, lulled by the purr of the
water against the boat. There was a feud between show-boat
troupe and tugboat crew. The actors kept the tugboat crew awake
at night with their music, their talk and laughter in the relaxed
hour following the performance; the tug crew with their early
daylight activity disturbed the actors' morning sleep. After the

show there was always a bit of supper to be prepared, each couple busy with their own saucepan or skillet over the spirit lamp; an egg, a bottle of milk; a cheese sandwich and a glass of beer. The heavy had a weak chest and his wife would heat liniment to be rubbed in and covered with a square of flannel. It was the Vincent Crummleses afloat.

The women made their own costumes. Beulah Adams' Chinese costume (Chu-Chu San, or approximately that) was cotton-back white satin, ordered by the yard from Sears, Roebuck, with silver braid complete and further enhanced with a sprinkling of diamants. It wasn't, perhaps, strictly Chinese, but the North Carolina audiences were enraptured.

The audiences were remote in type from anything that Chicago or New York had ever heard about. Their ancestors lay now in the little North Carolina churchyards, with beautiful English names engraved dimly on the tombstones and the vaults inside the crumbling churches. I had wandered through the churchyard at Bath. The old, old inscriptions were in Early English script with the letter s done with the flourish of the letter f. All the hardships and tears and hopes and fears of the struggling American Colonies could be pieced together from the reading of those weather-worn annals. It was here that I got the idea for the dashing Gaylord Ravenal's background.

Many of these towns were twenty, thirty, thirty-five miles from a railroad. As I watched the audiences I saw, in the dim-lighted auditorium, faces that might have stepped out of a portrait two hundred years old. I tried, in Show Boat, to describe these audiences. I am going to repeat that bit of description here.

Now the band struck up. The kerosene lamps on the walls were turned low. The scuffling, shuffling coughing audience became quiet, quiet. There was in that stillness something of fright. Seamed faces. Furrowed faces. Drab. Bitter. Sodden. Childlike. Weary. Sometimes, startlingly clear-cut in that half-light, could be glimpsed a profile of some gaunt Southern laborer or backwoodsman; and it was the profile of a portrait seen in some gallery or in the illustration of a book of history. A nose high-bred, aquiline; a sensitive haughty mouth; eyes deep-set, arrogant. Spanish, French, English? The blood of a

Stuart, a Plantagenet? Some royal rogue or adventurer of many many years ago whose seed, perhaps, this was.

The curtain rose. The music ceased, jerkily, in mid-bar. They became little children listening to a fairy tale. A glorious world of unreality opened before their eyes. Things happened. They knew that in life things did not happen thus. But here they saw, believed, and were happy. Innocence wore golden curls. Wickedness wore black. Love triumphed, right conquered, virtue was rewarded, evil punished.

They forgot the cotton fields, the wheatfields, the cornfields. They forgot the coal mines, the potato patch, the stables, the barn, the shed. They forgot the labor under the pitiless blaze of the noonday sun; the bitter marrow-numbing chill of winter; the blistered skin; the frozen road; wind, snow, rain, flood. The women forgot for an hour their washtubs, their kitchen stoves, childbirth pains, drudgery, worry, disappointment. Here were blood, lust, love, passion. Here were warmth, enchantment, laughter, music. It was Anodyne. It was Lethe. It was Escape. It was the Theater.

A dozen times a day Charles Hunter and I would arrange to settle down for that long talk in which he was to spread before me his store of river lore and show-boat experience. But there were rehearsals, for the season was just starting and the company was by no means up on all the parts. He was director as well as star. He wrote some of the plays, others he blithely adapted to his own use. The supine South lay green along the Pamlico shores. No sign of commerce marred the scene; no smoking factory chimneys; sometimes for hours no glimpse of habitation.

It was early on the morning of my fourth day that Charles Hunter and I settled down in the quiet sunny corner bedroom, he with a pack of cigarettes, I with a chunk of yellow copy paper and a pencil. He began to talk. It was a stream of pure gold. I sat with my eyes on him and my pencil racing across the paper, and wrote and wrote and wrote. Incidents, characters, absurdities, drama, tragedies, river lore, theatrical wisdom poured forth in that quiet flexible voice. He looked, really, more like a small-town college professor lecturing to a backward student than like a show-boat actor.

Sheet after sheet of yellow copy paper, crudely numbered in

[301]

the upper right-hand corner, littered the floor around my chair. Noonday came and went, it was three, it was four and time for the early dinner, but still he talked, and dinner was put off.

By the time he had finished I had a treasure-trove of show-boat material, human, touching, true. I was (and am) in his everlasting debt.

When I asked him what I could do to show my appreciation he said, "Send me a So Big with your name in it." When (perhaps not very tactfully) I accompanied this little gift with a check he pasted the check in the flyleaf of the book and wrote me: "If I ever need it I'll write and ask if it's all right to cash it. Who knows?"

Years later the James Adams Floating Palace Theater sank in mid-river, with every scrap of scenery, costumes, papers, furnishings. It was then that Charles Hunter cashed the check and I wish it had been double its size.

Early that summer I went to Europe and straight to St.-Jean-de-Luz, the little Basque seaside village in the Basses-Pyrénées. In a big bright room in the Golf Hotel, overlooking the Bay of Biscay, I began to write Show Boat. Through the open French doors leading onto the balcony I could see the blue water, the gay little floats and boats. I knew a kind of deep peace and contentment as I pulled my typewriter toward me, slumped unhealthily down on my spine, and began the first page of many months' work. The faint shouts of the bathers on the plage, the tinkling music of the little orchestra at the Casino did not disturb me. The gaufrette man cried his wares, and the fat Basque woman with the clean white apron over her vast front shrilled her, "Glaces! Vanille! Chocolat! Glaces!" There was something dreamlike, unreal, about the scene. It was right for the writing of Show Boat. No one could have dreamed that, ten years later, the cries of the vendors would be silenced by the deep-throated iron voice that boomed out just across the border and that at Hendaye, a few miles distant, you could actually see the Spanish Civil War being fought on the banks of Fuenterrabia and Irun, across the river. You had only to wade across the shallow river to be in the war itself.

For a full year the writing of Show Boat went on—in St.-Jean, in Paris, in New York. Again Gertrude Lane was publishing it serially in the Woman's Home Companion, before book publication by the Doubledays. Miss Lane's enthusiasm for the manuscript encouraged me enormously when my vitality was low after the long pull of work. Before two installments had appeared the motion-picture offers came tumbling in. I waited, however, until book publication and sold the book's motion-picture rights to the Universal Film Company.

Doubledays brought out the novel immediately following serial publication. It received superb reviews. There are writers who say they pay no attention to reviews of their books, never read them, and don't care whether they're good or bad. I am not one of these. I do read them and I do care, but I have played safe by never having subscribed to a clipping bureau. I was enormously touched and pleased by the Show Boat book reviews. I had feared that, after the tremendous book sale of So Big, this novel might come in for a bad time of it.

Here, to my surprise, was another best seller. I sometimes think that So Big, Show Boat, Cimarron and the rest were well received partly because all America was sick of the war. Myself, I wrote them, I suppose, quite unconsciously, as an escape from the war. Unless the writer went back to another day he found himself confronted with the blood and hate and horror of the years between 1914 and 1918. I had never deliberately figured this out; I seemed automatically to turn my thoughts away from this mad and meaningless hate and slaughter to a lovelier decenter day. In doing that I quite unconsciously followed the inclination of the reading world. Many writers wrote of the war years and ignored the war itself, as a tactful visitor avoids mentioning your uncle who was hanged.

So Big and Show Boat were written because I wanted terribly to write them. Until I began to write this rambling account of my writing life I never had reread them. Now, dipping here and there for a quotation line or passage, I find myself reading a page or even a chapter. And it is good to know that I need not blush for them today, twelve and fourteen years later. Show Boat has sold some three hundred and twenty thousand copies in the United States. It has been translated and published in Poland, Russia, Hungary, Czechoslovakia, Holland, Germany, France, England, Sweden, Norway, Denmark, Finland. In the twelve years since the appearance of the first installment in the magazine Show Boat has appeared as a novel, as a musical play, as a sustained radio program lasting over a period of about six years, and as three separate motion pictures with a fourth now in preparation. In that time there never has been a week when Show Boat was not being performed somewhere, in one form or another. It brought a fortune, I'm glad to say, to everyone who touched it; to Doubledays, to Florenz Ziegfeld, to Jerome Kern, to Oscar Hammerstein. For now along came Jerome Kern, the composer whose lovely nostalgic melodies are equaled by no one in America. He had to his credit an imposing list of successful musical plays, but when he suggested that I give him and Oscar Hammerstein the musical-dramatic rights in Show Boat I thought he was being fantastic. I never had met Jerome Kern, but I heard vague rumors of his feeling about the book's dramatic and musical possibilities. I rather resented the idea.

Since then I suppose I've heard the Show Boat music, and Ol' Man River especially, a thousand times. I must break down and confess to being one of those whose eyes grow dreamy and whose mouth is wreathed in wistful smiles whenever the orchestra—any orchestra—plays Ol' Man River. I've heard it played in the bar of the King David Hotel in Jerusalem, at Pré Catelan in the Paris Bois, at the Savoy in London (we writers get around). I never have tired of it. I just happen to think that when Jerome Kern wrote the Show Boat score he achieved the most beautiful and important light-opera music that has ever been written in America. And I consider Oscar Hammerstein's lyric to Ol' Man River to be powerful, native, tragic and true.

It was Alexander Woollcott who acted as schatchen in the marriage between the novel entitled Show Boat and the music of Jerome Kern. The happy union brought forth the musical play presented by Florenz Ziegfeld at the Ziegfeld Theater in 1927.

One night I went to a first night with Alexander Woollcott,

then dramatic critic on the New York Times. We saw Fred Stone in Stepping Stones at the Globe. After the first act we drifted out to the lobby and my courtly cavalier bounded off to talk with someone else, leaving me to my own devices, of which I had none. A pixie-looking little man with the most winning smile in the world and partially eclipsed by large thick spectacles now fought his way through the lobby throng toward Woollcott. He said (I later was told):

"Look, Aleck, I hear you are a friend of Edna Ferber. I wonder if you'll kind of fix it for me to meet her. I want to talk to her about letting me make a musical from her Show Boat. Can you arrange an introduction or a meeting or something?"

Mr. Woollcott, with a dreadful relish for the dramatic plum which had thus fallen into his lap (if any), said, musingly, "M-m-m, well, I think I can just arrange it if I play my cards right."

"Thanks," said Kern. "Thanks awfully, Aleck, I'll be——"

Woollcott now raised his voice to a bellow: "Ferber! Hi, Ferber! Come on over here a minute." Then, "This is Jerome Kern. Edna Ferber."

It was done. As the writing of the musical play proceeded (and its ups and downs were even more heartbreaking than those of most musical plays) I heard bits and pieces of the score. Once or twice everything was seemingly abandoned because Ziegfeld said he couldn't produce the play. Almost a year went by. I had heard Can't Help Lovin' Dat Man with its love-bemused lyric:

> *"Fish gotta swim, birds gotta fly,*
> *I gotta love one man till I die.*
> *Can't help lovin' dat man of mine."*

I had melted under the bewitching strains of Make Believe and of Why Do I Love You? and Gaylord Ravenal's insolent careless gambler's song. And then Jerome Kern appeared at my apartment late one afternoon with a strange look of quiet exultation in his eyes. He sat down at the piano. He doesn't play the piano particularly well and his singing voice, though true, is negligible.

[305]

He played and sang Ol' Man River. The music mounted, mounted, and I give you my word my hair stood on end, the tears came to my eyes, I breathed like a heroine in a melodrama. This was great music. This was music that would outlast Jerome Kern's day and mine. I never have heard it since without that emotional surge. When Show Boat was revived at the Casino Theater in New York just four years after its original production at the Ziegfeld I saw a New York first-night audience, after Paul Robeson's singing of Ol' Man River, shout and cheer and behave generally as I've never seen an audience behave in any theater in all my years of playgoing.

16

Somewhere between the writing of So Big and the completion of Show Boat I had managed somehow to do enough short stories (published in various magazines) to make a collected volume. Doubledays now brought this out under the title of Mother Knows Best. The short story of that name had appeared in Cosmopolitan Magazine in April 1925 and had created considerable to-do. It was thought that I had used Elsie Janis and her mother. The truth is that I had first thought of this short story in 1914 in Paris when Edna Aug, that superb raconteuse, told me something of the life of Mabel Hite. But no one to this day believes this.

That short-story volume entitled Mother Knows Best is rather varied in its themes and in its workmanship. Of its eight short stories five are, I think, good. And one of them—Every Other Thursday—brought me a heart-warming line from a writer whose books and plays had charmed and delighted me from the days of my young girlhood. He actually wrote that he wished he had written Every Other Thursday, that short story of the weekly Thursday holiday of a Finnish hired girl in New York. That same author, whom I had never even met, wrote me, too, a letter about So Big and Show Boat. I should like to quote it here because of all the happy and dazzling gifts that those two books have brought me, of all the letters I have received in all these years none has made me happier than this one letter which I cherish. Written in a neat and delicate hand, it says:

Adelphia Terrace House
Strand, W.C.2.
25 March 1928.

Dear Miss Ferber,

I was very pleased to find your inscription in my So Big and thank you heartily. Selina is as delightful a woman as I have met with in fiction for many a day and I wish I do that I could go out in the waggon to High Prairie and help her paint the house white with green trimmings. I am sorry that she didn't get back there without meeting the Hempel family that day she first went to market—I grudge their share in her and it did for Dirk.

I see that Show Boat is coming here in style, and I look forward to seeing it on the boards. A gorgeous work, my dear fellow author, and I've had happy hours with it. If you come over I hope you will come and see me.

Yours sincerely,
J. M. Barrie

The fates now decided that I'd had too much sugar and that a bit of acid might set me right. Practically everyone in America —or so it seemed to me—now threatened to sue me for something or other they professed to find in the novel Show Boat. River captains I'd never heard of said I had used their boats; descendants of riverside saloonkeepers announced that in using their ancestors' names I had defiled their fair escutcheon and wrecked their political careers; gambling-house owners threatened injunctions; and as a final horror there came a legal messenger from Cardinal Mundelein, of Chicago, saying that the chapter on the Chicago convent school to which Kim Ravenal was sent was an affront to the Church. Also, he pointed to page 327 as containing an innuendo so vile that when I heard it I couldn't believe my ears.

There was a meeting between my lawyer, Morris Ernst; the member of the Chicago law firm representing Cardinal Mundelein; and myself. We met at lunch, which nobody ate.

That page, the Chicago lawyer said, and a good deal of the chapter must be removed. Suit was pending and dire other penalties threatened, including a blacklisting of the book.

Suddenly I was filled with cold fury. The chapter had been written without malice or the faintest thought of disrespect to any creed. No meaning such as had been read into the disputed page ever had entered my mind. The Doubleday firm, on hearing of the threatened measures, had strongly advised me to delete.

"I won't change a line or a word," I said, while Morris Ernst's kind face beamed approval. "Sue and be damned!"

They did blacklist the book, and I had a dreadful time of it, what with name-calling in various papers and the like. But they didn't sue, and Cardinal Mundelein turned out to be rather a darling after all. Many years later I heard that when the news was brought him that I had refused to change the chapter, though my publishers had advised it, he had gone to the window and stood there a moment looking out in silence. Then he had said thoughtfully, "She seems to have very shortsighted publishers." This was told me recently by the Cardinal's own lawyer, and I find it very endearing.

Right here there should be a chapter about Morris Ernst, that gay, brilliant, wise and warmhearted friend. But Morris Ernst is a book, not a chapter. If I were really to go in for descriptions of him he would bob up on every page, like Mr. Dick's head of King Charles. Whenever I heed his advice I am the better for it; when I stubbornly or, in vanity, ignore it, I generally rue it. He came into my life in 1928, just too late to prevent me from signing a bad contract for the musical-dramatic rights in Show Boat, and a worse contract (with Jed Harris) for the stage production of the play, The Royal Family, written in collaboration with George Kaufman. Since that time I never have signed so much as a restaurant check without first consulting him—which is tough on Morris Ernst but extremely beneficial to me. Though he is a lawyer by profession I somehow never think of him—or rarely—in that capacity. I suppose Solomon the Wise was a lawyer, really, and a good one. Those bits about suggesting that the baby be cut in two to decide which woman was the mother would indicate a nice social and humor sense leavening the legal wisdom. This would apply as well to Morris Ernst.

He is far from being just a successful lawyer with a strong social sense. The world, seeing him lunching at the Algonquin, having supper at Twenty-One, enjoying life with the gusto of an undergraduate, knows little of the enormous scope and depth of his work for humanity. But many a Little Man knows, and the Big Man at Washington knows. Turn the pages of almost any important humanitarian movement of the past fifteen years and there, on the record, you will find the name of Morris Ernst, all the way from birth-control laws to book postal rates; from free speech to decent wages. He holds and wants no political office or position of power. He is the most informal, lighthearted, least pompous and the purest human being I have ever known. In his outlook on life, his compassion, his generosity, his integrity he is (and I mean no irreverence) a kind of gay Jesus.

While Jerome Kern and Oscar Hammerstein were up to their eyebrows in the work of bringing Show Boat to the stage, George Kaufman and I had decided to write a play about a glamorous theatrical family—no particular theatrical family, I hastily add—but an imaginary one that might be any family wedded to the stage. We did, however, plan to use one member of the Barrymore family—John; not as a whole, but bits of him. He was, of course, too improbable to copy from life. This family of ours was to have been in the theater for generations. It was to be the kind of stage family that thinks, talks, lives, breathes only theater.

It seems unbelievable now, but day after day, for eight months, George and I worked on the writing of The Royal Family. Every morning at eleven George would appear at my apartment in Central Park West. When I say eleven I mean, not one minute before or two minutes after—but eleven. We would start work. Lunch at one-thirty would be coffee and sandwiches or something equally portable, eaten on the march. My digestion is now a tottering wreck and George's is, I believe, not that of a hired man at threshing time. But for my part it's been worth it. I don't regret a single sweated hour. Better old age and soda-mint tablets than never to have written at all.

Considering that The Royal Family, is, after all, just a comedy, it is rather embarrassing to confess that eight months of work went into its writing. The wonder is that we weren't at each other's throats after that long grind. We actually emerged good friends. Gallons of coffee had been drunk, tons of sandwiches consumed, miles of floor had been walked, typewriter ribbons had been worn to rags, Jed Harris had come into the scene as producer—and still we two collaborators remained friends.

So many people have asked me what actual method of work we had used in our collaboration on Minick, The Royal Family, Dinner at Eight and Stage Door. I don't know, really, except in a sort of way. Not that the process is any twilight sleep. It just works itself out, finally, with the inevitability of a huge and intricate jigsaw puzzle.

Whatever the definition of the process, it never has varied. The work always is done at my apartment or house (with an occasional brief desperate leap into the fancied quiet of Brooklyn, Atlantic City or Long Island).

Shaved, brushed, pressed, shined, Mr. Kaufman appears at eleven sharp, wearing (among other things) one of his inexhaustible collection of quiet rich ties. I sit at the typewriter; George stalks. I mention the tie. He says it's really nothing. A few moments' light conversation about this and that—the newest bit of gossip, last night's party, if any, this morning's newspaper headlines, the play that opens tonight. One of us says, "Let's write the play!" Paper, carbon, we're off.

George jiggles the curtain cord; plays tunes with a pencil on his cheek which he maddeningly stretches taut into a drum by poking it out with his tongue; he does a few eccentric dance steps; wanders into the next room; ties and unties his shoestrings. He is a confirmed shoestring tier. In moments of irritation, puzzlement, embarrassment or special thoughtfulness he stoops, unties his carefully tied shoestrings and ties them again. He says they work loose.

No written word is safe from his gaze. A letter, telegram or note left lying about will sooner or later be read by the Paul Pry of playwrights. He can't help it. His curiosity is, seemingly, overpowering. I thought of a plan to punish him for this habit. Before he was due to arrive at eleven I typed a telegram on a Western Union blank and placed it face up on my desk almost completely covered by another sheet of paper. Only one corner of the telegram peeped out, folded and creased as though it had been read and reread. There wasn't enough of it exposed to make its reading possible, but one could see it was a telegram left open.

Immediately his gaze alighted on this. As we talked he stalked his prey. He would walk over to it and eye it hungrily. He would walk away from it, casting a longing glance over his shoulder. He bent his head and screwed it around to see if he couldn't thus make out a word or two. Finally, "Damn it, what's in this telegram!" he said. And picked it up.

I have heard that people's jaws drop with surprise. I never had hoped actually to see this. I saw it now.

This was the telegram I had typed:

GEORGIE KAUFMAN IS AN OLD SNOOPER.

His method of conserving his strength is carefully thought out, and it works. He concentrates. Aside from bridge (he is one of the most brilliant amateur bridge players in America) his interests are practically nonexistent outside the theater. The theater is his life. If there is a couch in the room—any room—he stretches out on it. He doesn't stay there long, but very few people know the refreshment that comes to muscles, heart and arteries in five minutes of repose, repeated at frequent intervals. During tough rehearsal sessions, when he is directing, you are likely to miss him for a few minutes. He's in a second box or at the back of the house or somewhere in a side aisle, stretched full length on the floor, relaxed and resting. He does almost no walking. From the Astor to the Music Box is a day's jaunt for him. He eats prodigious quantities of chocolate candy and pastry, which gives him energy. He smokes and drinks almost not at all. He talks little. He hates to be interrupted or forestalled when he does talk. His wit is devastating but rarely cruel. He is one of the most considerate of men. He rarely praises. In the years of our work together he has never paid me anything that could faintly

A More Impressive Equestrienne Off Than On the Horse.

Earning Breakfast at the Morris Ernsts' on Nantucket Island.

be construed as a compliment. This makes me very cross indeed. He himself likes praise. I never have known any very successful man who hadn't the encouragement of a brilliant and understanding woman. Anyone who knows Beatrice Kaufman will admit that this is true, too, of George.

Most of George Kaufman's collaborators have written articles about him. I don't recall any article that he has ever written about a collaborator. These have included Marc Connelly, Ring Lardner, Katharine Dayton, Moss Hart, Laurence Stallings. I think he might do quite a nice little series of sketches entitled Man Bites Dog.

I don't know anyone in the world with whom I'd rather work.

Of Jed Harris, the producer of The Royal Family, it is almost impossible to write. He is a five-foot shelf or a single paragraph. It would be useless to try to sketch in this strange, gifted and paradoxical creature fated to destroy everything he loves, including himself.

He had at that time produced Love 'Em and Leave 'Em; Broadway; he was the new Wonder Boy of the theater. Both George and I were fascinated by this emaciated, magnetic, omnivorous fellow. He had a trick of turning on charm as you'd flick an electric-light switch. As prospective producer he telephoned either George or me or both at all hours of the day or night. Four in the morning, midnight, eight in the morning. His appreciation, however, proved almost fatal. The Royal Family ends with the death of old Fanny Cavendish on stage. This should never have been. Every member of this stage family should have gone on to the fall of curtain, even though the audience might know that Fanny was going on the road to her death. We should have seen her starting off on her last road tour, vain, stage-struck to the end, gay and courageous.

The Royal Family, begun in November, was finished the end of June. When I say finished I mean that, except for perhaps twenty minutes spent in doing some additional off-stage dialogue in a scene that needed extra clamor, we never rewrote a line or a word of the play. At least our eight months had served that purpose.

[313]

Casting was a nightmare. We couldn't get anyone to play Julie Cavendish. We had hoped, in our innocence, that Ethel Barrymore would play it. She would have been perfection. We had sent her the first two acts. For five years thereafter she refused to speak to George or to me. We even heard that she had threatened to sue us. We never knew why. My notion of next season's heaven would be to see The Royal Family revived with Ethel Barrymore as Julie Cavendish, John Barrymore as Tony Cavendish, Ethel's daughter, Ethel Barrymore Colt, as Gwen. I'd rather fancy myself as Fanny Cavendish, but no one would permit it, I suppose.

Between June, when the play was finished, complete, and the early autumn, when we hoped to go into rehearsal, I again scampered off to Europe. I took with me my mother and my sister Fannie. London, Paris, the château country, St.-Jean-de-Luz, Biarritz. Louis and Mary Bromfield were spending the summer, as usual, in a house in the Basque country, perched on a cliff overlooking the Bay of Biscay, just across the water from St.-Jean. I've always planned to write the story of the Spanish bullfight in San Sebastian which turned out to be a series of unbelievably fantastic happenings, culminating in the three of us—my mother, Fannie and myself—finding ourselves locked in the bull pen; seated, chauffeurless, on the driver's seat of our car, amidst indescribable welter and gore, like three females in one of Mary Roberts Rinehart's Tish stories. I still can see the dead bulls being dragged gaily past our very feet, the donkey bells tinkling, the attendants' uniforms sparkling in the Spanish sunshine. Our fascinated eyes swiveled to the sight of these slaughtered animals being cut up on the spot, smoking hot, and sold as meat to the clamoring hordes pressing at the gateway, baskets in hand. And to my dying day I never shall forget the shock of incredulity with which I recognized a faintly familiar gesture in the midst of a group gathered round a tottering horse that had just been led, mangled, from the ring. The gesture was a housewifely one. My starting eyes then saw that of which I had heard but never had believed. Neatly, thriftily, they were sewing up this animal whose entrails had been dragging the ground, and when the operation was completed they shoved him back into the ring again.

That European trip was scarcely even a fair success. My thoughts were in New York. Sight-seeing irked me. The only sight I cared to see was The Royal Family in rehearsal. But back in New York George met me with the depressing news that the part of Julie Cavendish seemed impossible to cast. Ina Claire, approached, had announced that she wasn't going to be a walking ad for the Barrymores. Laurette Taylor refused it. Practically every well-known and personable actress between the ages of thirty and fifty in America turned down the part. Some of them said they were too young to play the part of a mother with a grown daughter who, producing a baby before the play's ending, makes her a grandmother. Others said that the part of old Fanny Cavendish would walk away with the play. Twice we went into rehearsal and twice we had to abandon the play. It was heartbreaking. The play, complete, could have been produced in late September. It did not open until the end of December and we lost half a season.

Busy with his production of Coquette, starring Helen Hayes, Jed Harris was by no means as upset as we were. Finally, shockingly late we arranged to have Ann Andrews play Julie. She did a valiant job and we were grateful to her, but the part was not altogether right for her. Hers was an incisive quality rather than the velvety glamorous one which the part required. Of all the parts, I never shall forget the perfection of Jefferson de Angelis' performance as Oscar Wolfe, the theatrical producer.

Now, with a bang, The Royal Family and Show Boat both went into rehearsal. I swung between the two like a distracted hen with her chicks. I had had little enough to do with the actual dramatizing of Show Boat, but I was fascinated by it, though not as much as by The Royal Family. There had been casting difficulties in Show Boat, too, but Kern and Hammerstein were triumphant with Charles Winninger as Cap'n Andy, Edna May Oliver as Parthy, Helen Morgan as Julie. Jules Bledsoe's rich baritone shook you with its organ tones in Ol' Man

River. Norma Terris was Magnolia, Howard Marsh a fine vocal (though perhaps not a pictorial) Gaylord Ravenal.

I was living a two-ring circus. The Royal Family was in rehearsal at the Plymouth, in West 44th Street; Show Boat was rehearsing at the New Amsterdam, in West 42nd. Both were utterly absorbing. I did a split.

Of course The Royal Family was more my own child; Show Boat had been adopted by foster parents and was being educated to be a glamour girl. Royal Family rehearsals were often a grisly business. The company would work itself ragged from eleven to five. There was an endless repetition of scenes, the theater was cold, Haidee Wright (our Fanny Cavendish) was threatened with bronchitis, we had changed directors midstream. Then, at five in the afternoon when the actors were limp with strain and exhaustion, in would glide Jed Harris, having just got up out of bed, fresh as poison ivy and wearing a three-day beard. He would start to rehearse from the beginning just as though the others hadn't been at it for six solid hours.

I would sneak through Shubert Alley and into the dim green cavern that was the New Amsterdam. The rehearsal of a musical play is, of course, a much more intricate process than that of a straight legitimate play. The dance director is working with one group; the music is being gone over by another; dialogue and business are being attended to in still another section. In one obscure corner of the vast New Amsterdam stage Charley Winninger would be industriously practising his falls for the play-within-a-play scene. He worked like an athlete. Clutching himself by the back of the neck he would throw himself head over heels to the floor; then he would scramble up and do it all over again. After a half-hour of this, red-faced and breathing hard, he would muffle himself in a heavy bathrobe, swathe his throat in a bath towel and subside. Over there Eva Puck and Sam White were practising their cakewalk steps. The girls of the chorus, in bathing suits or shorts or pinafores, were busy with their dance routine. Jerome Kern, at the piano, was clearing up a point for Norma Terris or Howard Marsh. Oscar Hammerstein had Edna May Oliver in hand. It was a blissful business.

Ready to drop with weariness (they never did) the rehearsal would sag a little. Florenz Ziegfeld would choose this moment to leave his office and come quietly down the aisle, an imposing figure, handsome, erect, broad-shouldered. Instinctively all on stage turned their faces toward the dim auditorium. You sensed that an electric personality had entered the house. Two seconds later you knew it. Ziegfeld's curiously flat plangent voice would come across the footlights:

"What the hell's this? You're dragging around like a lot of corpses. This is a rehearsal. You're supposed to play as if you were giving a performance. If you let down in rehearsal you'll do the same thing a week after we've opened. Any of you boys and girls too tired to go on please get out. Go home! And stay there." It was the showman cracking the whip. He didn't mean it. They all knew he didn't mean it. They didn't resent it. There was about him an engaging quality. The speech wasn't as brutal as it sounds. He served as an astringent. Toward the end the company actually was rehearsing twenty hours out of the twenty-four. They were heroic. No one knew whether the weeks of work would end in success or failure.

Much the same was true of The Royal Family. We tried out in Newark and in Atlantic City. Sometimes the play seemed brilliant, sometimes it seemed sodden.

Show Boat was scheduled to open in New York at the new Ziegfeld Theater December 27th. The Royal Family was due to open at the Plymouth Theater December 28th.

I dashed down to Washington to see the opening of Show Boat. It turned out to be something to see. I sat in the second row, center, with Jerome Kern on one side and Oscar Hammerstein on the other. The curtain went up at eight-fifteen and down at twelve-thirty. Not a person in the audience left the house. At nine o'clock next morning, in a drizzling rain, there was a line outside the theater that extended from the box office down the block, around the block and back again. I've never seen anything remotely like it. But we were not exultant. This was Washington. New York would tell the story.

For sheer endurance and bravery I've never seen anything in

the theater like that Show Boat company. After the opening night performance, with the play running an hour and a half overtime, they had stayed for notes. They knew that there would have to be terrific line cuts. A matinee was scheduled for the next day. A rehearsal was called for eleven in the morning. They took their cuts, rehearsed them and actually put them in at the matinee performance. The matinee ran until nearly six. There was another rehearsal after the matinee. More cuts. These went into the evening performance. They now were down almost to proper curtain time. By midnight of the second day they were standing on their ankles as they took the curtain calls, but they were smiling.

Back in New York for the Show Boat opening the final dress rehearsal was so chaotic that it seemed incredible that anyone could bring order out of this confusion in time for tomorrow night's performance. Costumes were wrong or missing; lights refused to work; Norma Terris and Howard Marsh, as the love-stricken Magnolia and Ravenal, struggled with the duet, Only Make Believe, while a vast vital figure hurled itself, shirt-sleeved, down the theater aisle.

It was Joseph Urban, the scenic designer. "Wo ist mein himmelblau!" he bawled to the electricians. "Gott verdammt! Wo ist mein himmelblau!" The famous Urban heaven-blue having been found the duet emerged more clearly.

I am now somewhat ashamed to confess that I never saw the opening performance of Show Boat or the opening performance of The Royal Family. I don't know why. I deeply regret it now. They were spectacular, they were enormously exciting events. I couldn't bring myself to go. It must have been a psychological quirk which I was powerless to overcome. I suppose I cared too deeply. Show Boat ran two years in New York alone and was revived almost as soon as it stopped playing on the road. The Royal Family threatened to be swamped with the flood of that week's openings, but it weathered the storm and became an enormous success. Show Boat's English company, with Paul Robeson as Jo singing Ol' Man River, played ten months in London. I never saw the English production which later toured England, Scotland and Ireland (I think I'd have enjoyed the incongruity of it in Dublin and Edinburgh). But I did see the French production in Paris and I hope never to witness such a grisly sight again in the theater of any land. It played at the Sarah Bernhardt Theater and I am sure that that gifted actress must have whirled like a top in her tomb. I went with Louis and Mary Bromfield who were living in Paris out near the Bois. We laughed until the tears rolled down our cheeks. The American idiom in French translation, the Parisian actor's conception of Cap'n Andy, the Mississippi River boatman, and the French orchestra's rendition of the Jerome Kern music were beyond description or bearing. We left, wisely, or I'm sure we'd have been thrown out.

I was a lucky girl. My New York friends all assured me of this fact, and they were right. "Two enormous hits in one week! What luck!"

I turned toward them a lackluster eye. Perhaps it was a reaction against the intensive work of the past few years. Suddenly, now, the job seemed done, the world empty, New York stale. I was suffering from success-poisoning. Off on a trip to Bermuda I was disappointed in this, too. To my sour eye the island seemed the spinster of the tropics, spare, bony, masquerading as a femme fatale with a poinsettia stuck coquettishly in her scanty locks, an onion between her teeth. I rode a bicycle, sprained my ankle, bought cashmere sweaters for more than I'd have paid in New York and came home, still disgruntled.

New York was full of parties. I seemed to be asked to all of them and went to almost none. Here at least I showed a glimmering of sense. The rich and social invited me to their houses. Now I do not despise people merely because they may happen to have too much money and care overmuch about social position. Perhaps money ambition and social ambition are traits as worthy as my own overpowering work drive. But the very rich and the very social are, almost always, the very stuffy. It always has seemed to me incredible that there are people who actually will dine at the homes of the rich for no reason other than that they are rich; not entertaining or gay, or companionable or intelligent or sympathetic—but just rich. I found, with one or two exceptions, that their libraries were too full of uncut leaves and sharp tapestries; that their dinners were dull and the cooking unimaginative. I found better food at home cooked by my own Mrs. Rebecca Henry, from Maryland, fount of fine cookery. Perhaps the very rich do not themselves know how to buy and prepare food; perhaps they aren't anxious enough to please the palates of their guests. A very large formal dinner at a very large formal New York house is usually, in choice of viands, wines, and in preparation and service, about on a par with a well-run public banquet at a second-rate hotel, than which there is nothing less piquant or stimulating. I was invited, not because of what I intrinsically was, but because of what I had done in a public way. I would have none of it.

The Herbert Bayard Swopes were rich, but they weren't then socially ambitious, and to that big hospitable Long Island country house we all flocked for week ends. It was likely as not that neither Margaret nor Herbert had yet risen when you arrived at five in the afternoon, but they would be down eventually, so it didn't matter. Croquet was in full swing, a bloody bitter game, no relation to the Victorian pastime indulged in by the average player. In and out, carefree as guests at an unbelievably luxurious clubhouse, were George and Beatrice Kaufman, Ethel Barrymore, F.P.A., Neysa McMein, Marc Connelly, Frank Sullivan, Irving Berlin, Harpo Marx, Bernard Baruch, Robert Sherwood, Margalo Gillmore, Ruth Gordon, Heywood Broun, or any combination of a hundred others. Tea was at six or seven, dinner at ten or eleven, supper at three or four. Good talk, laughter, games. Herbert buoyant and bellowing, Margaret acid in cream. It was fun, though you felt rather fagged next day. It was one of the two or three big houses to which I enjoyed going. Later, the Ralph Pulitzers', at Manhasset, was as stimulating and more restful. And for sheer beauty (and for the zestful valiant Molly Cazalet, its mistress) I loved Fairlawne, the Cazalets' place in Kent, England. For the most part I make you a present of the very rich; their conversation, their cookery and their contract.

In the spirit of sheer bad taste I should like to tell the story of Mrs. Wolcott (no relation; he spells it with two o's and two l's).

AT THE DRESS REHEARSAL OF "SHOW BOAT"

One of Those Restful Dress Rehearsals Before the SHOW BOAT
Opening.

Show Boat.

In the light (or darkness) of Hitler's goings-on, and the large (but not large enough) indignation arising from the same, the incident is timely and gives one what's known as pause.

There lived in New York a formidable old lady named Mrs. Wolcott. Her life's business was lion hunting. She was an inveterate and almost invincible dinner-giver. So Big, Show Boat and The Royal Family had made me fair game for her. Thus far I had escaped her careful aim.

Then, one day, when I was off guard, she said that she was giving a dinner for eight. Winthrop Ames had said he would come if I would. I welcomed the thought of sitting next him at a small dinner and having an hour of his stimulating talk and his gay glancing wit.

There was good talk and good food. Winthrop sat between the hostess and me. The conversation turned to books, someone mentioned G. B. Stern's novel, The Matriarch, which had been well received.

"That book!" shouted the hostess. "When I found it was about spawning Jews I threw it across the room."

A little silence fell. It was, I suppose, just about the nastiest little silence I have ever felt. I said, with laborious dignity, "It was a rich chronicle of a dramatic and cultured family. I loved it."

In leaped the gallant Winthrop. "Dramatic! That's it! I've often thought that if it hadn't been for the Jew in me I'd never have amounted to anything in the theater."

"*You,* Winthrop!" screeched Mrs. Wolcott.

"Certainly," he went on, equably. "Old Ameus, from whom we get our name of Ames. It's all in the book of the family tree in the library up at North Easton. Old Ameus, the Jew, who was thrown out of England and into Spain, and out of Spain back into England, centuries ago. Where do you suppose I get this profile, if not from him!"

"That," I put in, lamely, "is exactly the way I feel about anything I've done in the theater. We Jews, because we've been suppressed for centuries, have to express ourselves in the creative arts and sciences."

"Oh, are you Jewish—too?" faltered our charming hostess. "I didn't know——"

"Only," I replied cheerfully, "on my mother's and father's side, my grandmothers' and grandfathers', my great-grandmothers' and great-grandfathers', my great-great-grand——"

"There are Jews and Jews," interrupted Mrs. W., graciously.

"Yes, indeed. And Christians *and* Christians." With which I took my departure.

Now, that's the sort of thing that interests me, psychologically. This beldame probably never had talked to three Jews in her life, knowing they were Jews. Her resentment of them was as pathological and unsound as the fear of, say, high places. If you multiply this one woman's ignorance and prejudice by one or two millions you have a very nice little Hitler group snugly seated in your own lap.

There are, I think, many Mrs. Wolcotts in America, male and female. Unsure, they search for something upon which to establish their superiority. This woman, like many others, had fixed upon the Jews as a symbol. Unknowingly, she had worked herself into a lather to wheedle and coax to her table two people who were proud of their Jewish background.

17

BY NOW I had transferred the lemon-yellow chintz curtains, the piano, the lovely extravagant eighteenth-century writing desk and such other pieces as the place accommodated to a penthouse apartment in East 56th Street. A wood-burning fireplace made it homelike in the winter and a vast terrace on the nineteenth floor jutting out into space made it exhilarating in the spring and autumn. I discovered that New York penthouses are ovens in the summer. From that terrace I saw light after light blotted out by the stock-market crash of 1929. It was a dramatic thing to see building after building grow dim and dimmer. The dome of the Grand Central Station, lighted at night, had glittered like the Korean crown jewels; twin towers had sparkled from the Waldorf, diamond-encrusted; the Empire State Building, the Chrysler spire and a score of star-piercing shafts, glowing with thousands of electric lights in gorgeous designs, had made an Arabian Nights panorama of the New York sky line after dusk. Those dazzling towers symbolized the most extravagant and material period that this or any other country has ever known. If ever I live to see those lights blazing once more against the sunset sky I shall know that the thing we call the Depression is over. I'm not sure that I shall welcome the sight.

But 1928 knew nothing of 1929. Nineteen twenty-eight was Little Red Riding Hood, tripping through the buttercups and daisies, knowing nothing of the Big Bad Wolf. Show Boat and The Royal Family were zooming along. But I was still in the doldrums. Any writer will recognize the symptoms. I was wandering in a vacuum. I almost never went near the Plymouth or the Ziegfeld theaters except, perhaps, to see if a performance was slumping; and there were people much better suited than I to attend to that. Last year's work was done; irrevocably and completely finished; stale as last week's crusts for me. All New York seemed equally stale. I turned again toward the West.

I wasn't going any place in particular. Just away. I found myself sitting in the big front room at the William Allen Whites' in Emporia, Kansas. There, over the fireplace, hung the painting of the blue sky and the wheat fields. There were Sallie and Bill. Young Bill was home, too. He was working on the Emporia Gazette now and taking part in the political life of Kansas. No one spoke of the absence of Mary White, that brilliant and original girl whose untimely death had shocked a continent. Yet anyone who had known this household during her lifetime felt the void now. To know Mary one need only read William Allen White's editorial obituary about this, his daughter. It is one of the most poignant pieces of writing that I have ever read.

The talk was interesting and varied, as always. The best talk I've ever encountered anywhere in America; of people and politics and places and things of the spirit. It was like drinking from a cold pure stream after a day in the desert. The neighbors came in. I wandered around Emporia, the little railroad town squatting so flat on the prairie in the late winter sun. It wasn't beautiful. I liked looking at it. In its flatness, in the long stretches of the prairie that rolled on and on to the horizon, my city eyes, weary after months of cement and stone, of asphalt and brick, of endless towers and shafts blotting out the sky, found rest and refreshment. In the morning, early, I walked down Commercial Street to the Gazette office with Bill. The townsfolk, passing, greeted him, and he them.

"Hello, Mart!"

"Hi-yah, Mr. White!"

"Morning, Stan!"

"Fine day, Bill!"

Arrived at the office I gratefully sniffed the nostalgic smell of the small-town newspaper office. It hadn't changed since my Appleton Crescent days. But here the presses were larger and swifter, and the busy little job room boasted half a dozen lino-type machines.

The second evening they told me of a trip they had made in the autumn of the year. The three of them—Mr. and Mrs. White, and Will, Junior—had motored through Oklahoma. Their keen observant eyes, their brilliant humor sense, their trained reportorial noses had missed nothing of the fantastic, the dramatic, the tragic, the ridiculous in that bizarre common-wealth. Their stories stunned me.

Right here I must make a shamefaced confession. I knew literally nothing of Oklahoma until that evening. It was a state in the Union. That was all. I was as ignorant of it as I had been of show boats when first I had heard Winthrop Ames speak of them. I didn't know when the Indian Territory had become a state; I never had heard of the land rush of 1889. Either the Appleton public schools had been less advanced than I had thought them or I was a case of retarded development.

Now, as the Whites talked, sometimes one at a time, sometimes all together and with equal brilliance, for they are all great story-tellers, I would interrupt with exclamations such as, "Indians! You mean actually blanket Indians riding around in Pierce-Arrows! . . . Oil lands that made the Indians millionaires!"

The Whites went on with the fantastic story: "Yep! Herded them onto the reservation like cattle—it was the poorest piece of land in Oklahoma, you couldn't raise anything on it. And the reason turned out to be that it was the richest oil land in America. What a joke on a lot of dirty political tricksters! . . . Marble palaces and fifty-story skyscrapers where a buffalo mud-wallow lay fifty years ago. . . . They rushed into the Oklahoma Territory at the firing of signal muskets. Any land they took was theirs. . . ."

I listened to all this, open-mouthed. Or perhaps the Whites, in their dramatic way, made it seem spectacular for the first time.

"If it's all in the history books, I suppose it's true. Why hasn't someone written it? What a novel! Bill, you've got to do it."

"Me! No, thanks. Why don't you do it?"

I shivered at the thought. Show Boat had been a tough job. I didn't want to tackle another like it. "No, the story of Oklahoma is a man's job. From now on I'm going to write little stories about two people in a telephone booth. No more big open spaces for me. Let somebody else do the American-background stuff. Too hard work."

Then, as an afterthought, "But, oh, how I'd like to see it!"

"Done and done," said the Whites. "It's too early now. The Oklahoma roads would be mud-wallows out in the oil country. Come back West in May and we'll all pile into the car headed for Oklahoma."

In May, then, I came rushing back to Emporia, and, with young Bill driving, we started on our Oklahoma jaunt. Though it was May, the Kansas prairies were burgeoning and the Kansas sun was hot. We had planned to stop overnight at the Victor Murdocks' in Wichita. Now there is a romantic and spectacular family. A pity that the East knows nothing of the ways of a Kansas family like the Murdocks. It is difficult to describe that group without going off into adjectives that sound slightly silly. A handsome crew, first to last. First, there is Victor Murdock, editor, politician, scholar. He is a gigantic red-haired magnetic fellow, with the rich booming voice of the born orator, an actor's sense of the dramatic. A writer, a reader, a gourmet. They live well, these Kansans, make no mistake about that. Fine big houses, done with taste and comfort. They read the best, they know and love music, their tables are set forth with the most deliciously prepared foods, beautifully served. Next to the Californians, I should say the Kansans are the most gracefully hospitable people in America.

Mrs. Murdock looks the way you hoped your first duchess would look—white hair, pink-and-white schoolgirl skin, great chic. The Murdock girls are famous beauties. It is not an exaggeration to say that it is difficult to imagine greater wit, gaiety and beauty in any one household. If I were to pick three families in America who seem to me to contain all the rare qualities that should go to make up the best of life, I should name the William Allen Whites, of Emporia, Kansas; the Victor Murdocks, of Wichita, Kansas; and the Hepburns (Katherine's family, no less), up in Hartford, Connecticut. Each of these families contains, incidentally, just that sufficient dash of Sanger's Circus to make them perfect.

We had stopped at the Murdocks' not only for social reasons, but because Victor had seen Oklahoma in its early days, he knew a thousand land-rush stories and he told them with indescribable drama and gusto. On this visit he talked for hours as I listened, entranced. Blood-and-thunder tales, ludicrous and fantastic yarns poured forth, as golden a flood as that earlier one had been when Charles Hunter poured riches at my feet on the show boat that day in spring just three years before. Victor was suffering from a touch of gout or neuritis, I forget which. One foot was propped up on a cushioned footstool. But in the excitement of his story his actor's instinct would triumph over the flesh, and he would bound to his feet and hobble about the room, brandishing his stick, playing now Indian, now cowboy, now bandit, now pioneer. It was a great protean performance. It was then I heard the story of the American Southern Indians driven forth into exile by the American government—as fine an example of minority persecution and injustice as any historian would care to see.

For good measure I took my first airplane ride in Wichita, for that city at that time was placidly manufacturing more airplanes than any other spot in America. My choice was more thrilling than wise. A young test flier was bumbling about the field and I decided that this was as good a time as any to go up. The plane was the size of a footbath. It held the two of us snugly. We zoomed up into the blue Kansas sky like an oversize bumblebee. The wind tried to tear my hair out by the roots, the noise was horrendous, I kept leaning now right, now left under the innocent impression that I could keep the plane from banking. But I assumed that this was average airplane flying and never really learned the difference until I went up in a Handley-Page across the English Channel.

That night I went down to see the mail plane come in. I wanted to see the modern sight of the smallish-town youth of Wichita driving down to the flying field to see the night mail come in much as the boys and girls of Appleton, in my childhood, used to loaf on down to the depot just for the excitement and vicarious travel thrill of seeing the 7:52 train steam in from Chicago, northbound. The Appleton boys and girls had stared down the track, but these boys and girls looked up at the sky. The heavens were black, and an occasional lightning flash to the east presaged an approaching storm. Out of the blackness then a beautiful thing zoomed down in a circle of light. Out stepped a lean young kid with a bundle strapped to his back. Presently, gulping the last of a sandwich, he emerged from the shed and climbed into the cockpit again and was off to try to beat the onrushing storm that now was nipping at his heels. But even so, he was too American and too young and too zestful of life to resist circling above the field just once to show off before he darted toward the west and was lost in the blackness beyond and above us.

That little incidental visit gave me the short story, Meadow Lark, which is one of the group collected under the book title of They Brought Their Women. Full of Oklahoma stories and delicious Kansas food and the Murdock milk of human kindness, after a night's sleep in the cool fresh room with its mahogany four-poster, we were off for Oklahoma and the Indians and oil fields and the preposterous oil millionaires of Tulsa.

The Oklahoma novel, Cimarron, has been done once by me; certainly I shall not commit the error of repetition here. I spent three days in Oklahoma with the Whites and ten days there alone after they had driven off in the direction of Kansas and home. It was a fine friendly act of theirs—that of taking me into the Oklahoma country and giving me the gentle push that started me on the long, long road which I was to travel steadily in the next year and a half.

I saw sights which never were on land or sea. Many of them I used in Cimarron, many I was obliged regretfully to discard because, though true, they were too improbable for fiction. I stayed at millionaire ranch houses with log cabins de luxe embellished with grand pianos, peacocks; lavender, pink, green or yellow tiled bathrooms; camels, monkeys; buffalo meat and champagne —all mixed in an indescribable welter. There was Pawhuska, with its Osage Indian houses built of brick, filled with plush and taffeta and plumbing; and in the backyard were the tepees in which the owners preferred to sleep. The unbelievable town of Bowlegs with its oil fields smearing the landscape with grease and machinery. Tulsa, aping New York and Europe with its Italian headwaiters; its skyscrapers seemed anachronistic in the midst of a million acres of prairie. Forty years ago this was a buffalo wallow. Your mind rejected the whole picture even as your eye gazed upon it.

I buckled down to work in earnest after the Whites left. There were countless men and women, not particularly old, who had made the land rush in 1889. I talked to scores of these as they sat rocking comfortably on the front porch, tree-shaded now, where only clay and sage had been. Any man or woman of fifty-five or sixty could be an Oklahoma old pioneer. Sometimes the older ones talked on and on and on and I listened patiently, finding one pearl, perhaps, in a sea of brine. They talked of their childhood days in Ohio, Indiana, Illinois, so unlike this half-savage land to which they had come in search of adventure or land or peace. ". . . and they wasn't a tree in the whole town, if you could call it a town, only tents and maybe two wood shacks after a while. We staked our claim where the big liberry stands today, if we'd of hung onto it we'd be millionaires today, but sakes, I can't complain, I'd do it all over again if I . . ."

There were amazingly few written records of these early days in the Indian Territory. Such as there were I read. Walter Ferguson of Tulsa, a former newspaperman, sensed what I was seeking. He had collected old newspaper clippings and these, pasted in scrapbooks, were made available to me. Walter Ferguson's mother lived in a little Oklahoma town about sixty miles from Tulsa. At his urging I went to see her, for she had come a bride to Oklahoma, and her husband had been a small-town newspaper editor in the early days of the Territory. I found her an intelligent and alert woman, now editor of the newspaper her husband had bequeathed to her. I spent the night as her guest and we had two hours of fine rich talk about the early Oklahoma days. Next day I drove back to Tulsa. After the publication of Cimarron there appeared in various Oklahoma papers the statement that the character of Sabra Cravat and the newspaper background in the novel were founded on Mrs. Ferguson and her life. This was, of course, absurdly untrue, and it irked me, perhaps through vanity. Sabra Cravat was fictional, purely; and the newspaper background was my own, except for such imagined events and characters as I saw fit to create.

From Tulsa I went to Oklahoma City, and in the Historical Library there I found a set of paper-bound pamphlets made up of personal recollections, old letters, old settlers' speeches at public dinners, reminiscences and the like. I was able to buy one of these sets through the kindness of the curator of the Oklahoma State Library. I worked sixteen hours a day during those two weeks. It was now June; hot, dusty, enervating. I found myself weary almost beyond bearing and I decided to take my great envelopes full of scattered notes, my books, pamphlets and my mental pictures into any cool and reasonably quiet spot not too far away. And high. I longed for altitude as the thirsty pant for water.

I went straight to the luxurious Broadmoor Hotel at Colorado Springs, engaged a suite with a screened sleeping porch and a vast terrace high up overlooking the Rocky Mountains, the sweep of valley, and practically the Western Hemisphere. The Broadmoor was quiet and sedate in those days. The altitude of six thousand feet wasn't quite high enough for my peculiar make-up; but anything was better than the Oklahoma flatlands. Thus surrounded by luxury and the tools of my toil I proceeded to find out why I had been so low and joyless during those past winter months in New York. Anaemia, low blood pressure and too much work with too little rest. Which one had caused the other I didn't know.

I stayed in bed because I wasn't able to stand up. And it was mighty fine. There were the mountains; here were my books and notes; I knew no one; at night, from my balcony, the stars were lavish beyond belief. I read Oklahoma; I read Westerns; the life of the James boys, Sam Houston, Bat Masterson. I sorted and filed my notes and even started a rough scenario of my first draft of the novel. By September 1928 I was back in New York and up to my ears in Cimarron. All through that winter, all through the spring I plodded on, day after day.

A letter from the Bromfields described a little house perched just next to theirs on the cliff overlooking the ocean at Socoa, in my beloved Basses-Pyrénées, the Basque country. It was, they said, both quiet and gay. There was nothing between you and Coney Island but the Atlantic. Louis was deep in a novel. There was a little private bathing beach. The sun there, they assured me, contained more ultraviolet rays to the square inch than any other spot on the globe. The water was full of iodine to build you up; there was boule at the little St.-Jean casino, and langouste for gala evening dinners if we wanted diversion; Louis and Mary were painting a little and it was great fun; Victor Cazalet was coming over from London for a few days, later. Oh, come on!

I packed up Cimarron, grabbed a portable typewriter and caught the Paris for Havre.

Louis and Mary had been right; Socoa was at once peaceful and gay.

My train from Paris was, as always when headed toward the beloved Basses-Pyrénées, the famous Flêche d'Or, bound for Madrid. St.-Jean-de-Luz passengers like myself were dumped out at seven in the morning. And there on the station platform, in sleeveless jersey, crumpled white pants and Basque espadrilles, breakfastless but buoyant, was Louis Bromfield, come to meet me. A vast second-hand Hispano, snorting like a yellow grampus, took us up the precarious cliff drive to my temporary summer home. I had grown to love the district and the people and the

[331]

life there. After New York and Paris there was infinite peace and a kind of serene gaiety in the Basque villages with their houses, white and red, the Bay dimpling in the morning sunlight, the little fishing boats rocking gently at their moorings. As we bounded along in his car, Louis told the news of the day:

"You're coming to our house to dinner tonight. I've taught the cook to do Ohio food, she gives it a French slant and it's wonderful. . . . My sister Marie's visiting us. . . . Mary's found a little dressmaker in Biarritz who copies all the Paris models for practically nothing. . . . Basil Leng's down in his house and his garden is incredible, I don't see how he does it on that little rocky slope. . . . Victor's coming over from London to visit us a little later, and the Colefaxes, too. . . . I'm doing a novel too, but you've got to knock off at noon the way I do and get the sun and a bathe. The violet rays here are magic."

The Bromfields had engaged for me a Spanish cook (female) with a fine mustache; and a zany housemaid (local) the lighthouse-keeper's daughter. Housekeeping in a lighthouse must be light housekeeping indeed, for the housemaid's ideas on the subject were airy to the point of nonexistence. One thing she did expertly. According to the Basque custom this nymph waxed the cottage floors by skating on them. Her skates were felt pads strapped to her shoes. It was fascinating to watch and exhilarating to do, though I found I was only fair at it, in spite of my years of roller and ice skating in Appleton.

Every morning the cook left the house bound for the near-by market place of St.-Jean-de-Luz. Though I was a household of one in that little cottage, with only very occasional dinner guests, she went daily armed with a shopping list that looked like an army roll call. On her return she was practically ambushed by the baskets and bundles bursting with supplies sufficient for a village in a state of siege. Sticking out here and there I glimpsed delicacies evidently meant for palates other than mine, for I never again beheld them. The food bills made New York, in retrospect, seem a working girl's paradise.

I tried during the summer to remonstrate with her but my feeble French had not been founded on a knowledge of the

Spanish-Basque vocabulary. On leaving Socoa three months later, I made the rounds of the house to see that all had been left clean and in order. The cook was busy with her own private departure. On the kitchen table, on shelves, in boxes and on every available chair were jars whose plump glass sides glowed colorfully with the most appetizing display of fruits, vegetables, pickles and preserves of every description. I don't know whether she set up shop with them or just lived off them, with her large family, for the rest of her life.

But no household Harpy could spoil that good summer. Besides, my mother arrived for the month of August to do battle with the lavish provider, and during her stay at least the household bills dropped like a pricked balloon. Julia needed no knowledge of French (or any other foreign language) to best an extravagant cook.

In that summer I learned really to know and love the Bromfields; really to admire and respect the Basques. For the acid test of friendship there is nothing better than being thrown together for company on an isolated cliff in a foreign country for three months. Louis, Mary and I saw the worst and the best of each other. We came through it with colors flying. I never have encountered anyone with Louis Bromfield's capacity for enjoying life and his gift for communicating that enjoyment to others. Humor, amazing vitality, sympathy, a limitless zest for life all are his. In company with the rakish Julia Ferber he would go off to gamble a few francs at boule in the little Pergola casino at St.-Jean, and you would have thought he had in tow a combination of Mata Hari and Cleopatra.

Louis and I observed practically the same working schedule. With two small daughters in his house, Louis had taken a workroom outside the range of their activities. At the tip of our cliff that extended out into the ocean there stood a handsome and unused seventeenth-century fort, one of the many coast defenses that had been built by the brilliant engineer, Vauban. I wonder what he would have thought if he could have known that today it would serve as a yacht club for the fashion of that coast. But in 1929 it was occupied only by a caretaker and his wife, with their brood of barefoot children, cackling chickens and yapping dogs. In one ground-floor room of this massive edifice, Louis found refuge for the writing of his novel. The wife of the caretaker had swept and scrubbed it, and the room now held a bit of ragged rug, a chair, a table, a typewriter. But the unmistakable odor of the chickens, late tenants of the room, overpoweringly persisted. Visitors fled, their handkerchiefs over their faces. But Louis declared that he, an old Ohio farm boy, was accustomed to it and liked it, and drew deep gusty breaths in proof of this.

Louis was writing A Modern Hero, I was writing Cimarron. We worked from early morning until midday. Then we bathed and basked in the life-giving sun and went home to lunches much too good. The Harpy simply couldn't understand the American light lunch; and for some inexplicable reason (probably happiness and peace within) I found that I could not only digest her noonday banquets, but work after them. It is a land of fresh shrimps and baby langouste, of ripe vegetables, perfumed honey, wild strawberries and chicken casserole and sparkling pale golden Vouvray. If Cimarron had bounce and vitality it was because I, stuffed with sunshine and the Spanish one's food that summer, had too.

My house perched on the cliff's edge. Just below it was the roof of Basil Leng's lovely villa, Arrantegeia. Two or three hundred yards away was the Bromfields' substantial house, a true Basque one of white plaster with red-painted beams. To look out of any window was fatal while working, for sky and sea and mountains changed with every hour and each change seemed more ravishing than the last. After work was done, or just at sunset, it was marvelous to walk out to the end of the long breakwater that jutted so far into the Bay that you had all the feeling of being on a ship at sea, with none of a ship's discomfort. Peace slipped down over one like a garment of velvety feathers (especially if it had been a good working day). There were always Basque fishermen perched on the rocks below fishing for herring or for the region's favorite delicacy, the octopus or squid, whose very aspect, goggling and writhing its tendrils, turned me sick with horror. The Pyrénées were purple-blue against the sea and sky, the little houses clinging to the cliffs had the peaceful look of a day's work done.

Socoa, where we lived, and Ciboure, just below on the road to St.-Jean, were typical Basque fishing villages. There lived the mysterious handsome race whose origin no one knows, whose history is lost, whose language is unrelated to any other known European language. With the fishermen we sat in the little waterside cafés; we dined early or late in order to be able to dash down to the tiny harbor when the fishing fleet came in at sunset. We always were in time because we could see the saucy little boats, bright blue with scarlet funnels, flashing past our cliff on their way to the wharf. The wharf end would be a crowded chattering mass of wives, daughters, sweethearts, babies, dogs, all come down to witness the big news event of the region—the day's catch. The plump little blue boats would draw up alongside, the crowd would surge forward to see the mass of silver that lay gleaming on the deck. An hour later you saw the returned fishermen smoking their after-supper pipes in the village square. They had on their clean denims of the bright blue peculiar to that coast, the faces of the older men were the color of rich mahogany, their bodies were round and hard and firm, they stood with their legs somewhat wide apart, their feet planted as though they felt a boat's deck beneath, they seemed to sway a little with the earth's motion, gently, just as on shipboard they swayed with the sea. The younger men were slim and straight and strong, with fine level brows and ardent eyes; the women in their peasant black, quiet, serene, serious. A superb race, a people full of courage, dignity, integrity and beauty.

On fête days there was dancing in the little square at St.-Jean; the village band in scarlet coats played the fandango and everyone rushed forward to dance or look on. It was the most natural and unself-conscious dancing I've ever seen. White-haired grandmothers, big, full-bodied fishermen, boys and girls, children little more than babies, formed sets and leaped into the nimble intricate steps of the fandango. Fingers snapped like castanets, feet in their clean white espadrilles twinkled so fast that the eye could scarcely follow them. Louis Bromfield became very good at it. When we wanted a taste of *higlif* we could motor in less than half an hour over to Biarritz, about which we had a feeling of superiority and considerable scorn. There, at the Bar Basque and the little Café de Paris one encountered the society crowd strayed and slumming from their somewhat fly-specked Riviera; Michael Arlen, still excited at finding himself allowed in at the front door; the Cunards, the Russian grand dukes, the Mayfair bridge players. But the food at the Café de Paris was the very best type of French bourgeois cooking, than which there is nothing better in the world; the prices were moderate, the air superb, the scene vivacious and stimulating. We, with our own friends, would eat our very good dinner or lunch, with such big-town errands as were needed thrown in, and off we'd gallop again to the peace and security of our own beloved Basque cliffs and sea and mountains. We felt very smug about our hideaway. It was almost impossible to find it without explicit directions. Acquaintances whom we barely knew would hear of our being there and would send us telegrams to say that they were motoring over from Biarritz or on their way to or from Paris, and would we give them lunch or dinner or both. Working with great intensity as both Louis and I were, this sort of thing was impossible. Invited friends were another thing, but these self-invited guests would have made work and life unbearable. Our little cliff road was hidden. Often as not we would see the unwanted guests make the wrong turning and head straight for Spain which was only an hour or so distant. Then we would go contentedly back to work again.

The writing of Cimarron went steadily on in this gay but secluded environment. Nothing could have been farther from Oklahoma, not only geographically but in spirit, background and feeling. That was good, that was what I liked. Here there was nothing so real as to make an impact that would jar the reality of the Oklahoma in which I was really living. We walked on the cliffs, we picnicked, we lunched at Ascain, served with delicious Basque food under the cool arbor; we had tea and tennis at the enchanting villa of Roy McWilliams (American vice-consul) and Mrs. McWilliams, high on the cliff above the

Arizona Rodeo.

Top of the World, 1929.

sea at Bidart. Every month I mailed a great chunk of copy to Gertrude Lane of the Woman's Home Companion in New York. Sir Louis Mallett came to visit Basil Leng, and that was pleasant; the Thomas Lamonts stopped at the Golf Hotel in St.-Jean and came to our little eyrie for bathing and sun and good food and talk, and so did the London Colefaxes, which was even pleasanter. Then, one night (pleasantest of all) I heard a familiar British voice beneath my window. After a day of work and sun and fun I had gone to bed at nine with an interesting book and a face smeared with cold cream. The British voice came out of a pitch-black moonless night.

"Edna! Edna! Really, seclusion's very nice and all that, but this is going a bit too far."

It was Noel Coward and Gladys Calthrop come a-calling all the way from London. We gathered the Bromfields and talked until morning. If Louis and Mary and I had dreamed that they were within a hundred miles we'd have been willing to carry them up the cliffs. How they found the place in the dark is a mystery; and how they escaped death over the cliffs in the blackness is another. It would have been difficult enough to locate in the glare of noon-day.

"Nonsense, not difficult at all!" Noel said, airily. "We merely got into a fiacre and I told the driver in my best French to drive us to where those crazy Americans were living. He came straight as a carrier pigeon."

It was a good summer indeed, that summer of 1929, before the poisonous miasma of hate and terror and agony had swept over all Europe, and before the panic of Wall Street had depressed all America. A golden shining summer, the last happy one I was to know in France for ten years—perhaps forever.

Back in New York with Cimarron still unfinished I settled again to the grind, my face in the typewriter all day, day after day. By now I had long since passed the uphill stretch and was rolling downhill at the rate of a thousand words a day. It was, as usual, a treadmill, but it had its enjoyable aspects. I could see the end. I knew, now, to the day when I should have written my last thousand-word stint. It would be, I knew, about the tenth of November 1929.

All through that summer and autumn I had had a growing feeling of uneasiness about investments and money. Throughout the years of my writing life I had been thrifty and lavish at the same time. The thrift had consisted of three very simple rules which I have observed all my life. I never bought anything for which I could not pay in cash on the spot. I never borrowed a penny or owed a penny. I tried to put by at least something of each sum earned. I had seen the misery and fear that improvidence could cause. I wanted none of it.

Novels, plays, motion pictures, serializations, foreign rights had brought me enormous returns; at least, they seemed enormous to me. Part of this money I had, from time to time, invested as best I knew how, without speculation and without any desire to make money on the money itself. I knew that I could earn a living as long as I kept my health; I was strong, ambitious, I loved my work. I had tried to keep my life as simple as possible within the realm of comfort.

Now though all my energies seemed concentrated on finishing this book one small still voice was whispering a warning. As I plodded on I looked about me uneasily. I knew nothing (and know nothing) of finance. Investments and investing bore me. The stock market is a mystery to my unmathematical mind. But certain fundamental truths have penetrated even my untechnical intelligence. One of them is this: a top-heavy structure, if piled still higher, will tumble. The cop on the corner was leaving his beat to stroll over to the drugstore telephone booth where he called up his broker to get the last word on the last quotation on U.S. Steel and International Match and Anaconda. The elevator boys who took me up to my apartment asked me what I thought of Tel. & Tel. The masseuse had made three hundred dollars that day and was now pyramiding, she announced. One of her clients had given her the tip. The laundress had taken her lifetime savings out of the bank ($2,000) and had thrown them into the stock market about which she knew as much as her baby knew about calculus. Chambermaids, scrub-

women, clerks, errand boys, your doctor, your lawyer (but not
mine), your teacher, your banker, your every friend and acquaintance, all were babbling about that golden mystery called
The Market.

Though mine were never speculative investments the little
voice persisted. After all, it said, isn't it idiotic to work for years
and then be more careless about the money earned in those
years than about the purchase of a hat or coat! I decided that
I would finish Cimarron by early November, and then, free
from the daily grind, I would invest every penny I possessed in
good old United States government bonds and live happily ever
after, like someone in a fairy tale. It was canny instinct—perhaps
my German-Jewish banking ancestors—warning me.

Ten days before the finish of Cimarron the stock market
crashed. I lost more than half of everything I had saved. This
should have depressed me very much indeed. It didn't. I wasn't
disturbed for a moment—or for little more than a moment, at
most. Money lost is money lost. The whole scrambling screaming frenzied spectacle of that period seemed a saddening and
sometimes wryly amusing spectacle. I went calmly on finishing
my book, and when it was finished I found I had made a lot of
money all over again. Cimarron was published serially; it was
published as a novel and sold over 200,000 copies; it was made
into a superb motion picture, the finest motion picture that has
ever been made of any book of mine.

I was bitterly disappointed. Cimarron had been written with
a hard and ruthless purpose. It was, and is, a malevolent picture
of what is known as American womanhood and American sentimentality. It contains paragraphs and even chapters of satire
and, I am afraid, bitterness, but I doubt that more than a dozen
people ever knew this. All the critics and the hundreds of thousands of readers took Cimarron as a colorful romantic Western
American novel. Perhaps it will be read and understood in another day, not my day, if anything is left in the world.

Oklahoma—that was another thing. Oklahoma read the book,
stood up on its hind legs and howled. By now I had realized
that an American regional novel always is resented by the people

of its locale, unless, of course, all descriptions and background are sweetness and light. Oklahoma had all the self-consciousness and inferiority feeling of the new and unsure. A flood of letters poured in upon me. They ranged from remonstrance to vilification. Oklahoma newspapers published editorials from the mildest of which I can select a plum or two: "This Ferber woman is the most unpleasant personality that has ever come into Oklahoma. . . . Why doesn't she stay in the ghetto where she came from?"

I made up my mind that I definitely never again would write a novel of the regional type whose background required a long period of research, whose period embraced three or four generations, whose characters were varied and numerous. A book of that type was hideously difficult to write; one had to prepare with months of research; the characters, purely creative, had to appear real and dimensional; the writer, in order to accomplish an atmosphere of credibility and vitality, had to throw herself into the past. This was, for me, a physical, mental and emotional effort. I had lived every step of Cimarron and the journey had exhausted me.

By this time Oklahoma had relented toward me. Book and picture were enormously successful. Oklahoma decided that this was good publicity. I was invited to be a guest of honor (whatever that implies) at statue unveilings, banquets, old-home weeks. Oklahoma senators and congressmen in Washington telegraphed me to come to the Capital for the opening of the motion picture. I did not take advantage of these hospitable offers, but they made me thoughtful. Cimarron, wholly or in part, is now incorporated into scores of textbooks used in American schools and colleges and libraries. Life (I claim no originality for this statement) is very strange.

In this mood I went to spend a week-end with the Walter Lippmanns at Wading River, Long Island. Driving down the country road with Walter, I saw walking toward us against the background of a spectacular sunset a handsome black-haired young fellow. He was hatless, the color was high in his cheeks, he had a look of strength and vigor. But the native stock which still clings to that particular shore of Long Island (the unfashionable section) is rather meager of aspect; a bit on the barren and stony side, like the New England soil from which it sprang.

The handsome lad who swung along toward us had a foreign look. America, I thought, had probably not filtered through him for more than fifteen years.

"What's that?" I demanded of Walter. "That doesn't look Long Island, North *or* South Shore."

"That's one of the Polish boys. Polish farmers own all the land around here, you know, and a good deal of the North Shore, too. Truck gardens."

I was mildly interested. "You don't say! How long has this been going on?"

"Oh, about fifty years. The Poles came over by the thousands and settled in New England. All that Connecticut tobacco farming up around Brookfield and back of Danbury—that's done by Poles. They're magicians when it comes to making that stony New England farm land grow things. The early American settlers gave it up as a bad job and left the farms to rot. They moved on to Illinois and Indiana and Ohio and Kansas. Half of New England's Polish now. They're wonderful farmers. They live in the old New England houses that were built in the 1700s by hand, of the trees chopped down in the forests, and the bricks dug and kiln-dried on the place, and then left to rot when whole families went West to the rich farm land of Ohio and Indiana and . . ."

Well, there it was. American Beauty. My holiday was over. Just as when Winthrop Ames had happened to say show boat to me, starting me toward the South and the world of the Mississippi and the floating theater, and as William Allen White, with all a newspaperman's gift of observation and flavor, had given me that first exciting glimpse of the dramatic possibilities in Oklahoma, so now Walter Lippmann's brief comment set my imagination racing. Poles, eh. . . . The old New England farmhouses. . . . Windsor, Windham, Litchfield, Groton, village names smacking of England. . . . Tuthill, Oakes, Pynchon, Champion, English family names. . . . Now, on the rural-delivery mailboxes outside the chicken-littered Connecticut doorways, you saw Krupa, Osniak, Porzycki, Doborkowski.

I fought against writing it. I was tired; I didn't want to do that kind of book again. I wanted to do a play or a half-dozen short stories, just for a change. I did write a few short stories in a show of defiance. But the urge to write the New England novel was stronger than the desire to smother it. Perhaps I should have been stern about practising birth control on American Beauty. Conceived in careless love I hadn't meant to have it. But there it was.

Histories of New England. Histories of Connecticut. Annals of Brookfield, New Milford, Danbury. Cemetery gravestones. Books on New England architecture. Libraries. Libraries. Libraries. I steeped myself in New England. But I spent exactly three days in the Kent which was the region of my novel's background. For exactly three days I walked and drove about that section of Connecticut's tobacco country. The pores or antennae or whatever the means through which I am capable of absorbing in vast quantities every detail of that which I see and hear were working beautifully. I was able to recede into another period, I lost sight of myself, of today, I became a human being quite outside myself, I was a New Englander in the Connecticut of the eighteenth century. It was a charming company in which I found myself.

For my family I took the name of Oakes, and my family's founder was Orrange Oakes, a man of taste, imagination, power and courage. I ought to know. I made him. My house I built out of a hundred book illustrations of fine old New England houses, out of dozens of other houses which I had glimpsed in Connecticut and Massachusetts, and out of my own imaginings of what such a house should be. One book entitled Old Houses of Connecticut, of which only a thousand copies ever existed, was and is particularly rich in both writing and description. Very generously the authors of this fine volume gave me permission to use such material as I needed. It was like being given the hospitality of a gold mine. Out of all these sources, real and imagined, taking a fireplace here, a stairway there, a cornice from this, a drawing room from that, a doorway, a paneling, a pediment, a roof out of my own recollection or imagination, I constructed the Oakes house, bit by bit. It was a fine castle-in-Spain. It never existed. To this day I get letters from real-estate salesmen informing me that the house I described in American Beauty is now for sale, and wouldn't I like to buy it.

In explanation of the book's title I constructed, too, a letter, supposed to have been written (it never was) by Captain Orrange Oakes in this new Connecticut Kent to Sir Christopher Wren in the Kent of old England. He wanted to build a house as an American country gentleman's house should be built, and I caused him to forward some descriptions of the hills and forests and streams and meadows of the lovely Connecticut countryside:

It has, my dear Kit, a resemblance to our own Kent, but it is different. It is grander, bolder, vaster, more sweeping. The sky looms larger, the trees grow higher, the rocks seem more grim. It has, I may say, quite another kind of beauty. A kind of American beauty.

So then here I was, deep in another background novel. The book was slow in the writing. I was trying to draw a circle—not too neat a circle—but a circle nevertheless as I saw the pattern of the past two hundred years in Connecticut. The New Englanders were coming back now to the land they had left. Sociologically the design was fascinating. The incidental reading was an education. Two enormously fat blue-bound volumes entitled The Polish Peasant in America were alone more absorbing and exciting than any fiction I'd read in years. Certain frank outspoken Connecticut histories were eye openers. I peopled the book out of my own imagination, I invented the incidents, I made sure that my background and all factual matters were sound and authentic. Incidentally I learned an awful lot about tobacco-growing.

A year went by as I plodded on, page by page, sometimes slow, sometimes fast. The novel was published in 1931. Compared to the torrent of abuse that now engulfed me, the results of Cimarron's appearance were a mere trickle. I had not drawn

Connecticut as a mass of rose-embowered cottages half hidden by apple orchards, manned by broad-shouldered John Aldens and pretty Priscillas. Connecticut was hopping roaring mad. I myself found serious fault with the book, now that it was too late. The ending seemed to me false and sentimental. I hadn't meant it to be. But the body of the book was true and sound.

It seems I had committed lèse-majesté. Even staid Boston papers called me nasty names. What right had I to write about New England! How dared I vilify Connecticut! What right (one newspaper actually demanded) had a Jew to come into New England and write about it!

One tart-tongued spinster out Danbury way publicly announced, to my complete amazement, that I had used her house, her family, her very self; and threatened to sue. It's a lie! It's a libel! It's a piece of impertinence! shouted Connecticut. Then my Polish readers raised objections. I referred them to Polish Peasants in America, the finest and most complete and authentic survey of Polish immigrants in the United States; and to their own Polish Reymont's superb novel, The Peasants. They would have none of these.

The book received many unfavorable reviews; it was published in that subcellar depression period of 1931. It has sold just short of one hundred thousand to date. It was not a popular book. I was glooming about it when a letter arrived at the office of Nelson Doubleday, of Doubleday, Doran & Company. Though I never had met him I knew that Kipling had a reputation for being an infrequent letter writer and sparse with his praise. The letter was revivifying to my drooping spirits. He had read American Beauty and liked it. He wrote:

October 31st, 1931.

Dear Nelson:
I took Miss Ferber's American Beauty all in one piece last night. It's all right—very much so—and it has for me a personal interest because we were in New England just as the outside invasion began, and the last of the old mortgaged to death men were dropping off the naked farms. Mercifully, I didn't see the Poles move in. It was Italians in those days. They had finished laying down car-tracks in the small cities and were starting shops and restaurants there. The farms were derelict.

Holiday in the Basses-Pyrénées. A Scene from CAMILLE, *with Noel Coward's Necktie (Armand) Eclipsing Bernhardt.*

And she has handled the thing splendidly from the historical point of view. If it isn't an impertinence please give her my best congratulations. I don't think her own people realise her value as a historical painter—yet. They will later.

I haven't been very fit lately but I'm better now. Best love to you all.

Your affectionate
UNCLE RUD

I hope he is right. I should love to think that when I am dead the chronicles of my own country written by me because I so terribly wanted to write them will be my descendants, however puny and short-lived. We are all vain; we all want to perpetuate ourselves beyond the span of our own brief existence.

In the working-day life of a professional writer success or failure is very likely to sum up much the same at the end. I don't mean that failure is as pleasant as success. I've known both. Success stimulates the glands, revivifies the spirits, feeds the ego, fills the purse. Failure is a depressing thing to face. The critics rip your play to ribbons, audiences refuse to come to it; reviewers say your book is dull or trite, readers will not buy it. You read these things, you hear them, you face them as you would face any misfortune, with as good grace as you can summon. Success or failure, you go on to the next piece of work in hand. There may be a day of brooding or sulking or self-pity and resentment. But next morning there's coffee and the newspaper and your typewriter, and the world. What's done is done. Win or lose, success or failure, all's to do again. If a lawyer or a doctor or a merchant or an engineer fails in a task it is, usually, a matter of private concern. But the failure of a playwright, an actor, a novelist, a musician, is publicly and scathingly announced and broadcast and published over an entire continent and frequently over the whole civilized world. Often the terms of that announcement are cruel, personal or even malicious, though this last is rare. Yet next day or next week there he is, writing, acting, singing or playing again. That's being a craftsman.

18

THOUGH 1930, throughout the writing of American Beauty, had been spent surrounded by a wall of work, I emerged now and then to cast a not too bilious eye upon the world. A queer world it was, too. I remember an evening spent at the Herbert Swopes' in West 58th Street. As always, you might meet at the Swopes' apartment anyone from Dempsey to Bernard Baruch; from Helen Hayes to ex-Governor Smith. The talk, as usual in that year, turned on the Depression which by now was spelled with a large D, like a period of time such as the Paleozoic Era or the Pleistocene. The Depression, this was called, as differing from the Silurian Age or the Pre-Cambrian.

Those present said it was all economic. It would last five years. Depressions in America always lasted five years. Then the roses bloomed again and the birdies sang.

I volunteered (in a vagrant quiet moment somehow escaped from the trampling march of Herb Swope's verbal army) that the economic aspect of this Depression was only one small portion of the whole; that the real depression was a spiritual and moral one so deep, so cancerous, that the world probably would end by succumbing to its malignant growth. This was greeted with derision. Herbert went to the bookshelves and brought forth a book which proved with facts, figures and every sort of ironclad statistic that this Depression was a blood relation of every other American Depression. Its name was merely Nineteen Twenty-nine Depression instead of Nineteen Three Depression, or whatever first names its older brothers and sisters had.

It was at about this time that I received, to my astonishment, a large square envelope, very imposing and stiffly starched, whose engraved contents requested my company at dinner at the White House as a guest of President Hoover and Mrs. Hoover. The first Cabinet dinner of the winter.

I never had met the Hoovers. I learned from a private source that they had read my books, liked them, and hence the invitation. The old reporter sniffed the air. I never had seen the inside of the White House, I never had met a President, I didn't see how I would fit into any Cabinet, however roomy. But I welcomed a new experience, as always; packed my new Mainbocher white crepe, very smart yet girlish withal, bought a pair of long white kid gloves for whose like I never before had found a need, and took a train for Washington. In selecting the train I gave myself time for a prowl around the town before being obliged to dress for dinner. The prowl proved too fascinating or perhaps I fussed too much over the donning of the white frock. At any rate I found myself finishing up in a last-minute rush, grabbed my evening bag and the hotel-room key and leaped into the waiting motorcar. I reflected, smugly, that it was very pleasant indeed to know that if you put one little word down after another they eventually made a path that led you up to the brilliantly lighted portico of the White House. I love to see the inside of other people's houses, and always I mentally rearrange all the furniture to suit myself. I gave the White House a terrific overhauling.

The cloakroom was full of last-minute women guests. We went up the broad stairway. I was met by one of the aides, I gave him my name (very handsome he was, too) and I knew ten seconds later that his expression as he looked at me was not one of swooning admiration but of horrified disapproval. For as I entered the great white room with its throngs of dinner guests

I realized that I was the only bare-armed woman in the room. In my haste I had left my long white gloves in the drawer of my hotel bedroom. And long white gloves are not only de rigueur at a White House state dinner—they are obligatory. Anyone who has ever dreamed that dream of finding himself or herself naked in a crowded street will know what my sensations were.

As they used to say in the Victorian novels—I knew no more. Or, at any rate, very little more. As I placed my hand on the arm of the man who was to take me in to dinner I felt that surely he would as soon have welcomed a sprig of poison ivy as that ungloved member.

After dinner, as we women were finishing our coffee in the little Blue Room while the men settled the world (and now look at it!) in another, the President stood in the doorway. He came straight toward me. As I stood up and looked into his face I thought, "How tired you are! And what a bum time you're having at your own party."

"Well, what do you think of it?" Mr. Hoover asked, astonishingly enough.

I was taken off my guard; I hadn't expected so forthright a beginning to our conversation. "It's like Alice in Wonderland. Not very real and a little foolish—all this fuss in a democracy. I expect any minute to see the White Rabbit come down the hall. But perhaps that's because I, too, have forgotten my gloves."

He smiled a little wanly. "It isn't much fun," he said. "But it's part of the whole. One has to do it."

I seem not to cut a very graceful or splendid figure on these state or public occasions. In June of that year, after some three or four years of resistance (for I am of the opinion, perhaps ungratefully and mistakenly, that these things too are a little foolish), I received the degree of Doctor of Letters at Columbia University. We were thirteen men and one woman on the honorary-degree list. Harold Ross, editor of the New Yorker magazine and a notorious practical joker, threatened to come to the exercises, rush down the aisle and forbid the banns, shouting, "Doctor of Letters! Hell! She can't even spell!"

The real anticlimax was even more ludicrous than this. Dr.

Nicholas Murray Butler, presenting the various degrees, sono-
rously rolled off the names and titles and honors past and
present. They made an imposing list. Sir Ronald Lindsay, British
ambassador to the United States; Friedrich Wilhelm von Pritt-
witz und Gaffron, German ambassador to the United States;
Sir James Arthur Salter; Claude Moore Fuess; The Most Rever-
end James De Wolf Perry; Francis Pendleton Gaines. Graduate
of Oxford! Graduate of Harvard! Graduate of Heidelberg!
Graduate of Cambridge! Graduated at Amherst, at Columbia, at
the University of North Carolina. Then it was my turn. The
kindly Dr. Butler looked at his list, swallowed a little, announced
my name. "Trained in the—uh—mm—schools of Wisconsin,
and by the practical work of journalism." It sounded a little
flat, I decided, but Dr. Butler made the most of it, and I thought
of dear old Prof. Pringle of my Ryan High School days, and of
Sam Ryan of the Daily Crescent, and I made them both a little
bow, wherever they were.

In between novel writing, short-story writing, jaunts to the
West which so invigorated me, and to Europe which in those
years so rested me, or to Mexico or Honolulu or the Midwest,
George Kaufman and I had met from time to time to discuss
another play. The process was interesting but depressing, too. An
idea would pop up as a possibility. We would meet perhaps
three or four times on that idea, whatever it was, and talk about
it, try to shape it, turn it this way and that to see its most
dramatic pattern. We would run it right down into the ground
and bury it, with a headstone on top of it which might have
read, "Here lies an idea, stillborn."

But now one idea persisted in my mind, though we had discarded it years before. It was for a play called Dinner at Eight.
George said it was too tough a job. It called for a number of
scenes, each a playlet in itself, yet bound one to the other and all
making a whole. The play was simply the story of a dinner party
from the moment of its planning in the mind of the hostess until
the guests go in to dinner. The life of each guest in that interval
was to be sketched in and united, if possible, to the lives of the
other guests and the host and hostess. The play was, of course,

not meant to be merely the story of a dinner party; we had thought of it as a rather ironic commentary on the institution known as Society. It always has seemed to me completely incredible that whole pages of daily newspapers (for whose white paper giant trees have been felled, machinery has been moved, men have toiled) are used to announce that some dough-faced little chit is "coming out," or that the week-end parties are now beginning at Newport, or that ten people instead of the usual family three sat down to eat the food cooked at the home of this or that couple. It all sounded to me not only boring but anachronistic.

A half-dozen times we roughly blocked out the scheme of the play, but always we abandoned it as too complicated to be practicable. I had even told Winthrop Ames the plan and plot of the play, because I believed it could be done. He thought the idea good but the execution impossible. This now seems absurd. I was deeply disappointed. Our outline was, I thought, reasonably tight; the play could be done with economy of writing and close-knitting of the various allied themes and characters. But it was laid aside nevertheless.

Interesting and heartening things had been happening in my own family meantime. Jacob Fox, my brother-in-law; Fannie, my sister; and my two nieces, Janet and Mina Fox, had moved from Chicago to New York. The two little blue-eyed Foxes, whom I had thought of as charming babies always, now suddenly emerged as young ladies each with a definite personality and a plan of life. Not only that, my sister Fannie Fox, having reared these two, now calmly took a typewriter in hand and, out of the blue, began to write very good short stories indeed and, not only that, sell them for prices which I hadn't attained until after years and years of plugging. It was interesting to note that these stories did not derive; they had definite individuality of style and purpose; were completely different from the type of short story with which I had become identified. Astonishingly enough, in 1923 she had written a cookbook, of all things! She was a superb cook, but one never, somehow, thought of her in the role of professional in these culinary matters, probably because Fannie herself is a woman of definite chic; modern and witty. Writers of cookbooks one imagines as motherly matrons in steel-rimmed spectacles, their white hair smoothly parted above a round placid face.

Janet, seventeen and enrolled at a girls' school near Boston, now announced that she'd had enough of that nonsense; she was going to be an actress. There always had been mutterings of this, but the family hadn't taken it too seriously. She didn't, she said, expect to stamp onto the stage and immediately electrify an audience; she meant to learn the technique of the art for which she had definite talent. This she proceeded to do by enrolling at the American Academy of Dramatic Art in Carnegie Hall, New York. Now Mina Fox, thirteen months Janet's junior (they looked enough alike to be twins), finishing her freshman year at the University of Wisconsin, Madison, proceeded to make plain her own plans. She was quitting Madison at the end of the year; she wanted to be an advertising writer; Columbia University had a fine advertising writing course. And (she wrote) here I come.

Within a period of three years following this Fannie Fox's name appeared in most of the popular fiction magazines; Janet Fox was playing on Broadway; Mina Fox was a paid advertising writer. The Ferber family was running true to the Neumann matriarchal form.

While I wrote short stories as a ballet dancer does bar exercises to keep herself in condition I still had the thought of Dinner at Eight in my mind. On New Year's Eve, 1931, George and I met at his house. We had dinner and we talked and talked and talked about an idea (the latest) for a play. It had looked rather promising. By eleven o'clock, it, too, had joined its weak little brothers and sisters in the graveyard of stillborn ideas. Outside the house all New York was getting ready to celebrate within the next hour the advent of the new year, 1932. George and I, alone in the house, sat looking glumly at each other, and finding the prospect bleak there, stared into the glowing fireplace.

"Well," I said, with that grace and charm which so endears

me to a collaborator, "I still think you're wrong and Winthrop Ames is wrong and everybody's wrong who says we can't make a fine play of Dinner at Eight. It has stuck in my mind all these years. It can't be so bad."

"All right, all right," George said—a peace-loving man—"if you're still so stuck on it let's dig it up and have a look. But even if we do it now everybody'll say we're imitating Grand Hotel."

"They can't. We thought of Dinner at Eight years before Grand Hotel was produced."

"They'll say so anyway. After all, we didn't write our play."

He was right. But then, I was, too.

In the hour that was left before midnight should strike, ushering in the New Year, George and I began to talk. And now, as we talked, suddenly the difficulties that always before had beset the plan of the play seemed to melt away. We warmed to the idea, we sparked, we became excited about this scene, that character, we began to interrupt each other, to argue, we were both talking together and walking up and down the room, gesticulating in each other's face, acting out a bit as it came to one or another of us. It was fine, it was exhilarating, it was glorious fun. As I talked or listened to George I was dimly conscious of some outside noise which distracted and annoyed me. It didn't subside, it began to be a downright nuisance. George, too, faltered a little in a sentence.

In acute irritation I turned toward the curtained street window. "What in heaven's name is the matter with this street! What a neighborhood! You can't hear yourself talk! Is there a fire or something?"

George came over and imprinted a chaste kiss on my scowling brow. "Happy New Year to you, Miss F.! And success for Dinner at Eight."

Begun that spring, Dinner at Eight was finished in June. It was written with comparative ease and a great deal of enjoyment. In the scene of the suicide by gas of Larry Renault, the broken-down actor, I still can see the two of us, George and I, reeling around the room in which we were working, stuffing cracks with imaginary pillows, turning on the lethal jet, dying tragically for each other's approval. We were really just a couple of actors taking it out in being playwrights.

Casting Dinner at Eight was difficult indeed. Again we had trouble in finding an actress to play a woman of fortyish, and again Ann Andrews came to our rescue. Constance Collier arrived from London to play Carlotta Vance, the passée actress —another part with which we had had great casting difficulties. We had been a week in rehearsal by the time she arrived. She came straight up from the boat, and there was something re-assuring about the very way in which she walked sumptuously across the bare stage, wrapping her sables about her and drawl-ing, "George dah-ling ducky how ah you!" exactly like the character she was going to portray in the play.

Perhaps one unfortunate day I may be blasé enough not to have a feeling of high excitement and anticipation at the re-hearsal of a play in which I am actively concerned. I don't think so. I enjoyed every minute of the Dinner at Eight rehearsals, though there were, as always in any theater venture, disappoint-ments, maddening exasperations, difficulties, long weary hours of repetitious scenes; problems about the many sets (we had eleven scenes in all) and the difficult details of clothes for so large a company. We were to open at the Music Box Theater and it was there that we rehearsed. It is a theater I love, its size seems just right, its acoustics are suited to the sort of play that we had written. Perhaps these reasons don't really exist, perhaps I am sentimental about the Music Box only because I have known success within its walls.

George directed. If I never—or practically never—missed a day's rehearsal altogether it was because the process fascinated me. Stage-struck as always, I never tired of it: the darkened sheeted auditorium, the pilot a single spot of light in the dim-ness of the stage, the entrance of the company members as the rehearsal hour drew near, the lighting of the bare stage; the heightening of excitement, the stress of added work, the strain of anxiety as the opening night approaches. We had tried to foresee every possible difficulty. The many scenes had been planned and built before we went into rehearsal so that we actually were able to rehearse in the sets after the first week or so; the clothes had been discussed and planned and ordered in the first week. Yet the inevitable setbacks confronted us. It is this, perhaps, that contributes toward the fascination of the theater. You never know. And when that grisly night of the dress rehearsal finally comes round, and the strange figures enter the dim auditorium and grope for seats and whisper and mumble and creep about and you make out the dressmaker and the dressmaker's assistant and the girl from Bergdorf's (the star's clothes) and the girl from Saks' (the ingénue's) and the friend of the management, and somebody's uncle, and all the understudies sitting in the back row politely wishing the various principals would break a leg—it is then that everything goes suddenly completely and inextricably wrong and you realize that tomorrow night is just twenty-four hours away. You wonder if there is a boat due to sail in the morning so that you can be safely at sea, Europe-bound, before the catastrophe engulfs you. But you know very well that wild horses or tame tanks couldn't pull you away from the theater. One reassuring thing about Dinner at Eight was that the very complicated ensemble scene in the last act—the scene in which all the dinner guests assemble in the drawing room of their host and hostess—had magically unsnarled itself and went off with pace and dramatic impact. It was the last-act curtain; it had better be good. There were sixteen people on stage at one time in the scene; all talking at once in the before-dinner gabble of cocktail time. Watching George as he conducted this scene I discovered one day at rehearsal that there was something familiar about his gestures as he quieted this group on the left, brought up that group on the right, held in abeyance a third group upstage, brought out this single character down front. Unconsciously, he was using exactly the gestures of a leader who is conducting a symphony orchestra.

No play is, I suppose, important as importance is rated in the world. But to the playwright and the actor it is, during those three weeks of rehearsal, the one supremely important thing in life. Not that alone, it is the one thing on the planet. Markets may crash, dynasties fall, wars rage—the people of the theater live in their world bounded by the three walls of the empty stage and the blank of the proscenium, suspended in a vacuum above the planet Earth.

One thing alone made this play, for me, different from the rest and more important than any other theater-experience in my life. Janet Fox, Fannie's daughter, was making her first Broadway stage appearance. After finishing at the American Academy she had played briefly in stock at the Westport playhouse. In Dinner at Eight she was playing a maid, but it wasn't the usual maid's bit. Tina, the character she portrayed, was a blackmailing hussy, devious, hard, just the sort of maid that a rich vulgarian mistress such as our Mrs. Packard, the former hat-check girl, would employ. I was more deeply concerned about her than about anything else in the play. All through rehearsal I had carefully tried not to be the anxious auntie, had schooled myself not to hover. In fact, in my anxiety to avoid any show of favoritism I had rather overdone this and had been offhand to the point of neglect.

Now, for the first time, I sat right through the opening night of a play in which I had collaborated. I even had got a new dress, I can't imagine why. I sat crouched in an aisle seat in the last row of the balcony and I was hot and cold and moist with apprehension. I kept saying it's-only-a-play-it-doesn't-matter-don't-be-silly. But I didn't fool myself. I wanted the play to be a success, I wanted Janet Fox to come through. And it was and she did. The latter was more apparent to me than the former. For, while the audience that Saturday opening night in October definitely seemed to sit on its hands, Janet held up her end. I saw, with an eye that was hard, cold and critical in spite of my otherwise nervous emotional reaction, that she was giving a deft characterization; she got her laughs, every one; her timing (a thing that cannot be taught) was perfect; she possessed one invaluable part of a successful actress's equipment: when she was on stage you knew she was on stage. And I saw, too, that here was not only a young comedy actress but one who had the making, at least, of an emotional actress. Failure or not, the play was a success to me from that point and worth all the doing so far as I was concerned.

The stage-struck Ferbers had an actress in the family at last.

As this was Saturday night, and there would be no reviews until the Monday morning papers were on the streets, Sunday stretched ahead an endless yawning black abyss. Realizing this, Ralph and Peg Pulitzer had asked me to come out to their restful place at Manhasset to stay until Monday. They were having no other week-end guests. Haggard and apprehensive at midnight on Saturday, I awoke feeling refreshed (but still apprehensive) on Sunday morning. It was a gray autumn day, soothing to the eye. I had a walk in the woods and returned to the house to find that a well-known playwright had dropped in for lunch. He seemed sympathetic but regretful.

"I thought your play was very interesting," he said.

The death knell.

"Thanks," I croaked.

"Too bad about your lighting. And of course something could have been done about that second-act curtain. Even if you had called someone in at the last minute, that, at least, could have been fixed. Too bad. But it was interesting. A good try."

By teatime I was suicidal. Another walk in the woods didn't help. By six I was driving back to New York in the pelting rain. The Monday morning papers would be on the downtown streets by eleven that night. I took a taxi to the corner of Broadway and 46th and bought all the morning papers. I read them there, in the taxi, in the dim light from a ski-ball alley window.

Dinner at Eight was an unmistakable and smashing success.

19

Charles Cochrane, the London theatrical producer, had seen *Dinner at Eight* in New York and he wanted immediately to produce it in London. To George and me this seemed a fine idea, though we rather wondered how London would adapt itself to the swift American pace of this play.

George, as director, and Robert Sinclair, assistant director, went over to London in early November. I followed two weeks later, after a partial cast had been lined up. If casting in New York had been difficult it was almost unsurmountable in London. Miss Irene Vanbrugh was to play the role of Mrs. Oliver Jordan; and Laura Cowie had the Constance Collier part of Carlotta Vance, the rather shopworn and expatriate American actress. The hard-boiled Kitty Packard was played by the American actress Carol Goodner. Casting was rather a pleasant cozy business (in the beginning) up there in Cochrane's offices at the Princess Theater in Shaftesbury Avenue with a coal fire glowing in the grate and tea going round. Presently the casting got on our nerves, the tea got on our nerves, the coal fire we would gladly have swapped complete for one reliable very commercial second-hand American radiator. George began to cough, but I went the whole way. There was, at this time, a particularly black and virulent form of influenza going the rounds in London. This I proceeded to annex in larger and larger quantities.

We then discovered that Mr. Cochrane was completely absorbed in the trying out of a revue in which he was starring Delysia. They were opening in Manchester and to Manchester he now went, taking with him his entire staff with the exception of the peerless Frank Collins, stage manager, whose services he allowed us for a few—too few—days.

We were left to do all the odd jobs ourselves. We had no wardrobe staff, no costume director, no regular stage manager who would remain with us throughout, no property men. The clothes problem alone was enormous; and there were seven complete scene sets to be furnished. Our production date was three weeks off. Mr. Cochrane (in Manchester) was charm itself, but our howls of protest were not assuaged by that engaging quality.

The Princess Theater in Shaftesbury Avenue is a vast and cavernous edifice of approximately the dimensions of our own Hippodrome on Sixth Avenue, but more lavishly provided with galleries. It was completely unsuited to our brisk little play. One day, in a frolicsome yet boldly adventurous mood, George and I decided to make the journey up to the very last gallery whose outlines we could just see looming in the distance like a cloud-misted mountain peak. We bade the company good-by, gathered up imaginary ropes, picks, snowshoes, pemmican and spiked boots, and began the climb. George is afflicted with that disconcerting horror of high places; the topmost gallery of the Princess was actually a dizzying eyrie from whose heights the stage and its company looked a toy box inhabited by ants. Cautiously and despondently we crept down again.

The theater itself was icy cold. The doorman sat in his little cubbyhole drinking strong black tea all day long. The sun retired for the winter. The December fog began to roll in, soupier and soupier. Miss Vanbrugh announced that she wanted to wear pink lace lounging pajamas in the last scene of the second act. The very new and inexpert property man vanished for an entire day and turned up next noonday to say that he had visited every bookshop in London and couldn't find the volume mentioned in our script. Its title was Aspects of the Adult Mind. George and I had made it up. The book never had existed. Dressmakers produced frightening garments for our approval. Nevertheless that first week was fun, for there were supper parties with the English friends of whom we were so fond—the Masseys, the Colefaxes, the Cazalets, the Dicky Birds and a dozen others. We were stopping at Claridge's in lavish surroundings (far too lavish for me, I discovered, when, many weeks later, I paid my hundreds of pounds in hotel and doctors' bills).

By now I was staggering around with a temperature of one hundred and four, which was definitely silly. I was following the stage tradition and being a Brave Little Woman, a sentimentality which very nearly did for me.

Presently I gave up and went to bed, a sight. I not only had the regulation London flu of that season, I had a streptococcus throat and conjunctivitis in both eyes. Between swollen and blackened lids my eyes stuck out like hard-boiled eggs in a particularly unappetizing puff-paste.

From Adrianne Massey I had fortunately borrowed a maid who turned out to be a dear soul, as kind as she was British. The whole thing now assumed a comic aspect. From ten in the morning until midnight there literally never was a moment in which there were not at least three actresses, two dressmakers' assistants, a shopper and a couple of stray errand boys or girls in my bedroom. The bed was almost invisible under a turbulent litter of dress material, fringe, flowers (artificial), gloves, hats, slippers, bits of fabric samples, furniture coverings, trimmings, uniforms. In the midst of this my face, swollen and purplish with fever, peered out, growing more and more repulsive by the minute. I can't imagine why every woman in the company didn't catch one of my poisonous germs and come down with the flu. They did develop racking colds, but I attributed their immunity to the influenza germ to the fact that they all (as dress fittings revealed) were snugly sewed up for the winter in old-fashioned long-sleeved long-legged heavy woolen underwear of a kind I hadn't seen since my childhood days in

Ottumwa, Iowa, when I had dressed, shivering, behind the base-burner.

Whenever my temperature subsided a degree or two I got up, dressed and wove my way down to the theater, barking like a seal. I couldn't bear to be out of things. Besides, what else had I come over for! (A lie. I had wanted to come over.)

London newspapers published dreary columns of the names of people who had died of the prevailing influenza, and now and then these lists contained a name I knew. It appeared that if you had a weak heart you lost. Then, one morning, I inevitably found that not only could I not get up but I couldn't possibly have anyone come in. Noon came and Frank Collins telephoned to ask why I hadn't appeared at the theater. I was amazed to hear Ethel, the nice English maid, say, "Oh, Miss Ferber's very queer today."

I raised up on one elbow. "What do you mean by saying I'm very queer today!"

"Oh yes," said Ethel primly. "I do think you're very queer today and we ought to have the doctor in at once."

Queer, it turned out, meant ill, in a certain London vernacular. Down at the theater, however, George Kaufman hadn't this information. Frank Collins reported to him.

"I hear Miss Ferber's queer."

"Sorry you think so," said George, startled. "She isn't, really."

"Oh, but she is!" Collins insisted. "I just talked to her maid. She says she's very queer indeed."

"Not," George replied, with a kind of lame loyalty, "when you really know her."

If I'm ever again in London and develop so much as a sneeze I shall take the next boat home. Ever since the Sherlock Holmes stories, and before, I had read of Harley Street physicians, those stately wizards in frock coats and striped trousers who brought royalty round when death threatened. I had them all in. I've never been well since. There was the throat man who asked me where my brushes were.

"Brushes?"

"Haven't you brushes? So that I may swab your throat?"

I said that I had, indeed, no brushes; that in America brushes were not used for swabbing infected throats; and that the idea was the most revolting and antiquated I'd ever heard.

The eye man (titled) lost a spirit lamp, complete with cap, wick and stand, in the bedclothes and it's doubtless still there somewhere between the mattress and the luxurious downy satin puff.

I never saw the opening night of Dinner at Eight in London. George telephoned me, act by act, to tell me how it was going, and I tried to seem interested, but I scarcely heard what he said and didn't in the least care. The play was launched, it was a success, and George and Robert Sinclair left for New York.

The black fog rolled in. Days went by. I had kept the news of my illness from my family by the ruse of writing made-up letters all about mythical gaieties. I had planned to meet my mother in Naples and with her spend a few weeks in Egypt that winter. Now she sailed, blissfully unconscious of my state. The Rex would land her in Italy in little more than a week. London friends were kindness, were generosity and love itself. But I grew steadily worse. Then, suddenly late one afternoon, the engine seemed to cease working. It was a delightful sensation. A drifting floating feeling, a ceasing-to-be. A kind of peaceful nothingness enfolded me. It was, I later learned, the point at which most of the flu-afflicted Londoners had stepped quietly out of life and into the obituary column. The nurse (she had been called in some days before) must have noticed something odd in progress. Next thing I knew the Harley Street boys were in full force, it was evening, the peaceful floating sensation was gone and instead there was a hammering and pounding inside me, as though I had swallowed a pile driver. The Harley Streeters had slightly overdone the heart stimulant.

The black fog rolled in, thicker and thicker. Daylight and darkness seemed to blend inextricably. I told Harley Street that I was going to get up and dress and get out of there. I was meeting my mother in Naples, bound for Egypt.

"If you so much as leave your bed," they said, "you'll die."

"Die anyway," I retorted, "if I don't get out of this. There

A PECULIAR TREASURE

must be sunshine somewhere." I thought of lower New York in January, with the strong sharp sunshine slanting down like a glittering sword above the soaring towers along the Battery.

"We forbid you," they said, "to leave London. If you even leave your bed you do so at your own risk."

Ethel packed me. I booked a seat on tomorrow's plane for Paris. I cabled my mother on the Rex to the rather garbled effect that I couldn't get any good accommodations on that week's boat from Naples to Egypt; she'd better get off at Ville-franche and go to the Ruhl Hotel in Nice, where I would join her.

In a driving rain and a black fog I drove out to Croydon and stumbled into the big silver plane. Up, up we went into the murk (I learned later that this was the last Paris-bound plane out of London for ten days). Higher, higher, to escape the fog. Then, as always, the altitude began to buoy me. Suddenly, for the first time in weeks, I felt light, happy and almost well. I opened my eyes and looked out. We were far over the Channel. The fog had lifted. For the first time in six weeks I saw a ray of sunshine—a pale watery ray, but sunshine nevertheless—strike the tip of the plane's wing. I ordered a small brandy and a large roast-beef sandwich and I ate and drank them, every drop and crumb.

"Harley Street me eye!" I said aloud to my somewhat startled fellow passengers.

I met my mother in Nice. My wireless all about the boat accommodations had not fooled the astute Julia. She had known, she said, that something was seriously wrong and had instinctively felt that it was grave illness. My cable had arrived late at night. The Rex was due to land its France-bound passengers next morning, before proceeding on to Naples. She could not face the long hours of fixed apprehension alone in her cabin. So she had put on her shore clothes at midnight—suit, coat, hat, bag, gloves. Her luggage was packed, she had taken a seat in the big public corridor leading to the main stairway and there she had sat alone all night, ready to step off. Later I asked her why she had done this.

[362]

"Well," she said, "I knew you must be terribly sick or you wouldn't have cabled all that stuff about not getting the boat. It was late, and I didn't want to trouble anybody. But I couldn't sit there in my room thinking. I tried to read, but I couldn't keep my mind on it. So I sat where I could see people passing now and then—girls in pretty evening dresses, and like that— and it kept me from thinking too much. Everybody—the stewards and the little bellboys and the officers—were lovely to me. Lovely."

Nice was cold even when the winter rain wasn't pelting down. Someday someone really should expose all this myth about Riviera winter sunshine. We sailed for home on the Europa. It was January 1933. No one dreamed that it was the last time any self-respecting Jew would set foot on that big luxurious comfortable ship, or that its German flag would so soon be changed to an emblem which stood for despotism, bigotry, hatred and brutality beyond modern human imagining. We came majestically into New York Harbor on just the kind of morning I had pictured in my mind during those choking foggy London days and nights. The day was sharp and brilliantly clear and cold, but not too cold. The sun on the bay was liquid gold, and there on the dock I could see the dear face of my sister Fan and beside her Janet and Mina with that eager youthful glow in their faces that so warms the heart of the middle-aged. Behind them soared the piercing shafts of the New York sky line, up, up into the heaven blue. I began to cry then, weakly and happily.

I was alive. I was home. It was wonderful.

20

MARKING TIME, MARKING TIME, so as not to get out of step;
writing short stories which, in 1933, were to make up the book
of short stories entitled They Brought Their Women. Like almost every line I had written since my writing days began in
1911, these stories were about men and women who worked for
a living. These people of my quarter-century or more of writing
belong to the middle and lower-middle section, economically.
They are neither rich nor poor. Most of the world would call
them commonplace: clerks, hog drivers, scrubwomen, traveling
men, farmers, garage mechanics, small business men and women,
mill workers, housewives. For some reason which I can't explain
they interest me more than any other American stratum. Not
only do I find them interesting, but I like them better than any
other, and feel more at ease with them, perhaps because I really
am one of them. I never had analyzed my reason for writing
about working people. I wasn't even conscious of doing it. I
only knew that I'd rather talk to a truck driver than to a man
who drove his own Cadillac. The reason for this had nothing to
do with class consciousness or any of that applied varnish.
Simply, the conversation of the truck driver was more stimulating, saltier, had vigor and native tang. That went all up and

down the line. On transcontinental trains I always plan to lunch very late (selfishly, certainly, for it probably delays the dining-car and kitchen staff) so that I may eat in a car cleared of almost everyone but the colored waiters and porters, a few trainmen and the cooks. One of them who has eaten earlier waits on me. They are all relaxed, at ease. They must pay for their meal so they choose carefully, selecting the greatest bulk and nourishment for the least outlay. Bowls of today's lamb stew, full of good vegetables and gravy; hunks of French bread and tumblers of milk. Ham hocks and cabbage, rice pudding. Stuff that sticks to the ribs. They talk little as they eat, but what they say is invigorating and nourishing, too, like the food they eat. I like to look at the beautiful resigned faces of the Negroes. And there, too, one finds much more than is to be gleaned from the face of the chief steward, white, who sits apart, a dapper tight little man with pince-nez.

Though almost all native-born Americans have initiative and it is characteristic of them to resent regimentation and general bossing around, it is the middle-layer working people who have the real cockiness and flavor—or did have. Even these past ten years haven't served to deprive them completely of this trait. Our very rich are ganging up, in fear of losing their inherited wealth; our very poor, numbering actual millions, are flattened out with bewilderment, apprehension, resentment. But the man and woman with a job—or not too long without one—the gas-station boy, the truck driver, the taxi driver, the stone mason, carpenter, the farmer, the railroad brakeman, girl stenographer, clerk—they still retain a kind of primary American freshness and assertiveness. Who you shovin'? they say in the subway. Watch it, sister! on the road. Well, now, they argue, slowly, I figger it this way. . . . But now their faces, too, are beginning to wear that look of puzzlement, of dim resentment at some-thing they can't understand. They can't figger this one out, no matter how hard they try. They too are beginning to want to be led—to be shown the way. It may easily turn out to be the terribly wrong way—or the right one. The radio, the movies, the street-corner orator constitute their forum. Every lie, every infamy, every injustice, every prejudice shouted over the radio in America reaches millions of listeners. And those listeners are, for the most part, bewildered by the strange world in which they find themselves. Though possessed of none of the sheeplike quality of the German nation, they, too, want to be shown the way in the dark. Instead of bringing light that shouting torchbearer may start a holocaust as did that self-appointed leader of the betrayed Germans.

Down in Union Square one Saturday night I stopped to listen to a hoarse-voiced fellow. He talked rather well, he had the magnetic quality that serves to hold an audience. They were grouped about him, a hundred or more men, decent-looking fellows, hatless in the warm spring air, wearing their clean Saturday-night blue shirt, smoking a pipe or cigarette.

". . . and I want to tell you, fellow workers, that here in this country you aren't getting a square deal . . . rise up and demand your . . . Russia, the land of the free . . ."

They were listening attentively.

Suddenly, to my own enormous surprise, I found myself shouting from the fringe of the throng, "Hi, you! Have you ever been in Russia?"

"No, but——" The faces turned toward me.

"Well, I have. If you tried to talk for two minutes there as you've been talking here you'd never talk again. Or in almost any other country besides this one. It may not be so hot here just now, but at least they let you stand here and yell this stuff you've been giving out. Russia! You don't know what you're talking about! I've seen it over there. Communism is slavery. If you don't know that, you're a fool trying to make fools of these men here. . . ." I was off like a fishwife who is treating herself to a Fourth of July speech. I never had done a thing like that before in my life. As suddenly as I had begun I came to my senses and stopped. I slunk off. But the men in the crowd said, "You're damn right, sister! . . . That's telling him!"

I had stolen his show that night—but not the next or the next or the next. All over America they're listening, right or wrong. They want to know. And all over America this same fellow, or his like, Communist or Nazi or other democracy destroyer, is feeding the bewildered crowd his own particular brand of poison.

It was largely this sort of fellow who, ten years ago or thereabouts, discovered in America someone whom he called The Worker. I thought the working man had been here all the time (as a common noun like the rest of us) but it seems he appeared here only after the Russian Revolution and the establishing of Communism in that far-off land. A few years later, in Germany, Hitler discovered him. But Communist or Fascist they climbed on his broad back, clung to his shoulders, applied the lash, and even as they whipped him up they shouted to him, "See how strong you are! You are wonderful! Only see how you can carry me on your broad bent back! Go on! Go on! Faster! Faster! I am here close to you." And Democracy, who had been traveling with him, side by side, as best she could (though sometimes her foot slipped, and she stumbled), was being ignored; for The Worker, blinded by the sweat that poured from his brow and into his bloodshot eyes, could scarcely see her. "Wait for me!" cried Democracy. "We will walk side by side." But the Rider thrust out a booted foot and kicked her brutally.

All the Bright Young Men came to the defense of The Worker. Being themselves often weak they found self-justification in thus posing as protectors of the strong, much as a fussy little terrier, barking shrilly, thinks he is protecting a bull.

If the Bright Young Men are going to persist in posing as the protectors (and equals) of the strong, I wish they'd learn the habits and technique necessary to the role. They were out full force one night when I witnessed a performance of that stirring and courageous play, The Cradle Will Rock. Scores of them in the audience were giving a bad imitation of The Worker with whom they doubtless sympathized but about whom they seemed to know little. Certainly the result, while worthy, was not flattering. Shirts unbuttoned, tieless, shoes sockless, cheeks stubbled, they listened appreciatively to this fine play about the American working man. Now all the way from Ottumwa, Iowa, to New York, N.Y., I've known men who work hard, manually, for a living. I've seen and talked and played with them on Colorado mountains and Arizona desert; in towns, cities, prairies and farms. And I know that the American workman is a self-respecting man, with decent vanity in his normal make-up. Given half a chance and half a dollar, the minute his day's sweaty toil is finished he will wash up behind his ears and under his armpits and all up and down the front and back of him; he'll shave and put on his other shirt, clean, and his best pants and a collar, by God, and a tie and socks. Any truck driver, coal miner, factory hand, ditch digger, steel-mill puddler, machine tender, railroad fireman, section hand, bricklayer or stone mason I ever knew wouldn't be seen dead after working hours looking the way the Bright Young Men look as they go about imitating their betters.

Swedish Holiday.

21

As the poisonous bug acquired in that London winter seemed still to be scurrying about in my blood stream I decided to sail, in late June, on what seemed to be a dream boat for what sounded like a dream trip. The Swedish liner, Kungsholm, new, white, clean-cut as a Viking ship, was sailing on a cruise bound for Iceland, Finland, the North Cape, Sweden, Norway, Denmark, Russia. I had thought no one I knew was sailing, but by the time we pushed off into the Bay, bound straight for Iceland, there had assembled around the table loaded with smörgåsbord such gay and friendly company as Ralph and Peg Pulitzer, Russel Crouse and Alison, Art and Vivian Samuels, Marc and Madeleine Connelly, Bill Powell. From the first minute to the last the dream trip became a reality. No group of travelers ever had such a superb time. The civilization of the north countries—Sweden, Norway, Denmark, Finland, Iceland—astounded me. The poverty, dirt, crowding and confusion which I had seen in every other large city in Europe and America were here absolutely lacking. I looked in vain for slums. Even the Lapps camping for the summer in the fields near the fjords were more sanitary than our city slum dwellers. After four days in Russia I had to keep a firm rein on myself in order that the old reporting instinct should not trick me into writing at least one article on what the camera eye had seen. Those four days were the most completely interesting days I ever have spent anywhere in my life. And if I were very very rich (or even rich) I would ask every Communist in America to go to Russia at my expense and stay there as long as he liked it. (No return fares paid.) The North Sea would be alive with Communists swimming back. Luckily for us, Maurice Hindus and Walter Duranty both were in Moscow. Theirs were the only cheerful smiling faces I saw in my four days. Nor did I see in Leningrad, Moscow, or anywhere in the countryside and farmlands, one single horse, dog, or old man or woman. The grisly significance of that caused a chill to run up and down my spine. One couldn't step out of doors (or in) without being confronted with a sight utterly absorbing. It might be just a policeman directing traffic with majestic Delsartian gestures while a cigarette dangled from one corner of his mouth; or a funeral with the Comrade's remains being borne in a bright scarlet casket; or a complete silver dressing-table toilet set, massive, magnificent, emblazoned with a monogram which had nothing to do with the public dressing room of the Moscow Hotel in which it now lay spread; or men and women soberly singing in the Park for Culture and Rest; or the apartment houses rising incongruously out of the farm fields (you wondered if they parked the plow in the foyer, like the perambulators in a New York flat building); or a play, jeeringly irreligious; or Lenin, lifelike yet waxen in his glass house; or a company of soldiers, very tough and fit, marching across the Kremlin parade grounds (for the benefit of the tourists, or I'm a fool) and singing as they marched; or the grave of that erstwhile gay young New York blade, Jack Reed, so still now in the pompous dignity of the Kremlin Wall; or the tubs of caviar, the size of small skating rinks, served to impress the tourists; or the Comrades themselves, all of whom looked a little like Harold Ross, 1918 edition. Or the churches, prisons, farms, factories, palaces.

Fascinating. And I make you a present of it.

Back in New York in the early autumn of 1933 I found myself seriously concerned with an idea with which I had been flirting for a number of years. It was to write a novel of Wisconsin and Michigan, whose background and people had been so large a part of my childhood and young girlhood. I shrank from it because of three reasons: much of it I knew familiarly; some of it (the lumber camps and the whole vast woods life and industry) I knew not at all; and all of it would mean another year or two of plodding and indefatigable work.

December found me up in Ironwood, Michigan, trudging knee deep in snow (and an incongruous mink coat), eating in lumber camps, watching the giant pines crashing to their death in the forest slaughter, talking to the paper-mill millionaires whose names had been so familiar to me since my Appleton days; breathing in the dry cold air, lifting my face to the feathery snowflakes; saddened by the sight of the cut-over land with its miles and miles of rotting stumps where once a glorious forest had stood. The Grand Old Boys whose names and faces stood forth so prominently in the books on Wisconsin and Michigan pioneers and commerce and politics and wealth turned out to be not so grand, after all. Cutting and slashing, grabbing and tricking, they had seized and destroyed millions of acres of forest land with never a sprig replanted; they had diverted and polluted streams and rivers; had falsely obtained right-of-way on either side of trumped-up railroads and thereby got control of untold mineral wealth as well as woodland, water and farm lands. They, in the North, were only Wisconsin-Michigan reproductions of their brothers in the East—the Astors, the Vanderbilts, the Goulds, the Harrimans, the Morgans, the Fisks, the Rockefellers —oil, railroads, land, forests, waterways; and in the West had been the Huntingtons, the Hopkinses, the Hills, all solemnly embalmed now in libraries and museums and hotels and boulevards. The Robber Barons, ruthless, plunderers of a vast rich continent. And I marveled that, since we Jews have such a name for shrewdness and acquisitiveness, there was never the name of a single Jew among these despoilers of America.

In my search for information I had a rather nasty experience in the home of an American German-born lumber baron who lived in a fine house north of Ironwood, in the heart of the devastated pine-forest country. This was so recently after the coming of Hitler to power in Germany that I hadn't yet grasped the spread of his poisonous doctrine in America. The man was a real power in the community, he lorded it over vast tracts of land, he possessed a fortune, the place was a maze of colored-tile bathrooms, phonographs, radios, stuffed birds and animals, high-powered cars—and never a book from cellar to attic. Not one. At the bountiful dinner table I was shocked to hear this gentleman announce (with the immediate concurrence of the assembled company) that all the bankers in the world were Jews, that Jews possessed all the money in the world, that they were scheming to obtain control of the world—in short, I heard the incredible balderdash and vicious drool with which the German fanatic had fed his enslaved people. When I announced, quietly, I hope, that I was a Jew, there fell a malevolent silence, and as I looked at their faces I saw such hatred as I never before have seen on human countenances, except, perhaps, in photographs of the toadlike Goebbels. There was no rising grandly and leaving the house that night. I was forty miles from a railroad. I am a little embarrassed to confess that I locked my bedroom door that night and put a chair-back snugly under the doorknob. In the morning they did not speak to me. Also, they tried to prevent me from completing arrangements which I had made the day before for a tour of inspection in a near-by lumber camp. As I drove back to my hotel in Ironwood I realized that a poison, virulent and dreadful, was being fed into the veins of the free American people, and that unless an antitoxin was soon administered to counteract it the most dreadful convulsions might soon rack the whole body of the land.

The novel was called Come and Get It, a title which has a clumsy colloquial sound but which, I thought, possessed a double significance for the reader. It was published in 1934, sold about ninety thousand, and was about 70 per cent good. In it I committed a serious error. A little more than halfway through the book I killed the character called Barney Glasgow, and with his death the backbone of the book was broken. He was the most vital and engaging person in the story.

I now saw, somewhat to my surprise, that in the past ten years I had written five novels which touched at least the four points and the center of the United States of America. I hadn't in the least planned to do this, but I now was rather pleased with myself—an emotion which no one, least of all the book critics, shared with me. I took stock, a shade too solemnly. So Big (and The Girls, too, for that matter) had been about the Middle West; Show Boat had pictured the South; Cimarron was of the West; American Beauty had been New England; Come and Get It was a novel of the North. I had written these books because the American scene (hackneyed phrase) interested and stirred me more than any other writing material. Each one of them had been written with a definite underlying theme in mind, and this had, for some baffling reason, been almost entirely overlooked by the average reader. I found myself regarded as a go-getting best seller and a deft writer of romantic and colorful American novels. Curiously enough, this was not true among my European readers and critics. I found small comfort in that. Very cross indeed, I said to myself, well, that ends it.

I hope I meant it.

As always, when a long job of work is completed, I found myself looking longingly at boat sailings and train schedules. I was torn between taking a streamliner for the West which I knew and loved, or a ship for Egypt and Palestine which I never had seen and about which I had great curiosity. Palestine particularly seemed to me a place which I must see, and quickly; no matter how briefly. I decided for the East and sailed on the Conte di Savoia. I was gone weeks and I hated the whole trip except for three marvelously interesting and crowded days in Jerusalem.

The ship was enclosed in glass with no open deck space for walking; I felt like a hothouse plant. As we came into the harbor of Naples it was ever so jolly to hear the familiar clop-clop of heavy iron-tipped boots and to see the boys—mere downy-cheeked lads of eighteen, nineteen, twenty, born since 1918—being poured like cattle onto the transports that were taking the Italian troops to Ethiopia. Luckily for me there were on board ship a family of Egyptians whom I had met some years before.

The family name, Khayatt, was a well-known and important one in Egypt; it was associated not only with wealth and culture but with justice, humaneness and charity. The two young daughters, Dora and Naila, were perhaps half my age, but theirs was a training and background so cosmopolitan, so intelligent that to be with them on short trips and deck walks, to talk with them or dine with them was to learn. Theirs was the instinctive breeding of an old, old race. Arrived in Egypt they showed me everything from swank club life to the open bazaars, and including a half-day with that dazzling Prince Abbas Halim (cousin of the King) who had been thrown into prison for his efforts to organize the pitifully underpaid Egyptian working man. I'll not soon forget how the news went round the bazaars that he was with us, and how they swarmed from every shop and hovel and corner and hole to touch and embrace him, until he had to flee through a rear exit to escape the press and clamor of the adoring mob.

For the rest, I found to my intense surprise that I had taken a deep dislike to much of Egypt which usually elicited oh's and ah's from the tourist. I can't yet account for it. The fields seemed to me to be fertilized with old dried blood of past centuries. I looked with lackluster eye on the splendid and curious objects that filled the famous museum at Cairo. I saw the golden armlets, the jeweled and chased couches, the weapons, the wrought furniture and ornaments and utensils, the exquisite patrician busts and masks of Egyptian royalty (very Jewish-looking). And I didn't care a whoop. This, I have heard since, was the result of my own ignorance and lack of education. I am willing to believe it, since I have no better explanation for the fact that though I rode a camel and floundered in the sands of the Pyramids and beheld the Nile and ate strange and delicious Egyptian food, it all left me less than cold. I can only venture to say, at the risk of being hooted, that somewhere in Egypt a couple of thousand years ago I probably had a very tough time of it.

Palestine. That was quite another story. There I saw wonderful and touching things; there I saw human and growing things, reaching up toward the sun and a new life.

For centuries it has been said that the Jew is not an agriculturist, he knows nothing of the land, he cares nothing for the land. For those same centuries the Jew was denied the privilege of owning land. You can't be a farmer if you have no farm. The Jews, as a matter of fact, were the original farmers. I give you those two problem children, Cain and Abel. And I give you, in our own day, Aaron Aaronson, who, in the pursuit of his college thesis, elected to try to discover the lost plant, wild wheat, and who did discover it, and who thereby enriched the wheat (and the nations) of the entire world by untold millions. If one thinks of Jerusalem in connection with camels, praying walls, Mount of Olives and Biblical history, one is right. But in today's Jerusalem the Biblical frescoes and the modern murals, the filth of centuries and the sanitation of modern engineering, the hope of today's persecuted Jew and the hatred of yesterday's bigotry, all mingle in unbelievable chaos. The King David Hotel in Jerusalem is, for example, one of the most modern and comfortable hotels I've ever known. The cozy little bar of the King David Hotel is the local hot spot. It was there I heard one young Jerusalem businessman call to another seated at the next table:

"How about a game of golf tomorrow?"

"Sorry. I can't. I have to go to Nazareth."

The radio was playing dance music, and a few young couples were stepping briskly to the strains of Hi, Toots!

I know now why it was known as Jerusalem the Golden. It *is* golden. Houses and walls are built of a curiously golden stone, and the hills are golden, too, like the hills of California. The sky is strangely low, you feel, somehow, that you can reach up and touch it if you stand on tiptoe. Maybe that's why the old Prophets felt so close to their God, and at home with Him.

This mustn't be one of those travel talks that scream for the added boredom of an amateur movie camera. Yet I am helpless before the temptation to point with one hand to the Arab tents and the Arab huts, stinking with the odor of the camel who dwells as one with the family, sheltered with them indoors as for centuries in ignorance, disease and filth; and with the other to the farm colonies of those Jews who have fled from horror and unspeakable persecution in Europe. There, mile on mile, where once there had been only swamp or desert with never a growing thing, I saw fig trees, orange groves, vineyards; wheat and barley and rye and corn and oats. Planted and tended, every inch of it, by the hands of these same Jews of whom it was said that they knew nothing of the soil, cared nothing for the soil. I saw how they turned the scabrous and neglected earth once more into a land of milk and honey. I saw big-thighed women in shorts, their hair knotted beneath peasant kerchiefs, working like men with men in the fields. I saw them eating dry bread and milkless tea so that the butter and milk should go to their children in the model nurseries that had been built and maintained in every Jewish colony in Palestine. They were ready to drop with fatigue after a day's labor in the fields, yet their faces were stern with purpose and serene with the serenity of achievement. I saw the hospital in Jerusalem, manned now, thanks to Hitler, with the most magnificent staff of physicians and surgeons that the civilized world can provide. And in that hospital were Arabs and Jews and Christians alike being treated in wards and private rooms. And the hundreds of thousands of Arab babies whose blindness at birth was taken for granted in the days of Palestine's ignorance are now insured their sight because of the modern treatments dispensed to them in this hospital maintained by the Hadassah society of Jewish women of the civilized world. And as I saw these things I stood very tall and proud as a Jew. And I cried, as I now cry, shame on those officials high or low who have so fallen from their estate in the world of humanity as to try to deny these people the right to work and live and give to the impoverished world again of their rich storehouse of vitality and genius.

I talked to a woman, young, the mother of three, who had lately escaped to Palestine from hideous European persecution. And now, here in Palestine itself, unbelievably enough, the same savage torment was being brewed. The woman's face was stricken in its bewilderment. Her hands, toil-worn, were stretched out in despair.

"We came here," she said, "because in Palestine we thought

surely we would find peace and the right to work and the right
to live. And now here in Jerusalem I hear the same words, I see
the same deeds that I saw in those dreadful days that I thought
were past. Where, then, is the God of mercy and justice? Where,
then, is civilization?"

I am not a Zionist. I am afraid I know practically nothing about
Zionism. Ignorant as I am, and bewildered by the world in which
I find myself, I wonder if I know the difference between what
is right and what is wrong, what is good and what is evil. Who
does not think he has that knowledge?

I only know this, with increasing assurance: that if sufferance
has for centuries been the badge of all our race it is high time to
tear off that badge and to put in its place another—a new and
shining one which says that justice is the badge of all our race.
Myself, I have finished with turning that other cheek. I know
that the one thing stamped indelibly on my memory as my ship
came again into New York Harbor after those weeks of voyag-
ing was the look in the faces of those Jewish men and women of
Palestine who were laboring to carve a new civilization out of
their own past pain and suffering. And I know how that look
must have changed in these past months of savage renewal of
persecution even in that Promised Land.

Now we know that today's confusion is not racial or national
but world-wide. The whole human race is involved; fundamental
human decency is at stake. At first it was rather amusing. Two
strutters—the one with a comic-cartoon mustache, the other with
a prognathous jaw—both pretending, we thought, to be Alexander when they were only Smart Alecks. But from being merely
absurd they became rather amazing—then damned nuisances
and bores—then frightening—then catastrophic. It was as if the
Marx Brothers were suddenly to turn into a quartette of Al
Capones, with a gun poked into the ribs of each of us.

It is as though the world has retrograded spiritually in exact
proportion to its scientific advancement. Science has isolated the
typhoid germ and perfected the electric refrigerator; has lengthened prodigiously the span of life and conceived the radio. So
now a war correspondent is able to broadcast over the radio the

details of a battle he has himself seen that day. The civilians of a great city lie on the streets—dead and dying men, women, babies, animals—now only an indescribable mass and welter of rags and ooze. They have been killed by bombs dropped from the sky. We can actually hear it described as it happens. Almost you can hear the shells bursting and the screams of the mutilated. Civilization is truly wonderful.

I haven't set foot in Germany since the Nazi or ape-man regime came into power. A good thing for me, I suppose. I probably would step off the boat, slap a Storm Trooper's face and be shot before I could say Kalamazoo, Michigan. But I did manage to contain myself during those few days in Russia. It was difficult, though, to refrain from telling them not to bother. So far as I could see (it wasn't very far nor very deep, but a good reportorial look around, nevertheless, in that brief time) they all were out for the same things, those Comrade Communists. Behind the Stalins, the Five-Year-Plans, the clenched fist and sickle, the tomb of Lenin, the purges, the whispering, the fears, the spiritual and physical slavery, the pretense at freedom, the Park for Culture and Rest, the old newspaper eye sensed this: Everybody in Russia wanted, more than anything in the world, to have oranges and soap and leather shoes and a Ford car and a radio-phonograph and a fountain pen. I longed to say, "Look. In the United States in the ten years preceding 1929 practically everybody had all those things. But it didn't seem to work out so very well. I really wouldn't go to all this bother if I were you."

22

Simply because it had a high brick parapet all around it, like a garden wall, I now leased an all too grand apartment penthouse on Park Avenue. The roar of traffic bounces, baffled, off that parapet. It is the only really quiet apartment I have ever seen in New York.

Built on the roof of a tall apartment building, my new home was really a delightful one-story brick house set down in the midst of a garden. Originally it had been occupied by a strange and frightened man whose name was to be known round the world, first for his fabulous wealth, then for his gigantic knavery. Ivar Kreuger, in that garden penthouse, had used a little of the money so quaintly come by to plant the most fantastic trees and shrubs and vines. More fantastic still, they actually grew there. I often had passed that particular apartment building on Park Avenue and had seen unbelievable willow trees tossing great leafy hoopskirts in careless abandon over the parapet of the roof. I wondered who lived there, and how anyone could possibly afford to be so lavish as to plan, buy, plant and nourish such Aladdin-like flora on New York's sooty rooftops. The black loam alone, I decided, must have cost incredible thousands.

And so it had. But Kreuger's millions turned out to be made

of thin air. When a duped world discovered this the gambler played his last trick. Fortunately it was played in Paris, not New York. Now the New York apartment, empty and dilapidated following his death in Europe, was rebuilt, restored, redecorated, and I, moving into it, became Kreuger's sole heiress, really, for I alone benefited by his going. There were the growing things he had so lavishly caused to be planted in tons of rich black loam hauled into New York and dumped on a rooftop. There were willow trees twenty-four inches in circumference and fully forty feet high; there was a grape arbor thirty feet long and hung with clusters of grapes. There was a peach tree eighteen inches in circumference, which bore quantities of fruit; there were espalier apple trees, rhododendrons, wisteria, ivy, roses, lilac bushes, iris, forsythia, privet all growing on a penthouse sixteen stories high on Park Avenue. There were three fountains, a rock garden. It was all too lovely and too fantastic and—I discovered—too foolish. If the revolution had come in 1936 I'm sure my head would have been first on a pike. We planted rhubarb and strawberries and we had strawberry preserves, grape jelly and peach marmalade right off the farm on Park Avenue. New York's roar and rumble and siren screams rebounded, baffled, from the protecting brick wall that enclosed the garden with its flagstone paths, its tinkling fountains.

One autumn night I returned to my apartment at midnight after a road tryout of a play written with George Kaufman. We had been beset by difficulties, I was weary, discouraged. Entering my quiet home I breathed a sigh of relief and went to the kitchen for a midnight snack. There, ranged neatly on the pantry shelf, were rows and rows of jelly glasses. Evidently Mrs. Rebecca Henry had done up preserves in my absence. They shone richly ruby and golden. I looked at their neatly written labels. There, done in Rebecca's handwriting, I read:

FERBER FARM PRODUCTS. GRAPE JELL.
FERBER FARM PRODUCTS. PEACH MARMALADE.

If I never had heard of Ivar Kreuger I still should have known, seeing his former dwelling for the first time, that here had lived a frightened and apprehensive man; a man who knew that one day Nemesis would catch up with him. Though on a rooftop, every window was double, and the inner windows were dark brown and purple stained glass, through which no one could see, and through which no sunlight could penetrate. There were iron grilles and gates everywhere. Everything was in the most execrable taste. In the main bedroom a deep cornice near the ceiling concealed electric lights which cast scarlet, blue, pink, purple or green lights, as the mood dictated. All these bizarre and rather gruesome oddments were removed now. We pulled down partitions, built great French windows that let in the sun, tore out the iron doors, made the place gay and charming. But it was haunted, catastrophe dogged it; the story of my three years there would make a fine mystery thriller (which I never shall write).

The story of men such as he is as repetitious as history itself. For years a duped world, overcredulous, is tricked into accepting them at their face value. Secure, as they hope, in barred and patrolled eyries on Park Avenue or in Berchtesgaden, they weave their plots. Then, suddenly, one day, little Jack-the-giant-killer says, "Come down out of there! Out!" And there stumbles forth only that which always has been there—a bogy—a shell—a thing all lies, bombast and sawdust. And the world stands abashed at its own stupidity.

Arizona, Colorado, California, New Mexico—the West I so loved was a fine antidote for all this nonsensical make-believe. It was on one of these trips that I stopped off at last to spend ten days with Mabel Dodge Luhan and Tony Luhan, her Pueblo Indian husband, on the magic plateau that is Taos, New Mexico. I suppose no country in the civilized world could furnish so bizarre a ten days as I enjoyed that August. Mabel Luhan, as everyone knows who reads her books, is a spectacular, gifted and slightly improbable member of a conventional old Buffalo, N.Y., family. The story of how she came finally to marry a pure Pueblo Indian and to live with him in an adobe house high up on an eight-thousand-foot plateau in New Mexico is not for me to tell. Nor to describe the house itself, charming, original, richly furnished and capably managed. But throughout those ten days I had to keep telling myself that this was the United States of America in the year 1936.

It was staggering to see the amiable Tony, vast, dark, unloquacious, lolling in one of Mabel's rose-satin-brocade armchairs in the drawing room. On his feet, as he took his ease, were moccasins made by the Indians in the near-by pueblo. His light summer blanket was knotted round his great waist, his black hair hung in two long braids over his shoulders, the strands entwined with bright-colored tapes. Turquoise bracelets clasped his wrists, a turquoise chain hung round his neck. Two miles distant or thereabouts stood the pueblo in which Tony had lived and in which his tribal members and relations now dwelt. Said to be the oldest known human habitation in the western hemisphere, the many-storied edifice might have been a modern set-back apartment house built without the aid of machinery. The whole vast electric plateau, encircled by mountains that seem always farther and farther away no matter how swiftly you ride to approach and overtake them, stimulated and awed me.

I had heard about all this, I knew that Mabel Luhan liked to "will" to her mountain top such guests as appealed to her imagination or emotions or intellect. My invitation was of two years' standing. I knew, too, that she was very likely to wish her hapless guests out of the house two days after they had arrived, bag and baggage, for a long summer's stay. Knowing this, I traveled light and planned a fortnight's stop at the most. Sure enough, within three days my hostess was doing her best to urge me down the canyon toward Santa Fe. But I had come to see what I could see, and I was exactly as stubborn and unruffled as I had been in my old reporting days when a victim, in the process of being interviewed, suggested that I get out and stay out.

Tony Luhan and I got on famously. There lurked in his button-black eye a certain quizzical look, as though deep within he was mightily amused at all the goings-on in this household of his. Though breakfast could be had in the dining room, or out in the patio, or in one's bedroom, I usually elected to eat breakfast with Tony in the kitchen, off the end of the kitchen corner table. There it was cozy, the parrot chattered in his cage, the toast came piping hot off the kitchen range, buttered lavishly by the hand of Beatrice, the colored cook (who was writing her memoirs). Tony was almost talkative under these circumstances. I grew to like him enormously.

Relenting for the moment, Mabel Luhan gave a party in my honor and invited all the local lights—painters, writers, poets who basked the year round in the New Mexican sun and thin air. Frieda, too, was there—the Frieda Lawrence of Mabel's notable Lorenzo in Taos. I had been promised an Indian dance such as Mabel had frequently staged for favored house guests.

In the Luhan house the dining-room floor is of tiles, ox-blood red and waxed to a glassy perfection. A little flight of steps leads down to it from the drawing room. As we guests stood here there filed in eight Indians who formed a circle in the center of the polished tile floor. They stood naked as the day they were born except for the loincloth and the dazzling pinwheels of feathers which swirled about them like a Paine's fireworks display. Whorls of brilliant feathers, scarlet, green, blue, yellow, blazed on their backs, chests, wrists, ankles, heads. Little bells of silver jingled as they moved. Their bodies were lithe and hairless, the legs, arms, torsos were slim and smooth as a young girl's, the muscles beneath were not knotted but flowed easily with the movements of the dance. The steps they wove around and around the room were the repetitious and dull figures of the stomp. In one corner of the room, in a little huddle, sat Tony Luhan, blanketed, with two other Indians of about his own age. These made music with drum and gourd, monotonous and lugubrious as the dance itself. As the dancing Indians turned and whirled, the feathered pinwheels made a brilliant kaleidoscope; I thought of that first dazzling glimpse I had had of the Russian Ballet at the Opera in Paris; I was reminded, somehow, of Prince Igor and of Scheherazade.

Over this primitive scene, in the midst of a house filled with suave upholstery, paintings, rugs, china, glass, sculpture, presided Mabel Luhan in a white satin and lace hostess gown, the train sweeping in graceful folds. Six of the eight naked dancing Indians were her husband's cousins.

[383]

As I looked at this barbaric sight I thought, for the thousandth time, how strange life is in America—how varied, how dazzling and unique. And this was what the tyrants overseas were trying to mold into their wretched pattern of iron and steel and hate. As I looked suddenly the world that I knew down there below this strange plateau vanished, quite. Three hundred years and more of civilization vanished. The white man, so arrogant and ruthless, who had come overseas to take the land from the savages by every device of trickery and deception; the towering structures he had built to pierce the sky; the bridges, the dams, the gardens, the farms, the magic wires through which he heard and talked and saw a thousand miles distant—all these, white man's pride, were wiped away by some Horror in the Sky. And only the aborigines remained, to smoke their placid pipes, to fish again in the unsullied streams, to hunt on the plains where cities once had stood. They needed no skyscrapers, no radios, no streamliners, no airplanes. Though the centuries had passed over them, there they were in Mabel Luhan's tiled and clover-scented dining room, as naked, as barbaric, as changeless as on the day when Christopher Columbus had set foot on these lovely shores.

Drought and scourge and pitiless dust storms in the next two years swept over the West and Middle West that I so well knew and loved; storms and scourges a thousand times worse swept over Europe. It was in March 1938 that I was on a train bound for Arizona; depressed, world-weary. With my breakfast the porter brought a morning paper picked up along the route. There on its front page was the news of the Austrian Anschluss. Austria, the gay, the careless, the proud, the beautiful, had gone down like a delicate doe before the Nazi wolves. I knew then that those fangs, dripping blood, would range wider and wider, pounce again and again. Staring out at the bleak landscape of winter in Colorado and New Mexico, we were steadily climbing up, up; the giant engine was pulling the train high and higher; four thousand, five thousand, six thousand feet, and still the grade was steep. It was half raining, half snowing, a thin sharp sleet. We were passing the adobe houses of New Mexico; they

1936.

stood, little square boxes of clay, on the vast plateau. Then for a time there would be miles with no sign of human habitation visible. Sage, desert, sky. Now and then, against the background of blue and purple mountains, of horizon and plateau, suddenly and incongruously there would appear the plump scarlet-and-yellow sides of a transcontinental bus scampering along the sands like some strange lost prehistoric bird. Or, equally strange in that eternal landscape, I saw the sweeping light of an airplane beacon guiding a steel sky bird. Then, startlingly modern and unexpected with its many shining windows, its neat façade and trim walks, a new brick schoolhouse would appear like a clever trick, its bland face under a cocky cupola beaming out at the vast landscape. You wondered where the children lived that filled it. They must pop out of the earth every morning at half past eight, like sprightly gnomes. But I knew that every morning, in buses and good middle-class cars, they came from the little adobe houses hidden among the foothills and all about the plains of Colorado and New Mexico. There was something reassuring, heartening in the sight of these new bright schoolhouses. Here in America was a new generation being trained in such comfort as their fathers never knew and their grandparents never even dreamed of. I wondered if they, in these shining new houses of education, were being taught, fairly and honestly, something of the spirit on which this country was built. As I looked out at them I reflected, a little bitterly, that in the last decade it had become the fashion to sneer at the United States; love of country, of home, of parents was definitely not The Thing. Austria—Germany—England—Italy—France—Czechoslovakia—Rumania—Poland—Hungary—lost lands now. But America! For years we had allowed a jealous outside world to jeer and scoff at it; we ourselves had jeered and scoffed at our own laws, our own people, our own very reason for being. Well, I thought, that which we have and do not cherish we deserve to lose. And so perhaps we shall go with the rest, all of us—prairie and plain, desert and mountain; Radio City towering fantastically to the brilliant New York sky, little brick schoolhouse squatting so plumply in the midst of sage and sand. This

continent, which we should have worn proudly like a jewel on
our brow, we had kicked along in the dust as a careless schoolboy
tosses a shining pebble with the toe of his boot.

The train approached the Raton Pass, high, high. Suddenly I
sat up as though an electric shock had passed through me. The
sun had come out, not brilliantly but half hidden by a film of
gray clouds. At this height the light rain had frozen as it fell.
The bleak plateau had been transformed into a crystal fairyland.
The whole world—trees, shrubs, bushes, wild grass—was made
of spun glass through which the sun's rays shone with such a
dazzling glow of orange and blue and green and scarlet and
purple that a kind of ecstasy welled up within the beholder. I
felt I must share this beauty with someone or I should choke
with it. And at that moment there came a knock at my closed
door. There appeared in the doorway the car porter, a tall lean
serious fellow in spectacles.

"I jest wanted for you to see it on the other side!" he burst
out, excitedly. "I didn't want for you to miss how it looks on the
other side the car, because you got your door closed, pahdon
me."

I don't know why that made Austria—and life—easier to bear,
but it did.

In those two years—between 1936 and 1938—I had written
little. Deeply disturbed, emotionally and spiritually, writing
seemed not only difficult but unimportant unless that which I
wrote might be of some help, however slight, to someone or
something. With George Kaufman I wrote a play called Stage
Door, a rather gay and touching play about the hopes, ambitions
and struggles of the young boys and girls who loved the theater
and wanted to work in it. The theater, struggling for its life
against the motion picture, the radio, the motorcar, draws in its
belt another notch and goes on. I had seen and George Kaufman
for years had seen the young people who loved the stage meeting
rebuff, disappointment, uncertainty and downright poverty with
such gaiety and indomitable courage as would make the beholder
marvel at the tenacity and fortitude of the human race. Stage-
struck, all of them, and proud of it. I had seen hundreds of them

—I had seen, in my own family, Janet Fox, one of them—trudging from office to office, refusing to be obliterated by the managerial no. Success this season, failure the next, nothing the next —and start all over again. A sandwich and a cup of coffee at the Penn Drug Store. Did he see you? . . . No. . . . Is he casting? . . . Yes. . . . Do you think there's anything for me in it? . . . It's cast. . . . Who? . . . Oh well, she'll be good in it but I wish I could have . . . Who? . . . Are they casting? . . . Excuse me I've got to phone, I just . . .

Brush your hair until it shines. Not too much make-up. . . . Not the type? Oh, but I can make up for it. After all, that's why I'm an actress. I'm short in low heels, I'm tall in high heels, I can dye my hair brown, yellow, black, red. . . .

They kill me with their courage and their hope. So then we wrote a play called Stage Door, and it was rather good but not frightfully good. It was a success, and in the midst of the success Miss Margaret Sullavan left it, throwing about forty people out of work, and over that we draw a veil, dear reader, as the novelists used discreetly to say.

Then there was a smallish book made up of two shortish long stories. One was called Trees Die at the Top and it was good; the other was called Nobody's in Town, and it was better. In technique, theme and characterization it seemed to me to be the best piece of writing I had ever done. The two were too long to be called short stories, too brief to be called novels. Perhaps that was one of their faults.

The book sold exactly as much as Dawn O'Hara, my first novel, way back in another world called 1911.

Well! I said to myself. That's called being through, isn't it, Miss F.?

I went back, then, five years—ten—fifteen—twenty-five; and from that distance I took a long look at myself. Had I made the circle and was I right back at the starting point? Or had I arrived at my final destination; and must I set forth again on a new journey, or be content to stay here forever looking back on the road I had traveled for so many years?

It all sounded very solemn and a little dull. Whither are we drifting, and all that sort of thing. Yet I knew that the old habit was still with me of translating everything I saw and felt and heard into terms of writing. I was busy as ever tucking bits of lace and silk and feathers and ribbon and muslin into the old trunk in the mental storeroom. Perhaps that is why writers grow old and gnomelike rather early in life. The impact of life against their emotions is so constant. It is like being constantly fed with a stimulant. A walk down the street, a ride in a subway, a glance out of the window are, or may be, adventures to the sensitive writer. It is a gift that makes life richer and more difficult at once, for having it one must cherish it and protect it, as is true of all possessed treasures.

In all these years there was rarely a waking moment when I did not think, consciously or unconsciously, in terms of writing; of dialogue, character, situation. On a train, as I prepare to hang up my coat, the metal hangers strike the one against the other with the motion of the car. Immediately, like a mechanism which turns itself on, the mind goes to work. What was that sound? How would you describe that sound? Uh—the coat hangers whispering sibilantly together under cover of the train noises . . . mmm . . . too elaborate . . . uh . . . the thin whining music of the metal hangers singing in tune with the train . . .

I call to the young Italian-American working in my garden. As the sound of his name strikes his ear he whirls on his heel. It is the most beautiful co-ordination of brain and muscle, possible only to the very young and strong. You see it in trained pugilists. As he whirls I think, that was beautiful, and at once the impression goes into the storeroom trunk. A week later, a year, ten years, I need to describe the sound of thin metal against metal, or the look and action of a lad turning swiftly at a call. There it is, tucked away among the bits and pieces.

These years of successful writing have given me a false idea of my own importance. A very large number of people have read my books. I have enjoyed the kudos that goes with successful writing. It has been pleasant indeed to have that little edge of advantage in a highly competitive world. When, in Paris, I give my address for the sending of cobwebby handkerchiefs bought in the Rue St. Honoré, the little French salesgirl says, "Is it you who have written the book Show Boat?" I am frankly pleased. When the Russian guide in Leningrad spoke to me familiarly of So Big and Show Boat I was thrilled. And nothing gives me more sheer happiness than the knowledge that my novels and short stories are included in grade-school, high-school and college courses throughout the United States. That alone has been worth working for.

Twenty-three neatly bound volumes each bearing my name stand in a row on my bookshelf. I never possessed them all until Morris Ernst gave them to me, in finest leather and tooling, as a lavish Christmas gift. Nine of them are novels; nine are volumes of short stories; five of them are plays. Of the five plays one ($1200 a Year) was a failure. I pout a good deal over the fact that I never am mentioned as a playwright.

What of it? I said to myself. What now? Twenty-three neat little books standing in a line. I thought of the song with which my mother used to sing me to sleep in Kalamazoo:

> *Ten little Indians standing in a line,*
> *One stepped out and then there were nine.*

So then I began to make this inventory. Some of it has been exhilarating, much of it has been dull in the writing and doubtless will be in the reading. Throughout the process I have had a good deal of the feeling that one has on seeing a motion picture for the second time. It was all too familiar to me. Again and again I have wanted to rush up the aisle saying, "This is where I came in."

Perhaps I had been deceiving myself at the outset. This was not an inventory at all, but another escape. Deeply, horribly disappointed in the human race, I shrank, perhaps, from looking at the dark and frightening road ahead. Better to travel the road back.

Before book publication about half of this chronicle appeared serially in the Woman's Home Companion, a magazine with a large circulation. I wanted it read by millions who might not be book buyers. Immediately there poured in upon me a flood of letters from every part of the United States. Many of them began by saying, "This is the first fan letter I've ever written in my life." I liked that. Some were admiring, some stupid, some touching or really thrilling or abusive. I was relieved and delighted to know that these last were greatly in the minority. Any writer of any following (or, for that matter, any person in the public eye) receives abusive and often obscene mail. The world is full of border-line cases. I suppose nothing could better illustrate than the following two letters the difference between the decent, intelligent middle-class American and the propaganda-fed illiterate who, given a Storm Trooper uniform and a gun in his belt, would make the perfect Hitler follower. I suppose that the America of the future depends entirely upon which of the two classes (represented by the following two letters, picked almost at random from among hundreds) will survive the present economic and spiritual and political disorder. I had very little difficulty in making my choice. Others may, of course, not find it so simple. Neither of these letters is written by a Jew. The first contained the writer's name and address. The second was anonymous:

LETTER No. 1

MY DEAR MISS FERBER:

While waiting for my men folks to appear for breakfast this morning I started reading this month's installment of "A Peculiar Treasure" and came across this: "I have never heard a satisfactory answer to the riddle of the world's attitude toward the Jew."

Whom the Lord loveth he chasteneth. It has been my privilege to know several families of Jews, and those who suffered most, gave most; gave to charities, to the intellectual and spiritual poverty of their neighbors, by example helped other creeds to find a closer communion with our common God.

Your story is one that opens my mind, my eyes and my heart. I am soon forty-eight years old, so I am living again my own youth. It is delicious. I love your folks, and I know I shall find something to help me and something to delight me in what is to come as I have in what I've read so far. You are doing a service to our young folks also, for I've heard several comments on it by lads and lassies who entertained us at our P.T.A. meeting Thursday evening (Parent-Teachers Association).

[390]

A PECULIAR TREASURE

As a family we have read everything you've written that has come our way, and the wish speeds to you that you will have many more years to entertain and educate your public.

Sincerely yours,

BESSIE STROH BURGARD

(Mrs. Frank R. Burgard)

Sunbury, Pennsylvania.

LETTER No. 2

Edna Eob Ferber

Well in the first place your name is more than likely is a lie. You say, "two thousand years of persecution." Well that lets Hitler out quite a bit. Why are the Jews persecuted? Well, first for those things Hitler has accused them off. A few quotations, not Hitlers, not off his generation. "A peculiar people a dastardly people, hated and despised by all." George Borrow in the 19th Century (England). A returned missionary in Sept. 1938. "Jewish youth do not go to the synagogue. "Money is their God." from Palestine. You speak of your people's love for the theatre, I have seen "The Rothschilds" perhaps you were to cultured to see the lying cringing cunning deceit from beginning to end of that House of Rothschilds, "eating crusts of bread when the tax collector came around and roasts of beef under the cellar door. You have summed up the whole race in your "merchants Bankers." "glamorous background" and the Jews don't fly in airplanes nor invent them either. Germany will survive the loss of Jewish culture, parasites in any country. "The immigrant (supposedly Jews) made the United States what it is today)" Jew is the Jewish movies have made it to a what it is, the where the worse sordid literature comes out off. Well your whole summing up of the Jews is in your, "Children of six were allowed free. I was bundled up in a shawl for a supposed nap and told to make myself small. "She's big for her age. Which I undeniably was." deceit, cunning, what else is that. "Money is their God. Plagiarism. Yes any one could go the to the library and take notes from other writers and make a life of Napoleon. Your "A Peculiar Treasure" isnt even interesting, Disrealie was a sly sneek.

[UNSIGNED.]

I am not so naïve as to be oblivious of evil and ugliness, but I thought that the bulk of the human race wanted, deep down, to be good if only they could, somehow. A childish belief, perhaps. But I shrink from relinquishing it.

I am not astonished at brutality, nor at the weak yielding to it. I know that man belongs to the animal kingdom. But I know, too, that he is superior to other animals through the possession of that intangible something called the spirit. Just as I believe that God is Good and that Good is God, so I believe that Good (and therefore God) lives within each of us. Each one of us is not only an animal, but a spirit. And for that reason alone (though there are a thousand others) I marvel that every decent human being does not reject the spiritual murder which accompanies the scourge of Fascism, Nazism and Communism. Of the three, the Nazi plan will perish first, not because of the Nazi brutality, but because of the Nazi vulgarity and insolence. As in 1914 (and always) the German nation now reckons mathematically without considering the human equation. A mistake.

PHOTOGRAPH BY NICKOLAS MURAY, N. Y.

1939.

23

WHILE WRITING THIS ACCOUNT of my past years I have been building a house. I never before have built a house, I never before have owned land. The land is made up of one hundred and sixteen stony acres. They form an entire Connecticut hilltop. The house is built of field stone taken from the tumble-down stone walls that cut across unused fields and overgrown forest. From the house site one looks down over what seems to be the whole state of Connecticut, a thrilling and lavish panorama of woods and fields and hills; there, to the south, a glinting silver sword that is Long Island Sound; there, to the north, the foot-hills of the Berkshires. Inch by inch the two have struggled on— the book and the house—and now, after almost a year of double work, they are finishing neck and neck.

The land has been a farm, off and on, for two hundred years and more. And for most of that time it has been hideously neg-lected. When I took it over the hilltop was washed almost bare through erosion, the soil was starved for want of all the life-giving qualities, the old stone fences were tumble-down and overgrown with poison ivy, the trees had been chopped down and uprooted to make way for straggling feed-corn that had taken nourishment from the barren earth and given nothing in return. I have planted new trees, scores of them, I have fed the dying soil and coaxed it back to life, I have sown clover and timothy for strength, I have cleared the poisonous weeds, I have rebuilt the fences, I have made a staunch good house from whose sightly terrace one sees the soul-healing loveliness of the Connecticut landscape. Perhaps—who knows what the next year will bring?—I may never live in it. But it is good, nevertheless, to feel that at least one small piece of this continent is the richer for my having possessed it.

I do not expect to find a new life there. New life must come from within. As for contentment—I don't even want it. Contentment is for cows. But there is something amusing and invigorating in the change of viewpoint. It is October. A year ago I'd have been saying, well, a new fur jacket perhaps. One of those smart little short ones, just right for brisk autumn days. But now I find myself saying, "Three-fifty a yard seems to me very high for cow manure. . . . Don't you think we could find some good loam down in that south meadow? . . . No, we'll plant the white dogwood near the house to blend with the lovely white pointing in the stonework; and plant the pink dogwood farther away."

The make-believe farm on the top of the New York Park Avenue apartment building must go. Someone else will inherit the grape arbor, the peach tree, the espalier apples, the rhododendrons. Good riddance! Still, I hope I shall not miss too much the cozy neighborliness of New York.

Alfred, calling up at six to say, "What are you doing?" He and Lynn live just around the corner.

"Oh, nothing. Reading the evening paper in front of the fire. Come and have dinner."

"Oh, I've had my dinner. Lynn and I eat at six, you know, when we're playing. I can only stay ten minutes, but I thought I'd run over and show you the new design I've drawn for the dining-room wall panels."

Or Lynn's lovely drawl over the telephone, on a Sunday night: "Ducky, we're making Vichysoise, and we've got the most lovely leg of lamb cooked with a little coffee in the gravy, the way you like it. Come on over."

I shall miss Kate dropping in at nine while she's taking Cinnamon, the cocker, for his walk. The Foxes, just round the corner; Charley Towne calling up to say, "I know a wonderful little restaurant for dinner. . . ." Beatrice asking if I'm perhaps going to be in this afternoon, late; Peg bringing little Susan to call on the Nana's day out; Margaret Ernst coming in with Joan on the way home from school; or Morrie rushing in for a cocktail; Moss demanding duck and red cabbage for dinner. But I know that though late spring, summer, autumn may find me true to Connecticut, winter will see me in the New York that I love, as close to the theater as I can possibly snuggle.

And if I am to know neither house in Connecticut nor apartment in New York, it doesn't really matter now. I've had them. I have lived in the best of all possible worlds; the only world, so far as we know, on which human beings can live and have their being; it has been my privilege to be a human being on the planet Earth.

There is, for me, something fantastic in the idea of being here at all. Always I have felt a little incredulous of the whole business.

It was as though the Unknown Power, juggling these celestial globes in the air, some high, some low, some swift, some slow, had suddenly been seized with the whim to people one of them. He selected a nice medium-size star-ball and weighed it judiciously with His hands.

"There's a good ripe one," He said. "The Earth. I'll put two-legged animals on it, called people. The sun will be their heating system. Just to show my heart's in the right place I'll give them trees for shade, flowers for beauty, rivers and lakes and oceans for water, the blue sky as a roof. Nothing could be fairer than that. Wait a minute! I'll do more. I'll give them something that no other animal possesses; I'll give each one a soul and spirit. And as a last touch I'll endow them with a sense of right and wrong. Of course, the thing's only an experiment. It may not work. I'll give them a million years or so to get the hang of it.

At the end of that time, if they haven't made a go of it, I'll call the whole thing off and scrap it. But at least they can't say it's anybody's fault but their own, after all I've done for them."

Perhaps the dreaded moment has come now to call it a failure. Or perhaps the pulse that still beats here in these United States will save the body of the Earth from the death that hovers so close. This new world, vast, rich, brilliant, electric, is sick too with the other organs and members of the whole planet. A continent to which, for centuries, the persecuted, the frightened, the poor, the courageous, the ambitious, the unafraid could come by the millions to find freedom and a new life is now contaminated by the old-world sickness so that it cries, in its delirium, "Down with the rich, down with the poor! Down with the Jews, down with the Catholics! Down with the freedom of the press, down with freedom of speech, down with freedom of worship!" Down, then, with everything that brought to this country the Huguenots, the Pilgrims, the Quakers; the Methodists, the Presbyterians, the Lutherans, the Catholics, the Jews; the Irish, Italian, Turkish, English, Spanish, Swedish, Polish, Rumanian, Hungarian, Russian, Greek, German, Bohemian, Austrian people.

The North American continent they had for the taking; a vast world on which they were free to have such land as pleased them, where they might worship as they pleased, where they might walk, talk, laugh, sing, play, work as they pleased. I sometimes think, with pain, of what it might mean to the persecuted minorities of Europe today if suddenly, out of the Atlantic, there should rise a vast and gleaming virgin continent to which they, like our own ancestors here in America—yours and mine—could go for safety and healing. But there is no Columbus now, and no new land for refuge. And laughter has gone out of the world. A lovely sound, laughter. It has been banished by a madman with a comic mustache, himself subject for laughter. So perhaps millions will perish again for the lack of one spirit to revive the inner spirit of all. Sometimes, as I have listened to the wise and humane words of the man Franklin Roosevelt, I have thought that he alone, in these past five hideous years, has had the courage and the vision and the skill to try to devise a cure for a sick and dying world. But the measures he is taking require almost super-human effort, for he must fight the virulent hatred of the very rich, and the inertia caused by the white blood corpuscles of the very poor, and the curious indifference of the vast American middle class.

It is monstrous that a single pathological madman should, in a world we thought civilized, bring down indescribable agony, humiliation and death upon hundreds of thousands of people of one religion; a religion which, persecuted through the centuries, has welded its followers into something akin to a race. As though under some evil spell the countries of the world have stood by while this latest savagery has gone on. Of course the German Jew belongs in Germany as long as he cares to remain there, just as the Italian Jew belongs in Italy, the English Protestant belongs in England, the Swedish Lutheran belongs in Sweden. Suppose that the United States were dictator ruled (which is unthink-able). And suppose that that dictator were to announce to an amazed world that the Presbyterians or the Episcopalians or the Baptists or the Lutherans or the Catholics were the cause of all the ills that had come upon America; that they were swine, dogs, thieves, impure of blood—all that is vile; and that they must leave the country forthwith, penniless and homeless, to wander until they died.

This would be as reasonable, as just, as sane as that which has come upon the Jews of Germany, and which may well be visited upon the Jews of other European countries if this barbarism is permitted to go on. It is a world I do not recognize. I am like a woman disappointed in love—in her love of the human race. For myself it does not matter, for I have seen another world; the world that was before the year 1914. All my life I have lived, walked, talked, worked as I wished. I should refuse to live in a world in which I could no longer say this. Since 1933 the whole German people have been slaves. And in those years not a line of beautiful poetry, not a page of stirring or important imaginative writing, not a piece of great or even good music, not a single fine painting has come out of the German nation.

At the thought there floods over one an overwhelming gratitude for freedom of the spirit, freedom of the mind, freedom of the soul, freedom of the body.

It has been my privilege, then, to have been a human being on the planet Earth; and to have been an American, a writer, a Jew. A lovely life I have found it, and thank you, Sir.

So come Revolution! Come Hitler! Come Death! Even though you win—you lose.

"NOW, THEREFORE, IF YE WILL OBEY MY VOICE INDEED, AND KEEP MY COVENANT, THEN YE SHALL BE A PECULIAR TREASURE UNTO ME ABOVE ALL PEOPLE; FOR ALL THE EARTH IS MINE; AND YE SHALL BE UNTO ME A KINGDOM OF PRIESTS, AND AN HOLY NATION."